THE PICKERING MASTERS

SELECTED WORKS OF ROBERT OWEN

Volume 2. *The Development of Socialism*

SELECTED WORKS OF

ROBERT OWEN

EDITED BY

GREGORY CLAEYS

VOLUME

2

THE DEVELOPMENT OF SOCIALISM

Routledge
Taylor & Francis Group
LONDON AND NEW YORK

First published 1993 by Pickering & Chatto (Publishers) Limited

Published 2016 by Routledge
2 Park Square, Milton Park, Abingdon, Oxon OX14 4RN
605 Third Avenue, New York, NY 10017

Routledge is an imprint of the Taylor & Francis Group, an informa business

British Library Cataloguing in Publication Data

Owen, Robert

Works of Robert Owen. – (Pickering Masters Series)

I. Title II. Claeys, Gregory III. Series

335.0092

ISBN 13: 978-1-851-96088-0 (set)
ISBN 13: 978-1-138-64640-7 (hbk)

Typeset by Waveney Typesetters
Norwich

CONTENTS

OWEN'S AMERICAN DISCOURSES.

TWO DISCOURSES

ON

A NEW SYSTEM OF SOCIETY;

AS DELIVERED

IN THE HALL OF REPRESENTATIVES

At Washington,

IN THE PRESENCE OF THE PRESIDENT OF THE UNITED STATES, THE PRESIDENT ELECT, HEADS OF DEPARTMENTS, MEMBERS OF CONGRESS, &c. &c.

The first on the 25th of February, the second on the 7th of March, 1825,

BY ROBERT OWEN,

OF NEW LANARK.

LONDON:

Printed by Whiting & Branston, Beaufort House, Strand;

SOLD AT THE OFFICE OF THE LONDON CO-OPERATIVE SOCIETY,

18, PICKETT-STREET, TEMPLE-BAR.

[Price One Shilling.]

1825.

FIRST DISCOURSE ON A NEW SYSTEM OF SOCIETY[a] 1825

The subject which I shall now endeavour to explain is, without exception, the most important that can be presented to the human mind; and, if I have been enabled to take a right view of it, then are changes at hand greater than all the changes which have hitherto occurred in the affairs of mankind.

But if, on the contrary, I have been deceived in my ardent, and earnest, and honest endeavours to discover truth for the benefit of my fellow-men, then it behoves those distinguished individuals now before me, and all, indeed, who are interested in the improvement of our species, to take the most effectual means to show wherein I am wrong.

For believing, as I do most conscientiously, that the principles which I am about to explain are founded in fact, are in unison with all nature, and are abundantly competent to relieve society from its errors and evils, I must, while this conviction so remains, adopt every measure that my faculties and experience can suggest, to enable all men to receive the same impressions, and to act upon them.

It is, therefore, no light duty that is about to devolve on those who are to direct the affairs of this extensive Empire. For the time is come when they will have to decide, whether ignorance and poverty, and disunion and counteraction, and deception and imbecility, shall continue to inflict their miseries upon its subjects; or whether affluence and intelligence, and union and good feeling, and the most open sincerity in all things, shall change the condition of this population, and give continually increasing prosperity to all the states, and secure happiness to every individual within them. And this is but a part, and a small part, of the responsibility with which they cannot avoid being invested: for it is not merely the ten or twelve millions who are now in these states who

[a] First delivered before the Houses of Congress on 25 February and 7 March 1825. Another edn of the 'First Discourse', Philadelphia, 1825; Pittsburgh, 1825; Washington D.C., 1825; English edns, 1825; Manchester ?1839. Reprinted in *The New Harmony Gazette*, vol. 2, no. 29 (18 April 1827) – no. 34 (23 May 1827), pp. 225–6, 233–4, 241–3, 249–50, 257–8, 265–6, *New Moral World*, vol. 2, no. 11 (9 January 1836), pp. 81–4, no. 40 (30 July 1836), pp. 313–15, no. 41 (6 August 1836), pp. 321–3. Reprinted 1970.

will be injured or essentially benefitted by their decisions, but their neighbours in the Canadas, in the West Indies, and over the whole continent of South America, will be almost immediately affected by the measures that shall be adopted here. Nor will their responsibility be limited within this new Western world: the influence of their proceedings will speedily operate most powerfully upon the Governments and people of the old world.

If, upon a fair and full examination of the principles which I am to present to you, they shall be found true and most beneficial for practice, those who are appointed to administer the general affairs of the Union, and of the respective states of which it is composed, will have to decide upon the adoption of measures to enable the people of this continent to enjoy the advantages which those principles and practices can secure to them and to their posterity.

And, through long experience, I am prepared to say, that the advantages to be derived from these principles and practices, will be so superior to any now possessed by any people, that, if the Governments of the old world do not gradually alter their institutions, so as to permit the subjects of their respective states to partake of similar benefits, then will the population of the old world come to the new; for, within its limits, from north to south, there is an abundance of capacity to sustain and support, in high comfort, much more than all the present population of the old world. Therefore, the rulers of these states, in coming to a decision on this subject, will have to decide upon the destinies of the human race, both in this and in future generations.

The knowledge which I possess upon this subject has been derived from reading and reflection, from practice, and from personal communication.

To make myself acquainted with the facts to be collected from the past history of our species, I read, in my early life, at least five hours each day, on an average of twenty years. This reading was in English, the only language I have acquired, and I know it but imperfectly.

To ascertain whether the principles which the reading of those facts, and the reflections thereon, produced in my mind were true, and, if true, beneficial for practice, I commenced a series of experiments, which have now continued, without intermission, for nearly thirty-five years.

To make myself quite sure that I could not be deceived in the truth of these principles, in the results of the experiments, or in the advantages to be derived from their universal application to practice, I have employed a considerable portion of each year, of the last twelve, to mix freely with all descriptions of society, and to communicate, in person, confidentially, with the leaders of the various classes, sects, and parties, to be found in my own country, and in the most civilized parts of Europe. I have also, in the same manner, communicated with many strangers, of every rank and condition, who came as visitors from different parts of the world, to examine the results of the experiments which I commenced, more than twenty-five years ago, at New Lanark, in Scotland, where they continue in daily successful progress.

Among these strangers not a few were from this country; for the experiments were made for the benefit of mankind, and they have ever been open to the inspection of all my fellow-creatures, from every quarter of the world.

The result of such reading, reflection, experiments, and personal communication, has been to leave an irresistible impression on my mind, that society is in error; that the notions on which all its institutions are founded are not true; that they necessarily generate deception and vice; and that the practices which proceed from them are destructive of the happiness of human life.

The reflections which I was enabled to make upon the facts which the history of our race presented to me, led me to conclude that the great object intended to be attained, by the various institutions of every age and country, was, or ought to be, to secure happiness for the greatest number of human beings. That this object could be obtained only, first, by a proper training and education from birth, of the physical and mental powers of *each* individual; second, by arrangements to enable *each* individual to procure in the best manner at all times, a full supply of those things which are necessary and the most beneficial for human nature; and third, that *all* individuals should be so united and combined in a social system, as to give to each the greatest benefit from society.

These are, *surely*, the great objects of human existence: yet the facts conveyed to us by history, and the experience of the present, assure us that no arrangements have been formed – that no institutions exist, even to this hour, competent to produce these results. For, is it not a fact, that, at this moment, ignorance, poverty, and disunion, pervade the earth? Are not these evils severely felt in those countries esteemed the most civilized? Do they not now abound in those nations in which the arts and sciences and general knowledge, and wealth and political power, have made the most rapid and extensive progress? Then, permit me to ask, Why have these plain and simple, yet most important objects, not been attained? Why has so little real progress been made in the road to substantial happiness? My reading and reflection induced me to conclude, that man continued degraded, and poor, and miserable, because he was forced, by the prejudices of past times, to remain ignorant of his own nature, and, in consequence, that he had formed institutions not in unison, but in opposition to it – and thence proceeded the conflict between a supposed duty and his nature.

To aid me in discovering whether this conclusion was true or false, my attention was turned to the examination of facts calculated to assist in forming a right judgment upon the subject. A steady and persevering examination of these facts confirmed the early impressions made by reading and reflection.

The records of history informed me that human nature had been governed by force and fraud, and that a general conviction prevailed that it could not be otherwise controlled with safety or benefit to itself. Yet, from the most impartial consideration I could give to the past transactions of mankind, I was obliged to conclude that those principles of government proceeded from error regarding the real constitution of human nature.

It seemed to me that a government founded on justice, kindness, and sincerity, as soon as the world could be induced to admit of sincerity in its transactions, would be one more suited to human nature, and much more likely to improve the condition of any people. To enable me to ascertain the truth or error of these supposition, at the age of eighteen I commenced a series of experiments upon a limited population.

At that period circumstances occurred which placed five hundred persons – men, women, and children – under my management; and, from that time to this, I have had from 500 to 2,500, the present number, under my immediate direction.

Without any regard to the previous character of these people, I determined to govern them upon principles of strict justice and impartial kindness.

I wished, also, to have adopted a system of open sincerity with all of them; but the irrational state of their minds, of those around them, and of the public at large, at that period, rendered such a proceeding impracticable, and the attempt to introduce a practice so new and strange to the world, would have destroyed my usefulness.

I was, therefore, by the force of circumstances, compelled to reflect much, to speak little, and to practice extensively: and these were my habits during the first twenty years of these experiments. In all that period I did not intrude one sentence upon the world; for I deemed it a duty to make myself quite sure of the truth of all the principles upon which I acted, before I recommended them for the adoption of others.

But, during that period, I had a full opportunity of proving the truth and value of the principles which had governed my conduct.

These principles enabled me to proceed, from one step of success to another, until more was accomplished than the world deemed possible to attain in practice. Many would not believe, on any testimony, that such results could be produced, until they came to examine the facts for themselves; and even then it was with difficulty they admitted the evidence of their own senses, many of them exclaiming with astonishment, 'The beings before me do not appear to belong to the human nature I have been accustomed to see, or with which I have previously associated.'

They saw a population that had been indolent, dirty, imbecile, and demoralized, to a lamentable extent, who had become actively industrious, cleanly, temperate, and very generally moral, in all their proceedings. They saw the children of these people trained and educated, from two years of age and upwards, without individual reward or punishment; and they had never seen children who were their equals in disposition, habits, manners, intelligence, and kind feelings, or who appeared to enjoy an equal degree of active happiness. Yet this population had been so changed by an unknown and uneducated individual, without fortune and friends, and in opposition to almost every conceivable obstacle that the prejudices derived from ages of ignorance could unite, and while, comparatively, a few only of the circumstances most favourable to their well-being and happiness could be combined for their improvement.

It may now be the wish of many to inquire, Whence this influence? Wherein does its efficacy consist? And by what unheard of means, or magic power, are these beneficial, yet strange results, now brought to pass? I reply, by means the most natural, obvious, and simple, and the knowledge of which were obtained from the facts around us; from facts, too, which have been familiar to man in every stage of his existence, and which, as they are derived from the direct evidence of our senses, no intelligent mind will now dispute. For, is it not a fact, in accordance with the direct evidence of our senses, that infants at birth are ignorant of themselves, and of all things around them? Is it not a fact, that they are unconscious how their senses were formed, or any part of their organization was generated or produced? Is it not a fact, that the senses and organization of no two infants have ever been known to be alike, although all possess the same general principles of human nature; and that no two individuals have ever been made the same, although trained and educated under apparently similar external circumstances? Is it not a fact, that all infants are most powerfully influenced by the general and particular external circumstances which exist around them at birth, and through childhood and youth, to manhood.

Is it not a fact, that these circumstances may be so varied as to give an almost infinite variety of character to any infants, on principles as fixed and certain as those on which any of the sciences are founded; and that, by such varied circumstances, any, or all infants, may be trained to become ignorant or intelligent, cruel or humane, selfish or liberal – a Cannibal or Hindoo – a miserable being – or one whose existence shall be a life of happiness? Is it not a fact, that all infants are capable of being formed by the overwhelming influence of circumstances, acting upon their original individual nature, into any of these characters, provided their physical and mental organization be not imperfect; and that, in such case, as nature has been disturbed in her process, that the beings thus injured, physically or mentally, become objects for compassion and for increased care and kindness, in proportion to their malformation? And is it not a clear and evident deduction from these facts, that those who govern society possess the power, if they knew how to use it, to combine and regulate the circumstances which ought to influence and form the character of every individual of the rising generation? And thus do they possess within themselves the sure means of creating affluence, intelligence, virtue, and happiness, throughout the whole population.

These are living facts, confirmed by the history of every nation and people; and they are in strict accordance with whatever we know from the evidence of our own senses.

And it was in consequence of acting upon the belief in the truth of these facts, that the characters of those placed under my direction were so much changed for the better, and that their condition has been so materially improved.

With a knowledge of these facts, I could not be angry or displeased with any of those placed under my guidance on account of any original personal defects, for to me it was evident they could not have had the slightest influence in producing them. Neither could I be angry or displeased with them, on account of the injuries which they might have received from being surrounded with unfavourable circumstances, over which they could have no control, but which circumstances, formed their language, disposition, habits, sentiments, religion, feelings, and conduct. If these were defective and inferior, they necessarily created in my mind compassion for their misfortunes, and my thoughts were employed in discovering the circumstances which produced these unfavorable effects, and all my efforts were directed to remove them, and to replace them by others having a beneficial tendency. Having discovered that individuals were always formed by the circumstances, whatever they might be, which were allowed to exist around them, my practice was to *govern* the circumstances; and thus, by means imperceptible and unknown to the individuals, I formed them, to the extent I could control the circumstances, into what I wished them to become; and in this manner were the beneficial changes effected in the population under my care. In this process I could not be disappointed; for I did not expect any evil to disappear; until I had removed the cause or causes which produced it; nor will evil of any kind ever be excluded from society, until the cause which gives it existence shall be discovered and removed.

Here, then, have we before us the *natural* means by which, on sure grounds, society may be made virtuous, and immediately improved, to an extent that no one can limit; and, by a similar practice, the causes which generate all the inferior motives, and, consequently, actions of man, may be easily withdrawn; and, by the same means, universal charity, benevolence, and kindness, may be made to become the ruling principles in the government of mankind.

With a knowledge of the facts which I have enumerated, relative to the constitution of human nature, the error and childishness of praising and blaming each other, and of devising rewards and punishments, and of applying them, through a gross ignorance of our nature, to particular individuals, must become too obvious to admit of their longer continuance among those who have any real pretensions to rationality.

For what shall we praise or blame each other? Not, surely, for our personal qualifications, which we had no will in forming! Still less for being born within the circle in which Jewish, Christian, Mahommedan, or any other general impressions are, at an early age, forced into our minds! Or do we praise and blame each other because we have come into existence a member of any particular sect, class, or party, in any country within either of these large circles which now so effectually divide man from his fellow-man, and, in consequence, make him one of the most unjust and irrational of all beings? Or shall we praise or blame each other because we have been born of rich or poor, virtuous or vicious parents; or because the more or less favourable circumstances, existing in the place of our birth and training, made the population around us more or less wise or foolish, strong or weak? Or shall we praise or blame each other for any conceivable combination of our personal or acquired advantages or disadvantages?

In this irrational conduct, behold the real cause of almost all the evils that have ever afflicted humanity, save those extraordinary overwhelming dispensations of Providence, which seldom occur, and soon pass away.

Man, through ignorance, has been, hitherto, the tormentor of man.

He is *here*, in a nation deeming itself possessed of more privileges than all other nations, and which pretensions, in many respects, must be admitted to be true. Yet, even *here*, where the laws are the most mild, and consequently the least unjust and irrational, individuals are punished even to death, for actions which are the natural and necessary effects arising from the injurious circumstances which the government and society, to which they belong, unwisely permit to exist; while other individuals are almost as much injured by being as unjustly rewarded for performing actions for which, as soon as they shall become rational beings, they must be conscious they cannot be entitled to a particle of merit.

It is true that, from obvious causes, the great mass of the people, in all countries, have been so trained by the circumstances around them, that they have been forced, unknown to themselves, to receive notions which are opposed to the great and important truths which I have placed before you, and, in consequence, the most lamentable ignorance of human nature universally prevails, and poverty, and injustice, and vice, and misery, at this hour, every where superabound.

Vast numbers of men, and more particularly women, in all countries have been forced, from generation to generation, to receive in infancy, as true, various imaginary notions, long prevalent in those countries, and they have been taught that their happiness or misery depended upon their belief or disbelief in the truth of those notions. In various countries, these notions differ materially. In some they are in direct opposition to others, and, as all are trained to think that the notions taught in their own country are so true that it is impossible they can be deceived, and that those in opposition to them are so false that none but the most ignorant and weak will be made to believe in them, and that such false and wicked notions must produce vicious conduct. In this manner, every imaginable bad feeling that can be implanted in human nature, is generated and fostered. National, sectarian, and individual antipathies necessarily follow; division and counteraction of every description succeed; and the world is thus forced to become a chaotic scene of confusion, disorder, and misery.

It is so at this moment, and strange to say, it has been made to be so through those original qualities of our nature, which, whenever they shall be rightly directed, and justice shall be done to them, will produce the fullness of charity, and kindness, and sincerity, from each to all, until we shall become, in fact, and reality, a new people, having but one common interest; and then all the benefits of the world will be freely open to every one, and in consequence, all will be gainers, to an extent that no imagination has been yet trained to be competent to conceive.

The original faculties of our nature, which have been thus abused, are the natural love of truth, and the desire to benefit our fellow creatures to the greatest possible extent. These are the genuine feelings which *now* actuate the conscientiously religious in all the countries throughout the world. These are the sole motives which animated the *real* religious of all the past times, and which gave an inexpressible pleasure to the dying moments of martyrs of all sects, in every age and country. Why should these inestimable qualities of the human mind be longer abused, and forced to become the instruments of universal discord, confusion, and suffering? Is it wise in those that govern to allow this wretched error to continue?

Are there not men around me, even now, in the actual possession of tenfold more power and influence than are requisite to stem this torrent of error and misdirection of the finest feelings and best faculties of our nature?

I know there are, and I trust they will now manfully and promptly step forward, and place themselves in the gap between the present and the future, and from this Capital, in their collective capacity, say to the world, 'Now shall the government of force, and fraud, and disunion cease, and from henceforth, truth, and sincerity, and charity, and kindness, and union, shall take their place, and superstition and prejudice shall no longer have dominion here.'

This is the mighty deed that the intelligent part of the population of this country, and the enlightened men among all the nations of the earth, will expect at their hands. And can any position be conceived so important, or, at this moment, so highly to be desired, for the accomplishment of the greatest good to this country and to the world, as that to which the new administration of this empire has been just appointed?

Knowing well the favourable circumstances which, in the most extraordinary manner, have been combined, and are in full force to aid its attainment, I conjure them, on account of their own future feelings and reflections, but I conjure them, most particularly in the name of those innumerable beings throughout the world, who are now afflicted with penury and want, with ignorance, and vice, and superstition, with the inferior motives which have been instilled into their minds from infancy, and the consequent misery which they suffer, that they will not allow this inestimable opportunity to escape. If the leading men of these States, forgetting every little and unworthy party and sectarian distinction, will now cordially unite, they may, with ease, break asunder the bonds of ignorance, superstition, and prejudice, and by thus acting they could not fail to dispel error, and to give and secure mental freedom and happiness to the world. To effect this change, the greatest ever yet made in human affairs, no sacrifice on their parts will be necessary. If they possess, as I trust they do, sufficient moral courage to will this deed, and without delay to express that will openly and decisively to the world, then will mental slavery soon cease every where, and the victory over ignorance and poverty, and sin, and misery will be achieved. Here, fortunately for you and for the future destinies of the human race, no regal or legal power sustains ignorance, error, and superstition, and without such support, what chance of success can those have in opposition to the most valuable practical truths, derived immediately from the most obvious facts around us?

The Government and Congress of this new empire have only now, as I have previously stated, to will this change, and it will be at once effected; and by such act, they will give and secure liberty, affluence, and happiness, to America and to the world.

I have said, give liberty to America; but the natives of this empire have been taught to believe, that they already possess full liberty. I know it is *not* so; and in proof of this denial, permit me to ask, how many present feel they possess the power to speak their real sentiments, freely and openly, on subjects the most important to themselves and to the well being of society? Until this can be done, and done without any disadvantage whatever to those who do it, liberty has not been attained, and you have yet to work out for yourselves this, the most precious and valuable part of liberty. Many must be now conscious that they are to a great extent under the despotism of weak minds, who are themselves the slaves of superstition and prejudice. Until human beings shall, without any inconvenience whatever, speak openly and frankly the genuine impression of their mind on all subjects, they must be considered to be in a state of mental bondage, and in that condition all men have ever yet been, and to a greater extent perhaps, than you suspect, you are so even now. By a hard struggle you have attained political liberty, but you have yet to acquire real mental liberty, and if you cannot possess yourselves of it, your political liberty will be precarious and of much less value. The attainment of political liberty is, however, a necessary step towards the acquirement of real mental liberty, and as you have obtained the former, I have come here to assist you to secure the latter. For without mental liberty, there can be no sincerity; and without sincerity, devoid of all deception, there can be no real virtue or happiness among mankind.

My desire now is to introduce into these States, and through them to the world at large, a new social system, formed in practice of an entire new combination of circumstances, all of them having a direct moral, intellectual, and beneficial tendency, fully adequate to effect the most important improvements throughout society. This system has been solely derived from the facts relative to our common nature, which I have previously explained.

In this new social arrangement, a much more perfect system of liberty and equality will be introduced than has yet any where existed, or been deemed attainable in practice. Within it there will be no privileged thoughts or belief; everyone will be at full liberty to express the genuine impressions which the circumstances around them have made on their minds as well as their own undisguised reflections thereon, and then no motive will exist for deception or insincerity of any kind.

Every one will be instructed in the outline of all the real knowledge which experience has yet discovered. This will be effected on a plan in unison with our nature, and by which the equality of the mental faculties will be rendered more perfect, and by which all will be elevated much above what any can attain under the existing despotism of mind; and by these arrangements the general intellect of society will be enabled to make greater advances in a year, than it has been hitherto allowed to attain in a century. The innumerable and incalculable evils and absurdities which have arisen from the inequality of wealth, will be effectually overcome and avoided throughout all the future. By arrangements, as simple and desirable as they will be beneficial for every one, all will possess, at all times, a full supply of the best of everything for human nature, as far as present experience on these matters can direct our knowledge.

The degrading and pernicious practices in which we are now trained, of buying cheap and selling dear, will be rendered wholly unnecessary: for, so long as this principle shall govern the transactions of men, nothing really great or noble can be expected from mankind.

The whole trading system is one of deception; one by which each engaged in it is necessarily trained to endeavour to obtain advantages over others, and in which the interest of all is opposed to each, and in consequence, not one can attain the advantages that, under another and a better system might be, with far less labour, and without risk, secured in perpetuity to all.

The consequence of this inferior trading system is to give a very injurious surplus of wealth and power to the few, and to inflict poverty and subjection on the many.

In the new system, union and co-operation will supersede individual interest, and the universal counteraction of each other's objects; and, by the change, the powers of one man will obtain for him the advantages of many, and all will become as rich as they will desire. The very imperfect experiments of the Moravians, Shakers, and Harmonites,[a] give sure proof of the gigantic

[a] The Moravians were descendants of a 15th-century Bohemian church renowned for their simplicity, strong communal values, and pacifism. The Shakers were a sect of Quakers known for their ecstatic utterances and eccentric worship; led in America by Ann Lee (1736–84), who

superiority of union over division, for the creation of wealth. But these associations have been hitherto subject to many disadvantages, and their progress and success have been materially counteracted by many obstacles which will not exist under a system, founded on a correct knowledge of the constitution of our nature.

We cannot fail to be alive to the superiority of combined over individual efforts, when applied to destroy. We all know the increased power acquired by a small army, united, and acting as one body, over the same number of men acting singly and alone – and if such advantages can be gained by union to destroy, why should it not be applied to our benefit for civil purposes?

The new combinations proposed, will be associations of men possessing real religious and mental liberty, with every means for obtaining great mental acquirements; and these, it is expected, will rapidly increase among all the members.

Under this system, real wealth will be too easily obtained in perpetuity and full security to be much longer valued as it now is by society, for the distinctions which it makes between the poor and rich. For, when the new arrangements shall be regularly organized and completed, a few hours daily, of healthy and desirable employment, chiefly applied to direct modern mechanical and other scientific improvements, will be amply sufficient to create a full supply, at all times, of the best of everything for every one, and then all things will be valued according to their intrinsic worth, will be used beneficially, and nothing will be wasted or abused. I did expect, before this time, to have received from Europe models, upon a large scale, of these new combinations, and, without which, it is difficult to comprehend that which is so wholly new in principle and practice to you. I have here drawings of some of them; they are, however, upon too small a scale to be seen by the whole assembly, but I shall have pleasure in opening them after the meeting, for the inspection of any parties who may wish to examine them.

Well knowing the great extent of these advantages, my wish now is to give them, in the shortest time, to the greatest number of my fellow creatures, and that the change from the present erroneous practices should be effected, if possible, without injury to a human being.

With this view, I am prepared to commence the system on my own private responsibility, or with partners having the same principles and feelings with myself; or by joint stock companies, under an act of incorporation from the state governments of Indiana and Illinois, in which the new properties which

emphasised celibacy, spiritual rebirth and Christ's Second Coming; active in America from 1774, and highly successful, with at least 18 colonies formed before 1861; survived until recently. The Harmonites were followers of a small German Pietist sect led by George Rapp (1757–1847) of Württemberg, who emigrated to Pennsylvania in 1804 and relocated to Indiana from 1814–24, where their community was named Harmony.

I have purchased, with a view to these establishments, are situated[a] – or, by a general incorporated company, formed of the leading persons in each state, who could easily form arrangements by which the benefit of the system might be obtained, with the least loss of time, by all the inhabitants within each Government, belonging to the Union. Improbable, and impracticable, as I well know it must appear to you, and to the mass of the public, I do not hesitate to state confidently from this chair, from which you have been accustomed to hear so many important truths, that the system which I am about to introduce into your states, is fully competent to form them into countries of palaces, gardens, and pleasure grounds, and, in one generation, to make the inhabitants a race of very superior beings.

When the principles on which this new system is founded, and the practices to which they will necessarily lead, shall be so investigated as to be fully understood, it will be discovered that the present system of society must almost immediately give way before it.

The principles of human nature, on which its morals are founded, will render union and co-operation, to any extent, not only easy, but delightful in practice. The pecuniary effects which will be produced by union and co-operation, will make the division and combination of labour, in the same persons and interest, complete, and, in consequence, all individual competition must prove unavailing, and cause loss of time and capital.

I am therefore desirous that the knowledge of this change, being about to commence, should be speedily known over the Union, that as little capital as possible should be lost by its application to objects which might be rendered of no value by the new measures which may be soon carried into extensive execution in all the states. Many, who have partially considered this subject, and who are converts to the principles, and fully alive to the benefits to be derived from the practice, are, nevertheless, impressed with the belief that the system can advance but slowly, as other great changes have been effected.

This supposition is very natural; it is in unison with the experience of the past; but their minds have not yet had time to expand to the full extent of this subject, and to discover how different its character is from all former changes. These have been merely an alteration of the mode of acting, while the fundamental principles remained untouched; but, in the present case, there will be an entire change of the fundamental principles on which society has proceeded in all countries, from the earliest period of which we possess knowledge, to the present. Compared with the mighty consequences which must flow from this change, all former revolutions in human affairs scarcely deserve a name.

This is a revolution from a system in which individual reward and punishment

[a] The Harmony community.

has been the universal practice, to one, in which individual reward and punishment will be unpractised and unknown, except as a grievous error of a past wretched system. On this account, my belief has long been, that, wherever society should be fully prepared to admit of one experiment on the new system, it could not fail to be also prepared to admit the principle from which it has been derived, and to be ready for all the practice which must emanate from the principle; and, in consequence, that the change could not be one of slow progression, but it must take place at once, and make an immediate, and almost instantaneous, revolution in the minds and manners of the society in which it shall be introduced – unless we can imagine that there are human beings who prefer sin and misery to virtue and happiness.

Let the subject be sifted and examined with the most scrutinizing care and caution, and it will prove to be as I have now stated. The truth is, that the great principle on which the new system rests, is directly opposed to that on which old society has been founded; they lead to the same opposition in practice; and there is not the slightest connection between them, nor is it possible they can long exist together. For, whenever these two principles shall be brought into fair and open competition, one or other must speedily prove to be false, and a mere notion of the imagination. The one attributes merit and demerit to belief. The other gives neither merit nor demerit to any belief, because belief has never been under the will or control of man. The one generates in man anger and irritation, because his fellow man differs from him in sentiments, habits, and feelings. The other instructs how men are necessarily made to differ in colour, in language, in habits, in sentiments, in religion, in feeling, and in conduct, and thereby implants in every one the principle of universal charity, benevolence, and kindness, and withdraws all anger from the human constitution. The one separates man from man, individualizing the human race, and thereby creating endless causes of division and opposition of interest and of feeling, and thus generates and fosters all the inferior motives and bad passions and actions which have ever pervaded society. The other forms man at once into a rational being; and, by removing every cause of dislike and jealousy, prepares the most effectual means to unite him with his fellows, and to combine them in one general system of action for their mutual benefit. In short, the one is, in reality, an imaginary notion, which has ever been impressed in infancy on the mind of the human race, in direct opposition to every known fact; a notion derived solely from the ignorance of the darkest ages, and which has so perverted the human faculties, as, with slight exceptions, to keep the whole race of men almost continually involved in war and violence, in direct opposition to the real interest of every individual. While the other is a principle derived from experience, in unison with all facts, past and present – a principle which deprecates all war and violence, and punishment of every kind; which harmonizes every feeling and faculty of the human mind, rendering it rational and humane, and uniting all in one bond of interest and affection. Therefore, between this principle, and this imaginary notion, there can be no resemblance whatever; they must abjure each other – the one being the cause of all happiness to man, the other of all misery; and the time is now come, when the principle of good is about to predominate and reign triumphant over the principle of evil; and when, in consequence, society may be most easily arranged to exist without ignorance or poverty, or vice, or crime, or misery.

It is to effect this change that I am here this night; that, if possible, a mortal blow shall be now given to the fundamental error which, till now, has governed this wretched world, and inflicted unnumbered cruelties and miseries upon its inhabitants. The time has passed, within the present hour, when this subject can be no longer smothered or hidden from the public mind of this country. It must now be open to the most free discussion, and I well know what will be the result.

At this time a match has been applied to a train, that, if I mistake not, will dispel past errors, until old things shall pass away, and all shall become new,[a] and beautiful, and delighted, bringing unnumbered and unlimited blessings to every one. I trust, this subject just now appears paramount to every other; and that the necessity for a speedy examination of it, by the highest authorities, is equally evident.

Placed as it now is before the public, a day ought not to be lost in stamping it with its proper terms of truth and falsehood. The system now advocated can be of no equivocal character – it must be full of benefit or of evil to you all; I therefore beseech you, for your sakes, and for the public benefit, to ascertain its value, that the people may know whether I have brought them a vision to amuse them, or a substantial blessing. To effect this object, may I be permitted to suggest, that competent persons be appointed, under the name of commissioners, or committee, or any other name, to examine the whole subject, a mere outline of which, in this discourse, has been hastily and slightly sketched. That, after such examination, the parties appointed to investigate, make a report for the satisfaction of the public, whose interests are so deeply involved in the result.

In what has been said I have endeavoured to show, that the subject I have introduced, is the most important that can engage the attention of mankind; that the cause of all past and present evil in society is the notion that there can be merit or demerit in any belief whatever; that this error generates all the bad passions, keeps them in perpetual activity, produces nothing but unhappiness to the human race; and that, while it shall be allowed to irrationalize each succeeding generation, sin and misery must have dominion over the world.

I have stated, also, that by the undeviating constitution of our common

[a] See 2 Corinthians 5:17.

nature, each individual has hitherto been formed by the circumstances which have been allowed to exist around him from birth to manhood; that these circumstances have been uniformly opposed to our constitution, and, consequently, of a very injurious character, producing only various degrees of vice and misery. I afterwards explained what appeared to me to be the real constitution of our nature and state; that, when circumstances shall be judiciously combined by those who have acquired an accurate knowledge of it, that each individual of our species, without a single exception, may be trained to become virtuous, intelligent, and happy, to a degree much exceeding what has been experienced under the old system of society in any part of the world: and thus far only time allows me to proceed on the present occasion.

That which requires yet to be explained, to enable the public to form a right judgment of the entire system now advocated, is a detail of the circumstances which, in combination, are to possess sufficient power to produce the extraordinary results which I have promised, and a development of the means by which, without injury to any one, they can be carried without delay into national and general practice, so as to give, almost immediately, many of the benefits of the change to the whole population of the Union, by relieving them from poverty or the fear of it, and very soon, from ignorance, and all the lamentable effects which these two evils necessarily produce.

SECOND DISCOURSE ON A NEW SYSTEM OF SOCIETY 1825

In my former discourse from this place, it was stated, that the subject which was then brought before you was the most important that could engage the attention of mankind; that the world was in error, and that all its institutions partook of it; that this error was the notion that man formed his own belief; that merit and demerit belonged to it, and that as long as this error should be forced into the minds of each succeeding generation, at an early age, the human race must continue to be, as heretofore, irrational, and their proceedings to remain as they are, and ever have been – a complicated scene of disorder, counteraction, and confusion.

It was then explained what appeared to me, after much reading, reflection, and experience, to be the constitution of our nature; that it was formed, by the power which originally gave it existence, to be influenced by the circumstances which should surround it, so as to receive any opinion, whether true or false, in accordance with facts or opposed to them, and to become, in consequence, either ignorant or intelligent, miserable or happy; and, as these results were not produced by the will or consent of the individual, no one who experienced them could rationally become a subject of praise or blame; of reward or punishment.

It was likewise stated, that I had acted upon these principles for thirty-five years; that I was never disappointed in the results which they produced; that this experiment only confirmed the previous history of human existence, which demonstrated these principles to be unerring, and that whenever they should be judiciously applied in practice, they would always prove successful. The investigation of the subject was therefore strongly recommended to the executive part of the government and to the members of Congress, that, if the principles should be found true, the people of these states might be enabled, in the shortest time, to partake of the innumerable benefits which the principles are calculated to produce in practice.

The discourse was concluded by stating that many important parts of the subject remained unnoticed, because it was apprehended that the time for the continuance of such a meeting had expired.

It was my intention to have proceeded, the next day, to pay my respects to Mr Jefferson[a] and Mr Madison,[b] but many of the audience, who were present on the former occasion, having expressed considerable disappointment that the whole subject was not before them, I consented to remain, to have this opportunity of explaining more of the principles, and the means of carrying them into national and general practice. At the particular desire of some of the distinguished individuals who are present, I will also explain some of the details of the measure which were adopted to improve the character and condition of the population at New Lanark, more than twenty-five years ago. Upon this part of the subject, some kind friend has saved me trouble, for to my surprise, I found, at Mr Pishey Thompson's[c] since the last meeting, a copy, just published, of an American edition of some of my early writings, in which, twelve years ago, I gave a narrative of my proceedings in that establishment during the first twelve years of the experiment, and, before I conclude, I will, with your permission, read some extracts from this publication. It may be here remarked that, since that work was written, I have visited personally or examined the written details of most of the public institutions which have been established in Europe for the improvement of the poor and labouring classes; communicated, personally and confidentially, with the leading men of Europe, and passed through thirteen years of the most extensive of my practice; and I have now the satisfaction to state, that these united proceedings confirm, in a remarkable manner, the truth of the principles which, at that early period, I had been led to adopt, and have enabled me to become familiar with the new science of circumstances, by which, without any chance of failure, virtue, intelligence, affluence, and happiness, may be secured to every individual of the rising generations, and by which, much may yet be attained for the present generation.

As this subject is of such deep importance to every one of us, as well as to our children and their descendants, permit me, before I proceed to any practical details, to place shortly before you, for the benefit of the public, a correct statement of the broad principles of the science, and of the general consequences to which they will lead; because, if these are not distinctly impressed on the mind, so as to be fully comprehended and clearly understood, all I may endeavour to explain, relative to measures of detail, will be of little or no practical value.

Then it should be ever remembered that the first principle of the science is derived from the knowledge of the facts, *that external circumstances may be so formed as to have an overwhelming and irresistible influence over every infant that comes into existence, either for good or evil; to compel him to receive any particular*

[a] Thomas Jefferson (1743–1826): 3rd President of the United States.
[b] James Madison (1750–1836): 4th President of the United States.
[c] Evidently a Washington bookseller.

sentiments or habits, to surround him through life with the most agreeable or disagreeable objects, and thus, at pleasure, make any portion, or the whole of the human race, poor, ignorant, vicious, and wretched; or affluent, intelligent, virtuous, and happy.

And thus also form man to understand and to practise pure and genuine religion, which never did, nor ever will consist in unmeaning phrases, forms, and ceremonies; but in the daily, undeviating practice, in thought, word, and action, of charity, benevolence, and kindness, to every human being with whom we come into communication, or have any transactions, near or remote. Now this, and this alone, is true religion, and true, because it will lead to the greatest happiness that man can enjoy, and because it is consistent, and in unison with all the facts of which we have been permitted to acquire any knowledge relative to *our* nature, and to *all* nature. And, except in this consistency, there is no other criterion of truth.

But this is not the religion of any particular person, age, or country; it is the *universal religion* of human nature. It is *true*: it therefore requires no name for its support, for truth will always support itself, without any factitious aid; and a name can be of no other use than to sanction fraud or error. This universal religion, as I trust it will speedily become, is therefore justly called *rational religion*;[a] its base is simple truth, and it defies what man, through error, can do against it. For this rational religion, now for the first time declared amidst this enlightened assembly, composed of the most distinguished men of this country within its metropolis and within its capitol, I, as a citizen of the world, claim for it the full and complete protection which the American Constitution freely offers to mental and religious liberty. I claim this protection, however, not with the slightest feeling of hostility to a single individual of the human race; my intention is to do them good – to relieve them from the error and evil by which they are now on all sides beset; and my sole object in thus claiming protection for this new religion, is to introduce into practice, and permanently secure, peace and good-will among all mankind, by destroying the selfish, and establishing the social system.

If these principles proceed from error, they will come to naught; but if they are consistent with all facts, and therefore true, who shall prevail against them?

Having then discovered, as I believe I have, the science of the influence of circumstances, and a rational, and therefore a pure and genuine religion, the next important consideration is, to ascertain in what manner the new science, and the new religion, can be applied to produce the promised practical results. I have been frequently urged to apply these principles to the present state of

[a] Owen's idea of 'rational religion' is here clearly indebted to the tradition of 'rational Dissent' (especially Arianism and Socianism, and most notably Unitarianism), which attempted to reduce Christianity to a simple set of moral precepts.

society, and not attempt to disturb it, but endeavour to make them unite harmoniously together. To this request I would most willingly accede, if it was practicable. The inventor of the steam-engine might as well have been required to unite his new machinery with the inefficient and clumsy horse-engine, which, at that time, was commonly used to obtain mechanical force; or the inventor of the spinning-machinery, to unite it with the woollen and flax single-wheels; or the person who introduced the gas-lights, to combine it with the common candle. These things are impracticable, and every one knows that to attempt to effect any of them, would be a loss of time and labour; in like manner, were I to endeavour to unite the system which I advocate, with the present notions and practices of society, my time and labour would be uselessly employed.

The fact is, and I am most anxious that all parties should fully understand me, the system which I propose now for the formation and government of society, is founded on principles, not only altogether different, but directly opposed to the system of society which has hitherto been taught and practised at all times, in all nations; and, until the public mind can be elevated to this point, I shall not be understood; my attempt at explanation must fail to be comprehended, and an inexplicable confusion of ideas will alone remain. The error must be mine; I have not yet been sufficiently explicit; but upon this occasion, I must endeavour to put the contrast between the two systems, in such a point of view as not to be misunderstood. The old system of the world, by which I mean all the past and the present proceedings of mankind, presupposes, that human nature is originally corrupt – that man forms his own belief and his own character – that, if these shall be formed in a particular manner, the individual will deserve an artificial reward, both here and hereafter; but if this belief, and this character shall not be so formed, the individual will deserve an artificial punishment both here and hereafter. The theory of the old system is therefore founded on notions directly opposed to our nature, and its practice is individual rewards and punishments.

The new system presupposes that human nature is now what it ever has been, and will be, and what the power which produced it formed it to be originally; that man does not create his own belief, or his own character, physical or mental; that his belief and character are uniformly created for him, and that he cannot possess merit or demerit for the formation of either; that he is a compound being, formed by the impressions made by external circumstances, upon his individual nature, and, as he had no will, or knowledge, or power, in deciding upon the creation of either, he cannot become a rational object for individual reward or punishment; that man is a being formed to be irresistibly controlled by external circumstances, and to be compelled to act according to the knowledge which these circumstances produce in him; that a knowledge of this fact will compel him to make himself acquainted with the nature of circumstances, so as to understand the effects which they will produce on human nature, and, through that knowledge, compel him to govern all circumstances, within his control, for the benefit of his own and succeeding generations.

The old system has been influenced in all ages, by some imaginary notions or other, under the name of religion, but which notions have been, in all countries, uniformly opposed to facts, and, in consequence, all minds have been thereby rendered more or less irrational. The new system, as I have previously stated, adopts a religion derived from the facts which demonstrate what human nature really is, and which facts give to man all the knowledge he possesses respecting himself; it is, therefore, called rational religion, or a religion of demonstrable truth, of intelligence, and of universal charity and benevolence, and derived from the evidence of our senses.

The old system keeps its votaries in ignorance, makes them mere localized beings, and the perpetual slaves of a combination of the most inferior and worst circumstances, and, in consequence, society is a chaos of superstition, passion, prejudice, poverty in many, and ignorance of their real interest in all; while the new system makes man familiar with his true interests, and, in consequence, gives him the knowledge and power to combine and govern circumstances in such a manner as to secure it, and unerringly to produce happiness to himself and others.

And this is the practical point at which I wished to arrive to produce benefit from this discourse. In my former address, I stated that, to produce the greatest happiness for the greatest number, three things were necessary:

1st. A proper training and education, from birth, of the physical and mental powers of each child.

2d. Arrangements to enable each individual to procure, in the best manner, at all times, a full supply of those things which are necessary and the most beneficial for human nature; and

3d. That all individuals should be so combined in a social system, as to give to each the greatest benefits from society.

Now, practical arrangements to produce these results have never yet been formed, or any thing, approaching to them. They cannot be found in any single and detached dwelling, in any village, town, or city, in any part of the world. I am, therefore, justified in saying, that, like old machines, when a new one of very superior powers has been invented to supersede them, separate dwelling houses, villages, towns, and cities, must give place to other combinations.

Now, if circumstances possess an overwhelming and irresistible influence over the whole human race, so as to make every individual either happy or miserable, is it not of the last importance to all of us, to become learned in that science, an accurate knowledge of which will enable the present generation to remove misery from the succeeding one, and secure happiness to their posterity?

What other subject can be brought into comparison with this? Or rather, when compared with it, do not all other subjects either lose their value or become extremely insignificant?

If I am right, the first and most important inquiry for human beings ought to be, to ascertain *what* circumstances produce *evil*, and what *good*, and *how* circumstances can be arranged to *produce* the *latter*, and *exclude* the *former*. To become learned in these matters of the deepest interest to my fellow men, has been the study and practice of my life; and as the result of such study and practice, I submit for your most serious consideration the new combination of circumstances which are now before you. They have been very hastily put together by Mr Hutton of this city,[a] since our last meeting, and cannot be expected to give more than a very imperfect sketch of the outline of the plan, as it will appear in actual practice.

I am now prepared to say, with a confidence that fears no refutation, and which nothing, except being fully master of the whole subject, could so impress on my mind, that all existing external human or artificial circumstances must speedily give place to these. And, as the essential interests of each one, whatever may be his present rank, station, or condition, in the world, will be promoted to an incalculable extent by the change, I trust that one and all who are present, and the whole American population, will now begin to study the subject, and, when masters of it, assist each other with all their power to remove, speedily, the present wretched and irrational circumstances, and to replace them by others which must, of necessity, make them intelligent and happy.

A model of the combinations to produce those beneficial results is now before you, and such buildings, with a variation of architecture, according to local circumstances, and the views of the parties who form them, placed within 1,000 or 2,000 acres of land, cultivated like a garden, and laid out as pleasure grounds, will be, I presume, the future habitation of the human race.

I express myself thus decisively, because, by a combination of singular circumstances, by long study and experience, I have been permitted to acquire some knowledge on this subject unknown to others.

The model before you contains an arrangement, purposely formed, to enable each individual to possess in perpetuity, and enjoy through life, without anxiety, the three objects which have been enumerated, and it may be justly considered to be a new machine for performing, in a superior manner, all the purposes of human life.

Before any rational arrangements could be made for an improved society, it became necessary to ascertain what number of persons could be associated together, to give to each the greatest advantage with the fewest inconveniences; that is, to combine the most desirable benefits which the country and

[a] Hutton cannot be identified with any certainty.

cities afford; adding to these the best arrangements for education, from infancy to manhood, the best and most economical arrangements for producing from agriculture and manufactures, for consuming their productions; then uniting the whole to form a social system in which there should be but one interest, and in which each individual should go on continually from one step of improvement to another, acquiring thereby the highest and purest enjoyments of which our nature is susceptible.

Such are the principles on which the arrangements before you have been formed.

The model represents a square of buildings, each side of which is 1,000 feet in length, and each side contains every domestic arrangement that can be required for 5,000 persons. The square is also intended to contain a complete school, academy, and university, in which a superior education will be given from infancy to maturity, and it will comprise the first combination of circumstances which has yet been formed to do any thing like justice to the physical and mental powers of any human being. The four buildings within the square, one of which projects from the centre of each of the sides, contain the culinary arrangements, the dining apartments, stores, washing, drying, brewing, and every other domestic accommodation, arranged in a superior manner, by men of great science and practical experience. The schools, lecture rooms, laboratories, chapels, ball and concert rooms, conversation rooms, committee and other public rooms, are in the centres and angles of the building. The private dwellings of the inhabitants are between the centres and angles, and occupy the first and second stories. The third story contains the dormitories for the unmarried persons, and children above two years of age. There is a communication under cover, from each dwelling to every other, and to all the public rooms, throughout the whole extent of the square. Each apartment will be heated, cooled, ventilated, supplied with gas lights, and hot or cold water, at the will of the occupants, by merely turning a cock or moving a slide. All the apartments may be cooled in warm weather much below, and warmed in cold weather much above, the temperature of the atmosphere, and, under these scientific domestic arrangements, one person, chiefly employed in an interesting direction of mechanical and chemical operations, will perform as much as twenty, under the separate individual system, can accomplish in the same time. By these new arrangements, two essential objects will be secured; the operative, or producer, will be better trained and educated than the working, or any class, has been heretofore, and they will be supported at a less expense than must be incurred under any individual system, which can afford but one-half of the advantages that these new arrangements will secure to every one, even from the commencement. Under these circumstances, therefore, manual and mental power would be produced of a superior quality, and maintained at a less expenditure than under the separate, or individual system; consequently, all other circumstances being supposed to be the same, whatever these united labours produce, whether from agriculture or manufactures, will be better and cheaper than similar productions can be brought to market by any individual, seeing that the cost of all productions consists in the value of the labour they contain. Upon this principle, now universally admitted, the present buildings in the country, in villages, towns, and cities, will as rapidly disappear as the new combinations before you can be introduced into practice.

This combination, however, will not only create a superior quality of labour, and support it in more comfort at a much less expense than any individual system, but it will place the parties under the most favourable circumstances for gardening, agricultural and manufacturing operations, which will be so united as to enable each to assist the others, at the different seasons of the year, in such a manner as to secure seed and harvest operations with one-fourth of the favourable weather required in farms and gardens under the present system.

In short, the advantages of this new combination, for health, for forming a superior character; for producing, for consuming, for securing, free from all pecuniary anxieties, the chief benefits, without the disadvantages, of a country, city and college life, and for enjoying the best society in the most convenient manner, will be discovered to offer such overwhelming temptations to human nature to change from the present system, that I conclude it will be impracticable to provide these new abodes of rational improvement and enjoyment, as speedily as society will desire to possess them.

When these buildings, gardens, and pleasure-grounds shall be formed, the next important inquiry is, how are they to be governed?

To explain this part of the subject, I will, with your permission, now read some rules and regulations*[a] which were drawn up, two or three years ago, for an independent society, to be formed of the operative classes, upon the supposition that they borrowed all the capital.

Such are the rules and regulations which are proposed and recommended for an association of the operative classes, on these new principles of union and co-operation; and I have no doubt but the plain good sense and practical knowledge of many among those classes, will be found, with very little assistance, sufficient to understand the principles, and to carry them into successful execution. And, if they were to carry them into practice upon borrowed capital, what security could be offered superior to that which they could give? namely, land well chosen for their purpose, and bought at its present value; buildings erected, to be much more convenient, and therefore, in the same proportion, more valuable than any existing buildings; the land annually improving, by an extensive and improved cultivation, and manufactures established under the latest improvements; these, added to the security of an

* See at the end.

[a] See *Proceedings of the First General Meeting of the British and Foreign Philanthropic Society* (1822), pp. 46–56.

association of from 1000 to 2000 industrious and temperate persons, each aiding and none opposing each other, would present such an aggregate of substantial security, continually improving, as is not to be found, perhaps, under any other circumstances. I hope the Governments of all the States composing the Union, will investigate the whole of this subject, in such a manner as to enable the citizens of each State to become fully satisfied, that the principles on which it rests are so true, that error cannot be found in them, and the practice so beneficial, that it will be evidently the interest of one and all to adopt it without the least delay, that not one day more of unnecessary anxiety and suffering should be experienced by the inhabitants of this country. But, whatever others may do, my purpose is fixed; I mean to carry these measures of amelioration, to the full extent of my means and influence, into immediate execution.

With this view, I have purchased from the Harmonite Society the settlement and property of Harmony, in the States of Indiana and Illinois. The settlement, or town of Harmony, is upon the Wabash, in Indiana; it is composed of log, weather boarded, and brick dwelling houses; of infant manufactures, of wool, cotton, leather, hats, pottery, bricks, machinery, grain, distilleries, breweries, etc with granaries, and two large Churches, and other public buildings, laid out in regular squares like all the modern American towns. It does not, however, form such a combination as the model before you represents, and therefore it will serve only a temporary, but yet a useful temporary purpose, for the objects which I have in view. It will enable me to form immediately a preliminary society, in which to receive a new population, and to collect, prepare, and arrange the materials for erecting several such combinations, as the model represents, and of forming several independent, yet united associations, having common property, and one common interest. These new establishments will be erected upon the high lands of Harmony, from two to four miles from the river and its Island, of which the occupants will have a beautiful and interesting view, there being several thousand acres of well cultivated land, on a rich second bottom, lying between the high lands and the river. And here it is, in the heart of the United States, and almost the centre of its unequalled internal navigation, that that power which directs and governs the universe and every action of man, has arranged circumstances which were far beyond my control, to permit me to commence a new empire of peace and good will to man, founded on other principles, and leading to other practices than those of the past or present, and which principles, in due season, and in the allotted time, will lead to that state of virtue, intelligence, enjoyment, and happiness, in practice, which has been foretold by the sages of past times, would, at some distant period become the lot of the human race! Do not the dissatisfaction of all minds, in all countries, with the existing circumstances; the evident advance of just, kind, and benevolent feelings, and the universal expectation of some great change in human affairs, indicate and foretel this change? Do they not give assurance that the time is at hand when evil shall give place to good – division to union – war to peace – anger to kindness – superstition to charity, and pure practical religion – prejudice to intelligence – and pain and misery to enjoyment and happiness? Assuredly they do, and it will be wise and prudent in us to be prepared for the event.

I have, however, no wish to lead the way; I am most desirous that Governments should become masters of the subject, adopt the principles, encourage the practice, and thereby retain the direction of the public mind for its own benefit, and the benefit of the people. But, as I have not the control of circumstances to insure success in this public course, I must, as I have stated, show what private exertions, guided by these new principles, can accomplish at Harmony, and these new proceedings will commence there early in April. It was currently reported, when I arrived in this country, that Harmony was unhealthy, and, in consequence, I had nearly given up the intention which I entertained of purchasing it; but having crossed the Atlantic with the intention of examining for myself, and knowing from personal experience, how little truth is generally to be found in reports connected with any thing new in society, I proceeded to the place and examined the facts in person. I then discovered, that for the first three years after the Harmonites made the settlement, the colony was very unhealthy, and this naturally gave rise to the reports. From that period, however, the settlement has become every year more healthy, and for several years past, it has been remarkably so, until the year before last, out of 800, five died, and last year, from the same number, two only died. The change has no doubt arisen from the land being well drained and cultivated, and the woods being extensively cleared. These operations will be now soon more extended, and I conclude that the future inhabitants of Harmony, under their rational mode of life, will be as healthy as the same number of persons in any part of the world.

I have drawn out a prospectus of a preliminary society to be established at Harmony, until arrangements can be formed to enable the parties who meet there to commence the new system according to its genuine principles and practices.

I have been asked, what would be the effect upon the neighbourhood and surrounding country, were one or more of these societies of union, co-operation, and common property, should be established?

My conviction is, that, from necessity and inclination, the individual or old system of society would break up, and soon terminate; from necessity, because the new societies would undersell all individual producers, both of agricultural productions and manufactured commodities; and from inclination, because it is scarcely to be supposed that any one would continue to live under the miserable, anxious, individual system of opposition and counteraction, when they could with ease form themselves into, or become members of, one of these associations of union, intelligence, and kind feeling.

If, then, it has been further asked of me, these societies spread by their successful commercial operations, and the increased comforts and advantages which they offer to the whole population, what effects will they have upon the government, and the general prosperity of an extensive empire?

I again reply, that, a country, however extensive, divided into these arrangements of improved social buildings, gardens, and pleasure grounds, and these, occupied and cultivated by persons possessing superior dispositions, habits, and intelligence, will be governed with much more ease than it can be with the same number of inhabitants, scattered, irregularly over the country, living in common villages, towns, or cities, under the individual system. And that the expense of the government would be diminished as much as the trouble and anxiety. It is not unlikely that these would be diminished to one-tenth of their present amount. The effects which would be produced on the general prosperity of the country would be equally important and beneficial.

It may, perhaps, with confidence be stated, that any country will be prosperous in proportion to the number, and physical and mental superiority of its inhabitants. Now, the system of union, common property, and co-operation proposed will from the same soil, support, in high comfort, double numbers, at the least, and hence its commercial superiority over the individual arrangements of society. And by this improved system, especial care is taken that each child, without a single exception, shall by a superior training and education, under the most favourable circumstances, have full justice done to all his physical and mental faculties, and by these means a whole population will be formed, each full of bodily and mental health and vigour. There will be, therefore, upon the same soil, a double population, each of whom, through a wise arrangement of circumstances, will be a superior being, when compared with the mere localized man, which the individual system has hitherto formed, and while it is retained, must everywhere produce.

For defence against the attack of such irrational nations as may surround a country so peopled, the boys, while at school, for their exercise, might be taught military and naval tactics in the best manner, and they would soon become, and present such a force as to be impenetrable from without, and they would have minds too rational, intelligent, and benevolent, ever to be led into offensive warfare.

These communities are in complete union with the principles on which the constitution of this country is founded. The constitution is essentially a government of the union of independent states, acting together for their mutual benefit. The new communities would stand in the same relation to their respective state governments, that the states do now to the general government, and in consequence, the arduous duties of both will be most probably materially diminished.

I may further add, that the system is one of genuine liberty and equality, being in fact, the only system which contains the principles that can produce sufficient individual and general practical virtue to admit of the full enjoyment of the inestimable blessings of full liberty and equality. Ignorance and vice require restraints, but virtue and intelligence need them not.

Such then being the overwhelming advantages of the united social, over the individual selfish system, permit me to ask, what can support the latter much longer against the former? And why should not the united social system be now adopted by every intelligent mind?

Allow me to add, that in supporting the new system in opposition to the old, to do justice to the former I am frequently under the necessity of using strong expressions, and I fear I must occasionally hurt the feelings of persons who have been trained to have a high respect, and even veneration, for what I am obliged to think the errors of the old system. If there be any such present, I request their forgiveness, and I assure them that except in the cause of a high and important duty, paramount to every other consideration, it is quite contrary to all my feelings and principles, to say any thing to offend those from whom I am obliged to differ in opinion, and if I have so offended any one on the present, or former occasion, I beg it may be attributed to the real cause, the love of truth, and an ardent desire to relieve my fellow-men from the sufferings which they experience.

[Here Mr O read from a work, of which he had met with a copy at Mr Thompson's Book Store in this city, an account of the experiment at New Lanark, its schools, etc][a]

This was the origin of the new infant schools which are now spreading rapidly over the British isles. The singular good effects which were seen to arise from these, induced Mr Brougham,[b] Mr John Smith, MP,[c] the Marquis of Lansdown,[d] and other gentlemen, to form one at their own expense in the metropolis, to exhibit to the public the incredible results which they could be made to produce.[e]

[a] Published accounts of New Lanark at this time included: John Brown, *Remarks on the Plans and Publications of Robert Owen Esq. of New Lanark* (Edinburgh, 1817); 'Christianus' [John Minter Morgan], *Mr. Owen's Proposed Villages for the Poor Shown to be Highly Favourable to Christianity* (1819); Henry Gray Macnab, *The New Views of Mr. Owen Impartially Examined* (1819); [John Minter Morgan], *Remarks on the Practicability of Robert Owen's Plan* (1819); *A Vindication of Mr. Owen's Plan for the Relief of the Distressed Working Classes* (1820).

[b] Henry Brougham (1778–1868): Whig lawyer, MP and friend of Owen's for nearly fifty years; Baron of Brougham and Vaux after becoming Lord Chancellor in 1831.

[c] John Abel Smith (1801–71): banker and Whig MP 1830–59, 1863–8; campaigned for Jewish emancipation; also a member of the British and Foreign Philanthropic Society, and aided the Orbiston community.

[d] Henry Petty-Fitzmaurice (1780–1863), 3rd Marquis of Lansdowne: leading Whig, free trader, liberal reformer; friend of Bentham.

[e] One of Owen's teachers at New Lanark, James Buchanan, was hired for the purpose. (See *infra*, vol. 4, pp. 193–5.)

For this purpose they were supplied with a master from New Lanark, about four years ago, and he remains at the head of that establishment.

From this infant school many similar ones have been formed, and are now in active operation, both in London and many of the provincial towns, and also in some villages. Experience induces me to say, that this is the most important step, imperfect as it is, that has yet been made in a rational system of instruction. The good effects of them are incalculable, and the expense is very inconsiderable.

A NEW SOCIETY IS ABOUT TO BE COMMENCED AT HARMONY, INDIANA

The direct object of this association is to give and secure happiness to all its members.

This object will be obtained by the adoption of a system of union and co-operation, founded on a spirit of universal charity, derived from a correct knowledge of the constitution of human nature.

The knowledge thus derived will be found abundantly sufficient to reconcile all religions and other differences.

But to insure success in practice, a preliminary society will be organized, and directed by those who understand the principles of this system, and who have already proved them by a partial yet extensive practice.

Into this preliminary society respectable families and individuals with capital, and industrious and well disposed families and individuals without capital, will be received.

Those who possess capital, and who do not wish to be employed, may partake of the benefits of this society on paying a sum annually, sufficient to recompense the society for their expenditure.

Those without capital, will be employed, according to their abilities and inclinations, in building, in agriculture, in gardening, in manufactures, in mechanical trades, in giving instruction in elementary or scientific knowledge, or in some one useful occupation, beneficial to the society. In return for which, they will be provided with the best lodging, food, and clothing, that the circumstances of the establishment will afford: they will experience every attention during sickness and in old age. All the children will be brought up together, as members of the same family, and will receive a good and superior education.

At the end of every year, a certain amount, in value, will be placed to the credit of each family, and each individual, not being a member of the family, in proportion to their expenditure, and to the services rendered by them to the society.

Any persons may leave the society at any time, and take with them, in the productions of the establishment, as much in value as shall be placed to their credit, at the annual balance immediately preceding the time when they cease to become members of the society.

During the continuence of the preliminary society, any family or individual, whose conduct may be injurious to the well being and happiness of the association, and obstructs its progress, will be removed; but it is expected that the spirit of charity, justice, forbearance, and kindness, which will direct the whole proceedings of the society, and which will be soon diffused through all its members, will speedily render the dismissal of any one unnecessary.

As soon as circumstances will permit, it is intended that a society shall be formed, consistent in all respects with the constitution of human nature, the general principles and practices of which are explained in the prefixed paper, entitled, 'An outline of a new system of society, recommended for immediate and general practice by Robert Owen, of New Lanark:'[a] and in this society, all will be equal in rights and property, and the only distinction will be that of age and experience.

Members of the preliminary society, who shall acquire such a knowledge of the principles of the new system, as to enable and induce them to apply them to practice, may become members of this more perfect association, in which, it is anticipated, from experiments already tried during thirty-five years, that almost, if not all, the causes which have hitherto produced evil in the world will be gradually removed.

GENERAL RULES AND REGULATIONS,

Proposed by Mr Owen for an Independent Community, subject to such alterations as circumstances may indicate.

IT IS PROPOSED, –

I. THAT the Community shall consist of persons who have agreed to co-operate, with their labour and skill, in measures for producing, distributing, and enjoying, in the most advantageous manner, a full supply of the necessaries

[a] No separately published work of this precise title is known.

and comforts of life; and for securing for their children the best physical and intellectual education.

II. That, at the commencement, the number of persons shall not much exceed five hundred including their families.

III. That, as it is of great importance that the Community should produce within itself a full supply of the first necessaries of life, there shall be attached to the establishment a sufficient extent of LAND to render it essentially *agricultural.*

IV. That a Village, to be situated as near the centre of the Land as local circumstances may permit, be built according to the plan and elevations given in the engravings.

In this village the dwelling-houses, dormitories, etc form the sides of a large square; in the centre of which are placed the requisite public buildings, surrounded by public walks and exercise grounds. This form has been adopted as giving superior accommodation to the dwelling-houses, and admitting the application, at the least expense, of scientific improvements in all the departments of domestic economy.

V. That the manufactories, work-shops, granaries, stores, washing and drying houses, be placed at the most convenient distance beyond the gardens which surround the village; and that the farm offices be situated according to the localities of the land.

VI. That, whenever the capital advanced by its own members shall have been repaid, and the education of all be sufficiently advanced, the management of the establishment shall be confined to a Committee, composed of all the Members between certain ages; as, for example, between forty and fifty. But that, until *such period*, the Committee shall consist of twelve persons, to be elected at an Annual General Meeting; eight to be chosen from among those Members who have advanced capital to the amount £100 or upwards, and four from the other Members. The Committee to be empowered to elect the Treasurers and Secretaries.

VII. That the Treasurers be empowered to receive all monies due to the Community, and pay its disbursements on orders signed by the Secretary. That they balance and report their accounts every week to the Committee, who shall appoint two of their number to examine and pass them under their signatures.

VIII. That the Secretary be directed to keep a regular detailed daily statement of all the accounts and transactions of the Community, and that such statement be presented weekly to the Committee, and submitted to the examination of two of their number, who shall pass it under their signatures, with such observations as may occur to them.

IX. That the books of accounts and transactions of the Society be open to the inspection of all its Members.

X. That the business of the Community be divided into the following departments:

1. Agriculture and gardening.
2. Manufactures and trades.
3. Commercial transactions.
4. Domestic economy: comprehending the arrangements for heating, ventilating, lighting, cleaning, and keeping in repair dwelling-houses and public buildings of the village; the arrangements connected with the public kitchens and dining halls; those for the furnishing of clothes, linen, and furniture, and for washing and drying; and the management of the dormitories.
5. Health, or the medical superintendence of the sick, including arrangements to prevent contagion or sickness.
6. Police, including the lighting and cleansing the square; the repairing of the roads and walks; guarding against fire, and the protection of the property of the Community from external depredation.
7. Education, or the formation of character from infancy: to this department will also belong the devising the best means of recreation.

XI. That, for the general superintendence of these departments, the Committee appoint Sub-Committees from their own number, or from the other Members of Society; each of the Sub-Committees shall lay a weekly report before the Committee, to be examined and passed, with such observations as may be deemed necessary.

XII. That, should there not be at first a sufficient number of persons in the Community fully competent to the management of the different branches of industry, which it may be desirable to establish, the Committee be empowered to engage the assistance of skilful practical men from general society.

XIII. That in regulating the employments of the Members according to their age, abilities, previous acquirements, and situation in life, the Committee pay every regard to the inclinations of each, consistent with the general good; and that the employment be so ordered as to permit every individual, who may be so disposed, to occupy part of his time in agriculture.

Great facilities will be afforded to agriculture by the power which the Community will always possess of calling out an extra number of hands, at those times and seasons when it is of the utmost importance to have additional aid.

XIV. That, as under the proposed arrangements, every invention for the abridgment of human labour will bring an increase of benefit to all, it be a primary object with the Committee to introduce, to the utmost, practical extent, all those modern scientific improvements, which, if rightly applied, are calculated to render manual labour only a healthy and agreeable exercise.

XV. That the first object of the Community be to produce a full supply of the necessaries and comforts of life for domestic consumption; and, as far as localities will permit, directly from their own land and labour.

XVI. That, in regard to domestic consumption, each Member of the Community shall be fully supplied with the necessaries and comforts of life.

XVII. That, within the Community, all the Members be in equal rights and privileges, according to their respective ages.

XVIII. That, to avoid the evils arising from a system of credit, the commercial transactions of the Community be conducted for ready money or barter only; that these transactions, on the part of the Community, be always performed in good faith, and without the slightest attempt to deceive buyer or seller; and that, when any individuals with whom they deal show a disposition to impose upon the Community, all dealings with such individuals shall from that time cease.

XIX. That the surplus proceeds of the united exertions of the Community, which remain after discharging rent, interest, taxes, and other expenses, be regularly applied to liquidation of the capital borrowed upon the establishment; and when this debt is cancelled, it is proposed that the future surplus be invested to form a fund for the establishment of a second Community, should the increased population of the first require it.

XX. That, in the domestic department, the following arrangements and regulations be adopted:

1. The heating, ventilating, and lighting of the dwelling-houses and public buildings shall be effected according to the most approved methods.
2. An ample supply of water shall be provided and distributed to each building, for domestic purposes and as a security against fire.
3. Provisions of the best quality only, shall be cooked in the public kitchen, and it shall be a special object to those persons who have the direction of this department, to ascertain and put in practice the best and most economical means of preparing nutritious and agreeable food. Any parties being ill, or desirous of having their meals alone, may have them sent to their private apartments.
4. The furniture of the dwelling-houses, domitories, and public buildings (as far as the same be provided out of the public funds), shall be devised in reference to intrinsic use and comfort. A similar regulation will apply to the clothing of the Community. Among the children, very essential improvements may be introduced, which will not only save much useless expense, but be the means of increasing, in a very high degree, the strength of the constitution.
5. The dormitories designed for the children above two years of age, and those for the youth of the Community, until the period of marriage, shall be divided into compartments, and furnished with accommodations suited to the different ages.

XXI. That the employments of the female part of the Community consist in preparing food and clothing; in the care of the dwelling-houses, dormitories, and public buildings; in the management of the washing and drying-houses; in the education (in part) of the children, and other occupations suited to the female character. By the proposed domestic arrangements, *one* female will, with great ease and comfort, perform as much as *twenty* menial servants can do at present; and instead of the wife of a working man, with a family, being a drudge and a slave, she will be engaged only in healthy and cleanly employments, acquire better manners, and have sufficient leisure for mental improvement and rational enjoyment.

XXII. That it be a general rule, that every part of the establishment be kept in the highest state of order and neatness, and that the utmost personal cleanliness be observed.

XXIII. That the following objects and regulations, connected with the department of health, be attended to and adopted.

1. That, on the first appearance of indisposition in any of the Members, immediate attention be given to it, and every possible care be taken of the patient till complete recovery; the prevention of serious complaints being, always far more easy than to effect a cure after the disease has fixed itself in the constitution.
2. The complaint of indisposition by any individual, shall place him or her on the invalid list, on which the patient will remain until the medical attendant pronounce complete recovery.
3. The arrangements of the apartments for the sick shall be such as to afford every possible comfort to patients, and provide much more effectual means of recovery than their private dwellings could admit of.
4. Removal to the apartments for the sick shall be at the option of the individual.
5. As the health of the Community may be materially improved, or injured, by the interior plan of the dwelling-houses, by their situation with respect to other buildings, by dress, food, employment, the temper and general state of the mind, and by various other circumstances, the attention of the Sub-Committee of this department shall be constantly directed to this important consideration.

XXIV. That as the right education of the rising generation is, under Divine Providence, the base upon which the future prosperity and happiness of the Community must be founded, the Committee shall regard this as the most important of all the departments committed in their direction, and employ in its superintendence those individuals whose talents, attainments, and dispositions render them best qualified for such a charge.

The children of the Community shall be educated together, and as one family, in the schools and exercise grounds provided for them in the centre of the square; where they will at all times be under the eye and inspection of their parents.

By properly conducting their education, it will be easy to give each child good tempers and habits; with as sound a constitution as air, exercise, and temperance, can bestow;

A facility in reading, writing, and accounts;

The clements of the most useful sciences, including geography and natural history;

A practical knowledge of agriculture and domestic economy, with a knowledge of some ONE useful manufacture, trade, or occupation, so that his employment may be varied, for the improvement of his mental and physical powers;

And lastly, a knowledge of himself and of human nature, to form him into a rational being, and render him charitable, kind, and benevolent to all his fellow-creatures.

XXV. That when the youth of the Community shall have attained their sixteenth year, they be permitted either to become members, or to go out into general society, with every advantage which the Community can afford them.

XXVI. That intelligent and experienced matrons be appointed to instruct the young mothers in the best mode of treating and training children from birth until they are two years old, (the age at which it is proposed to send them to the schools and dormitories) that their constitutions, habits, and dispositions may not be injured during that period.

XXVII. That, in winter and unfavourable weather, a sufficient variety of amusements and recreations, proper for the Members of such a Community, be prepared within doors, to afford beneficial relaxation from employment and study.

XXVIII. That, as liberty of conscience, religious and mental liberty, will be possessed by every Member of the Community, arrangements be made to accommodate all denominations with convenient places of worship, and that each individual be strongly recommended to exhibit in his whole conduct the utmost forbearance, kindness, and charity towards all who differ from him.

XXIX. That in advanced age, and in case of disability from accident, natural infirmity, or any other cause, the individual shall be supported by the Community, and receive every comfort which kindness can administer.

XXX. That on the death of parents, the children shall become the peculiar care of the Community, and proper persons be appointed to take the more immediate charge of them, and as far as possible supply the place of their natural parents.

XXXI. That the Committee of Management shall not be empowered to admit a new Member without the consent of three-fourths of the Members of the Community, obtained at a general meeting.

XXXII. That, although at the period when all the Members shall have been trained and educated under the proposed arrangements, any regulations against misconduct will be unnecessary; and although it is anticipated that the influence of these new circumstances upon the character of the individuals whose habits and dispositions have been formed under a different system, will be sufficiently powerful to render any serious difference of rare occurrence among them; yet in order to provide against such, it shall be a law of the Community, that, when differences arise, they be referred to the decision of arbitrators, to be elected by the Society, who, after hearing the parties, shall decide upon the case.

XXXIII. That if the conduct of any individual be injurious to the well-being of the Community, and it be so decided by three-fourths of the Members assembled at a general meeting, the Committee shall explain to him in what respect his conduct has been injurious, and at the same time intimate to him that, unless the cause of complaint be removed, they are instructed to expel him from the Community.

XXXIV. That any Member wishing to withdraw from the Community, be at full liberty to do so at any time; and the Committee shall be authorized to allow any such gratuity as the circumstances of the case may require.

XXXV. That the Committee form arrangements by which all the Members shall enjoy equal opportunities of visiting their friends elsewhere, or of travelling for information on other objects.

XXXVI. That the Committee appoint duly qualified persons to travel, from time to time, to collect scientific and other information for the benefit of the Community.

XXXVII. That, in order to extend the benefits of a system of union and co-operation, which is applicable to mankind in every part of the world, measures be adopted by the Committee to disseminate a knowledge of the new principles and arrangements.

XXXVIII. That, as this system is directly opposed to secrecy and exclusion of any kind, every practicable facility shall be given to strangers, to enable them to become acquainted with the constitution, laws, and regulations of the Community, and to examine the results, which these have produced in practice.

XXXIX. That the Committee be charged with the duty of communicating, on all occasions, to the government of the country, an unreserved explanation of the views and proceedings of the Community.

ADDRESS

DELIVERED BY ROBERT OWEN, OF NEW LANARK[a]

I am come to this country, to introduce an entire new state of society; to change it from the ignorant, selfish system, to an enlightened, social system, which shall gradually unite all interests into one, and remove all cause for contest between individuals.

The individual system has heretofore universally prevailed; and while it continues, the great mass of mankind must remain, as they comparatively are at present, ignorant, poor, oppressed, and, consequently, vicious, and miserable; and though it should last for numberless ages, virtue and happiness cannot be attained, nor can man, strictly speaking, become a rational being.

Until the individual system shall be entirely abandoned, it will be useless to expect any substantial, permanent improvement in the condition of the human race; for this system ever has been, and must ever remain, directly opposed to universal charity, benevolence and kindness; and until the means were discovered, and can be brought into practice, by which universal charity, benevolence and kindness, can be made to pervade the heart and mind of every human being, a state of society in which 'peace on earth and good will to man'[b] shall exist, must remain unknown and unenjoyed by mankind.

These invaluable blessings can be obtained only under a social system; a system derived from an accurate knowledge of human nature, and of the circumstances by which it is, or may be, governed.

This knowledge has been, until now, hidden from man; he therefore knew not how to put the social system into practice; for without this knowledge, the social system is utterly impracticable. The slight attempts which have been made, in ancient and modern times, to procure some of the innumerable advantages, with which the social system abounds, have not proceeded from this knowledge, but have been founded on some artificial or unnatural view of our nature, and in consequence, only partial and temporary benefits have been obtained.

---

[a] Published in the first issue of the journal of the New Harmony community, *The New Harmony Gazette*, vol. 1, no. 1 (1 October 1825), pp. 1–3, with the title, 'Address by Robert Owen, of New-Lanark, on Wednesday, the 27th of April, 1825, in the Hall of New-Harmony, Indiana. Together with the Constitution of the Preliminary Society founded 1st May 1825'.

[b] See Luke 2:14.

The knowledge of our nature, and of the circumstances which govern the character and conduct of man, are to be acquired only by attending to the facts which exist around us, and to the past history of the human species.

These facts and this history, demonstrate, that all men are formed by a creative power, and by the circumstances which are permitted to surround them from birth; and that no man has ever had any will, or power, or control, in creating himself, nor in forming the circumstances which exist around him at birth, in his childhood, in youth, or in manhood. He is a being, then, whose general nature, whose individual, or personal nature, and whose artificial acquirements, or character, have been formed for him. He cannot, therefore, become a proper subject for praise or blame, nor for artificial reward or punishment, or artificial accountability; but he becomes a being capable of being formed into the extremes of good or bad, and to experience the extremes of happiness or misery, by, and through the circumstances which shall exist around him at birth, in childhood, in youth, and in manhood: he cannot, therefore, become a rational object for anger or displeasure of any kind; but in whatever deplorable circumstances he may be found, and whatever may be the character which nature and these circumstances may have formed for him, he is a being who justly claims our compassion, care, attention and kindness, in proportion to the extent of the evil and misery which he has been made to experience; and to this rule there can be no exception.

These fundamental principles being understood, and the real nature of man being thus laid open to us, the proceedings requisite to produce good instead of evil, and happiness instead of misery, become obvious and easy of practice.

I have bought this property, and have now come here to introduce this practice, and to render it familiar to all the inhabitants of this country.

But to change from the individual to the social system; from single families with separate interests, to communities of many families with one interest, cannot be accomplished at once; the change would be too great for the present habits of society; nor can it be effected in practice, except by those who have been long acquainted with each other, and whose habits, condition and sentiments, are similar; it becomes necessary, therefore, that some intermediate measures should be adopted, to enable all parties, with the least inconvenience, to change their individual, selfish habits, and to acquire the superior habits requisite to a social state; to proceed, if I may so express myself, to a halfway house on this new journey from poverty to wealth; from ignorance to intelligence; from anxiety to satisfaction of mind; from distrust of all, to confidence in every one; from bad habits and erroneous ideas, to good habits and a correct mode of thinking in all things; in short, from a combination of wretched, irrational circumstances, most unfavorable to every one, to new arrangements in unison with our nature, and most beneficial to all; and the only difficulty against which we should have to contend, will be while we shall have to remain in this halfway house, in which we shall have to give up the old habits acquired under the individual system, for the new habits requisite for the social and improved state of society for which we are now preparing.

NEW-HARMONY, the future name of this place, is the best halfway house I could procure for those who are going to travel this extraordinary journey with me; and although it is not intended to be our permanent residence, I hope it will be found not a bad traveller's tavern, or temporary resting place, in which we shall remain, only until we can change our old garments,[a] and fully prepare ourselves for the new state of existence, into which we hope to enter. It is, however, no light thing for men and women of all ages, to change the habits to which they have been accustomed from infancy; and many difficulties must be at first encountered, and many struggles made with our old feelings while the work of regeneration shall be going forward; but these contests with our old habits and feelings will be of short duration; and I trust that even these struggles may be made useful to ourselves and to others. In this halfway house, the accommodations, as you perceive, are unequal, and all, therefore, cannot be alike accommodated; this circumstance will present some obstacles at the commencement of our proceedings; yet, when the principles of the system shall be so understood, as to create the true spirit which ought to guide our actions, this very inequality, both in this and some other particulars, to which I shall afterwards refer, may, by wisdom and prudence, be turned to a beneficial account. – It is my intention, as soon as circumstances will permit, to have every thing here of the best description, in agriculture, manufactures, domestic arrangements, education, and in whatever appertains to the most improved state of society, founded on rational principles: to accomplish this important object, and to effect it in a short time, it is necessary that I should obtain the aid and assistance of men of science, and of great experience, as instructors and directors in the various departments, in which superior qualifications are requisite. Such individuals are now accustomed to certain accommodations, which they will not be inclined to relinquish; and unless such accommodations can be afforded them, they will not be induced to come, however serviceable and necessary their skill and talents may be to the progress of the establishment, towards the point of perfection which I am anxious it should attain.

I must, therefore, very contrary to my own feelings and inclinations admit, for a time, a certain degree of pecuniary inequality; and in consequence, submit to the certain and necessary evils which must continue so long as inequality exists; but I admit of, and submit to, this evil, because it cannot be avoided without sustaining a greater evil, though I consider it one of the *last* evils we shall have to encounter. After these parties have had an opportunity of witnessing how much more happiness may be experienced under arrangements in which inequality will be unknown, they will soon be reconciled to

---

[a] See Genesis 35:2.

the change, and wish of their own accord to possess the full benefits of equality; yet although some *pecuniary* inequality will be unavoidable at first, and for a temporary arrangement, there will be no *personal* inequality, or gradations of rank or station; all will be equal in their condition, and I shall never consider myself one step higher, nor any better, than any other individual; neither is it my wish that any more deference should be paid to me, than to any other individual of the same age and experience: all should be treated with equal sincerity and kindness. I mean to practise this myself towards others, and I hope in due time, to receive such in return, that it may be general among the whole population, and then we shall speedily lose every idea of personal inequality, except that which naturally arises from age and experience. Ardently as I long for the arrival of that period, when there shall be no artificial inequality among the whole human race – yet, as no other individual has had the same experience as myself in the practice of the system about to be introduced, I must for some time, partially take the lead in its direction; but I shall rejoice when I can be relieved from this task, by the population of this place becoming such proficients in the principles and practices of the social system as to be enabled to carry it on successfully without my aid and assistance: in fact, I now live but to see this system fairly established in the world, well knowing that this alone is wanting to secure permanent happiness to all my fellow-creatures.

We are now about adopting the intermediate measures – to exhibit to the inhabitants of this country, and the world, the practice by which good dispositions, good habits, high intelligence, kind feelings, and a superior conduct in all the affairs of life, can be given to the rising generation, and by which, also, a considerable approach may be made to this state, even by those of the present generation.

To prepare, in the best manner, for this practice, I left my concerns here, and proceeded to Washington, for the sole purpose of laying before the government, this nation and the world, in the most public manner the principles on which this new social system is founded, and the results they will produce;[a] that if any parties could find error in the principles, or evil in the practice, they might have the opportunity of doing so, and of guarding the public against their consequences. I purposely put this new system to this fiery ordeal, because I felt confident that upon a full and fair examination of it, the most acute and comprehensive minds, which this, or any other country has produced, or may hereafter produce, will find the principles to be true, and the results to be highly beneficial to mankind. Until I had thus, in the most public manner I could devise, openly and honestly declared my sentiments, and published them, I did not agree to accept of a single family or individual; for I

[a] See *infra*, pp. 3–37.

would, if possible, have no one deceived, in any manner, who shall be admitted into our new association.

My sentiments in relation to the errors and evils of the individual state of society, which now every where prevail, and my belief in the incalculable superiority of the social system over it, to produce real wealth, virtue, intelligence and happiness, are distinctly before the world; it now remains for it to shew wherein I am wrong, or to admit the truth of all my statements.

In my second discourse in the House of Representatives, before the General Government of the United States, in the city of Washington,[a] I stated the principles on which the preliminary societies are recommended to be formed, as well as the general principles recommended for the government of the first regularly constituted communities; these principles we mean to adopt here, and we shall to-morrow commence with the Preliminary Society. I will now read its Constitution, and the Rules and Regulations of the Independent Communities of Equality.

THE CONSTITUTION

OF THE PRELIMINARY SOCIETY OF NEW-HARMONY; MAY 1, 1825

The Society is instituted generally to promote the Happiness of the World.

This Preliminary Society is particularly formed to improve the character and condition of its own members, and to prepare them to become associates in Independent Communities, having common property.

The sole object of these Communities will be to procure for all their Members the greatest amount of happiness, to secure it to them, and to transmit it to their children to the latest posterity.

Persons of all ages and descriptions, exclusive of persons of color, may become members of the Preliminary Society.

Persons of color may be received as helpers to the Society, if necessary; or if it be found useful, to prepare and enable them to become associates in Communities in Africa; or in some other country, or in some other part of this country.

The Members of the Preliminary Society are all of the same rank, no

[a] See *infra*, pp. 18–37.

artificial inequality being acknowledged; precedence to be given only to age and experience, and to those who may be chosen to offices of trust and utility.

The Committee. – As the Proprietor of the Settlement and Founder of the System has purchased the Property, paid for it, and furnished the capital; and has consequently subjected himself to all the risk of the establishment, it is necessary for the formation of the System, and for its security, that he should have the appointment of the Committee, which is to direct and manage the affairs of the Society.

This Committee will conduct all the affairs of the Society. It will be, as much as possible, composed of men of experience and strict integrity, who are competent to carry the system into effect, and to apply impartial justice to all the Members of the Society.

The number of the Committee will be augmented from time to time, according as the Proprietor may obtain the assistance of other valuable Members.

At the termination of one year from the establishment of the Settlement, which shall be dated from the first day of May next, the Members of the Society shall elect, by ballot, from among themselves, three additional Members to the Committee.

Their election is for the purpose of securing to all the Members a full knowledge of the proceedings of the Committee and of the business of the Society; but it is delayed for one year, in order to afford time for the formation of the Society, and to enable the members to become acquainted with the characters and abilities of those who are the most proper to be elected.

It is expected, that at the termination of the second year, or between that period and the end of the third year, an Association of Members may be formed to constitute a Community of Equality and Independence, to be governed according to the General Rules and Regulations contained in the printed paper, entitled '*Mr Owen's Plan for the permanent Relief of the Working Classes*:'[a] with such alterations as experience may suggest and the localities of the situation may require.

This Independent Community will be established upon property, purchased by its associated Members.

The Preliminary Society will continue to receive Members, preparatory to their removal into other Independent Communities.

Admission of Members. – Every individual, previously to admission as a Member, must sign this Constitution, which signature shall be regularly witnessed.

The Members must join the Society at their own expense.

The Society shall not be answerable for the debts of any of its Members, nor

[a] Presumably *infra*, pp. 31–7.

in any manner for their conduct, no partnership whatsoever existing between the Members of this Preliminary Society.

The Members shall occupy the dwellings which the Committee may provide for them.

The Live Stock possessed by Members will be taken and placed to their credit, if wanted for the Society; but if not required, it shall not be received.

All Members must provide their own Household and Kitchen Furniture, and their small tools, such as Spades, Hoes, Axes, Rakes, etc and they may bring such provisions as they have already provided.

The General Duties of Members. – All the Members shall, willingly, render their best services for the welfare of the Society, according to their age, experience and capacity; and if inexperienced in that which is requisite for its welfare, they shall apply diligently to acquire the knowledge of some useful occupation or employment.

They shall enter the Society with a determination to promote its peace, prosperity and harmony, and never, under any provocation whatever, act unkindly or unjustly towards, nor speak in an unfriendly manner of, any one either in or out of the Society.

Members shall be temperate, regular and orderly in their whole conduct, and they shall be diligent in their employments, in proportion to their age, capacity, and constitution.

They shall show a good example, it being a much better instructor than precept.

They shall watch over and endeavor to protect, the whole property from every kind of injury.

The General Privileges of Members. – The Members shall receive such living, advantages, comfort, and education for their children, as this Society, and the present state of New-Harmony, afford.

The living shall be upon equal terms for all, with the exceptions hereafter to be mentioned.

In old age, in sickness, or when an accident occurs, care shall be taken of the parties, Medical aid afforded, and every attention shown to them that kindness can suggest.

Each Member shall, within a fixed amount in value, have the free choice of food and clothing: to effect this, a credit (to be hereafter fixed by the Committee) will be opened in the store for each family, in proportion to the number of its useful Members, also for each single Member, but beyond this amount, no one will be permitted to draw on credit. – The exceptions to this rule are the following, viz:

1st. When the proprietor of the establishment and the Committee shall deem it necessary for promoting the system, and the interest and improvement of the Society, to engage scientific and experienced persons to superintend some of the most difficult, useful, or responsible situations, at a fixed salary, then such individuals shall have a credit upon the store in proportion to their income.

2nd. When any peculiar, or unforeseen case may arise, a general meeting of all the Members shall be called by the Committee, who shall state the particulars of the case to the Meeting: the Members present shall then deliberate upon the subject, and give their vote by ballot, and the question shall be decided by the majority.

Each Family and individual Member shall have a credit and debit account, in which they will be charged with what they receive, at the prices the Harmonians usually charged for the same articles, and credited by the value of their services, to be estimated by the Committee, assisted by the persons at the head of the departments in which the respective individuals may be employed; the value of their services, over their expenditure, shall be placed at the end of each year to their credit, in the books of the Society; but no part of this credit shall be drawn out, except in the productions of the establishment, or in store goods, and with the consent of the Committee.

Members may visit their friends, or travel whenever they please, provided the Committee can conveniently supply their places in the departments in which they may be respectively employed.

To enable the Members to travel, they will be supplied with funds to half the amount placed to their credit in the books of the Society, not however exceeding $100, in any one year, unless the distance they have to travel from home exceed six hundred miles.

Members may receive their friends to visit them, provided they be answerable that such visitors, during their stay, do not transgress the rules of the Society.

The children will be educated in the best possible manner in the day schools, and will board and sleep in their parents' houses. Should any Members however prefer placing their children in the boarding school, they must make a particular and individual engagement with the Committee; but no Members shall be permitted to bind themselves nor their children to the Society for a longer period than one week.

All the Members shall enjoy complete liberty of conscience, and be afforded every facility for exercising those practices of religious worship and devotion which they may prefer.

Should the arrangements formed for the happiness of the Members, fail to effect this object, any of them, by giving a week's notice, can quit the Society, taking with them, in the productions of the establishment, the value of what they brought, which value shall be ascertained and fixed by the Committee; the Members may also, in the same manner, take out the amount of what appears to their credit in the books of the Society at the end of the year immediately preceding their removal; provided that amount still remain to their credit.

Dismission of Members. – Any Families or Members contravening any of the articles of this Constitution, or acting in any way improperly, shall be dismissed, by the Committee, from the Society and Settlement, upon giving them the same notice by which they are at liberty to quit the Society.

Persons who possess capital, and who do not wish to be employed, may partake of the benefits of this Society, by paying such sum annually as may be agreed upon between them and the Committee; always paying a quarter in advance.

Persons wishing to invest capital upon interest in the funds of the Society, may do so, by making a particular agreement with the Committee.

Such is the Constitution of the Preliminary Society.

The next consideration is, what are the practical measures by which the Preliminary Society is to be carried into execution?

This will be effected by the appointment of a Preliminary Committee, who have been chosen from among those who were here, who were the most experienced in these new measures and who were recommended for their sincerity and strict integrity.

This Committee has been chosen, that impartial justice shall be administered to every one, as far as it is practicable, under the unequal circumstances in which we are temporarily placed: to this Committee which will sit daily, those who wish to become members of the Preliminary Society will apply, and by them they will be informed of every particular relative to admission.

At the end of this year, when half our number may be expected to have arrived, and to be generally known to each other, the Society shall, by ballot choose from among themselves, three more members to be added to the Committee; and at the end of the next year, when the Society may be expected to have their full number, the characters of each to be in some degree known, and when all will be more or less familiar with the principles and practices of the social system, they shall also, by ballot, choose one half of the members of the Committee. The next step, and which I calculate we shall be prepared for in the following year, will be, to constitute the Community of Equality, with equal rights, property, and means of improvement and enjoyment; when I trust, we shall for ever bury all the evils of the old selfish, individual system.

This is all which I had intended to state at the present meeting; but understanding that many parties who are present, and who have not time now to remain to make the inquiries from the Committee, wish to be informed respecting various particulars, I will, as far as I am prepared, endeavor to meet their wishes and enable them, on their return home, to answer the inquiries of their neighbors.

It is recommended for the benefit of each member of the society, that their consumption shall be as much as possible, without being disagreeable to them, in those articles which are the productions of America, that the society may speedily become solely dependent upon its own labor and means. In such cases as will admit, private gardens will be added to the houses; when this cannot be done, the best means which can be devised will be adopted to supply the family with useful vegetables. The houses within and without, are to be kept clean and neat, and the gardens are to be kept free from weeds, and always in good order.

The change *now* proposed is intended solely for the happiness of the members. When this cannot be enjoyed by them, they may leave at any time on giving one week's notice; and if the conduct of any one, or more, should interfere with the happiness of the Society, the Committee is to possess the power of dismissing them from the town and settlement.

But to prevent any misunderstanding, the Rules and Regulations will be read over to each, who, upon admission, will be required to sign his or her consent to govern their conduct by them.

Until a sufficient number of members are placed in the different departments, the Committee will have to make the best temporary arrangements they can.

All differences between the members of the Society will be settled by arbitration; but the Rules of the Society will not admit of drunkenness, disputes, or quarrelling, not of any angry or disagreeable language from one member to another; all anger and ill will being quite contrary to the fundamental principles of this new social system.

It was very much my inclination to have discontinued the distillation of whiskey, and all ardent spirits; but I find this is impracticable for the present: whenever it can be done, however, and the habit of using it shall be overcome, it will give me the greatest satisfaction to put an end to the manufacture.

As it is necessary the country should be defended in the best manner, if attacked, and as the laws of the country require it should be defended by its inhabitants, formed into militia, measures will be adopted here to train the children (with the exception of those whose parents may, from conscientious scruples, object,) while at school, in a proper knowledge and practice of the drill, and to give the young men, for the benefit of their health, the means of being formed to practice in militia companies, in order that the members of the new social communities may become, in all respects, the most efficient members of society; but while they will be thus prepared for any irrational attack, their principles and conduct will prepare the young for universal peace: for war and the social system cannot exist together.

It is due to the Society who formed, and until now occupied this settlement, to state, that I have not yet met with more kind-hearted, temperate, and industrious citizens, nor found men more sincere, upright and honest in all their dealings than the HARMONIANS.

ORATION CONTAINING A DECLARATION OF MENTAL INDEPENDENCE[a] 1826

Delivered in the Public Hall, New Harmony, Indiana at the celebration of the Fourth of July 1826.

We meet to commemorate the period, when the inhabitants of this new world attained the power to withdraw from the control of the old world, and to form a government for themselves.

This event is likely to prove, in its consequences, as important as any which has occurred in ancient or modern times. It has been the means of preparing a new era in the history of man, and of producing such a change in circumstances as will admit of the introduction of measures to change, entirely, the character and condition of the human race.

The revolution in America, sanctioned and secured by the Declaration of Independence in 1776, gave to a people advancing towards civilization, the first opportunity of establishing a government, which would, by degrees, permit them to acquire that greatest of blessings, MENTAL LIBERTY.

This was, indeed, a most important point gained: it was the first time such privilege had been ever possessed by mankind.

Its fruits have been visible in the gradual advance towards mental liberty, which has been made during the half century which this day completes from that memorable event. But, I conclude, it will be in the next half century, now about to commence, that the wondering world will learn justly to estimate the value of the high achievement which was then attained.

It was not the mere political liberty then conquered from the old world, that was the real victory gained by the inhabitants of these vast regions; for political power had been often wrested from one party and obtained by another: But, it was the right which they thereby acquired and used, to establish the liberty of freely extending thought upon all subjects, secular and religious; and the right

[a] Published as a pamphlet and in *The New Harmony Gazette*, vol. 1, no. 42 (12 July 1826), pp. 329–32. French translation, 'Déclaration de l'indépendance mentale', *Mémorial Catholique*, 7 (1827), pp. 149–59. Reprinted in 1970.

to express those thoughts openly, so soon as the existing prejudices, derived from the old world, could be so far removed as to direct the mind of the multitude to investigate facts and reject the mysteries of disordered imaginations: to teach them to discern the value of the former, as they always direct to the development of real knowledge; and instruct them rightly to estimate the evil of the latter, as they lead to those errors which have made man a compound of folly and a recipient for misery.

Yes, my friends, the Declaration of Independence, in 1776, prepared the way to secure to you MENTAL LIBERTY, without which man never can become more than a mere localized being, with powers to render him more miserable and degraded than the animals which he has been taught to deem inferior to himself. It is true, the right of mental liberty is inherent in our nature; for, while man exists in mental health, no human power can deprive him of it: but until the Revolution in 1776, no people had acquired the *political power* to permit them to use that right, when their minds should be so far freed from early imbibed prejudices as to allow them to derive benefits from its practice. No nation, except this, even yet possesses the political power to enable the people to use the right of mental freedom.

This right – this invaluable right, you now enjoy by the Constitution obtained for you by Washington,[a] Franklin,[b] Henry,[c] and the other worthies associated with them.

You have indeed abundant reason to rejoice in this victory, obtained over the thick mental darkness which, till then, covered the earth.

The collision of mind which produced that victory, and which was produced by it, elicited a spark of light, which enabled the prominent actors in those scenes to discover a glimpse through the long night of error and misrule, with which the inhabitants of all the earth had been previously afflicted.

Still, however, these men, whose minds were in advance of the age in which they lived, were encircled by the prejudices which they and their fathers brought from Europe, and which had descended to the inhabitants of those regions through many ages of despotism, superstition and ignorance. And although a few of these highly-gifted men of the Revolution saw a stronger and clearer light at the distance, as they supposed, of some ages before them; they were too conscious of the extent of the old errors around them to attempt more than to secure the means in the Constitution which they formed, by which their successors might work their way to the superior distant light, and gain for themselves the innumerable advantages which real mental liberty could bestow upon them.

It is for YOU and YOUR successors now to press onward, with your utmost

[a] George Washington (1732–99): 1st President of the United States.
[b] Benjamin Franklin (1706–90): philosopher, inventor, diplomat, philanthropist.
[c] Patrick Henry (1736–99): revolutionary statesman and orator.

speed, in the course which, by so many sacrifices, for your benefit, they have opened for you. They discovered some of the innumerable impositions which had been practiced on your predecessors; they saw more of them, than in the temper of those times, they could venture publicly to expose; but they have left such decided proofs of their own feelings and views regarding them, that none, who reflect, can doubt the strong desire they felt to attack and destroy still more of them, and, if possible, to annihilate all the arts and mysteries by which the few had so long held a pernicious, despotic sway and control over the many.

These wise men were withheld from going beyond the line determined upon at the Revolution, apprehending that, by attempting to gain a greater advance upon ignorance and superstition, they might put to hazard the benefits they found they could secure; and herein they evinced their knowledge of the times in which they lived and acted.

These worthies knew, that their descendants, starting from the point which they had gained, could, in due time, without such risk, make other and still more important advances toward mental liberty – toward that which will, when fully attained, enable man to remove the cause of all crime, and the misery which arises from the commission of crimes. To attain this mental liberty, in its full extent and highest purity, and to be secure in its permanent possession, will be the greatest victory that man can gain.

My friends, it surely cannot be your wish, that any good and great cause should be effected only by halves, – and more especially when that which remains to be done, is, beyond all calculation, the more important? There is a noble object before us, to be won by some party or another in this or in some other country. It is no less than the destruction of the threefold causes which deprive man of mental liberty, which compel him to commit crimes, and to suffer all the miseries which crime can inflict. Could we but gain this object – soon would rational intelligence, real virtue, and substantial happiness, be permanently established among men: ignorance, poverty, dependence, and vice, would be forever banished from the earth.

Let me now ask, –

Are you prepared to imitate the example of your ancestors? Are you willing to run the risks which they encountered? Are you ready, like them, to meet the prejudices of past times, and determined to overcome them at ALL hazards, for the benefit of your country and for the emancipation of the human race? Are you, indeed, willing to sacrifice your fortunes, lives, and reputations, if such sacrifices should be necessary, to secure for all your fellow-beings, the GREATEST GOOD, that, according to our present knowledge, it is possible for them ever to receive?

Are you prepared to achieve a MENTAL REVOLUTION, as superior in benefit and importance to the first revolution, as the mental powers of man exceed his physical powers?

If you are, I am most ready and willing to join you in this deed – the last and most daring that has been left for man in his irrational state to perform.

But, my friends, knowing, as I do, the immeasurable magnitude of the GOOD which this Mental Revolution will effect and permanently secure for human nature through all future ages – I deem the continued existence, a little longer here, of a few individuals to be of no consideration whatever in comparison with its attainment; and, therefore, as I cannot know the present state of *your* minds, and as the continuance of life at my age, is very uncertain, I have calmly and deliberately determined, upon this eventful and auspicious occasion, to break asunder the remaining mental bonds which for so many ages have grievously afflicted our nature, and, by so doing, to give forever FULL FREEDOM TO THE HUMAN MIND.

Upon an experience, then, of nearly forty years, which owing to a very peculiar combination of circumstances, has been more varied, extended and singular, than perhaps has ever fallen to the lot of any one man, and, during which period, my mind was continually occupied in tracing the cause of each human misery that came before me to its true origin; – I now DECLARE, to you and to the world, *that Man, up to this hour, has been, in all parts of the earth, a slave to a* TRINITY *of the most monstrous evils that could be combined to inflict mental and physical evil upon his whole race.*

I refer to PRIVATE, OR INDIVIDUAL PROPERTY – ABSURD AND IRRATIONAL SYSTEMS OF RELIGION – AND MARRIAGE, FOUNDED ON INDIVIDUAL PROPERTY COMBINED WITH SOME ONE OF THESE IRRATIONAL SYSTEMS OF RELIGION.

It is difficult to say which of these grand sources of all crime ought to be placed first or last; for they are so intimately interlinked and woven together by time, that they cannot be separated without being destroyed: – each one is necessary to the support of the other two. This formidable Trinity, compounded of Ignorance, Superstition and Hypocrisy, is the only Demon,[a] or Devil, that ever has, or, most likely, ever will torment the human race. It is well calculated, in all its consequences, to produce the utmost misery on the mind and body of man of which his nature is susceptible. The division of property among individuals prepared the seeds, cultivated the growth, and brought to maturity all the evils of poverty and riches existing among a people at the same time; the industrious experiencing privations and the idle being overwhelmed and injured by wealth.

Religion, or Superstition, – for all religions have proved themselves to be Superstitions, – by destroying the judgment, irrationalized all the mental faculties of man, and made him the most abject slave, through the fear of nonentities created solely by his own disordered imagination. Superstition forced him to believe, or to say he believed, that a Being existed who possessed

[a] Some debt to John Bunyan's *The Pilgrim's Progress* (1678) is possible here.

all power, wisdom and goodness – that he could do and that he did, everything – and yet, that evil and misery superabound; and that this Being, who makes and does all things, is not the direct or indirect author of evil or misery. Such is the foundation on which all the mysteries and ravings of Superstition are erected in all parts of the world. Its inconsistency and inconceivable folly have been such as to keep the world in continual wars, and massacres, to create private divisions, leading to every imaginable evil; and it is probable that Superstition has caused more than its third of the crimes and sufferings of the human race.

The forms and ceremonies of Marriage, as they have been hitherto generally performed, and afterwards supported, make it almost certain, that they were contrived and forced upon the people at the same period that property was first divided among a few leading individuals and Superstition was invented: This being the only device that could be introduced to permit them to retain their division of the public spoils, and create to themselves an aristocracy of wealth, of power, and of learning.

To enable them to keep their children apart from the multitude who were to be kept in poverty, in ignorance, and consequently without power, – and to monopolize all wealth and power and learning to themselves, – some such contrivance as Marriage, with mysterious forms and ceremonies, to hide their real intentions from the ignorant, was absolutely necessary, that they might, through the influence of their wealth, learning and power, select the most beautiful and desirable women from among all the people, – and thus enslave and make them, in fact, a part of their private property.

This was the commencement of that system which led to such endless crimes and miseries and degradation of the human faculties, by tempting the inexperienced to barter their feelings and affections for wealth, trappings, and power; when too late for their happiness, they discover they have been deceived, and that wealth, learning and power, can make no amends for the want of those natural feelings and affections, in the union of which, all feel the present happiness of life to consist.

Among the truly intelligent, Marriage will be respected only when it shall be formed between those who are equal in wealth, education and condition; who are well acquainted with each other's habits, minds and feelings, before they enter upon the engagement; and who know also, that by their nature the continuance of affection does not depend upon the will of either, but that it will diminish or increase according as they produce pleasurable or disagreeable sensations in each other. Marriage, to make it a virtuous and happy connexion, must be contracted by both parties, solely with a view to their happiness. As, then, it is a law of nature that our affections are not at the control of the will; and as happiness can be enjoyed only when we associate with those for whom we cannot avoid having the most esteem, regard and affection; it should be as reputable, and equally authorized by law, to dissolve marriage when the esteem and affection cannot be retained for each other, and when the union promises to produce more misery than happiness, as to form the marriage in the first instance. When however the parties are on a perfect equality in wealth, condition and education, and intimately acquainted with each other's thoughts and feelings before marriage; and when no motive whatever exists but genuine affection to induce the parties to unite; it is most likely that marriages so formed would be more permanent than they have ever yet been. But the present and past character of man, formed by the inconsistent and incongruous circumstances around him, have made him so artificial in his feelings, views and conduct, that a decisive conclusion cannot be drawn upon this most interesting part of the subject. Be this, however, as it may, we may be sure, that as soon as man shall be trained rationally, and surrounded by those circumstances only which are in unison with his nature, he will act only rationally; that is, in such a manner as to secure the highest and purest happiness to himself and his fellow-creatures.

The revolution , then, to be now effected, is the DESTRUCTION of this HYDRA OF EVILS – in order that the many may be no longer poor, wretched beings, – dependent on the wealthy and powerful few; that Man may be no longer a superstitious idiot, continually dying from the futile fear of death; that he may no longer unite himself to the other sex from any mercenary or superstitious motives, nor promise and pretend to do that which it depends not on himself to perform.

Upon the experience of a life devoted to the investigation of these momentous subjects, I fearlessly now declare to you, from a conviction, as strong as conviction can exist in the human mind, that this compound of ignorance and fraud, IS THE REAL AND ONLY CAUSE OF ALL THE CRIME, AND MISERY ARISING FROM CRIME, WHICH CAN BE FOUND IN HUMAN SOCIETY.

This threefold, horrid monster, has been most speciously gilded and decorated with external trappings, to awe the ignorant multitude and deter them from examining the black venom and corruption within. It was in sundry times and places made death for any mortal, except the initiated, to approach these hidden mysteries; and nothing short of the Inquisition with the aid of that fearful unmeaning term SACRED, could have, for so long a period, kept man, – irrational as these terrors made him, – from discovering the imposition which was practised upon him for the sole purpose of keeping him in mental slavery and bondage.

For nearly forty years have I been employed, heart and soul, day by day, almost without ceasing, in preparing the means and arranging the circumstances, to enable me to give the death-blow to the tyranny and despotism, which, for unnumbered ages past, have held the human mind spell-bound, in chains and fetters of such mysterious forms and shapes, that no mortal hand dared approach to set the suffering prisoner free. Nor has the fulness of time, for the accomplishment of this great event, been completed until within this hour, – and such has been the extraordinary course of events, that the Declaration of Political Independence, in 1776, has produced its counterpart, the DECLARATION OF MENTAL INDEPENDENCE in 1826 – the latter just half a century from the former.

Rejoice with me, my friends, that your Mental Independence rests now as secure as your Political Independence; for the overwhelming power of TRUTH over Error is such, that as soon as arrangements can be formed to admit of the full development of Truth to the world, and it is once publicly promulgated, no art, or falsehood, or force, can ever afterwards return it back into forgetfulness, or unteach the truths which it has taught.

Under the circumstances in which this Mental Revolution has been made, no human power can undo, or render nugatory, that which has now been done.

This Truth has passed from me, beyond the possibility of recall: it has been already received into your minds: speedily it will be heard throughout America, and from thence it will pass North and South, East and West, as far as language is known, – and almost as fast as it shall be conveyed, human nature will recognize and receive it. In countries, in which ignorance and despotism hold their sway over the multitude, arts will be used to keep it from being heard among them: but neither armies, nor barriers of any kind, can now prevent a great and important truth from finding its way, by some means or another, into the darkest recesses of error and deception.

Rejoice, then, with me, my friends, that this light is now set upon a hill;[a] for it will increase daily, more and more, until it shall be seen, felt, and understood, by all the nations of the earth.

Rejoice, with me, that we now live under a government unconnected with any of the superstitions of the dark ages of ignorance; a government established purposely to give man his natural rights; to give him the full power to obtain mental liberty as soon as he could disburthen himself of the prejudices of his ancestors.

The individuals who compose a great majority of your present general government are happily free from the weakening and deadening influence of Superstition; their experience is too extensive, their minds are too enlightened, to be longer held in slavery and bondage by imaginary notions unsupported by a single fact. They will therefore rejoice to see their fellow-citizens and their fellow-men throwing off the yoke which has hitherto kept their finest faculties in bondage, and they will look forward with increased hope to the advantages which the rising generation, freed from these errors, will acquire and possess.

All who are deeply versant in human nature can readily estimate the

[a] See for example Matthew 5:14.

difference between a generation, whose judgment shall have been carefully cultivated from infancy, and whose best faculties shall have been early called into full action, and one in which the judgment has been forced to become subservient to a misguided imagination, and in whose mind all natural facts have been distorted and made to bend and support mysteries only calculated to blind the understanding and call forth the weaker and worse feelings of human nature. Your government, and all the enlightened men of these States and of other countries, now look to the improved education of the faculties of children, to produce a race of rational beings, whose minds will be freed from the superstitions, prejudices, and errors of past times; and I trust, that in this respect, no parties will be disappointed.

In furtherance of this great object we are preparing the means to bring up your children, with industrious and useful habits, with natural, and of course rational ideas and views, with sincerity in all their proceedings; and to give them kind and affectionate feelings for each other, and charity, in the most extensive sense of the term, for all their fellow-creatures.

By doing this, by uniting your separate interests into one, by doing away with individual money transactions, by exchanging with each other your articles of produce on the basis of labor for equal labor, by looking forward to apply your surplus wealth to assist others to obtain similar advantages, and by the abandonment of the use of spirituous liquors, you will in a peculiar manner promote the object of every wise government and of all really enlightened men.

And here we now are, as near, perhaps, as we can be in the center of the United States, even, as it were, like the little grain of mustard seed;[a] but with these GREAT TRUTHS before us, with the practice of the social system, as soon as it shall be well understood among us, our principles will, I trust, spread from Community to Community, from State to State, and from Continent to Continent, until this System and these TRUTHS shall overshadow the whole earth, – shedding fragrance and abundance, intelligence and happiness, upon all the sons of men.

I would that you, and those who now live in this and other countries, could partake, for many years, of all these enjoyments.

[a] See Matthew 17:20.

THE SOCIAL SYSTEM[a]
1826

The world has now been governed for 6,000 years under a system of individual rewards and punishments, emulation and separate interests; a system which has arisen from a supposition in the human mind, that each individual forms his own character, is a free agent, and responsible to the power that formed him for his conduct.

The object of the following pages is to prove that this system has its foundation in error; that it has necessarily made mankind irrational and keeps them so; that it has ever produced only misery to the human race, and that it is now the direct or indirect cause of all the evils of which men complain: that the error upon which it is founded, *is, in fact, the origin of evil upon earth.* It is likewise intended to shew, that the period is arrived, when it is practicable without danger or difficulty to introduce in its place a system of social arrangements founded upon principles derived from the highest evidence our nature is capable of attaining, and which soon after their introduction shall prevent the existence of evil in society, except that which may arise from accidents, disease and death.

CHAPTER I

MAN NOT RESPONSIBLE TO THE POWER THAT CREATES HIM

That the character is formed by the individual, and that the individual is responsible for its formation has been an early imbibed notion, received into the human mind, before it possessed any accurate knowledge derived from

[a] Though written in 1821, 'The Social System' was not published until 1826. It was first published in *The New Harmony Gazette*, vol. 2, no. 8 (22 November 1826) – no. 24 (14 March 1827), pp. 57–9, 105–6, 113–14, 129–30, 137–8, 145–6, 153–4, 161–2, 169–70, 177–8, 185–6.

experience. This is apparent, when the formation of the human character is examined through the medium of the evidence of our senses. And this evidence, supported as it is, by every historical narrative, is so strong and decisive, that the existence of a belief, which is in direct opposition to it, can be accounted for only, by its having been adopted previously to experience, when men could have no judgment, and by the tenacity with which human nature adheres to old established errors, however grossly absurd.

The combining of various ingredients to form an individual animal, vegetable, mineral or other compound, is termed its creation; the compound itself, the creature or the created; and the power that combines these ingredients the Creator or God. The whole creation is in perpetual movement; all things created, are coming into compound existence, termed being formed or growing, or going out of compound existence, denominated being decomposed or dying.

It appears that no two of these compounds are alike, that in those with the same general or external forms, there is a distinctive variety, and that each individual compound is made in some respects to differ from all similar compounds.

All things thus created, exist, think, will or act, each according to its nature, or in virtue of the peculiar compound, which constitutes its particular existence. Every compound then, exists in form and quality, as created by God, or the power that brought it into existence.

That which is created, it is evident, cannot form itself, its qualities are not in any degree its own; it cannot possess merit or demerit for their formation, it can have no control in choosing the ingredients, or in proportioning them to form the compound, which makes it what it is: and unless prevented by some other power, it must exist and act according to its nature.

The same laws apply to the whole of creation. Man, except in his own imagination, is not exempt from these, or from any of the general laws of nature. He is born, the evidence of our senses informs us, with faculties, qualities and propensities peculiar to his nature as man, and to himself as an individual of his species, in the same manner as all other animals, approximating to him in their general formation are born; in this respect there is no perceptible difference at birth, except that he is the most helpless of all the animal creation. But for the compound which makes him what he is, he is not, nor ever can become responsible.

The term itself as applied to any thing created is an absurdity. If responsibility have any meaning at all, it applies solely to the Power that creates having a will and choice in creating, and in this case it must eternally remain the only responsible Power in existence. How can that which is created possess any power that is not given to it, or act otherwise than according to the degree of that power, whatever it is, whether it be more or less?

Man then, does not form himself at birth, physically, mentally or morally;

and if left entirely to himself, he would act according to his general nature, as man, and to the particular qualities given to him as an individual of his species. For so doing, the evidence of our senses informs us, no responsibility could attach to him any more than to any animal, vegetable, mineral, or any other compound, existing or acting according to the qualities given to them by the creating Power. For if man were left entirely to himself, he would know no more of duties as they are called, than the Ouran Outang, the Lion or the Tyger. – Now who prevents him being left to himself? Not himself surely; for at his birth he has no power of thinking, willing, or acting.

Yet whatever may be the peculiar qualities of the individual at birth, the evidence of our senses informs us, he is capable of being almost infinitely varied after birth, physically, mentally and morally, by education, which in its true signification means all the circumstances which may subsequently act upon him. All animals, vegetables, and minerals are equally subject to this law of nature, and may likewise be almost infinitely modified by the varied circumstances with which they may be surrounded. Man then may be said to be a twofold compound, formed of the qualities given to him at birth, and the qualities derived from education, or the circumstances which surround him after birth, and these combined make the individual what he is at every moment of his existence. He grows, and at all times feels, thinks, wills, and acts, through the medium which is thus created, and as this is, so is the infant, child, or man.

According to the different circumstances in which the human being is placed, whatever may be his original character, or that which he received at birth, he may be compelled to become a cannibal, to delight in devouring his own species, or to loathe the eating of any kind of flesh. By these circumstances he may be formed to be one of the most passionate or one of the most patient of men; the most malevolent or the most benevolent; the most active, physically and mentally, or the most indolent; to delight in falsehood or to detest it; to be intemperate or temperate; ignorant or intelligent; to be of any of the religions professed in the world, a pagan, or of no religion; to die and glory in dying in defence of any one of these religions, or to die and glory in dying in opposing all these religions; to be the most cruel and hard-hearted wretch known in the history of mankind, or to be the most kind and charitable being to all his fellow-creatures; in short, to be healthy, rational and happy through life, or to have an irrational mind in a diseased body and be miserable through every period of his existence. Such, then, is the overwhelming influence of circumstances over human nature. And yet it is most evident that the individual has not the smallest control in all this, for in fact, he possesses nothing of his own creation. There is not the shadow of a substance in which merit or demerit can be supposed to exist. No part even of the original compound which is called human nature has ever been under the control of the individual, and there is the same rationality in attributing merit and demerit or responsibility to the Ouran Outang, the Lion, and all animals, vegetables, minerals and other natural compounds, as to the human species: all other animals have wills of their own, as the term is, as well as human beings; and if the latter are responsible on that account, so are the former.

But nothing created has a will of its own; the will and mind and all that is possessed, come from another Power, and are no more the work of the individual to whom they belong, than of any other individual, who is in fact as much to be praised or blamed for them as the immediate possessor. The individual no more made nor could make his own mind and body, than he could make the mind and body of an elephant, nor can he become by any process whatever more responsible for the one than the other. As it is impossible that a human being could ever form the smallest part of his nature, to say that he is naturally bad, is only saying that God created him with a bad nature; and as God has created the tyger and the hyena with apparently worse natures, why not make them responsible beings also, and prepare a worse place of future torment for them?

From what has been said, it is evident beyond any rational contradiction,

That nothing created can form any part of itself; that it must exist, think, will, or act, according to the qualities given to it, whether ignorance shall term them good or bad:

That that which is created, whether it be good or bad is the immediate and sole work of the Power that created it, and it will remain what it is until it shall be changed or decomposed:

That if there be responsibility in the work of creation or the operations of Nature, it most be wholly in the creating Power, – for no sophistry of language can give to a sound or rational mind, any idea by what legerdemain process that which is itself created can become responsible for the qualities which it has received from its Creator.

It is a characteristic of human nature that it may be taught to believe any thing, however absurd and contradictory. The history of mankind up to this hour and the evidence of our senses inform us that man has been, and is now taught in all parts of the earth, to believe what is inconsistent, and opposed to all facts or experience. He has been taught, that although he does not make his faculties, qualities and propensities, that is, his mind and body, yet that he becomes at some undefined period of his life responsible for the thoughts of the one and the actions of the other.

It has been demonstrated that the supposition of *infant* responsibility is in opposition to the most clear and direct evidence of our senses. Man is not then responsible for the faculties, qualities and propensities which God has given him at birth, – for the creating Power can alone be responsible for them at that period. When fairly stated, this is a truth so self-evident that no one surely will now deny it. But it is alleged, that man becomes responsible for his thoughts and actions *at some period subsequent to his birth.*

At what period then, and in what manner does he become responsible for his second nature, or that part of his character which is the effect of education on his first or created nature?

For knowledge that can be of any utility on this part of the subject, it is necessary to apply again to the evidence of our senses. This evidence informs us, that any infant at birth is capable of being formed into an almost infinite variety of character, as respects dispositions, habits, manners, religious belief, thoughts and actions; and that these are determined by all the circumstances in which he is placed, acting upon the character which is given to him at birth.

It is evident, as far as we are capable of judging, that no two compounds in nature, mineral, vegetable, animal, have been formed, precisely alike, and that according to this apparently universal law of nature, no two infants at birth possess exactly the same combination of physical and mental qualities. The same circumstances, or education, therefore, if it were possible to subject two infants to them, which it is not, would not produce characters alike, hence the minor differences observable in children of the same country, district or family. Yet it is most evident that education, or all the circumstances in which the infant is placed from birth, acting upon his peculiar created nature, make the individual, at every moment of his existence, in all respects what he is. Now the evidence of our senses informs us, that none of these circumstances for a considerable period can possibly be in any sense under the control even of the faculties, qualities and propensities, which have been given to the infant at birth, but which be it remembered, are in fact no more the *infant*'s choosing or forming than they are yours, reader, or mine, or any other animal's in existence, – for they were made for him and he was compelled to have them, without his knowledge, consent, or approbation.

But to shew the utter absurdity of all the popular notions on this vital subject, let it be supposed, for the sake of argument, that the human being after birth is responsible for the use he makes of the peculiar faculties, qualities, and propensities, which he possesses; but which, nevertheless, are altered, improved, or deteriorated, by the circumstances in which he is placed after birth. To make the created being responsible, it becomes requisite that he should have the power of choosing these circumstances, otherwise he cannot be answerable for the effects which they are sure to produce on his first or original nature. Has he this power? Can he in any degree determine the place of his birth? whether it shall be in Europe, Asia, Africa or America: whether he shall be placed in the midst of Jews, Hindoos, Christians, Mahometans, Pagans, or Cannibals: among the learned or illiterate: among the wisest or the most foolish: among the tyrants or the slaves of mankind: among those who have been taught the most correct manners, as they are called, or among the very outcasts of society. The evidence of our senses informs us, that in all these respects, the infant has not the shadow of a choice; that he is as to all these as passive a being as any other compound existing in nature. Before he can think, speak, or act, circumstances, irresistible to him, have placed him in a situation in which he will be compelled to learn the general language, manners, and religion, of the district in which he is born or into which he may be conveyed and allowed to remain.

This also, when clearly stated, is a truth so self evident, that no reasoning can disprove it. But, some parties will say, admitting all this to be true, the individual, *when his judgment is ripe*, is quite competent to overcome the effects of these early impressions on the young mind, and to judge between truth and error; and therefore he becomes at this period responsible for the opinions he may entertain and for the actions which proceed from these opinions.

The evidence of our senses informs us however, that those who are born and remain in any particular country, and who are early forced to receive the popular notions of the parties around them, not only imbibe those notions in infancy, but with few exceptions, which may be easily explained, they retain them through life. Thus all who are born within certain geographical limits are forced to receive the doctrines of *Fo*;[a] of the myriads, thus circumstanced, not one probably in a million, has ever doubted the truth of their early instruction. While all those who are born and remain within other geographical limits, are forced to believe the doctrines of Mahomet, which they as uniformly retain through life. In like manner all those who are born and remain within the limits of Christendom, are compelled to believe the mysteries of Christianity, which they retain through life in the same manner as the others hold their respective creeds. So also do other multitudes of our fellow-creatures who live in certain districts of Asia, receive and retain through life the doctrines of Bramah; millions of whom worship the great uncouth log called Juggernaut,[b] and many of them annually sacrifice their lives under the pressure of the wheels on which he moves, to evince the perfect devotion to him with which they are impressed. The inhabitants of almost all the remaining parts of the earth are also forced to receive other early instruction which makes them through life Pagans, believing in the divinity of the most hideous monsters.

These, then, the evidence of our senses informs us are the effects of the overwhelming influence of circumstances, by which human nature is controlled, and rendered whatever they made it. Thus are men forced to believe the popular notions, however erroneous, of the district in which they are born and live. They are taught that these notions are alone true, and that those taught contrary to them in other districts are false detestable impositions, and so truly absurd, that it is most extraordinary how any rational creature could be made to believe in them. These impressions are uniformly made on the minds of the inhabitants of all the various districts in the world; and in consequence those

[a] Fo, or Foe, was a Chinese idol imported from India, c. AD 65, linked to the doctrine of the transmigration of souls.

[b] Large cart associated with Vishnu cult, dragged annually by thousands of followers.

of each district are found to believe that all their fellow-men, who are born and live in all the other districts in which mysteries different from their own are taught, are poor, weak, irrational creatures, who deserve only their pity, contempt, hatred or detestation.

If human nature has not hitherto been completely under the control of the circumstances in which it happens to be placed, why have the inhabitants of China, for so many centuries, been disciples of Fo and Confucius? Why have the inhabitants of Hindostan been Hindoos? of Christendom Christians? of the districts governed by Mossulmen, disciples of Mahomet? and the remainder of the world, Pagans – worshippers of animals or imaginary monsters, or still mere savages?

If men, at any period of life, can judge for themselves between truth and error, and if any one of these general doctrines be true, why have not all men long since discovered this invaluable knowledge, – and become satisfied, content, and happy under its influence? So far from this being the case, however, the evidence of our senses informs us that there is not *one* fact, with which we are acquainted, which does not go to prove, that man ever has been the creature of the particular faculties, qualities, and propensities, which he has been forced to receive at birth, and of the circumstances in which he has been forced to exist after birth. Man therefore never was, nor can he ever become a free agent or a responsible being. The old system of society, from the earliest periods of which we have any record, has been formed on the supposition, that man *is* a free agent, and consequently responsible for this thoughts, words, and actions.

The old system of society is, therefore, false in principle.

CHAPTER II

Before the astronomical discoveries of Copernicus and Galileo there had been a general impression throughout the world, that the earth was flat and immoveable. In like manner there is now a universal belief in all countries, that man forms his own character, is consequently a free agent, and therefore responsible for his thoughts and actions, – and that the world could not be governed, if this doctrine were not universally taught.

In the former Chapter, it has been demonstrated, that this doctrine is unfounded. Our next object is to shew, that the fundamental notions according to which old society has been formed, have ever been as pernicious in practice as they are false in theory.

The supposition that man was a free agent, and responsible for his thoughts and actions, put him at once under the dominion of his imagination. In consequence, this faculty of the human mind has ever been unnaturally cultivated, and the reasoning powers have been made subservient to it. The first great class of evils which was thus created, arose from the consequent belief that he was responsible to some superior Powers, and that homage of some kind was due to them. This notion gave activity for ages to the faculty of imagination, during which almost every kind of conceivable deformity was produced by it, to be worshipped as a divinity by those, whose wild fancies created these monsters of the human brain. Hence arose Paganism, the Mythology of the ancients, and the various Religions, which now degrade and oppress the human race. These, as far as possible, transformed men into the monsters which their imagination had created. The human being was filled with hatred and every evil feeling against all those who could not imagine the same distortions that he had conceived or been taught to conceive. Believing, as he did, that his fellow-man was a free agent, and could command his thoughts, he concluded that such as would not see the truth which he alone had discovered, were obstinately blind, and that it was his duty to compel them to think as he did. Hence all divisions, persecutions, massacres, wars, and burnings on account of religious opinions. Hence the universal separation of the world into innumerable religious sects. Hence the detestation with which each sect is regarded by other sects. Hence the uncharitable thoughts and vile actions of each sect against all other sects with whom they come into communication. Hence the consummate vanity, egotism or spiritual pride, of each religious division in favor of its own mild imaginations. These evils, the details of which, through the past periods of human existence would fill innumerable volumes and appal the stoutest heart, have each immediately proceeded from the notion of man's free agency and responsibility. No error of less magnitude could have produced such a continued repetition of dire effects to the human race, – rendering them probably more miserable and less rational, than any other species of animals.

To the same source may be directly traced another large class of evils, – of which, however, as of the former, it is not within our present limits to give more than a very slight and imperfect sketch.

There is but one mode by which man can possess, in perpetuity, all the happiness which his nature is capable of enjoying, – that is, *by the union and cooperation of* ALL *for the benefit of* EACH.

But one of the necessary consequences of the belief in free agency and responsibility was to individualize mankind, – to create self-interest, from which immediately sprung the institution of private property, an ever fertile source of *disunion* and misery. Private property produced inequality of condition, – exclusive arrangements, intended to benefit a few at the expense of many. Hence vanity, pride, luxury, and tyranny on the one hand, and on the other poverty and degradation. Hence jealousies, hatred, traffick, insincerity, deception, robbery, murder, and a system of law or artificial justice, covering the grossest injustice.

It is this belief which has perverted all the faculties of the human mind, – compelling it to call vice, virtue; virtue; vice; good, evil; and evil, good: which has rendered men so totally blind, that with the strongest desire in all to secure their own happiness, each is compelled through life to think and to act in such a manner as to prevent the possibility to himself and others of attaining this universal object. In short, the evils, which this error has engendered, are all those with which our nature has been afflicted. To enumerate and detail the whole, would be to state all the miseries experienced by those who have starved for want of the common necessaries of life, and the sufferings of those who have lived in continual dread of this appalling fate; would be, to narrate the crimes which these feelings have generated, the various punishments they have caused to be inflicted, including the history of the individual horrors of each prison, gallows, guillotine, and other places and instruments of torment and torture, which have been devised by one irrational portion of the human race to harass the less fortunate of their fellow-creatures; would be, to detail the evils created over the world by trafficking, – the insincerity, deception and fraud which it engenders; the bankruptcies, or the perpetual fear of them, which it occasions; the vices to which so many resort to avoid them, and the innumerable ramifications of suffering to which all these give rise, and of which not the individuals themselves alone are the victims, but their families, connexions and friends; would be, to describe the slavery and degradation of the manufacturing classes, the majority of whom are doomed to an unvaried toil in the most unnatural and disagreeable situations, in the midst of continued disease and death, – and to aggravate the evils of this miserable existence, are the slaves of a system, under which all parties are necessarily engaged in an unceasing contest with each other, which gives rise to all the bad passions and feelings that opposition of interests, poverty, suffering and disease can foster and cultivate in human nature.

In enumerating the fatal results produced by the practical application of the theory of man's free agency and responsibility, we cannot overlook the desolation, bloodshed and revenge attendant upon war. In short, to do common justice to this part of the subject, it would be necessary to give the history of the pain and sufferings experienced through the life of every human being that has yet been born, whether he has been rich or poor, tyrant or slave, the oppressor or the oppressed. Unless, therefore, the world, through the sufferings and miseries which this error inflicts upon all classes of men, can be enabled to view it in the hideous light in which it ought to appear, ignorance will be perpetuated through all time, the human race, endowed with superior powers, must continue degraded below the animal creation, and to their mental and physical pain and affliction there will be no end. Ignorance, poverty, and mental darkness, and universal contest must for ever be their lot.

Let us then at once set aside this origin of evil upon earth, and in future make the only use of the miseries it has produced, to which they can now be rationally applied. Let an impartial history be compiled of the past transactions of men, and let it be given to our children through all succeeding generations, that they may know the horrid mental and physical degradation to which their predecessors were subjected by a single error of the imagination. Formed from infancy free from this error, they will discover that the volume transmitted to them, contains the history of human nature through the irrational period of its existence, during which the imaginary notion of free agency and responsibility produced in practice a system of punishments, rewards, emulation, separate interests, continual warfare and misery to all. That the abandonment of that notion was the commencement of a new era, when, by the knowledge of the influence of circumstances over human nature, a system was established which exhibited in practice the union and cooperation of all for the benefit of each: when scientific arrangements were first introduced to secure for every child that was born good habits and dispositions, the highest intellectual attainments, and a superfluity of all things necessary to his happiness. Let this be done and the whole earth will gradually acquire a new aspect; old habits, vices, difficulties, sufferings and miseries will disappear, and the human race, emancipated from that error which has hitherto counteracted every attempt to ameliorate its condition, will start forward in a course of real and uninterrupted improvement.

CHAPTER III

It having been discovered that man at birth is wholly formed by the power which creates him, and that his subsequent character is determined by the circumstances which surround him, acting upon his original or created nature, – that he does not in any degree form himself, physically or mentally, and therefore cannot be a free or responsible agent: the first practical effects of this knowledge must be, to banish from the mind of man all ideas of merit or demerit in any created object or being, – to extirpate from his constitution all the feelings to which such ideas give rise; and thus at once to reconcile him to human nature, to himself, and to all his fellow-creatures. His mind will thus be prepared to enter calmly and fearlessly into the investigation of truth, and to receive real knowledge from every source whence it can be derived. He will acquire a new interest in all the various circumstances by which he and his fellow-creatures are surrounded, and attentively regarding the effects which each of these produces on himself and others, will consider, how, with the least injury or inconvenience, those which create unfavorable results may be withdrawn and replaced by others, the influence of which must be beneficial. As he cannot fail soon to perceive that whatever leads to exclusion in the conduct of mankind necessarily terminates in misery, he will cease to be an exclusive being, or to desire that a single individual in any part of the world should not possess, equally with himself, whatever can contribute to his well-being and happiness.

Since he can no longer blame, he will view with pity all the aberrations from rationality, which the human mind has been compelled to make in the various parts of the world, and animated with the spirit of genuine charity, he will not merely commiserate their condition, but be irresistibly impelled to use every kind expedient to disabuse them of their errors, and to relieve their misery; he will cease to be a localized being of class, sect, party, or country, or to retain any wish to benefit or aggrandize himself and a few others, confined by accidental circumstances within a particular district, at the expense of those whom other circumstances have placed without it. Patriotism, to him, will clearly appear to be practical injustice; and perceiving the folly and madness of all national contests, – the bad feelings and passions which they engender, the endless crimes which they create, the countless miseries which they inflict upon the victors and the vanquished, and the utter impossibility of improving mankind while this system continues, – he will earnestly devote himself to remove the causes which produce such irrational conduct.

What has been said may serve to indicate generally the spirit of philanthropy, which a right knowledge of ourselves and of human nature is calculated to inspire. As the subject opens upon us, the prospects which this knowledge discloses to our view with reference to the progressive advancement of our species, are as boundless as they are animating and delightful to contemplate. The science of which the principles have been explained, and as it appears to us irrefragably established in the preceding pages, at once unveils to us the sources of ignorance and poverty, and of all their attendant vices, crimes and miseries; and with unerring certainty developes the means by which these evils may be removed. We shall discover that it is not only practicable, but that it is an object of comparatively easy attainment to place the rising generation under the influence of circumstances which shall render it impossible that they can fail to acquire the kindest dispositions, the best habits and manners, the most correct language, and high intellectual attainments, united with a sincere desire to exert all their physical and mental capabilities for the benefit of society.

The world will thus be governed through education alone, since all other government will then become useless and unnecessary. To train and educate the rising generation will at all times be the first object of society, to which every other will be subordinate; and those who possess the highest qualifications will direct and superintend in this department. Under the present system of physical weakness, mental imbecility, and moral evil, created by the irrational notions respecting man's free agency and responsibility, the education of the young has been generally one of the most arduous and disagreeable of all occupations, and in consequence it has usually been committed to inferior agents, and most frequently to those who possessed the least knowledge and experience of human nature. The belief that man forms his own character, naturally led to the persuasion that rewards, punishments and emulation were the only instruments with which it was possible to influence the inclinations, and effectually to control the self-willed perverseness of infancy and childhood. Anger, hatred, jealousy, revenge, and every evil disposition, were thus necessarily implanted and cultivated both in the teachers and the taught. Ignorance sowed the tares which smothered the growth of the kindly feelings of our nature. It created the evil passions, and then ascribed their existence to some occult cause, – a phantom of the imagination, to which was given the name of original sin.

But truth will at length prevail. Already we behold the dawn of a better day, when human nature shall be vindicated from the reproach which has been laid upon it; when man shall do justice to man, and society understand its true interests. Man shall be acknowledged to be good, not bad by nature; a delightful compound, containing the germs of unalloyed excellence, and which require for their due developement, only a kindly soil and careful cultivation. Education will then cease to be a perpetual contest with and counteraction of our best feelings; it will be directed assiduously to cherish and to expand them. The knowledge of the overwhelming power of circumstances in the formation of character, will enable us to place every individual from birth under a system of training and instruction in all respects congenial to his nature, and under the influence of which his interest, his duty, and his inclination, will become and appear to him continually but as one and the same sensation. Rewards and punishments and the unjust and horrid expedients which have emanated from false views of human nature, and which are calculated only to make man a demon, and the earth a Pandemonium, will give place to a treatment of undeviating kindness and impartiality.

To educate the young under such a system will become a sport and a pastime, affording equal pleasure to those who give and to those who receive instruction. And this easy and delightful task being performed, every obstacle to human happiness at once disappears. Man will then be formed with powers and dispositions to produce and preserve an abundant supply of whatever he can require or can wish to enjoy. The miseries arising from ignorance and poverty will be utterly unknown except through the history of the past or irrational period of our species.

It will then be discovered that all that has been written respecting the wealth of nations, and what has been called the science of political economy is worse than useless; that the theories which have been latterly promulgated on this subject, proceed upon data which exist only in the imaginations of the well-meaning authors of them; that so far from its being true that the means of subsistence cannot be made to keep pace with the highest possible rate of increase in population,[a] the very reverse of this proposition must hold good for at least many centuries to come; that by a system of union and cooperation, society will possess the power of creating wealth to an unlimited extent, and that it need no longer to be regarded as an object of contest or individual desire any more than water or air is at present.

Thus will a new state of society gradually arise out of the old, founded on the knowledge of the principles which regulate the formation of the human character. The doctrines of freewill will be superseded by the doctrine of necessity, reduced into the most enlightened and beneficent practice. It was probably the anticipation of superior minds having a knowledge of this doctrine and of the practice to which it would eventually lead that gave rise to the expectation of the millennium upon earth. Certain it is, however, that by its universal adoption almost all that has been predicated of that happy period of human existence may now be realized.

It may be here remarked that to give to one generation the knowledge of the means by which the character of the succeeding generation may be determined, is perhaps the happiest expedient which could be devised to destroy in man effectually and universally all cause of pride, vanity and ambition, – anger, hatred, jealousy and revenge, – murders, wars, and all uncharitableness.

The science of the influence of circumstances over human nature, is, like other sciences, susceptible of a gradual and unlimited progress towards perfection. But as it will soon be acknowledged to be beyond comparison the most useful and valuable of all, it is capable from its universal application of being carried in a short period to a higher degree of advancement, than any science has yet attained.

The application of it which is now proposed to be developed for the benefit of the existing generation, has been suggested by the past history and experience of our species. And although in the present stage of society the arrangements we are about to recommend will produce very important advantages to all ranks and descriptions of men, yet, as they have been projected in the earliest dawn of this new science by an ordinary untrained individual, it may naturally be anticipated that when the whole well-trained strength of the human mind shall be directed to the subject the most extensive improvement will rapidly follow.

Under all the disadvantages however which necessarily attach to a new undertaking, we proceed to make the first essay to apply the principles of this science to practice.

[a] See T. R. Malthus, *Essay on Population* (1798), Bk 1, ch. 1.

CHAPTER IV

It is required then to form on the basis of these principles a system of social arrangements, by which mankind may with ease and certainty attain all the desired objects of life, and effectually prevent the recurrence of those evils with which they have hitherto been afflicted.

There is but one mode (as has been already observed) by which man can possess in perpetuity all the happiness which his nature is capable of enjoying, – that is *by the union and co-operation of* ALL *for the benefit of* EACH. While mankind remain congregated in large cities and towns, or live in single families apart from their species, each having distinct and opposite interests, no substantial improvement can be effected in the condition of society. To obtain the full advantages of cooperation, men must be associated in small communities, or large families, all the members of which shall be united by the bond of one common interest; the same bond of union connecting each community with every other established on similar principles. The members to be associated in a community should be confined within certain limits; if too large, the evils of towns and cities; crowded dwellings, an unwholesome atmosphere, unhealthy occupations, and other inconveniences, could not be avoided. If, on the other hand, the numbers were below a certain amount, the full benefits of combination could not be attained.

As the result of much consideration on this subject, it is proposed that each community shall consist of from 500 to 2000 persons, according to circumstances. The form of a large square, or parallelogram, seems to present the most eligible disposition for the domestic accommodations of the society; the dwelling houses occupying the sides of the square, and the public buildings being placed in the center.

This plan combines all the advantages of a town and country residence, without the inconveniences of either, and admits of the best and the most simple and economical arrangements for heating, ventilating, lighting and cleaning; for cooking and eating; for instruction and recreation, and for every domestic object. Engravings have been made which will explain the general outline, and detail of the most essential parts of the plan, and from which workmen in any part of the world may form similar arrangements, adding to them any improvements that experience may suggest. – Around the establishment there must be a sufficient quantity of land to supply its members with a surplus of the best or most wholesome food. Accurate experiments, continued for a series of years, have satisfactorily proved, that a comparatively small extent of land, when the powers of the soil shall be adequately called forth under a proper system of culture, will amply satisfy the wants of such a population.

At a short distance from the gardens which will surround the parallelograms, may be placed the workshops and manufactories, washing and drying houses, granaries and store-rooms. With the aid of the embellishments which trees properly disposed afford, the whole of this combination may be made in almost any situation to present an animated, cheerful scene of great rural beauty.

These arrangements are intended to comprehend all the facilities which modern science can afford to the every day business of life, in order to render it healthy and agreeable, that intelligent and superior minds may no longer regard it as either irksome, degrading, or incompatible with the highest intellectual pursuits, and that no necessity may exist for the formation of any *lower class* in the new state of society. Mechanism and chemistry will in future become the slaves of mankind. As there can be no permanent happiness in any society in which inequality is not excluded, each individual will possess equal advantages. There will therefore be an equality in their houses, food, clothing, instruction, employment, and treatment, except that those who, at birth, are the least favored by nature, shall experience from infancy, increased kindness and attention, in proportion to their natural inferiority.

Individuals thus circumstanced having lost one and the same interest, to the promotion of which their whole concentrated powers of body and mind will be steadily directed, will command the means of producing much more than they can require, or desire to consume. They will always have in store a surplus of the necessaries of life to protect them against unfavorable seasons, and an excess of some kind of useful produce, in return for which they can obtain from their neighbors, such commodities as their own territory may not permit them to create advantageously. There will be no waste of labor, materials or skill in attending to or producing what is useless or pernicious. All things will be estimated by their intrinsic worth, nothing will be esteemed merely for its cost or scarcity, and fashions of any kind will have no existence. With regard to dress, an object upon which so large a share of the industry of civilized states is now so uselessly and injuriously expended, the members of the community, having once ascertained the best materials and the form best adapted to the health of the wearer, will have no disposition to introduce afterwards any of the frivolous, fantastical and expensive varieties that may be current elsewhere. They will adopt the rational course of employing the time which the manufacturer of such useless decorations would consume, in the pleasures of social intercourse, and intellectual pursuit, and in healthful recreations. They will well consider what will tend most to their permanent comfort, as respects food, clothing, dwellings and other objects; and, in every case, they will act on the principle of supplying their wants in the best and most direct manner, with the least loss of labor and capital. All the powers of production which can be derived from science may be beneficially called into action. The introduction of a machine for the abridgment of human labor, will not, as at present, have the miserable effect of wringing from the laborer an increased amount of exertion in return for diminished means of subsistence; but on the contrary will give him increased advantages in return for less labor.

The gifts of science will no longer be perverted, and rendered a curse to the great mass of society. Under the arrangements proposed, the magnificent discoveries and inventions of the last half century will give to man an almost unlimited power of creating whatever can be serviceable or beneficial to him. Manual labor, with these aids, will be converted into healthy, pleasant, and desirable occupation, while each individual will possess ample leisure for intellectual improvement and social enjoyment.

Economy will then have a different signification from its present meaning: to produce and use only the best of every thing will be discovered to be true economy. Poverty, or the fear of poverty, being under such circumstances entirely out of consideration, parsimony in using, when benefit can be derived from the use, will become evidently an error; and, as in these communities every thing will be for use, and nothing for accumulation, except to protect the members against accidents or bad seasons, no individual can have any motive or desire to possess a surplus of any kind of wealth.

This new order of things will gradually supersede the commercial system. The evils which necessarily arise from the practice of commerce in the present advanced state of the sciences, are incalculable. Since the termination of the last war, the period when its profitable continuance expired, it has annually destroyed many millions of capital, and the process of destruction is still going on. Manufactures, trade and commerce can yield a profit only as long as the demand exceeds the supply, or is barely equal to it. But society has now acquired the means of producing far more than the population of the world can advantageously consume. To render the existing system profitable, therefore, it would be necessary to destroy so much of the power of production as should reduce the supply within the demand, and continually to restrain that power. But it is directly contrary to the interests of mankind that this power should be checked or restrained.

Various circumstances connected with the late war gave a peculiar impetus to the powers of production in Great Britain, of which the developement was commensurate with the wants occasioned by the gigantic armies of the contending powers. But at the termination of this wide spread contest, when so formidable a demon of waste and destruction ceased its active operation, and the world was allowed to be at peace, peace could not be enjoyed, because a full stop was put to trading and commercial prosperity, by the excess of supply beyond the demand.

So deep-rooted are the notions which make men cling to the commercial system as the only means by which the wants of the world can be supplied, that they will resort to every expedient to uphold it, notwithstanding the frightful sacrifices of capital and the extreme distress in which the attempt is hourly involving them; nor will they cease their efforts until their ingenuity, again and again baffled, shall at length be exhausted. They will then, perhaps, ask themselves this simple question: Why should we wish to reduce the supply within the demand? When the mind can be divested of the prevailing prejudices on this subject, the true interest of society will be found to consist, 1st, In the discovery of what those things are, which are necessary to give the greatest happiness to human nature, and 2d, In the adoption of the best means by which a redundant supply of them may be produced, and be accessible to all, that no cause may remain for opposition of interests, or for individual and national contests. But the present trading system is incompatible with such a state of society; the sooner therefore it shall be abandoned the better. All parties are at this moment suffering grievously from its effects, and none more than the individuals immediately engaged in it, millions of whom for the sake of a bare subsistence are subjected to every kind of degradation and wretchedness; while by the proposed arrangements each individual would be enabled to possess and enjoy all he could desire through every period of his life.

In consequence of their numbers and union, the members of the new associations, even at first, will have to sell and purchase far less than individuals under the existing system: and in the same proportion will the risk and expense of their commercial transactions be diminished. To prevent loss and law-suits, as well as the evils arising from a system of credit, these transactions shall always be in money or barter, and be finally settled in the shortest time that circumstances will admit.

As the number of these communities increases, the exchange of products with each other will gradually supersede the necessity of having recourse to common society for the supply of their wants. This exchange in the earlier stages of their progress may be advantageously effected on the principle of estimating the value of commodities, by the quantity of labor required for their production: the quantity with reference to each article being previously ascertained and mutually agreed upon and fixed for defined periods. And for convenience this labor may be represented by notes or community bank paper bearing the value of one or any number of days labor. But after a sufficient number of communities, within a moderate distance from each other, shall be in action to create a full supply of all the articles required by each, any such medium of exchange will be found neither necessary nor desirable.

The connection subsisting between the several associations being founded on the same common interest by which the members of each are united together, they will cordially cooperate in forming arrangements which shall place the production and consumption of the whole confederation upon the most permanent basis. All that can be necessary in order to attain this object, will be, 1st, To regulate the productions of each community according to its localities and to the general wants; and 2ndly, as each community will produce a surplus of certain products, beyond its own possible wants, to establish periodical conveyances by means of which these various surplus products may be regularly interchanged. In this manner will the public stores of each association always contain an overflowing stock of all those things which can minister to the comfort and gratification of rational beings; and the time at length arrive when poverty can have no existence, and when every individual may obtain whatever he can require without money and without price.

Men placed under such circumstances, it is evident, can have no conceivable motive for individual accumulation, nor as a society, can they be influenced by any desire to amass wealth beyond what may be amply sufficient to protect them against every contingency – except with a view to extend to others the means of acquiring those advantages which they possess themselves. And so long as any of their fellow-creatures shall continue to suffer under the evils of the anti-social system, they will cheerfully devote whatever they can spare of their substance, to the cause of humanity.

It cannot fail to be perceived that the harmony and stability of the new institutions will mainly depend upon the training and education of the young. In regard to this subject of paramount importance, the principles which have been developed in the first part of this work, will guide us with unerring certainty, to sound conclusions and correct practice.

We have shewn what human nature *is not*, and what *it is*. We have shewn that man is not a free agent, having the power to will and act independently of circumstances, or in other words to form his own character; but that his character is entirely and in every sense formed *for him*; that it is the result of the particular qualities, faculties and propensities which he receives at birth and of the circumstances in which he is afterwards placed: that these combined make him what he is at every moment of his life; that as he has no power to determine what shall be his peculiar organization at birth, so neither does he possess any control over the circumstances with which he may be surrounded after birth; and we have proved that it depends upon the influence of these circumstances, whether the individual shall become a civilized man or a cannibal, – a charitable or a ferocious being, – enlightened or ignorant, – happy or miserable.

The knowledge of this law of our nature conducts us at once to the easy attainment of all the great objects of education regarded in its most comprehensive sense. It lays the foundation of a science, not less exact in its principles, and infinitely more important in its application than any which has arisen out of the past experience of mankind; a science which comes home emphatically to the business and interests of men; since, without its aid, all other acquirements must ever fail to give them happiness, and the bounties of nature be showered upon them in vain. It is the distinguishing feature of the new arrangements, that being throughout consistent with the principles of this science, they at once place the rising generation beyond the influence of those circumstances which in every existing state of society are continually operating to produce irrationality, and consequently vice and misery. By the very act of introducing a child into a community constituted in the manner we have described, we shall have surmounted all the great obstacles which are at present interposed to his right training, education and future well-being. The course which remains to be pursued is simple and straight-forward. His instructors will regard him, as a being upon whose plastic nature, education, as it is well or ill directed, may stamp the best or the worst impression; in whom, under one system of treatment, may be implanted, in his earliest years, the seeds of jealousy, hatred, revenge, and every evil passion; while under another, these feelings shall be for ever excluded, and their very names remain unknown to him. Rewards and punishments, emulation and partialities, are the characteristics of one; the other accomplishes every thing by reason and kindness alone.

The former system, with the utmost difficulty and labor to all concerned, effects the very worst possible results; reason and kindness on the other hand are sure to produce only the best, without labor or difficulty of any kind. And had not the grossest ignorance prevailed in society, no other would ever have been applied to human beings. Is it rational to punish a child because nature has endowed him with inferior powers, or because circumstances over which he could have no control have impressed upon him a character which is displeasing to us? or is it more rational to reward another, to whom nature may have been more liberal, and circumstances more propitious? – Is punishment a likely method of reforming the one? or can reward have any other effect upon the latter, than to pervert his good qualities, (the possession of which in no degree depended upon himself) to render him a vain conceited being, and to lead him to despise his less fortunate fellow-creatures? Can charity be expected in men, when the elements of all uncharitableness are thus effectually instilled into the minds of children?

If there be one object which society should steadily bear in mind above every other consideration, it is the necessity of rigidly excluding from the sphere of infancy and childhood all those circumstances which tend to impress them with the notion, that for any qualities they may possess, or any actions they may perform, they deserve either praise or blame, reward or punishment. In other words, it is the necessity of imbuing their minds with a right knowledge of themselves, and of human nature; for there is no other foundation than this, upon which genuine charity can be reared; that charity which suffereth long and is kind, which envieth not, which vaunteth not itself, and is not puffed up;[a] that divine charity, without which, though we understand all mysteries and all knowledge, and have all faith, so that we could remove mountains, we are nothing.

[a] See 1 Corinthians 13:1–4.

Such are the views which will be uniformly acted upon in regard to education in the new state of society. The children of each community will be brought up together and literally be as one family, in which partialities and distinctions will have no place. They will eat at the same table, wear the same dress, enjoy the same means of amusement, receive the same instruction and be treated in all respects with the same undeviating kindness. – No circumstances will exist around them which can excite in their young minds a single antisocial thought, which can possibly lead them to imagine that the happiness of each does not consist in the happiness of the whole. Long before verbal injunctions can be intelligible to them, they will act instinctively, as it were, in the very spirit of the precept, 'Love thy neighbor;'[a] and why will they act thus? – Because, under the system in which they are trained, no motives will be infused into their minds, which can give rise to any other conduct.

But this result cannot depend upon the children themselves. For we might place them under such circumstances as should with great certainty force them to hate each other. Love and hatred are feelings which are not in any degree at the control of the individual: he *must* hate the object which is hateful to him, nor can he help loving that which produces upon his mind the contrary impression.

In vain, then, do men under the present system, reiterate precept upon precept. All their proceedings towards children bear the character of irrationality. When they single out some for punishment, and distinguish others by reward, – when by every possible expedient they excite a spirit of emulation in all, which is in fact, making each strive to obtain advantages over his companions; no wonder that their precepts of love and good will so seldom produce any beneficial practical effects; no wonder that these little beings soon learn to hate and deceive, and acquire evil and injurious dispositions.

The system of *Instruction* which will be adopted under the new arrangements, will differ essentially from that which prevails at present. It is a mistake to suppose that there exists in children any repugnance to acquire knowledge, and to imagine that the business of tuition is necessarily an irksome task; and that what it is proper for them to learn most needs be forced upon them. The truth is, that at no age is the desire of knowledge stronger. In childhood, all the objects which surround the human being possess the charm of novelty, and the feeling of curiosity is intense. but as in our other proceedings under the existing system, we are continually counteracting nature, so do we likewise in the present case; always in a greater or less degree, but very generally the principle of counteraction is carried to its uttermost limits. Either the matter of instruction is such as cannot be interesting to the young mind, being adapted to a more advanced age, (very commonly indeed it is such as can be interesting,

[a] See Leviticus 19:18.

to no rational mind at any age, and absolutely pernicious) or the manner of conveying it is ill-devised and repulsive. It most frequently happens that the worst matter and the worst manner are conjoined. The child however must receive what is offered to him, or if he act more rationally than his teachers and refuse it, he is punished.

That the office of instructor may be rendered agreeable and his services efficient and acceptable, and that none but the most delightful feelings may be created between him and his pupils, it is necessary to present to them the objects of their instruction in the order which corresponds with the natural developement of their faculties; and instead of disgusting them with confused notions, by endeavoring to give them ideas of things through the medium of written language only, to convey to their minds clear and distinct perceptions, and correct knowledge by the aid of sensible signs with oral explanations. More especially is it necessary to withhold from them any dogmas, regarding the truth or consistency of which their previous attainments do not enable them to form a rational opinion; for to act otherwise tends directly to weaken and destroy the most valuable of their intellectual powers, to incapacitate them for any process deserving the name of reasoning, to render them the mere recipients of every wild and incongruous doctrine, and to convert them into the slaves of the grossest prejudices and the most uncharitable and absurd imaginations: in short, it is effectually to deprive them, through life, of religious and mental liberty; and *to this cause is it owing that mental and religious liberty has never yet been enjoyed by any human being.* Let it be the first great object to store the young mind with undisputed facts, and to guard against the entrance of any ideas not founded on facts, and still more against any actions which are in opposition to facts.

If we follow the dictates of Nature in our treatment of children, instruction will ever be blended with amusement, in order that the mind may be beneficially relaxed. We cannot be more ready to communicate than they to receive information. From their earliest years the pursuit of knowledge will constitute their chief delight, and give the purest zest and highest animation to their whole existence. For in that state of society to which we are looking forward, the interchange of ideas and sentiments will be free from the restraints and consequent deceit created by the existing artificial system.

We shall not however do justice to human nature, if we cultivate the intellectual at the expense of the physical powers. That the individual may enjoy the highest degree of happiness of which he is susceptible, a sound mind must reside in a sound body: nor is it saying too much to assert, that under a right course of training, the new race of men will excel their forefathers as much in physical capabilities as in intellectual strength and attainments. The powers of the body and of the mind will in every individual under the proposed arrangements be cultivated with equal care, and a due proportion of time be allotted to the exercise and improvement of each.

One great obstacle to the general diffusion of knowledge is the variety of languages in the world. Much time and labor must be spent before the knowledge elicted by one nation can be communicated to another. The friendly intercourse between different countries is impeded, and that locality of feeling, so adverse to the happiness of mankind is increased. It is proposed therefore that one general language, to be hereafter fixed upon, shall be taught to the children in the communities in all countries at the same time with their own; and thus in one generation, after communities shall have become general, this language may be adopted in every part of the world and supersede all the others.

Political economists have hitherto totally misunderstood their subject. They have in all cases supposed that the sole object of society was the accumulation of riches, and that men would necessarily obtain all they required in proportion as their wealth increased. They have always reasoned as though man were an inanimate machine, without the capacity of suffering, understanding or enjoying, and have consequently recommended those measures, which were calculated to reduce the mass of mankind into mere implements of production and to deteriorate the general powers, physical and mental, of each individual, that some small part of his faculties might be unnaturally and most injuriously cultivated. Thus have they led the public, step by step, from one error to another, until at length they can proceed no farther, for the fact is become too evident, that men can easily produce more than they know how to distribute or consume advantageously. At this moment, the chief suffering of mankind arises from *an excess of wealth*, with, if the expression be allowable, *an excess of ignorance*.

The science of political economy is, or ought to be only another term for the science of human happiness, for if it does not promote this, it is of no value whatever. As it has been hitherto taught, however, it is directly opposed to it, nor is it calculated to attain, in the best manner, even the inferior object which it professes to have in view. – It recommends, as its fundamental principles, the most minute division of labor, and separate or individual interests among the whole human race; while the first dawn of real knowledge respecting the means of promoting the well-being and happiness of mankind, will make it evident that these principles are at once opposed, 1st, to the most advantageous creation, distribution and preservation of wealth; and 2dly, to the best formation of the human character, physically, mentally and morally.

No one can doubt that it is for the interest of mankind that abundance of the most useful and intrinsically valuable products should be created with the least labor and the greatest benefit to the producers and consumers; that this wealth should be distributed in the best manner throughout society, in order that each may possess a full supply; that that which remains for future consumption and reproduction should be the most easily preserved; and that every individual should be trained to be capable of enjoying in the highest degree the use of these productions.

But not one of these essential objects can be attained under a system of which the characteristics are a minute division of labor and separate or individual interests. The effect of the first of these erroneous principles is, to form man into a creature far inferior to an inanimate machine; to deprive him, except in a single point of little comparative value, of all excellence as an intelligent and rational being, and to render him an unequal competitor with the harder materials of wood, brass and iron, to effect often the most useless result. The second of these principles destroys all the supposed advantages arising from the first, by preventing, to an incalculable extent, the adoption of the best means for distributing and preserving wealth after it has been created, and, together, they render it impossible that the population of the world can ever become under their influence as rich, healthy, intelligent, moral or happy, as it easily might be under another system.

Political economists have hitherto been entirely ignorant of human nature, and consequently of the very elementary principles, on which the science of political economy, in any rational signification of the term, is founded.

How to create the largest supply of the most valuable products with the least expense of labor and with the greatest amount of benefits to all – is the problem which this science is required to solve.

A correct knowledge of human nature is all that is now necessary for the attainments of each of these objects in a high degree of perfection, and if that knowledge be acted upon, poverty or the fear of poverty will no longer counteract the happiness of society. But instead of pushing the division of labor so far as to mutilate[a] (if we may so speak) the character of man, to reduce him in fact to a small fraction of an intelligent human being, it will be the great object of all our arrangements to place him under circumstances in which all his valuable powers both physical and mental will be so well and equally trained from infancy, that he will speedily acquire a new character full of excellence; be, as it were, recreated, or born again, and possess not only the ability and inclination to create abundantly whatever can be necessary to the highest degree of comfortable existence but the capacity to understand all human knowledge and to enjoy or make the best use of the advantages he possesses.

At this hour, with great industry and application and much good intention, the modern economists from wholly mistaking their subject, are producing throughout civilized society so much suffering and evil that it is probable they are unintentionally the most mischievous spirits, now in action in any part of the world. – They have assumed it as an incontrovertible position, that wealth is created of a superior kind, and more abundantly, is more easily distributed, better preserved for future consumption or reproduction, and more advantageously used, under the present system of separate and opposing interests

[a] See Adam Smith, *Wealth of Nations*, Bk 5, ch. 1.

than it would be under one of mutual aid and cooperation, or of united interests. And although the reverse were the case, they have also supposed that it is impossible to unite mankind to act cordially and beneficially for the general good; in short, that human beings could not be stimulated to exertion except through the influence of individual separate and opposing interests.

No greater proof, than these conclusions afford, could be exhibited, of the utter ignorance respecting human nature, and the elementary principles of the science in which the economists are involved.

Everyone at once admits the superiority of an army well organized, and abundantly supplied with all the materials of war, over the same number of individuals, unconnected, untrained, unsupplied with arms or necessaries for the contest, and each being obliged to think and act and provide for himself, not only unaided but opposed by his comrades. The different effects to be produced by the same numbers, under these opposite circumstances, scarcely admit of a comparison. Union and cooperation in war obviously increase the power of the individual a *thousand fold*. Is there the shadow of a reason why they should not produce equal effects in peace; why the principle of cooperation should not give to men the same superior powers, and advantages, (and much greater) in the creation, preservation, distribution, and enjoyment of wealth?

But it may be urged that men cannot be made to unite for the purposes of creating, preserving, distributing, and enjoying wealth and happiness, in the same manner as they have been associated to *prevent* the creation of wealth, to *destroy* it when created, to overwhelm their fellow-creatures with poverty and ignorance, to inflict upon them every species of suffering, and to render them destitute and miserable. These and such notions are surely a libel on poor human nature, and have arisen solely from a misconception of what it really is – a misconception which has already been traced to its true source, and exposed at some length in the preceding chapters. The experience of the writer has removed all doubts from his mind on this subject, and he hesitates not to say that the time is now arrived when it will be far more easy, (as much more so as it will be more beneficial) to unite men heartily and cordially in measures for promoting and securing their well-being and happiness, than it has been, through the past ages of the world, to induce them to act in numbers as one mind for the purpose of inflicting misery and destruction upon each other. Men can be compelled to cooperate for the latter purpose only so long as they are made irrational and kept in that state. To produce a general union for the attainment of all the desired objects of life, nothing more is necessary than to train men from infancy to be rational; and this will be easily accomplished under the proposed arrangements.

It remains to be explained, in order to complete the outline of these arrangements, in what manner the local government of the new communities may be the most advantageously conducted.

A certain period of time, it is evident, must elapse before the new system can have produced that regeneration in the human character, which, when in full operation, it is calculated to effect. During the change from the old to the new state of society, it will therefore be necessary to adopt regulations that will be altogether superseded at a more advanced stage. The administration of affairs in the first instance, must be delegated to a select committee or body of men, composed of such person or persons, as the knowledge of the parties concerned may point out as being the best qualified to superintend the different departments.

Individuals, who, in order to escape from the misery and wretchedness of the existing system, have agreed to unite their powers for their common benefit, convinced, that this is the only mode by which any relief can be obtained, will, it is concluded, feel every disposition to concur in such preliminary regulations as circumstances may call for. Nor is it to be apprehended that they will fail to select generally those to whom the management of their common concerns may be most fitly entrusted.

When however the members of the association shall all have received the advantages of the system of training and education, to which we have referred, each will then be fully competent to undertake the charge of any of the departments. And a very simple mode suggests itself by which every individual may, advantageously for all, participate equally in the business of government, may in fact acquire, without even the semblance of contest, his just proportion of the government of the world.

The future committee may be composed of all the members of the society between certain ages, of those for instance between thirty-five and forty-five, or between forty and fifty. But it is of little moment which period of life may be fixed upon. From what has been said, it is easy to foresee, that in such a state of society, the business of government, in regard to the task it imposes, will be little more than nominal. The only distinction among them will be that of age or experience; it is the only just and natural distinction; any other would at once be rejected by rational beings.

If any evils in practice should be found to arise at first from inexperience in the application of the science of the influence of circumstances over human nature, immediate measures will be adopted to discover the cause from which they originated; and it may be safely predicted, that there will be no difficulty whatever, in extirpating every evil almost as soon as it appears. When the period shall have arrived, in which the new principles can be acted upon in all their purity and consistency, it will be utterly impossible that evil or error can arise in the conduct of any individual.

While each community will, in its internal affairs, be independent of all other communities, there will yet exist for general purposes, a cordial union among them. The same spirit which unites the members of each will necessarily lead to the most amicable alliance between one association and every other.

As these institutions multiply, in the same proportion will an increase of benefits accrue to all who are placed in the sphere of their influence. National distinctions and prejudices will gradually subside and cease to form a barrier to the establishment of a friendly intercourse and a free communication and interchange of inventions, discoveries and improvements among the great family of mankind. The happiness of one portion of the human species can never be permanently founded upon the sacrifices and miseries of another.

Hitherto, the great mass of the population of the world has been doomed to a life of ignorance; the rich mine of human intellect has been neglected and remained comparatively unexplored. Even that small portion of intellectual power which has yet been called forth has not received the most beneficial direction. To what an incalculable extent, then, will our dominion over creations be enlarged, and our means of happiness be increased, when society shall adopt the principles of the science developed in the preceding pages; by the right application of which, the character of every individual, without exception, may with ease be so formed, as to render him the wisest, the best, and the happiest being that his nature and the existing state of knowledge will permit him to become.

CHAPTER V

The next consideration, which will naturally arise in the mind of the reader, is, how can these communities be generally established without prematurely disturbing the present order of society.

Among those who have long been convinced of the evils and misery which exist under the present system, and of the benefits to be derived under the proposed arrangements, there have been various opinions respecting the best mode of effecting the changes from the one to the other; the majority, perhaps, have wished to unite the principles of the old system, with the practice of the new. In compliance with these opinions, and from a sincere desire not to hurt the feelings of any portion of mankind, this part of the subject has been considered frequently with great attention; some steps were taken in conjunction with several well-disposed and intelligent individuals to combine them, and a certain progress was made in preliminary arrangements.

But after the most calm and patient investigation of the proposals made by the members of old society, who were pleased with the effects produced by a very slight approximation to the new system in practice; the writer of this work is very reluctantly obliged to acknowledge that he cannot discover any means by which the principles of the one may be united with the practice of the other.

The principles of old society have necessarily produced the practice of old society, and the principles of the new system can alone create that practice which these individuals propose to unite with and produce from their principles. They require therefore impossibilities. The notions of free-will and responsibility have engendered ignorance, poverty, vice, crime, punishment and misery; and while the same doctrine shall be taught, these evils must continue. To separate the one from the other, would be to disunite cause and effect: to annul the everlasting laws of the universe; as well might we expect to produce heat from cold, or light from darkness, as to create genuine kindness, benevolence and charity, in the hearts of those who are forced to believe in the doctrine of man's free agency and responsibility. With this conviction strongly impressed upon their minds, it would be worse than hypocrisy in those who clearly see the errors of the old, and the truth of the new system to hold out any, even the most distant expectation that they can be made to approximate. No, if mankind are now to be substantially benefitted, it must be by a fair, full and open declaration of the truth; for whatever obstacles may be opposed to it, truth will prevail.

The principles and practice of old society are before the world, and their effects are abundantly known and felt. Let then the principles of the new system be fairly tried in practice, as an experiment of the deepest interest to mankind; and let their truth or falsehood be proved by the result.

This is a proposal which no good man who desires to know the truth, and who sincerely loves his fellow-creatures, can object to. If the experiment should fail, the world will be relieved from a dangerous error; if it should succeed, the world will obtain an incalculable good. It is confidently believed that the principles which are now advocated are true; that they will bear the test of every examination, and that when they shall be fully adopted in practice, they will secure the permanent happiness of mankind.

It is therefore proposed to those, who sincerely desire the happiness of their fellow-creatures, and who are not afraid of truth from whatever quarter it may come, that they lend their aid to the formation of societies for instituting this great experiment, for adopting measures to try whether man cannot escape from the afflictions with which he is now threatened to be overwhelmed, and that, not by pestilence, plague, or famine, but by the excess of the bounties and benefits which have been showered upon him.

The rules and regulations of the projected societies have been so framed as to admit the assistance and cooperation of the intelligent of every rank, class, sect and party; and it is hoped, that setting aside all sectarian notions, and party feelings, individuals of such description will cordially unite in this good work.

The individual who makes the proposal, has proceeded on no slight grounds. There appeared to him to be a fundamental error in the constitution of society: He for years carefully examined and considered the opinions and practices of past ages; an investigation which tended only to confirm the impression, his mind had received. He instituted experiments upon an extensive scale both in England and Scotland for upwards of twenty years to try the practical effect of a principle in direct opposition to that which had hitherto influenced the proceedings of men, and which as it appeared to him, was continually producing disappointment and misery.

The results of these experiments, in every instance, exceeded his most sanguine anticipations. Several years were then spent in personal communication with a large portion of the leading men among all sects, classes and parties, to discover if the present age possessed any knowledge on this important subject which had been denied to former ages; and this intercourse was to a sufficient extent to ascertain the limited boundaries of human attainments in a science so necessary to the happiness of mankind. He then enlarged the sphere of his experiments, and continued them ten years longer up to the present time,* the result of which combined with his former experiments and information has been to remove every doubt from his mind, and enable him to say with confidence to the world, that it is and ever has been governed under a system as erroneous in principle, as it is pernicious in practice.

Under this conviction, he in the most public manner, declared his views and opinions, and solicited a fair and full examination of the measures he had to propose from the governments of Europe. In this effort, to limit the period of human suffering, he did not succeed, although his communications were in general favorably received and the truth of the principles generally admitted. Other attempts were subsequently made to bring the subject before the British Parliament, as the most effectual mode of giving it universal publicity; but an efficient investigation was not obtained for it, although it was supported by some of the most intelligent members.

Knowing the magnitude of the change which he proposed, and being well aware that the established habits and prejudices of men were opposed to it, and that the principles they had imbibed in infancy precluded them from considering it practicable to carry his plans into execution to the extent he wished, he could not feel much surprise or disappointment at these preliminary failures. He was fully prepared to encounter the opposition which had been excited, and steadily persevered in measures to enlighten the public mind on a subject which seemed to him preeminently important; and the right understanding of which could alone lead to any substantial improvement in the condition of society.

He trusts it cannot be deemed either unreasonable or presumptuous in him to entreat the public to try upon a scale sufficiently extensive the principles and practice which in his hands, under every discouraging circumstance, have

* 1821, and six years most interesting extensive confirmative experience has since been obtained.

created benevolence, plenty, good conduct and happiness, generally speaking, where previously, there existed squalid wretchedness, continual quarrelling, immoral conduct and misery. – That doubts and prejudices have been raised on this subject, in consequence of the many reports which have been spread abroad concerning it, he is fully sensible. It could not be expected to be otherwise, for the social system is directly opposed to the apparent interest of every class, sect and party, although in reality it will secure the happiness of every one. He never wished to deceive the public, or to lead men blindfold to the happiness which awaits them. In promulgating his principles, he has uniformly disclosed the effects which they would produce; and he again declares to the public, to those who govern, as well as to those who are governed, that the principles and plans which he advocates are calculated ultimately to effect (though gradually, and without requiring from any individual any sacrifice whatever) the greatest conceivable change in the feelings, manners, habits and conduct of mankind. He contemplates with peculiar pleasure the arrival of the period when those circumstances which are now continually creating vice and misery, shall give place to others which shall with equal certainty produce none but the most beneficial results upon individual conduct, and upon the character of society at large.

These are the grounds upon which he asks the cooperation of all men, and claims a fair trial of the proposed arrangements. Pecuniary loss (if such a consideration should have any weight in a question of this momentous import) cannot occur where the individuals do their duty to each other. The capital will be invested in buildings, in useful manufactures, and in the cultivation of the soil.

To prepare individuals for these communities, measures should be adopted according to the localities, character and condition of the parties who are to form them, but when they shall be ready to enter upon the practice required to give success to these associations, the writer proposes as an outline, the following Rules and Regulations, and for the most important of them he subjoins the reasons for the recommendation.

CONSTITUTION, LAWS AND REGULATIONS OF A COMMUNITY

It is recommended,

I. That the community consist of persons who shall have agreed to unite their labor, skill and capital for mutual benefit, to cooperate in measures for producing and distributing, in the most advantageous manner for all, a full supply of the necessaries and comforts of life, as well as in forming arrangements which shall enable them to enjoy in the highest degree the use of those productions, and secure to their children the best training and education.

II. That, to avoid on the one hand, the evils and inconveniences resulting from the congregation of mankind into large masses, and on the other hand to preserve that limit, below which, the full benefits of combination could not be attained, the number of persons composing a community shall not (including their families) exceed 2,000, nor be less than 500.

III. That, in order to provide for an increase of population, the numbers at the commencement shall not considerably exceed the minimum, or 500.*

IV. That the community buildings be arranged in the form of a square or parallelogram, the dwelling houses, dormitories, etc occupying the sides, and the public buildings, comprising kitchen and dining halls, library and committee rooms, schools and lecture rooms, being placed in the center. The vacant spaces of the area may be ornamented with trees, and laid out in public walks and exercise grounds for the children. Gardens are proposed to be formed around the exterior of the square.

The plan should be arranged to admit of the most beneficial application of scientific improvements in all the departments of domestic economy, to afford increased comfort and enjoyment, at a less expense of labor and capital, to give superior accommodations to the dwelling houses, and to render the external circumstances of the establishment in a high degree agreeable and favorable to health.

V. That the village be situated as near to the center of the land to be occupied by the community as local circumstances may permit.

VI. That as exclusive employment in manufactures and all occupations carried on within doors, as incompatible with a sound state of health, and as the union of agriculture and manufactures presents many facilities to both, and as it is also of great importance that the community should produce within itself, a full supply of the first necessaries of life, the land attached to the establishment shall be of sufficient extent to render it essentially agricultural.

VII. That the manufactories, workshops, granaries, stores, washing and drying houses, be placed at the most convenient distance beyond the gardens surrounding the village; and that the farm offices be situated according to the localities of the land.

VIII. That as cordial union and cooperation never have existed and cannot exist under a system of family and individual interests, or inequality of condition; there shall be a full community of interests among all the members of the society, and as much equality as can be advantageously introduced into practice during the change from the old habits to the new.

IX. That when all shall have been equally well educated, and the society shall have repaid such part of the capital, invested in the establishment, as may have been advanced by its own members, a full and complete equality shall prevail; the necessary and natural inequality of age, being the only distinction existing; and to advanced age every advantage, comfort and deference being given.

* In many situations the number associating together *at the commencement* may with great advantage be much less than 500.

X. That the community shall at this period be under the direction of a committee composed of all the members between certain ages of those, for example, between 35 and 45, or between 40 and 50.

XI. That in the mean time, the management of affairs be vested in a committee consisting of twelve persons, to be elected by all the members of the community.

XII. That the committee be elected annually, the members of the old being eligible for the new committee.

XIII. That the committee elect from the members of the society two treasurers and a secretary, who shall be members of the committee in virtue of their offices.

XIV. That the committee meet every Monday, and oftener when particular circumstances require their attention, such extra meetings to be called by the secretary or by any two of the members.

XV. That the oldest member present, exclusive of the treasurers and secretary, preside at these meetings, and that the minutes of proceedings at each be signed by him.

XVI. That the treasures be empowered to receive all moneys due to the community, and pay its disbursements on orders signed by the secretary; that they balance and report their accounts every week to the committee, who shall appoint two of their number to examine and pass them under their signatures.

XVII. That the secretary be directed to keep a regular, detailed, daily statement of all the accounts and transactions of the community; and that such statement be presented weekly to the committee and submitted to the examination of two of their number who shall pass it under their signatures with such observations as may occur to them.

XVIII. That the books of accounts, and transactions of the society be open to the inspection of all its members.

XIX. That the business of the community be divided into the following departments.

1st. Agriculture and gardening.

2d. Manufactures and trades.

3d. Commercial transactions.

4th. Domestic economy: comprehending the arrangements for heating, ventilating, lighting, cleaning, and keeping in repair the dwelling houses and public buildings of the village – the arrangements connected with the public kitchen and dining halls, those for the furnishing of clothes, linens and furniture, and for washing and drying and the management of the dormitories.

5th. Health, or the medical superintendence of the apartments for the sick and lying-in apartments, and general arrangements to prevent contagion and sickness.

6th. Police, including the arrangements for lighting and cleaning the square – for the repair of the roads and walks, and for watching to guard against fire and to protect the property of the community against external depredation.

7th. Education, or the formation of character from infancy; to this department will also belong the means of recreation, or of mental and physical exercise and improvement for all ages.

XX. That a weekly report from each of these departments be laid before the committee at their weekly meetings to be examined and passed with such observations as may be deemed necessary.

XXI. That, for the general superintendence of the departments the committee appoint subcommittees from their own number or from the other members of the society.

XXII. That in case there be not at first a sufficient number of persons in the community fully competent to the management of all the operations in the different branches of industry which it may be desirable to establish, or in any other department, the committee be empowered to engage the assistance of skilful, practical men from common society, until the increased experience of the members of the community can advantageously dispense with such services.

XXIII. That in regulating the employments of the members according to their age, abilities, previous acquirements and situation in life, the committee, at the same time, pay every regard to the inclinations of each, consistent with the general good; and that the employment be equalized as far as possible, and so ordered as to permit every individual who may be thus disposed to occupy part of his time in agriculture.

Great facilities may be afforded to agriculture by the power which the community will possess of calling out an extra number of hands, to assist in its operations at those seasons and moments, when it is of great importance to have the command of additional aid.

XXIV. That as under the proposed arrangements, every machine, invention and expedient for the abridgment of human labor will bring an increase of benefits to all, it be a primary object with the committee to introduce to the utmost practicable extent in every department of the establishment, all those scientific improvements of modern times, which if rightly applied, are calculated to render manual labor only a healthy and agreeable exercise.

XXV. That the productive powers of the community be applied in the first place, to create a full supply of the necessaries and comforts of life for domestic consumption, and as far as localities will admit, to obtain them directly from their own land and labor.

XXVI. That the system of garden cultivation be gradually introduced as the population increases, and as it shall be found to be advantageous.

XXVII. That the surplus products of the community, which will be derived from manufactures and the useful trades and agriculture, more or less from each, according to the peculiar circumstances of the establishment, shall consist of intrinsically valuable and staple commodities; to be regulated by the demand of the neighboring markets.

XXVIII. That the persons, whom the committee appoint to conduct the commercial transactions of the community, be instructed to buy and sell for ready money only, to avoid the evils arising from a system of credit; that these transactions on the part of the community be always performed in good faith, and without the slightest attempt to deceive in any respect, buyer or seller; and when any individuals with whom they deal, shew a disposition to impose upon the community, all dealings with such individuals shall from that time cease.

XXIX. That in regard to domestic consumption, each member of the community shall be equally supplied with the necessaries and comforts of life.

XXX. That all the members of the community be equal in rights, privileges, and accommodations, according to their respective ages.

XXXI. That the surplus proceeds of the united exertions of the community, which remain after discharging rent, interest, taxes, and other expenses, be regularly applied to the liquidation of the capital borrowed upon the establishment until it shall be repaid; and when this debt is cancelled, it is proposed that the future surplus proceeds be invested to form a fund for the creation of a second community, as soon as the increased population of the first may require it.

XXXII. That in the domestic department, the following arrangements and regulations be adopted:

1st. The heating, ventilating and lighting of the dwelling houses and buildings in the square shall be effected according to the latest and most approved methods.

2d. An ample supply of water shall be provided and distributed to each, for domestic purposes and to guard against fire.

3d. Provisions of the best quality only shall be cooked in the public kitchen: and it shall be a special object for the attention of the subcommittee of domestic economy, and of the superintendent who has the immediate direction of this department to ascertain and put in practice the best and most economical means of preparing the most nutritious and agreeable food.

Any parties being ill, or having an aversion to eat with their friends in the public dining hall, may have their meals sent to their private apartments.

4th. The furniture of the dwelling houses, dormitories and public buildings (as far as the same is provided for out of the public funds) shall be such as to afford every accommodation, which persons living in such a community can require, being devised with reference to intrinsic use and comfort and not mere fashion or capricious ornament.

5th. A similar regulation will apply to the clothing of the community. The best materials shall be provided, and that form of dress adopted, which may be best calculated to promote the comfort and health of the wearer. With regard to the children, whose habits are yet to be formed, very essential improvements may in this respect be introduced, which will not only save much useless expense of labor and capital, but be the means of increasing in a very high degree the strength of the constitution.

6th. Modern scientific improvements, which supersede the necessity of any severe or disagreeable manual labor, shall be applied to the processes of washing and drying.

7th. The dormitories, designed for the children above two years of age, and the youth of the community until the period of marriage, shall be divided into compartments, and furnished with accommodations suited to the different ages.

XXXIII. That the employments of the female part of the community consist in preparing food and clothing – in the case of the dwelling houses, dormitories and public buildings – in the management of the washing and drying houses – in the education (in part) of the children – in the lighter operations of gardening, and other occupations suited to the female character. By the improved domestic arrangements proposed, one female will with great ease and comfort perform as much as twenty menial servants can do at present; and instead of being the drudge and slave which the wife of a working man with a family has hitherto been, she will be engaged only in healthy and cleanly employments, and possess sufficient leisure for mental improvement and the rational enjoyment of life.

XXXIV. That it be a general rule, that every part of the establishment be kept in the highest state of order and neatness, and that the utmost personal cleanliness be observed.

XXXV. That the following objects and regulations connected with the department of health be attended to and adopted.

1st. On the first appearance of indisposition in any of the members, immediate attention be given it, and every possible care taken of the patient till complete recovery; the prevention of serious complaints being always far more easy, than to effect a cure after the disease has fixed itself in the constitution.

2d. The complaint of indisposition by an individual shall place him on the invalid list, on which he will remain, until the medical attendant pronounce his complete recovery.

3d. The arrangements of the apartments for the sick shall be so formed and conducted as to afford every possible comfort to patients, and provide much more effectual means of recovery, than their private dwelling could admit of.

4th. In the lying-in apartments the best accommodations shall be prepared for the quiet and recovery of the female members of the community during their confinement.

5th. Removal to the apartments for the sick, as well as to the lying-in apartments, shall at the same time be at the option of the individual.

6th. As the health of the community may be materially improved or injured by the interior plan of the dwelling houses, by their situation with respect to public buildings, by dress, food, employment, the temper, and general state of the mind, and by various other circumstances, the attention of the subcommittee of this department shall be continually directed to these important considerations.

XXXVI. That, as the right education of the rising generation is the corner stone upon which the future prosperity and happiness of the community must be founded, the committee shall regard this as the most important of all the departments committed to their direction, and employ in its superintendence those individuals, whose talents, attainments and disposition render them best qualified for such a charge.

From the nature of the subject which the present section embraces, it is necessary to develope at some length, the principle upon which the committee ought to proceed, and the arrangement proper to be adopted.

It is only by acting upon a correct knowledge of human nature, that the objects which mankind have in view in the training and instruction of children can be attained. The principle of the formation of the human character must be understood, before any rational system can be devised and successfully reduced to practice, for the education of human beings. All admit to a great extent the influence of circumstances upon the character and conduct of man; yet the notion of human free will and responsibility is still retained and acted upon in contradiction to that admission. For it is clearly contradictory to admit that man is influenced by circumstances, and at the same time to maintain that he is a free agent, or that he forms his own character, since if the latter proposition were true, he would in all cases *control circumstances*, instead of being *controlled by circumstances*. But it has already been shewn that there is no foundation whatever for the supposition that he is a free agent, or has the power to form his own character. The evidence of our senses, our present experience, and knowledge of the past establish it as the most certain of truths, that the character of man is in all respects formed *for* him, that it is at all times a combination of the qualities and powers which are given to him at birth, and of the circumstances in which he is afterwards placed. The influence of the latter over human nature may indeed be said to be overwhelming; to so great an extent, is the character of the rising generation under the control of the present.

Under this view of human nature it should be the object of society to place all children under those circumstances which are known to be the most favorable to the formation of a good character, or, in other words, to form each child into the best, the wisest and happiest being that his original faculties and qualities, and the present state of knowledge, will permit.

This great end can only be attained under a system of social arrangements, such as are now proposed, or such as shall be founded on the same principles.

By the plan of training and instruction to be adopted in the communities, undeviating kindness in the treatment of children will supersede rewards and punishments, and all those distinctions and partialities, which, having arisen from a misconception of what human nature is, are calculated only to produce discord and jealousy, where harmony, love and good will should prevail; and under the name of education, to counteract as far as possible, the formation of good dispositions. If any distinction be permitted, it will consist only in bestowing increased attention upon a child in proportion to his natural inferiority.

Knowledge will be communicated in the order which nature prescribes in the development of the human faculties. In certain branches of instruction, the objects themselves will be presented to the pupil, as far as circumstances admit, and in other cases clear perceptions of those objects will be conveyed, by means of sensible signs or representations accompanied by a verbal explanation from the instructor. No dogmas, or mere opinions will be inculcated, concerning which, children do not possess data to enable them to form a rational judgment, the main object being to furnish them with valuable, and undisputed facts; with distinct and consistent ideas. The effects of this mode of proceeding will be, to give them a knowledge of things as well as of words, to experience the powers of reasoning, instead of burthening the memory with mere sounds without any defined or useful meaning; to delight instead of disgusting them with the process of instruction; to direct that curiosity or desire of knowledge, which nature gives them, to the most beneficial purpose; in short, to render the business of tuition, not a task, but a source of equal gratification to the teacher and to the taught.

The children of the community will be educated together, and as one family, in the schools and exercise grounds provided for them in the center of the square, where they will at all times be under the eye and inspection of their parents. By conducting their education upon the principles which have been explained; it will be easy to give to each child –

Good dispositions and habits;

As sound a constitution as air, exercise and temperance can bestow;

A knowledge of the objects of nature around him, beginning with the most simple and proceeding as his faculties expand;

A knowledge of the outline of natural history and geography;

A knowledge of himself, and of human nature to render him charitable, kind and benevolent to all his fellow-creatures, and to form him into a rational being;

A facility in reading, writing, accounts and grammar;

Daily exercises in dancing, gymnastics, music and drawing;

A knowledge of mathematics, mechanics, chemistry, astronomy, anatomy and general history;

A knowledge of domestic economy, political economy (in its true signification) and government;

A knowledge of the theory and practice of agriculture; and lastly, a practical knowledge of some one or more useful manufacture, trade or other occupation, that his employment may be varied for the improvement of his mental and physical powers.

To improve and perfect this system of training and instruction will at all times be the chief object in every community; and such will be found to be the human power of simplifying instruction, that ere long it will be discovered that children, *in the mass*, at twelve years of age, will possess far more essentially valuable knowledge, than any body of men have yet been permitted to acquire, and with this increased knowledge will be combined superior habits and dispositions.

As the infant, child, and youth will be thus trained and instructed in the daily practice of all the moral virtues, in the elements of the knowledge hitherto attained, and with his mind stored with useful and valuable ideas, all consistent with each other, and with the whole of nature, and as he will thus for the first time in the history of human nature be formed into a rational creature, he will be well prepared to examine the opinions of his predecessors on all hitherto disputed points, to pass a sound and mature judgment upon them, and at once to discover which are rational. And thus for the first time also will *liberty of mind* be acquired. He may now safely in all things be allowed to judge for himself.

To most persons the successful execution of so comprehensive a plan as that which has been described, will no doubt seem at first sight impracticable. But it will appear so only because they have themselves been trained and instructed under the influence of different and opposite principles and arrangements. The latter indeed could never effect what may with perfect ease, order and certainty be accomplished, when human nature shall be placed under proper circumstances.

But whatever scepticism may exist on this subject, surely there is no one who would not desire to see a fair experiment of a plan, the principles of which have never yet been, even plausibly, refuted. Nothing can be worse than the effects produced by the existing system: almost any change, therefore, must be for the better.

It is proposed, in the next place,

XXXVII. That when the youth of the community shall have attained their eighteenth year, they be permitted to become and declare themselves members; or to go out into common society, with every advantage which the community can afford them.

XXXVIII. That parties wishing to be united in marriage, give notice of their intention in writing, signed by each, to the committee, at one of their weekly meetings; that at the end of three months they renew this notice, signed also by two witnesses; upon the receipt of which the secretary of the committee shall call a meeting for the next day of the members of the community, and at this meeting the parties shall appear with their witnesses, and openly declare themselves husband and wife, and from that time be admitted into the class of married persons and obtain a separate dwelling.

It must be evident to all who reflect, that the object of marriage is to promote the happiness of the parties who marry and of their offspring. The arrangements of the Social System have been devised with a view to these important results. Should, however, the precautionary measures proposed, not be, in every instance, sufficient to insure the happiness of the parties; but, on the contrary, should the union prove the cause of misery to them, then it is recommended that a notice and ceremonial similar to those by which they were united, shall be allowed to separate them again, in order to prevent the increasing evils which must arise to those who are compelled to live together when they can no longer retain the affection for each other which is necessary to their happiness.

Under the proposed arrangements, it is expected that the judgment of the parties will be so well cultivated from infancy, and their knowledge of human nature will be so accurate, that they will seldom, in forming the marriage union, err in the choice of a partner; but when they do err, there is surely no good reason why they should be prevented from rectifying their mistake.

Although this form of marriage and separation be adopted in the community, it cannot, of course, supersede those prescribed by the laws of the country in which the community may be situated: but it may be considered as that simple mode of proceeding on these occasions which the parties conceive to be alone consistent with their principles.

It is confidently predicted, that the married life in the new communities will present a striking contrast to that which is exhibited in common society. The causes of misery in the latter arise from an education fundamentally defective; from an inequality of condition; from the parties not being thoroughly acquainted with each other before marriage, in consequence of the artificial and insincere character created by the present system; from various changes which occur in the character of the parties after marriage, and which the existing state of society has a constant tendency to produce; from a change in pecuniary circumstances, from a difference of family habits and associations of ideas: from inexperience in the management of children and the difficulties which at present exist in their education, and from ignorance of the causes which influence the affections. In devising the whole of the new arrangements, these considerations have been especially attended to, and it will be found, upon an attentive examination of them, that they are calculated to exclude all the fruitful causes of misery which have been enumerated.

XXXIX. That experienced and intelligent matrons appointed to instruct the young mothers in the best modes of treating and training and children from birth until two years (the age at which it is proposed they shall be sent to the schools and dormitories) in order that their constitutions, habits, and dispositions may not be injured during that period.

XL. That in winter and unfavorable weather, a sufficient variety of amusements and recreations, proper for the members of such a community, be prepared within doors, to afford beneficial relaxation from employment and study.

XLI. That as liberty of conscience, religious liberty, and mental liberty, are to be possessed by every member of the community in the most ample manner his previous education may admit, – arrangements be made to accommodate all denominations with what they themselves may consider convenient and suitable places of worship: and that each individual be strongly recommended to exhibit, in his whole conduct, the utmost kindness and charity towards all who differ from him.

XLII. That, to secure real liberty of conscience, religious liberty, and mental liberty, to the rising generation, it be recommended to parents, not to force any dogmas on the minds of their children; and, in conformity with this principle, not to send them to any place of worship, until their minds shall be well stored with undisputed facts, and their judgments sufficiently matured to enable them to draw sound, correct and rational conclusions from the data placed before them.

XLIII. That in advanced age, and in cases of disability from accident, natural infirmity, or any other cause, the individuals shall be supported by the community, and receive every comfort which kindness can administer.

XLIV. That on the death of parent or parents, the children shall become the peculiar care of the community and proper persons be appointed to take the more immediate charge of them, and as far as possible supply the place of their natural parents.

XLV. That the committee of management shall not be empowered to admit a new member, without the consent of three fourths of the members of the community, obtained at a general meeting.

XLVI. That although at the period when all the members shall have been trained and educated under the proposed arrangements, any regulations against misconduct will be unnecessary, and although it is anticipated that the influence of these new circumstances upon the character of individuals whose habits and dispositions have been formed under a different system, will be sufficiently powerful to render any serious differences of rare occurrence among them; yet in order to provide against such, it shall be a law of the community, that when differences arise, they be referred to the decision of arbitrators (to be elected by the society) who, after hearing the parties, shall decide upon their case, viva voce.

XLVII. That if the conduct of any individual be injurious to the well-being of the community, and it be so decided by three fourths of the members assembled at a general meeting, the committee shall explain to him in what respects his conduct has been injurious, and at the same time intimate to him, that unless the cause of complaint be removed, they are instructed to expel from him the community.

XLVIII. That any member wishing to withdraw from the society be at full liberty to do so at any time, and after three months' notice to the committee be permitted to take out the capital he may have advanced, with common interest upon the same, and that in case his capital and interest should not amount to $100 he shall receive as a gratuity such a sum as the committee may deem proper in the particular circumstances of the case.

XLIX. That the committee form arrangements by which all the members shall enjoy equal opportunities of visiting their friends elsewhere, or of travelling for information or other objects.

L. That the committee appoint duly qualified persons to travel from time to time, with a view to collect scientific and other information for the benefit of the community.

LI. That in order to extend the benefits of a system of union and cooperation, which is applicable to mankind in every part of the world, measures be adopted by the committee to disseminate a knowledge of the new principles and arrangements.

LII. That, as this system is directly opposed to secrecy and exclusion of any kind, every practicable facility shall be given to strangers, to enable them to become acquainted with the constitution, laws and regulations of the community, and to examine the results which these have produced in practice.

LIII. That the committee be charged with the duty of communicating on all occasions to the government of the country, and unreserved explanation of the views and proceedings of the community.

CHAPTER VI

The preceding sketch of arrangements exhibits the great leading circumstances under which human nature, to be either rational or happy, must exist.

Consistent principles, and consistent practice are now promulgated to the world; and if there be power in truth to triumph over prejudice and error, the individual who makes the appeal, feels strong in the assurance that it will not be made in vain.

Let the reader who has attentively considered the practical measures which have been proposed, reexamine that part of the subject upon which early prepossessions would in the first view of it, preclude the exercise of a calm judgment.

Can it be denied, that the main principle to which it is the object of the present essay to direct the attention of society, is established on the most indisputable grounds? Is it not consistent with all the evidence that can be brought to bear upon the point, with the evidence of all past and present experience, that the character of man is in every sense formed *for* him? That he is literally throughout his whole existence the created being which the powers and qualities given to him at birth, and the circumstances which subsequently act upon him, irresistibly determine him to be? And that when he seems most to be directed by his own will, as it is termed, he is at that moment as much controlled by those circumstances as he is constrained to see when objects are presented to his sight, or to hear when sounds press upon his ear, or to feel when he suffers pain or experiences pleasure? Every fact which comes within the cognizance of our senses, proves beyond the possibility of doubt that man does not – that he cannot possess any, even the smallest conceivable power of his own, and that of himself he cannot do any thing whatever. All his thoughts, feelings, propensities, words and actions are preordained for him. If he cannot create his own mind and body, or the peculiar organization which constitutes what is called his nature, – and if he can, as little, create any of those circumstances that necessarily determine the particular phenomena which that organization shall afterwards exhibit, – is it not evident that his character cannot be, in any respect, of his own formation? It is not only true that man cannot possess power or any thing of his own, that he must ever be passive, and that his conduct in every instance is merely a reaction *necessitated* to be what it is by the circumstances which previously acted upon him, but it is evident that if this law did not apply to man, as well as to the whole of nature, the world could not be governed, and order would no longer reign in the universe.

Omniscience in the creator, and the existence of the smallest portion of independent power in the created are irreconcilable. If it be believed that the creator knows all things past, present and future, it does not accord with this belief to attribute an uncontrolled will and power of action to myriads of human beings. If each thought, feeling, word and action of every individual be previously known and consequently determined, by what refinement of sophistry can it be made to appear that he is still free to decide what those thoughts, feelings, words and actions should be? Or, in other words, how can it be made to appear that his approval or disapproval can have any influence whatever over that which has been eternally and irrevocably fixed?

The universe is formed by a universal creating and uncreating power, possessing omniscience, or not possessing it. If the former conclusion be adopted, it follows that all men, at every moment of their lives, must act without the smallest deviation according to knowledge existing unnumbered ages before they were born; and in this case the notions of human free-will and responsibility become as truly absurd as the most incongruous ideas which could be put together by any mind the most estranged from reason. If on the other hand, this universal power does not possess omniscience, then is the universe governed by eternal unchanging laws of nature, and each existence including man and all things created, is a necessary effect produced by all the previous acting causes, and becomes in its turn a cause to produce other endless necessary effects. Upon this supposition also, these notions are as much opposed to reason and to fact as in the former case. Yet such has been the effect of the circumstances in which men have hitherto been trained from infancy, that the doctrine of free-will and responsibility is not only implicitly believed in by the great mass of mankind, but is considered as the very foundation stone of the social fabric. They will therefore regard with a natural horror the individual, who now attempts to disabuse their minds of so gross an error. Many too will participate in this feeling, whose reason has already detected the falsehood of this doctrine but who have not yet discerned the beneficial effects which an enlightened application of the opposite doctrine of necessity is calculated to produce.

The intellectual energies of men have been paralyzed by the influence of the circumstances in which they have existed; they have been deterred from exploring the only path which can ever lead to virtue, intelligence and happiness. Had it not been for this influence, those individuals upon whom nature had bestowed a more than ordinary strength of understanding, and who perceived the utter impossibility of reconciling the popular notions with reason or experience, would have advocated the cause of consistent principle and practice, and exposed the endless miseries to mankind which flowed from those errors. They saw however only a small part of this important subject; they were placed in a painful situation, being permitted to discover the fallacy of the prevailing creed, yet not to perceive that the practice which proceeded from it, necessarily led to ignorance, poverty, vice, crime and misery, and that the world must be cursed with these evils so long as that creed should obtain and be acted upon.

At this hour a belief impressed upon the human mind by all the prejudices of past ages almost universally prevails, that the doctrine of free-will and responsibility is necessary to the existence of a well-regulated society; that withdraw it from the minds of the multitude, and they would instantly become ungovernable by any authority; vice and crime would reign triumphant, pervade all ranks, overwhelm all institutions; and injustice, war, rapine and devastation would cover the earth.

If this view of society were indeed well founded, and the belief in the doctrine of free-will and responsibility were really a safeguard against such evils, then it would be the highest degree of temerity, folly and madness, in any one, however false that doctrine might be, to bring any question regarding it in any way before the public. No! if such be its mighty efficacy, it ought to be held too sacred for men even to whisper a doubt of its divine origin. If indeed it be a truth that this doctrine produces all the practical good, which mankind enjoy, and protects them against innumerable evils which they have not yet experienced, – and if on the other hand, the doctrine of the influence of circumstances over human nature is calculated to create alarming evils in practice, and to prevent the enjoyment of many benefits, – then ought the latter to be considered most pernicious, however true, and the former be deemed invaluable, however false. But should it appear that the notions of free-will and responsibility are the immediate cause of all the evils which the world has hitherto suffered, and that the science of the influence of circumstances over human nature is calculated to prevent that suffering, – in this case, our sentiments regarding them must undergo a corresponding change.

Let us then examine what are the necessary practical effects arising from the human mind being forced from infancy to believe in the supposition that the character of man is formed by himself, and that he is consequently a free agent and a responsible being?

In the first place man is then deprived of all knowledge respecting the causes which make him what he is, which create his thoughts and will, and control all his feelings and actions. – He remains throughout life in total ignorance of himself, his fellow-creatures and human nature. He can make no proper use of experience; millions of the most obvious facts, perpetually before him, present results directly opposed to the belief, which has been forced upon him, and yet he continues entirely unconscious of the incongruity which characterizes all his thoughts and actions. Supposing that each of his fellow-creatures possesses a self formed character, he applies to it through the distortions of his imagination, the epithets of good and bad, and gives him praise or blame, and apportions rewards and punishments accordingly. This he does without hesitation, while he is kept in such mental bondage and degradation that he is totally incompetent to know what is good or bad, and almost uniformly praises and rewards that which perpetually occasions the greatest evil to mankind, and blames and punishes that which, in a rational state of society, would create and secure the greatest good.

In consequence, all the practical proceedings which would produce a good and happy character in every individual, place him far beyond the dominion of ignorance, or the fear of poverty, and unite him cordially with the whole of his species, are entirely neglected; and almost every practical measure which can be conceived is adopted, to form each individual into a being hostile to his fellow-creatures; to render him irascible and jealous of others; to fill him with pride, vanity, ambition, bigotry and superstition; to compel him to believe that the most crude absurdities which have been forced into his mind are divine truths, which as such, it is his duty to force into the minds of others; and that the notions, not however more absurd than his own, which others have been compelled to imbibe in infancy as divine truths, also, are gross impositions and ought to be eradicated, yet without being the least conscious that it was owing to the mere geographical circumstance of his birth that he was not obliged to venerate the very same absurdities and to be equally anxious and imperative in urging others to receive them.

To assign to man the attributes of free-will and responsibility, as they do not belong to his nature, is to surround him with a snare and a temptation to do all manner of wrong, under the notion that wrong is right, and to render his reasoning powers a curse and not a blessing. – It places these faculties under the sole dominion of imagination which distorts everything around him. He becomes not a rational creature who acquires wisdom from experience, but a being governed by passion and caprice, and by the most wild and inconsistent notions. And as all facts must be opposed to inconsistent notions, experience instead of being a safe guide to direct him to a knowledge of what is true, serves only to puzzle and confound his intellect still more. He is then made less rational, probably, than the greater part of those he denominates the inferior animals; and as these live according to their nature, while man, a social being, exists under institutions which separate his individual interests from the interests of his species, and are therefore directly opposed to his nature, he is probably more miserable than any of them. For the doctrine of free-will and responsibility by individualizing the human race, necessarily creates what is called self-interest in society, and deprives it of the advantages of cooperation. Every individual is compelled to acquire property from the mass by which he is surrounded, and afterwards to preserve it from the attacks of all who like himself are perpetually engaged in a struggle to keep what they have gained and increase their store. A continued contest and warfare among mankind is thus maintained, by which every kind of evil is engendered and the worst and meanest passions excited and kept in constant action.

Such is the origin of private property and of all the evils and crimes connected with the existing truly absurd arrangements for the creation, preservation and distribution of wealth.

Mankind are compelled, unaided and opposed, to procure as they can, every thing for themselves, and to attain knowledge each through his own individual experience, or to receive the most pernicious errors. An immense proportion die in greater ignorance than did many of their forefathers several thousand ages past; while, in a rational state of society, each child would acquire more knowledge and wisdom than any of his predecessors: and the improvement of mankind during every succeeding generation would be almost incalculable.

The doctrine of free-will and responsibility most effectually precludes the existence of universal charity, benevolence, peace and good will upon earth. They can never exist while human beings are taught to praise and blame, reward and punish each other; or to think that they have merit and are entitled to recompense for believing what they have been forced to believe, or that others deserve censure or deprivation because they have been forced to believe something else; or while it can be supposed that any individual can possess merit or demerit for any belief whatever, seeing that the most absurd imaginations can be forced into the mind of every child that comes into existence.

While doctrines thus opposed to existing facts, to reason and to all experience shall be impressed upon human nature, no one must look for peace and good will upon earth, or for the period when swords shall be turned into plough shares,[a] – these happy results, these necessary preludes to the millennium, can never be obtained.

To talk of sincere love and kindness and the doctrine of free-will and responsibility existing at the same time over the earth, is to speak as rationally as to say that we may be at the same instant in the full blaze of light, and be overwhelmed with thick darkness. To imagine that real virtue and this doctrine can exist together is as wise as to suppose that men can love and hate, esteem and despise the same thing at the same time.

There is in short as much real understanding evinced by those who think they are doing God a service by placing themselves to be crushed under the wheels of the log Juggernaut, as there is by those who deem themselves the salt of the earth, and imagine they serve God by forcing their fellow-creatures to receive the notions of free-will and responsibility for divine truths. The former suffer individually for an instant of time and their afflictions cease. But the others by a far more lamentable error perpetuate every evil that the human race has been heir to. The doctrine which they teach is the greatest enemy that man has known; and fortunate is it for this and succeeding generations that its reign of ignorance, terror, superstition and misery is about to terminate for ever. No power can now retain it. That it was necessary for a time, is certain, or it would not have existed. But the eyes of the world are at length opened to the dreadful moral, mental and physical effects which it has so long produced, to all the evil propensities and passions which it has engendered and kept in full action throughout society, and to the public and private acts of insanity, with which it has [been] filled from beginning to end, the histories of all nations.

So gross is the error of this doctrine, and so obvious, after the discovery is made, is the necessary connection between it and the miseries of mankind, that it seems as extraordinary as any thing yet known to us, how we should, for so many ages have suffered from a cause which will now be removed with so much ease and with the hearty cooperation of every human being.

How often have the best and most intelligent human beings sighed for equality and liberty to act according to their nature, without which they knew that neither excellence or happiness could be attained! How often has the human mind, through every danger been urged prematurely to attempt their attainment, while the doctrine of free-will and responsibility governed the world! How many lives have been vainly sacrificed in these attempts, and how much misery have these useless efforts inflicted upon mankind! These sufferings and disappointments could not have been experienced, had the acting parties in these conflicts been permitted to know that liberty and equality, and the doctrine of free-will and responsibility could never coexist in practice; no,

[a] See Isaiah 2:4.

not for an hour. The latter necessarily enslaves and degrades; it enfeebles the human faculties and powers, or perverts them, and can create only a tyrant or a slave; nor is it easy to pronounce which of the two becomes the more degraded and miserable creature, or more deserves the commiseration of a rational being.

If it be desirable that tyranny and slavery should no longer exist; that wars, massacres, burnings and public violences should terminate; that anger, hatred, revenge, pride, ambition, avarice and self-interest and every bad passion in private life should be eradicated; that ignorance, poverty, mental and physical imbecility, vice, crime and misery, should cease to prevail among us, then must the error of that doctrine be exposed, and be no longer permitted to scourge the earth with these evils.

If on the contrary, it be desirable to introduce sincerity into the world; to induce all men cordially to love one another; to secure permanently peace and good-will among them; to improve their intellectual and physical powers; to give them the best habits and dispositions and as much knowledge as experience has yet discovered; to withdraw all motives to the counteraction of each other's well-being and happiness, and to make the whole human race but one people, having but one language, and animated with one spirit, given a universal impulse to never-ceasing improvements; then should it be proclaimed throughout the world in the shortest possible time, yet in the language of genuine charity, what human nature really is, and what those circumstances are, under which alone it can become, either rational or happy.

Can it still be maintained that whether the doctrine of free-will and responsibility be true or false, it is impossible to govern the world without forcing the belief of its truth on every child that is born? that otherwise, there could be no foundation for good conduct, no security for persons or property, and that crime would universally abound?

At what period in the history of mankind has the influence of this doctrine prevented the commission of the most atrocious crimes? Can a time be mentioned when fraud, deception, violence, injustice, wars, murders, and oppression, did not superabound? Where, in what part of the world, has this doctrine made men sincere, charitable, kind and benevolent? Or rather where has it not created in them every bad feeling and passion that could be given to human nature? What is the present aspect of the world? Is it not full of strife and contention, and every evil thought and action? What is the present state of Christendom, and what has been the character of its inhabitants through every period of its history? The only reply which truth can make to these questions irresistibly establishes the conclusion, that the doctrine of free-will and responsibility has *not* the effect of preventing crime.

But do not all crimes proceed from individual interest creating selfishness under all the forms of pride, ambition, anger, revenge, injustice, oppression, – and from bigotry, producing spiritual pride and the evils of superstition, and perverting from infancy all the reasoning faculties? And is it not the notion of an independent, self-existing, and self-willing power in each individual, that has given birth to these errors, crimes and evils? Does it not as certainly as any cause ever produced its effect, fill him with all the self-sufficiency of a being having a power to create, direct and control his own will, thoughts and actions, lead him to attribute a mighty consequence to himself, and a right to judge of the feelings, thoughts and conduct of all other men and to decide whether they are good or bad?

Now, as it has been demonstrated that man cannot create any thing for himself, that there is not even the shadow of any thing that proceeds from himself, and that he cannot be entitled to the smallest personal consideration for any thing he possesses; poor and helpless as he thus really is, it is easy to imagine what a wretched, vain, irrational, and miserable being he must be made by filling him with notions of his own individual importance, and giving him the attributes of a creator of his own will, thoughts and actions, and that too while he remains wholly ignorant of the origin of any of those, or of what they are, except by the effects which they produce on himself and others.

Being thus set wrong from birth on all these subjects, he is formed into the degraded, inconsistent creature called man, forced continually to think and act, as far as it is possible to make him, *contrary to* his nature, while he is perpetually impeded by his natural faculties and propensities, which he could not decline receiving, to act *according to* his nature, and in this manner is a war created within himself, and between himself and all mankind.

Neither man nor any living thing can be happy except when they act in unison with their natures. Being compelled to receive the unnatural and erroneous notions of free-will and responsibility, man is urged from infancy to endeavor to think and act in opposition to his nature; and where he is made to succeed the best in this perverse course, he becomes nothing better than a miserable inconsistent hypocrite.

But no treatment which has hitherto been devised has deprived man of his natural feelings and propensities: and in most circumstances and situations, he is irresistibly impelled to act in obedience to them; and his actions viewed through the fantastic medium created by the doctrine of free-will and responsibility are called crimes, and in consequence every conceivable kind of evil has been introduced and perpetuated in human society. Had it not been for this original error, not one of these crimes and evils could have been conceived; being solely the effects of imagination uncontrolled by judgment, they could not have existed, and the world would have been spared the suffering which it has so long experienced. A social system in unison with human nature would have been established. No individual would ever have been angry at or blamed another for any thing thought or done. Simple, straight-forward measures would have been adopted to make every one without a single exception, good, wise and happy. The knowledge of the formation of human character would have been familiar to all, and each generation would have advanced in wisdom and in happiness. The terms wickedness and vice would have remained unknown, for they could have had no meaning. If defects existed in any individual, all would know that they proceeded either from his natural faculties and propensities, which he could not create, or from the circumstances in which their possessor was placed and which the preceding generations had arranged for him, and consequently that the individual required our greater aid and commiseration, but could not be in any respect an object for blame and displeasure. In a very few generations, however, after man shall be taught to think and allowed to act rationally, it may be reasonably anticipated, that both natural defects at birth, and the errors created by circumstances afterwards, will entirely disappear, and that each human being will be formed sound in body and mind and trained to become intelligent, wise and happy.

As soon as the ever-to-be dreaded doctrine of free-will and responsibility shall be exploded, the folly and evil of neglecting to train and place under proper circumstances every child that shall be born, will be too apparent to admit of such insane conduct. These little beings will be received and cherished as the most precious gifts that can be bestowed on man, since with so much ease and certainty they can be rendered capable of enjoying a high degree of happiness themselves, and become the instruments of distributing happiness to all around them. And in this view of human nature it will be impossible, at least for many centuries to come, to have as many of them as can be made essentially to contribute to the improvement of the world and the well-being and happiness of mankind.

But some parties may yet exclaim: Would you indeed! at once and without preparation, withdraw the restraints which have so long acted so powerfully on the human mind? – False in principle and pernicious in practice, as the doctrine of free-will and responsibility has been demonstrated to be, – would you indeed proclaim its error and evil to the multitude, without taking one step to guard against the reaction which would follow when human nature is relieved from this restraint upon its conduct? Surely, universal confusion would inevitably ensue, and only a madman could thus intend to act.

Such exclamation and fears however, arise solely from the irrationality which the doctrine has created. The knowledge which unveils its error and mischievous effects, will in the same instant open to view the immense benefits which man will attain by acting rationally; and the desire to attain happiness will at once make him the rational being he has ever been destined to be; nor will any practical evil ensue. The invaluable knowledge that man will thus acquire of himself and his species, will prevent any of the anticipated dangers from its public promulgation, even to the lowest and most degraded of our fellow-creatures; for as soon as they can be made to comprehend it, they will also be made rational and will act like reasonable beings. Those who have been already permitted to acquire and to act upon this knowledge would not hesitate, from their own experience to explain the full truth regarding it, to any number of the most vicious individuals at present to be found in the British empire, and afterwards to trust their persons and property to their mercy. – And they would do so without entertaining the least apprehension of any disagreeable result. On the contrary they would anticipate such a change for the better in their whole character and conduct, as common or old society could account for only by some supposed miracle, or by resorting to some other of their superstitious notions. For men, as they have been hitherto educated, are incompetent to form a correct or sound judgment on any subjects except those which are connected with the certain sciences, in which they have been instructed. On all others, in consequence of being compelled from infancy to receive the absurd doctrine of free-will and responsibility, they have necessarily been rendered irrational.

Error and falsehood never promoted virtue, and there never has been a more demoralizing imposition practised on mankind than that of covering this doctrine with divine authority.

So far is it from being true that the exposure of it will open the flood-gate to vice, – this doctrine itself is at this hour the sole cause of the wars, murders, deceptions and oppressions, with which mankind are afflicted; nor can it be too speedily removed for their well-being and happiness. It is this bugbear that has hitherto frightened all men out of their right senses, or they would see that no one has been benefited, but that all have suffered grievously under its dominion; and that not an individual now exists upon whom its instant annihilation would not be the means of conferring incalculable blessings.

No man, whatever may be his present situation, possesses in property or person, one part out of a thousand of the advantages he would immediately obtain, were this doctrine withdrawn, and new arrangements formed for the government of mankind in unison with those principles which it has been the object of the preceding pages to establish.

ADDRESS
TO THE AGRICULTURISTS, MECHANICS, AND MANUFACTURERS, BOTH MASTERS AND OPERATIVES, OF GREAT BRITAIN AND IRELAND[a]
1827

[*To the Editors of Country Newspapers*

The importance of the facts detailed in the Letter of Mr OWEN, and the necessity which exists, that statements so vitally affecting the greatest interests of society should be canvassed in every quarter, induce the Editor of '*The Sphynx*' earnestly to request that this Letter, which is now first printed, be copied by all the Journals of the United Kingdom. The objects of Mr OWEN's calculations and reasonings have no connection with party principles, and they cannot be viewed in the spirit of party. The evils which are depicted in them are perfectly apparent; but they have seldom been painted with such force and precision as in the Address before us. The remedies which Mr OWEN proposes can only be tried by the test of fact and experiment. At any rate, the discussion of such a subject must operate as a great public good, and it is with this conviction that we repeat our anxious desire, that these views should be put before the world as extensively as the power of the Press will command.
Editor of The Sphynx]

Two years ago I left you in apparent prosperity;[b] you then thought that war only could stop the progress of your success; you have remained at peace, and yet you have passed through a period of more distress than the oldest of you had previously experienced.

[a] First published in *The Sphynx* newspaper, 7 September 1827. Reprinted in *The New Harmony Gazette*, vol. 3, no. 9 (3 December 1827) – no. 10 (12 December 1827), pp. 65–6, 73–4, *The Correspondent*, vol. 2, no. 15 (3 November 1827), pp. 234–54, *Birmingham Co-operative Herald*, nos 7–8 (October–November 1827), pp. 25–30.

[b] Owen left the US for Europe in August 1825.

You were subjected to these severe sufferings when your industry was at its height, when capital was overflowing, and when both islands were full of whatever could be required to support in comfort a much larger population.

Your distress, therefore, did not arise from a deficiency of food or clothing in the islands, from a want of industry in masters or servants, from a want of capital, of raw materials, or of finished productions of any kind; but, on the contrary, because the country superabounded in the necessaries, comforts, and luxuries of life, even to saturation, until all markets, both at home and abroad, were overstocked by your industry,– and yet were you taught to believe that you were to look for relief only from an increase of those markets.

To those who have been accustomed to observe what has been in progress for some years past, your sufferings created no surprise; indeed they were anticipated and distinctly foretold. As the same cause which produced your distress is still in full action, it is natural to expect that the same effect, at no distant period, will again follow; but as this cause is daily growing in magnitude, it may reasonably be anticipated that the succeeding distress will be more severe than the last.

This distress, however, falls chiefly on you, the industrious producers of abundance; and it behoves you well to understand how this unfavourable result follows from your best-directed efforts, that you may attain the knowledge of the means by which you may not only prevent its recurrence, but learn also how to acquire a fair share of the abundance which you create.

You are deeply interested in probing this subject to its foundation; in ascertaining why, contrary to the usual laws of nature, a superabundance of all the necessaries, comforts, and luxuries of life should uniformly afflict you, who produce them, with extreme poverty and misery.

I will endeavour to trace this subject in such a manner as to make its progress obvious to every one who has been accustomed to reflect.

Your labour is the support of yourselves and families; all the wealth which you and the other classes consume is produced by it; and under the existing arrangement of society, you have to sell your labour as any other commodity is sold, and upon its merchantable value in the general market of commerce your prosperity or adversity depend. When it is of low value you are in poverty, and when it is in high estimation you are in comparative affluence.

There is, however, a silent and almost unnoticed change in progress, which has reduced, and will further reduce, the value of your labour.

For, all artificial operations which supersede manual labour come in competition with your powers of producing; and if such artificial operations should be continually extended, they must, while the existing organization of society remains, sooner or later reduce you to the lowest stage of existence.

Machinery, after it has been introduced to a certain amount, comes in direct competition with your labour; and as machinery is extended through the various departments of production, the value of your labour must diminish; and hence the sole cause of your pecuniary distress for some years past. The different causes which have been assigned for your distress were nothing more than the immediate mode by which superabundance produced the embarrassment.

Prior to the revolutionary war of France,[a] the population of various countries frequently suffered great privations from war, or famine occasioned by war, or by a succession of unfavourable seasons.

It was, however, in the midst of that war, somewhere about the year 1810, that the population of these islands were first afflicted with the evils of superabundance.

Mechanic and other scientific improvements had been so greatly extended at that period, that even under the enormous waste of a wide-spread and most destructive war, they were found amply sufficient to supply that enormous waste, to saturate all the foreign markets open to your legal and contraband trade, and to over-supply the home markets.

You, then, for the first time, experienced the paralysing effects of a superabundance, for which the present organization of society does not admit of any other remedy than time, to dissipate or waste, in foreign markets, the superabundance which you toiled to produce; while your labour, for this period, becomes of little, and, in many instances, of no value; and you are compelled, in consequence, to experience all the privations of famine and evils of poverty; while yet, during this period, you are surrounded with a superfluity of necessaries, comforts, and luxuries, of which the present arrangement of society in civilized life forbids you to partake.

You again experienced the dire effects of superabundance after the termination of the war in the years 1815 and 1816, when the cessation from waste and destruction left you so much production on hand, that you were thrown out of employment and plunged into poverty. You suffered from the same cause in 1818 and 1819, again in 1821, and lastly in 1825; and as long as the present organization of society shall continue, these periods of distress will occur frequently; and the evils which they will occasion will be more severely and extensively felt, until your sufferings, in the end, will become so unbearable, as to create a necessity which, through wisdom or violence, will effect a radical change in the general structure of society.

Thus, then, during the French revolutionary war, you passed a boundary never before reached in the history of man; you passed the regions of poverty arising from necessity, and entered those of permanent abundance, as soon as your affairs shall be directed by foresight and wisdom.

You commenced a new era in the progress of civilization; and thus have you attained the means to insure the 'Wealth of Nations,' the object so long sought for by legislators and political economists.

---

[a] The Napoleonic Wars lasted from 1793–1815.

It is now no longer necessary, except through ignorance, that 'man should earn his bread by the sweat of his brow;'[a] for the inventions and discoveries which have been matured, and which are now in full practice, are more than sufficient, with very light labour, under a right direction, to supply the wants and insure the independence of all, without real injury to any.

To understand this part of the subject, your best attention is requisite, because it is not only new to you, but it appears to be so also to legislators and political economists; for they continue still to direct their efforts to instruct the world how to *increase* its wealth, while the real difficulty against which society has to contend is, to discover the means by which an *excess* of wealth, now so easily produced, can be prevented from injuring all classes, who experience from it precisely the same effects which have been heretofore engendered by poverty.

Legislators and political economists seem to be many years behind the real advance of science, and the general knowledge which has been diffused among the people. They still think and act upon the principles advocated by Adam Smith, who lived and wrote before the introduction of the new mechanical and chemical manufacturing system, which has already essentially altered the relative condition of all classes in Britain, and which, in its natural progress, cannot fail to force a greater change in human affairs than has been effected by all the previous revolutions which have agitated the world.

The enormous power and silent progress of this new system appear to be unknown and unheeded by modern political economists; and without a knowledge of both, they may as well attempt to enlighten the public on the science of political economy, as to attempt to develope the principles of agriculture, without having regard to the influence of the sun on vegetation.

When Adam Smith[b] wrote his celebrated Essays on the Wealth of Nations,[c] men were struggling against a deficiency of the powers of production in society to supply all their reasonable wants; and the principle of division of labour, which he so ably advocated, was well calculated by its practice to lessen the difficulty. But he could not then imagine that in less than half a century the improvements effected by the combined sciences of mechanism and chemistry should set aside the necessity for the division of human labour to create the requisite wealth for happiness. It is now, however, obvious, that as long as the necessity for a minute division of labour existed, the happiness of the human race could not be attained.[d]

---

[a] See Genesis 3:19.

[b] Adam Smith (1723–90): philosopher and political economist whose plea for 'natural liberty' is usually regarded as founding the modern school of free trade economics. His chief disciples during Owen's life were the 'classical' political economists, notably David Ricardo, James Mill, John McCulloch and John Stuart Mill.

[c] Adam Smith's *Enquiry Concerning the Nature and Causes of the Wealth of Nations* was published in 1776.

[d] See Adam Smith, *Wealth of Nations*, Bk 1, ch. 1.

Since the time that Adam Smith wrote, the extension of mechanical contrivances, and the discoveries in chemistry, combined with the progress and diffusion of general knowledge, have rendered a minute division of human labour, for the creation of wealth, as unnecessary as experience has proved it to be deteriorating to the physical and mental faculties of man, and, therefore, always opposed to his happiness.

Mechanism and chemistry have been directed to multiply the number of scientific hands, far exceeding the conception of ordinary minds.

By these means, the powers of production have been increased in Great Britain alone, since the days of Adam Smith, more than *one hundred times*; or, in other words, these artificial powers have been so directed, as to produce the same effect as would arise from adding one hundred additional pair of hands to each producer, and these artificial hands have been *better* formed for their peculiar object of production, than the hands formed by nature.

In consequence, the new powers of production created in Great Britain and Ireland since the days of Adam Smith, are now little, if any, short of the labour that could be obtained from 600 millions of active men, previous to that period; or, the working classes of Great Britain and Ireland can now, aided by mechanical and chemical improvements, finish as much work of the kind to which their labour is directed, as could be completed in the days of Adam Smith by *three times the whole manual power of the world!*

And this power, which our legislators and political economists seem to disregard in all their reasonings and calculations, is annually increasing in a continually increasing ratio, for new discoveries are daily made in the mechanical and chemical sciences.

It is this power which is hourly encroaching on the value of your labour, that has thus far oppressed you by the facility it affords to *over*-production; while the existing organization of society has been formed solely to counteract the evils of *under*-production.

At the periods when the existing arrangements of society were formed, no one could suspect the possibility of any evil from over-production, and, in consequence, no remedy for it has been provided.

This extraordinary state of matters has arisen in the natural course of events, ending towards important improvements, and evidently not designed by any lass or by any individuals. It is useless, therefore, to blame any parties; but most necessary, in practice, to adopt such measures as will counteract these vils, and enable society to enjoy the benefits of all our discoveries and nprovements.

It is acknowledged that a state of society has now arisen, which puzzles and onfounds all statesmen and political economists. All who reflect are deeply ngaged in attempts to discover the cause of, and the cure for, the temporary vils which the late rapid progress in physical knowledge has produced. There therefore, now much mind at work on the subject, which is too important to be neglected by any party; and no doubt the truth, ere long, will be elicited, and your condition will be ameliorated. The fact is, all existing governments are too timid, and are afraid to probe the subject to its foundation: – this work must be accomplished by the union of men of high intellectual acquirements, and of great moral courage.

Having attempted to explain the cause why you are so frequently poverty-stricken in the midst of overflowing abundance, and while you possess the means of increasing that abundance without limit, I will endeavour to point out the means by which you may not only arrest the evil, but turn the cause which now generates it into a new channel, by which, if I am not mistaken, this evil shall be made to produce only unmixed good to yourselves and fellow-creatures.

I have already stated that every invention, discovery, and improvement, in physical science, facilitates production; and that, under the present organization of society, whatever facilitates production diminishes the value of your labour in a relative proportion to the amount of production, as long as the arrangements of society render it necessary for you to dispose of it as a merchantable article, upon the principle of buying cheap and selling dear, and bartering it in this manner to the highest bidder. By this procedure you aid in bringing your labour in direct competition with mechanism and other scientific improvements, by which, as experience proves, you must continually sink in the contest, until you will ultimately descend to the lowest possible stage of existence; and until a few very wealthy families will retain you, under the fallacious notion of being free, in a more hopeless and helpless state of slavery than are the negroes in the West Indies[a] and America, who have, what you would want, a direct claim for food, clothes, and habitation, on the master by whom they are reared or purchased.

Instead of selling yourselves to the public for money, by which your labour receives the most useless and injurious direction, would it not be more rational to apply your physical and mental powers directly for your own use, in a fair exchange among yourselves, of value for value, or the amount of labour in one article, against the same amount in another?

By this simple and just mode of transacting business, labour, and not money, would become the standard of value; and, without much difficulty, the value in all articles might be represented by notes of labour for an hour, a day, a month, a year, etc. Arrangements might be devised to prevent any change in the value of these notes, which might be made to represent real wealth remaining in store; for when the articles which the notes represented were taken for consumption, or deteriorated by keeping, notes to the amount of the labour or deterioration in those articles might be destroyed.

[a] Owen visited Jamaica in October 1828, on his way to Mexico. There is an account of his visit there in *Robert Owen's Opening Speech, and His Reply to the Rev. Alexander Campbell* (Cincinnati, 1829), pp. 184–226.

Some difficulty might arise at first, in discovering the amount of labour which *ought* to be in every article; but this process is nothing more than ascertaining the real prime cost of articles, which truly consists in the labour required to produce them. But as one person will take more time than another to perfect the same kind of article, the time required by a workman possessing an average degree of skill and industry, should be the principle by which the calculation should be made.

This mode of conducting business will introduce principles of justice and equity in all transactions between man and man; it will gradually destroy every motive to trick, deceit, and chicanery.

And by its adoption, Poverty, or the Fear of Poverty, will be for ever removed from the producers of real wealth.

The necessity which the present system inflicts on all, to endeavour to sell their own labour dear, and to buy the labour of others cheap, contaminates and debases the character throughout all the departments of life. In fact, no one who has studied human nature, will ever expect to find a pure mind, or real virtue in society, as long as the business of life is one continued attempt to buy cheap and sell dear, by the intervention of money, which itself is daily altering in value.

Any difficulties, however, which may arise from exchanging labour for labour among the producers through the intervention of labour notes, will be but of short duration; for the knowledge, which will accompany this change, and which in some degree will grow out of this practice, will speedily lead to a very improved state of society; – to one, in which, through a more enlightened system of education, the rising generation will be taught the practice of a much better mode of production, distribution, and consumption, by the means of which they will be enabled to form their children into a very superior order of beings, by training them from infancy to know themselves, and to organize a society in conformity to that knowledge, which will permit and direct them to enjoy, at the point of temperance, all their physical and mental faculties, in evident accordance with the laws of their nature.

For your benefit I now request to ask our Legislators and political economists, how it has occurred that you should have received, in about half a century, an aid to your natural powers of production equal to the assistance of 600 millions of well-trained labourers, who tire not, who never refuse to work, who require neither food nor clothes, and yet that you should experience a dire necessity to extend the time of your daily labour just in proportion as these millions came to your assistance, from 9 hours per day, of comparatively light and healthy occupation, to 10, 11, 12, 13, 14, and as I am told, in the manufacturing districts to 15, and sometimes even to 16 hours per day, of severe and often unhealthy employment, – and that you do not now receive the same advantages in return for the 14 or 16 hours of hard labour per day, that you readily obtained for your 9 hours of comparative easy labour, before the introduction of these enormous artificial powers?

I now require them to account for the additional productions of these 600 millions of labourers, who are now in full work, without requiring food, or clothing, or education, and to account for your present pecuniary condition, as well as for your very natural fears for the future. I also request them to inform you, why measures have not been recommended, and adopted in practice, to produce the very reverse of these lamentable results? – why, in proportion as these new powers were brought to your aid, your labour did not gradually diminish from 9 hours per day, to 8, to 7, to 6, to 5, to 4, and to 3? – and why the 3 hours of labour per day should not now be of more value to you, as they might easily be made more productive, than the 9 were before the introduction of these enormous mechanical and chemical powers of production?

I request them to inform you how it is, that, under this mighty power, if rightly directed, to produce wealth, promote knowledge, and secure independence, ample beyond the wishes of rational beings, for every one of a population tenfold or twenty-fold more numerous than the present numbers in the British islands; – how is it that you, the actual producers of all wealth, should be stricken with poverty, and with the most fearful forebodings for the future – how, that the poor-rates have increased so enormously, – and how, that crime has extended in every direction? It will be no answer to these questions to say, that 'your numbers have increased,' for you bring with you at birth the powers to produce with ease, far more than you consume; and, therefore, under a right direction of these powers, an increase of your numbers ought to increase still more your surplus productions, and consequently require less daily labour from each of you.

And, except where laws and institutions, founded in ignorance, compel the industry and mental faculties of man to take a vicious and unnatural direction, the surplus productions *have* increased everywhere with the increase of population; and they will continue to increase, as numbers multiply, until every acre of the earth shall be fully cultivated, although there should not be another improvement or discovery made in the sciences of chemistry or mechanism beyond those already known and secured to the public.

Another and a better reply, in answer to the foregoing questions, that 'an increase of your numbers' must, therefore, be given to account for the strange anomaly which Great Britain and Ireland present, – of an empire superabounding, through the industry and inventive powers of its inhabitants, in all the necessaries, comforts, and luxuries requisite for human happiness; while the mass of its most industrious population is in hourly fear and trembling for the support of a precarious existence, being overwhelmed with poverty, with poorrates, and with crime.

London, September 7, 1827 ROBERT OWEN

P.S. Other principles than those by which this empire has been governed, occurred at an early period of life to me to be true; and, without any motives of faction or of personal consideration, I have never ceased to endeavour to ascertain, whether those early imbibed principles were derived from facts, and therefore founded in truth, or whether my mind had been deluded by error. In the progress of this search after truth I proved the real value of those principles, for I tried them early in life in directing extensive practical measures among a large population in Manchester, and afterwards at New Lanark;[a] and I never found them to lead me astray from nature, or to be unsuccessful in the result, except when they were opposed by the ignorance and prejudice which our ancestors naturally and necessarily transmitted to all of us. These proceedings in Manchester and in New Lanark were not hidden from the public, and are well known; in the latter place, I advanced with these experiments to the extent that the ignorance or want of experience of the present times would admit. The principles which appeared to me to be true, would not allow of a further advance in practice, without the probability of exciting a greater degree of irritation, anger, and ill-will, than I wished to create in a search after truth for the benefit of my fellow-creatures. And about this period circumstances very unexpectedly occurred to make it probable that these principles could be more easily tried to their full extent, in the new settlements in America, than in an old established empire, in which the leading notions by which the policy of the country was governed, had been unchanged for many centuries. As the chief object of my life became at this time a desire to ascertain not only the truth of the principles which had been impressed on my mind, but their applicability to practice also, I crossed the Atlantic, and purchased New Harmony in the State of Indiana, a property in many respects well-suited for the experiment which I had in view. This experiment had been twenty-five months in progress when I left New Harmony on the 1st of June last; and as the whole of my proceedings in America are full of interest to that portion of the public who prefer truth to error, and happiness to misery, I mean to publish a sketch of these transactions as soon as time can be obtained to admit me to complete it.

I further propose, at an early opportunity, to communicate to the public, a more full development of my general views.

[a] See *infra*, vol. 4, esp. pp. 80–151.

MEMORIAL

OF

ROBERT OWEN

TO THE

MEXICAN REPUBLIC,

AND TO THE

GOVERNMENT OF THE STATE

OF

COAHUILA AND TEXAS.

LONDON: PRINTED BY WILLIAM CLOWES, STAMFORD-STREET.

MEMORIAL, TO THE MEXICAN REPUBLIC[a]
1828

INTRODUCTION

Some Proprietors of extensive grants of land in the province of Texas, having applied to Mr Owen to take an interest with, and to assist them in colonizing their districts, consisting of many millions of acres, he proposed to them to institute measures to establish an independent state of communities on the social system, in which all the laws and institutions should be in conformity with the principles on which that system is founded, and which are necessary to its success.[b]

To this proposal, after due consideration, the Proprietors, and those who represent them here, assented. Communications were then made to the proper authorities, who are in this country, acting for the Mexican and the neighbouring Republics; and there appears to be a real desire in all these parties to promote the plan.

In consequence, Mr Owen has prepared a Memorial on the subject, to be presented to the Mexican Republic of which the following is a Copy.

MEMORIAL

I address you on a subject entirely new, and in the character of a citizen of the world.

You have established your Republic to improve the condition of the inhabitants of Mexico.

[a] Also printed with *Robert Owen's Opening Speech, and His Reply to the Rev. Alexander Campbell* (Cincinnati, 1829), pp. 178–83, and in the *British Co-operator*, nos 1–2 (April–May 1830), pp. 21, 48, 69–71.

[b] Owen's own account of the project is given in *Robert Owen's Opening Speech, and His Reply to the Rev. Alexander Campbell* (Cincinnati, 1829), pp. 175–226.

You have already discovered obstacles, of a formidable nature, to retard, if not to prevent, the execution of your intentions to the extent you anticipated.

All other people experience difficulties in their progress to improvements, and desire to remove them.

I propose measures for your consideration, which shall enable you to remove your own difficulties, and assist others to remove theirs.

At an early period of my life, I discovered that the foundation of all human institutions was an error; and that no permanent benefit could be obtained for the human race, until that foundation should be removed, and replaced by a better.

That the prejudices of all nations were formed by their education, or those general and particular national circumstances by which they were surrounded from infancy to maturity.

That, to remove these prejudices, a new course of proceeding must be adopted, to enable the population of the world to perceive the errors in which they are involved, and the extent of the evils which they continually generate for themselves and their posterity.

After much reading and reflection upon these subjects, I instituted extensive experiments to ascertain, by fact, *truth* from *error*.

These experiments have continued without ceasing for nearly forty years, and they disclose the cause of the perplexity and disappointment of all people.

They demonstrate that the *real nature of man* has been *misunderstood*, and, in consequence, that he has been trained from infancy to think and to act erroneously, and to produce *evil* instead of *good*.

That man is not a being capable, of his *own power*, to believe or disbelieve truth or falsehood, or to *love* or *hate persons* or *things* in opposition to the sensations which they produce on his individual organization.

That even until now he has been supposed to possess these powers, and he has been *trained, educated* and *governed* accordingly.

That he has been thus made to believe that his character has been formed BY himself; while all facts demonstrate that it is, in every case, formed FOR each individual of the human race, whether in China, Turkey, Europe, America, or elsewhere.

That, through this error, the character of man has been formed, in all countries, at all times, on a *defective model*.

That the means now exist by which it may be formed, for every individual, on a *model* so *improved* as to be superior to any before known.

These experiments, and others which are in progress, also demonstrate that *the power of producing wealth* or real riches is now *superabundant for all human purposes*; and that it is annually advancing in a continually increasing ratio, and that no limits can be assigned to its augmentation.

That this power requires but a *right* or *intelligent* direction to relieve the inhabitants of all countries from poverty, or from the fear of not obtaining at all times, in security, a full supply of everything experience shall prove to be the best for human nature.

Upon the facts developed by these experiments, the knowledge of *two sciences*, the most important to human happiness, may be obtained.

The first, the science of forming a superior character in every child to whom the science shall be applied in his education and circumstances.

The second, the science by which every child, to whom it shall be applied, from infancy to maturity, shall be so trained and placed, that he shall enjoy the best of everything for his individual life in security, from birth to death.

But that neither of these sciences can be applied to full practice under any of the existing governments, whether of long standing or recent formation. Consequently, *a new district, free from all the existing laws, institutions, and prejudices, is now required, in which to exhibit this new state of society.*

The Government and People of the Mexican Republic possess such a district, most applicable for the purpose, in the state of Coahuila and Texas.

Its position, soil, and climate, with the present state and condition of its population, render it the most desirable point on the globe on which to establish this model-government, for the general benefit of all other governments and people, but more immediately for the benefit of the South and North American Republics.

Your Memorialist asks the province of Texas, and its independence to be guaranteed by the Mexican Republic, the United States, and Great Britain, as a free gift, to a society to be formed to accomplish this great change in the condition of the human race. He asks it from the Mexican Republic under the following considerations: –

First, That it is a frontier province between the Mexican and North American Republics, which is now settling under such circumstances as are likely to create jealousies and irritations between the citizens of these states, and which most probably, at some future period, will terminate in a war between the two Republics.[a]

This consideration alone, in the opinion of many experienced statesmen, would render it a wise measure in the Mexican Republic to place this province under the new arrangements about to be proposed.

Second, That this province, by being placed under the government of this Society, would be speedily peopled with persons of superior habits, manners, and intelligence, and whose main object would be, not only to preserve peace between the two Republics, but to exhibit the means by which the motive to war between all nations would be withdrawn, and all the objects expected to be attained by the most successful war secured to every nation.

[a] A boundary between the US and Mexico was fixed in 1828. Texas was independent between 1836–45, and war finally occurred between the US and Mexico in 1846–7.

Third, That the improvements which would commence in this new state, by the introduction into it of great numbers of men, selected for their superior industry, skill, capital, or intelligence, would cause a rapid advance in science, or real knowledge, throughout all the states of the Republic of Mexico, and the other Republics in its neighbourhood, by which a progress hitherto unknown would be made in a new civilization, as superior to the old as truth is to error. And, lastly,

That an instructed and well-disposed population will be of far more value to the Republic of Mexico, than territory without people, or with a population of inferior character and acquirements.

It is expected, also, that the new model-government will speedily demonstrate, that all the new states have more territory than they can advantageously people or employ for many centuries.

For these reasons and considerations, your Memorialist entertains the expectation that you will discover full and sufficient cause to grant the province of Texas to the Society, the nature and constitution of which your Memorialist will now explain.

The Society is to be formed of individuals of any country, whose minds have been enlightened beyond the prejudices of all local districts; whose single object will be to ameliorate the condition of man, by shewing in practice how he may be trained, educated, employed, and governed in unison with his nature, and with the natural laws which govern it.

It will be, therefore, a society to prepare the means to put an end to war, religious animosities, and commercial rivalries, between nations; – competition between individuals; – to enable the existing population of the world to relieve themselves from poverty, or the fear of it; – to create an entire new character in the rising generation by instructing them, through an investigation of facts, in a knowledge of their nature, and of the laws by which it is eternally governed; and thus to produce in *practice*

'Peace on earth and good-will to man.'[a]

This practice, so long promised to the human race, can never be obtained under any of the governments, laws, or institutions, in any known parts of the world; because they are, one and all, founded on the same original notions of error regarding human nature, and consequently of the mode by which it can be advantageously governed.

The increase of knowledge, the advance of science, and more especially the overwhelming progress of mechanic inventions, and chemical discoveries, superseding the necessity for much manual labour, now demand a change in the government of the world, a moral revolution, which shall ameliorate the

[a] See Matthew 10:34.

condition of the producers, and prevent them from bringing destruction, through a physical revolution on the non-producers.

The Memorialist will be enabled to advise in the forming of the arrangements to effect these great objects, and to assist in organizing the society to execute the measures, by reason of his long and extensive experience, solely directed to these objects.

By his experiments in England and Scotland, he has ascertained the principles of the sciences by which a superior character can be formed for all children not physically or mentally diseased, and by which a superfluity of wealth can be created and secured for all, without injury to any.

By his late experiments in the United States, he has discovered the difficulties which the existing institutions and prejudices have created in the present adult population, to make the change from the old to the new state of society under any of the existing laws or forms of governments.[a]

These experiments have also instructed him in what can, and what cannot be effected, with the different classes of society, as their characters have been formed under the existing systems.

He has thus ascertained the necessity of commencing this improvement of the condition of the human race in a new country, in which the laws and institutions shall be all formed in conformity with the principles on which this great amelioration is to be achieved.

All the governments of the world are deeply interested in these proceedings. The general progress of intellectual acquirements, and scientific discoveries, render a moral or a physical revolution unavoidable in all countries.

The experience of the Republic of North America has fully demonstrated to the intelligent in those states of which it is composed, that any government founded upon popular elections has within it the seeds of continued irritation, divisions, and corruptions; and that it can be tolerated only as the best known means of leading to an advanced state of society, by a superior education of all classes, fitting them to enjoy, in the most rational manner, the wealth which they will learn so easily, and so pleasantly, to create by *systematic scientific arrangements*.

Therefore, by the establishment of the proposed model government in the Texas, revolution in old or new states will be rendered unnecessary. It is most desirable for all parties that forced revolutions should never occur, but that the improvements, advancing with the age in which we live, should be made without violence, by the established government of every country deriving its knowledge from the experience of a country devoted to national improvements, without being impeded by any of the errors and prejudices of past ages.

---

[a] The New Harmony community had collapsed amidst considerable acrimony. For an account of its failings, see A. E. Bestor, *Backwoods Utopias. The Sectarian Origins and the Owenite Phase of Communitarian Socialism in America, 1663–1829* (2nd edn, Philadelphia: University of Pennsylvania Press, 1970), pp. 160–201.

Thus may the Republic of Mexico not only derive incalculable advantages for itself, but be the efficient means of securing them for all other states and people; thus presenting to the world an example, – as it has already done, when in its early formation it decreed the abolition of slavery from its soil,[a] – worthy of general imitation.

The Memorialist asks the means only to apply his past experience for the benefit of his fellow-men. He asks not, he wants not any thing for himself.

ROBERT OWEN

London, 10th October, 1828

[a] The Mexican Constitution of 1824 abolished slavery. This was reinforced by a further measure in September 1829.

THE

ADDRESSES

OF

ROBERT OWEN,

(AS PUBLISHED IN THE LONDON JOURNALS),

Preparatory to the developement of

A PRACTICAL PLAN

FOR THE

RELIEF OF ALL CLASSES,

WITHOUT INJURY TO ANY.

LONDON;
STEPHEN HUNT, 4, YORK STREET, COVENT GARDEN,
SOLD BY ALL BOOKSELLERS,
(And to be had at the Co-Operative Bazaar, Greville St. Hatton Garden.)

Price Eighteen-pence.

1830.

KING'S COLLEGE PRINTING OFFICE, HELMET COURT, 337, STRAND.

THE ADDRESSES OF ROBERT OWEN[a]
1830

TO THE GENTLEMEN WHO DIRECT THE LONDON PRESS

From an impression, early imbibed, and confirmed by daily experience, that all classes, sects and parties, in all countries, have emanated from notions of error relative to human nature, I have never connected myself with any of them except by kind feelings and good will impelling me to attempt an amelioration of their condition. Having also recently disconnected myself from all private commercial interests,[b] I have been induced to employ my time in an attempt to penetrate and unveil the mysteries which have induced such extraordinary anomalies as now exist in the most civilized countries, but more especially in the British Empire. I have endeavoured to ascertain the real cause why the British population, with a power of production new in the history of mankind, and capable, if they were rational in their proceedings, and the power rightly directed, of over-supplying the wants or desires of 10, or 20, or 30 times its present numbers, so large a majority of this population should be at the present moment contending, with all their energies, to obtain an increase of property, while a considerable number are in want of the first necessaries of life.

Disregarding the theories and prejudices of all, I have been induced to examine carefully such facts connected with the subject as my intimate acquaintance with various classes, sects, and parties, enabled me to collect and compare together, without being influenced in my decisions by the educational or national feelings or prepossessions of any of the local divisions of which society is composed. The result of this investigation I have submitted to the consideration of the British Cabinet, and await its decision.

[a] The pamphlet comprises eighteen addresses published from 4 January–4 February 1830 in various London newspapers, including the *Morning Advertiser*, *Morning Herald*, and *The Star*. Reprinted in *New Moral World*, vol. 2, nos 17–31 (20 February–28 May 1836), pp. 130–1, 138–9, 146–7, 150, 162–3, 170–1, 178–9, 187, 203, 211, 219, 235, 244.

[b] Owen sold his interest in New Lanark in 1828. Thereafter it was managed by the sons of his former partner, John Walker.

I am strongly impressed with the conviction that the Government of this country will not, that it cannot, much longer suffer the population of the British dominions to continue to be overwhelmed with an abundance which, as circumstances now are, necessarily inflicts with poverty and various unjust hardships the producers of that abundance, while, at the same time, the empire contains dormant manual and scientific powers sufficient to increase the real wealth of the population twenty, fifty, nay, more than a hundred-fold.

This is an irrational state of existence, which it is greatly for the best interest of every individual, whatever may be his rank, station, or condition, to terminate in the shortest period practicable, without creating by the change permanent evils of magnitude.

Such is the object which has been attempted in the *exposé* which has been presented to the British Cabinet.

The subject, however, is necessarily most extensive, and in its results will materially affect the feelings, the interest, and condition of every individual in the British dominions, and, ultimately, of those who inhabit other countries.

A subject so comprehensive requires much elucidation to enable the population to understand its practical effects, through all its ramifications, upon their respective conditions, occupations, and employments.

In addition to the subject, as submitted to the consideration of Government, I have prepared addresses to the various existing classes, explanatory of their situation and of the manner in which they would be affected by the proposed change in the condition of society.

These addresses are as brief as the subject of each will admit; many of them will not occupy more than half of one of your columns, some not so much, but a few of them will require a fuller development.

There is no private interest or party object in the slightest degree connected with them – they are solely intended for the public good.

Upon this ground alone I request the use of your columns for one of these addresses every alternate day until the meeting of Parliament, that, by that period, its Members and the public may have the subject fully before them.

You, as well as the public, have a deep stake in this matter; and when the whole subject shall be placed fairly before you it will be open to your scrutiny, and I desire it may receive your support, or call forth your censure and opposition, as it may appear to you to merit the one, or deserve the other.

Jan. 4

ADDRESS TO THE GOVERNMENTS OF EUROPE AND AMERICA

In September 1818, I presented to you a memorial; and in the October of the same year I presented another,[a] through the late Lord Castlereagh,[b] to the Allied Powers, assembled in Congress at Aix-la-Chapelle.

These memorials related to the general state of the civilized world, as it existed at that period; and to these I beg to refer you for an explanation of the causes that have created the general changes which have occurred in Europe and America from that time up to the present period.

Upon perusing these memorials you will perceive that, without the alteration of a single word, they describe the exact condition of the leading powers, and their respective populations, in Europe and America, as they exist at this moment.

In the first of these memorials it is stated that – 'A period has arrived in which a greater change in human affairs will be forced on the world than the world has yet witnessed; but, in all its extent, the change will be highly beneficial to every individual and to all States. It is a period when the errors which have hitherto perplexed mankind are about to be unravelled; and, in consequence, the obstacles which stood in the way of human improvement and enjoyment will be removed.

'The immediate causes which make this change certain and necessary are, the overwhelming effects of new scientific power, and the rapidly-increasing knowledge of all classes of men.

'The former will soon render human labour of little avail in the creation of wealth, while the latter will make evident to the people the absolute necessity, which has thus arisen for them to give a different direction to their powers, and will inform them, also, how the change is to be effected.

'To this day the means of consumption, or of obtaining the necessaries of life, by the working classes, have been acquired solely through the medium of their labour, the value of which the new power has already much diminished. And the certain consequences of the undirected progress of this power will be to reduce the exchangeable value of manual labour until it falls below the means of procuring a wretched subsistence for any large proportion of the working classes, while the remainder of them must be starved out of existence.

'Such is the nature of the contest, which has already continued for some time, and which now exists in full activity, between scientific power and

[a] See *infra*, vol. 1, pp. 253–67.
[b] Robert Stewart, Viscount Castlereagh (1769–1822).

manual labour – between knowledge and ignorance; but no one, who comprehends anything of the subject, can for one moment doubt the result.'[a]

The period has arrived when this change has become inevitable throughout the British dominions; and the causes which have produced the necessity for it in these countries are in active progress in the United States, in France, over Europe generally, and in many parts of Asia.

The new scientific powers of production, which, during the late revolutionary war of France made such a progress in Great Britain, as by their efforts to astonish her allies, her enemies, and the world, have now taken deep root in the United States, and in many of the nations of Europe; and this new power, which no human effort can now arrest in its continually increasing progress, is already sufficient, or may be made superabundant, to supply the physical wants of the human race, however rapidly the population of the world may increase.

Such is already the dominion which science has acquired over the productions by which the physical wants of mankind are supplied.

It is unnecessary, therefore, that poverty, or the fear of it, should be longer numbered among the evils to which humanity is liable, except through the want of knowledge, and consequent misrule of those who govern.

The most ample means to secure permanent abundance for the population whom you govern, and whose happiness or misery depends upon your knowledge or ignorance, are now at your disposal, and wait only for you to give them a right direction.

In the words, then, of the second memorial, to which I have already referred, it is strictly true that – 'The period has arrived when the means are become obvious, by which, without violence, fraud, or disorder of any kind, riches may be created in such abundance, and advantageously for all, that the wants and wishes of every human being, relative to real wealth, may be more than satisfied.'[b]

But the still more important knowledge has been acquired, and is now offered for your consideration by means of which you would be enabled to remove, from among the people over whom you rule, and from their descendants to the latest posterity, the cause of all intellectual and moral evil ever experienced in human society.

The inhabitants of the world have heretofore lived under the impression that the thoughts and the convictions of each individual were of his own formation; and that they depended upon his will, which they supposed to be an independent part of his nature. They have, therefore, been angry because of each other's thoughts and convictions; and have, consequently, been, without exception, ignorantly cruel and unjust, individually and nationally.

The inhabitants of the world have also existed, to the present time, under

[a] See *infra*, vol. 1, p. 246.
[b] See *infra*, vol. 1, p. 250.

the impression that each individual possesses a power, of his own formation, to like or dislike things, and to love or hate persons at his pleasure.

They have, therefore, been angry with each other when they did not like or dislike, and love or hate, according to the fanciful or arbitrary notions of individuals or nations.

Experience has now proved that these are impressions, arising, not from facts, but from imaginary notions opposed to all facts; and that hence alone has proceeded all the intellectual and moral evil; or, in other words, all the irrationality which the world has ever known.

The cause of all the misery which has existed is thus before you; and you possess the most ample power to remove that cause in this generation, without injury to yourselves or others.

Will you not, then, remove it, and thereby withdraw all the evil and misery from among yourselves, and all those whose well-being and happiness are under your guidance and control?

Will you unite among yourselves for your safety, and seriously deliberate what measures may be most beneficially adopted under the new circumstances which have arisen, and the knowledge of which can be no longer withheld from the general population of the world?

Can all your present wealth and power procure a higher enjoyment than that of becoming the active instruments of securing the future happiness of the human race?

To accomplish the object of all my exertions, it is necessary for me to economise time and money; and when the end to be attained is the permanent well-being of mankind, ceremonies become less important.

I feel myself therefore obliged to make this communication to each Government through the medium of the public press; in which form I beg each of you to accept it with the same kind feelings and attention which my former communications experienced from many of you.

Jan. 6

ADDRESS TO THE BRITISH NATION

Fellow Countrymen, – After having visited various countries I find you on my return increased in wealth, and also in poverty and distress.

That the public wealth has greatly accumulated may be inferred by the improved state of the roads and the higher degree of cultivation visible in every part of the kingdom, by the increase of the large towns and the superior character of the new buildings, and by the multiplied productions of every description which are now created.

That poverty and distress also more extensively prevail, is equally evident from the increased appearance of wretchedness visible among the lower orders, and from the degree of corroding anxiety and care depicted upon the countenances of the great majority of both the middle and working classes; producing among the population of these kingdoms an appearance of less satisfaction and more misery than is to be seen among any other people, whether free or enslaved, in any other part of the globe.

And these results are produced in a country superabounding with means for the creation of wealth; and in one where public opinion has a greater influence in directing the measures of Government than in any other, perhaps, excepting the United States of North America.

It becomes, then, most interesting to ascertain how it is that there exists such extraordinary means of creating wealth, and of securing pecuniary independence to all within the British dominions: and yet, that there should at the same time prevail so much poverty and misery among a large portion of the population, and so much dissatisfaction with the existing order of things, both at home and abroad.

The cause is in yourselves, and from you the remedy must proceed.

The scientific knowledge of the educated part of the inhabitants of this country greatly exceeds that of their moral and political knowledge. For, by means of scientific knowledge, powers have already been obtained, sufficient, if rightly directed, to saturate with wealth not only the British dominions, but the world at large; while the deficiency in moral and political knowledge is so great, that these powers of production, instead of being applied to the creation of the most valuable wealth for all the population, are now so unwisely directed as to make a few individuals greatly too wealthy, either for their own or the public benefit, and to render poverty and crime, and their consequent misery, unavoidable to a large portion of the community.

The remedy for these evils is to be found, therefore, only in the introduction of more correct moral and political knowledge among you. An accurate knowledge of these subjects would enable all parties to discover the great and lamentable errors into which mankind have hitherto fallen in directing the powers of society; and to perceive that, in order to govern a country well, it is necessary that all its physical and mental powers should be applied to form the best character for the whole population, that it may be enabled to produce the greatest amount of the most valuable wealth, and to distribute it in such a manner as to secure the greatest degree of happiness to the whole population.

These desirable results, it is evident, have never hitherto been obtained for any portion of the human race; and all are effectually prevented from attempting to introduce into society such measures as would secure them, by the mistaken system of morality which they have been forced, from infancy to receive.

To give a right or beneficial direction to the new scientific powers of production, a union of feeling and of action is necessary; and that union cannot be permanently effected among any portion of the human race by any moral or religious system founded on the notions upon which all the past and present moral and religious systems of the world have been established.

Is it then desirable that for the sole purpose of keeping men in ignorance and misery, that they may be more easily governed by the few, while the few, also, are essentially injured, that moral and religious errors which generate disunion and a want of charity, and of kindness among the human race, and which prevent the enjoyment of a very high degree of happiness among all people, shall be longer allowed to be considered sacred in the estimation of the public?

My conviction is, that now there is no wisdom whatever in thus continuing to destroy the superior faculties of the human race – that there is not one individual, whatever may be his station, who is not grievously injured by this deception – and that for the safety, well-being, and happiness of all, it is necessary now to unmask the hypocrisy of a system by which so many evils of the most lamentable description are entailed upon the population of all countries.

It is the moral courage to effect this object that is alone wanting, in order to relieve the world for ever from poverty, or the fear of poverty; and to remove the obstacles which now prevent a superior character being formed, and rendered permanent among mankind.

Shall we, then, of the present generation, who have been permitted to perceive these great truths, be deterred, by fear of man, or by any temporary consequences, from performing the greatest duty that ever can be performed for the human race?

Shall we, for want of bestowing a rational education upon the people, and giving a right direction to their industry, see Ireland in misery, and agitated from its centre to its circumference?

Shall we see the middle classes rapidly sinking into the lower, and the lower incompetent by their utmost exertions, to secure a reasonable support? And shall we see the whole population, from the highest to the lowest, educated under false notions, and surrounded by the most vicious or futile circumstances, and not attempt to remove these evils, when the means of removing them for ever from the world have become obvious?

Shall we see nations opposed to nations,[a] striving to obtain some small territory, when the earth is still a wilderness for want of people to cultivate it; or contending for the privilege of disposing of some of their useless productions to distant countries, while their industry would become ten-fold more beneficial to themselves if it were wisely applied at home?

Shall we see nations inflicting, through war, almost every kind of evil upon

[a] See for example Genesis 10:32.

many millions of their respective populations, for the mere chance of obtaining some uncertain commercial profit, while these nations possess the most ample means to gorge the world with the most valuable and substantial wealth?

Shall we, I ask, see these enormous evils advancing day by day, many of them hourly increasing, and distinctly perceive the cause which generates these sufferings, and, from fear of an ignorant interested public opinion, take no open and effectual measures to remove that cause?

Whatever circumstances may exist to prevent others from now coming forward to aid in this great work for the regeneration of mankind, none exists to deter me from thus performing the highest duty that man can perform for man. Perceiving the extent of the evil, its cause, and its remedy, I can no longer refrain from placing them before the public; and from calling upon all nations and people to put far away from them the cause of their ignorance, their imbecility, and their vices, and to apply the remedy in their power for the innumerable sufferings proceeding from these evils.

For man is incompetent to think as he pleases, or to feel as he likes; yet all the moral and religious systems known have been made to rest solely on the contrary supposition. This single error is the origin of evil among mankind, and alone generates all the evil existing at this hour among the human race. If the supporters of these systems can discover error in what is here advanced, let them now openly come forth and prove wherein that error consists.

The time has arrived when it has become unavoidable that the question should be for ever set at rest, and that the truth or error of these respective systems be made manifest to the world.

If it be true that man is forced to believe according to the strongest conviction made upon his mind, and to feel according to the impressions which external circumstances make upon his individual organization, then a very superior moral, political, and commercial system, for the practice of the world, may be immediately adopted, and evil and suffering may be altogether removed from human society. But if, on the contrary, man does possess the power to believe as he likes, and to feel as he pleases, then must the present wretched condition of the human race continue without ceasing; for experience has abundantly proved how man, under these notions, has thought and felt, and how necessarily evils and sufferings have followed from these thoughts and feelings; and thus no hope would remain for the future.

But a new day is opening in Britain, which will extend its light from these islands, until it shall illumine every continent and every island where man dwells.

For the first time in the history of Britain, truth may now be publicly spoken on subjects the most interesting to man, without the individual being liable to be burned or imprisoned, or without his experiencing any other inconvenience than the being called, by ignorant or interested persons, a visionary or a madman. And when truth can thus be publicly spoken, and have a fair chance of being heard, it will be seen how soon error will disappear before it, and how rapidly every mind will advance in the acquisition of real knowledge. Man must believe according to the strongest conviction that can be made upon his mind, and truth must, therefore, sooner or later, prevail over error.

Under the impression, then, that every fact connected with the subject will prove that all human evil proceeds from the erroneous supposition that man has been formed with powers to believe as he likes and to feel as he pleases, and that this origin of evil must now give place to the superior knowledge that man is forced by the unchanging laws of his nature to believe in obedience to the strongest conviction that is made upon his mind, and to feel in obedience to the impressions made by external objects upon his individual organization, I have developed a new moral, political, and commercial system for the British dominions, founded on this change of moral principle; which system will, in the first instance, be submitted to Government for their calm consideration, and afterwards be laid before the public, as it must, ere long, be adopted, to relieve you from the dire effects of immorality, and a misdirected scientific power.

The plan recommended is, to supersede the vicious circumstances which pervade the moral, political, and commercial system now in practice, by other circumstances of a more favourable character, formed in accordance with the now-ascertained law of human nature, that belief and feeling are alike independent of the will of the individual. Such a combination of circumstances would at once relieve the world from all the misery entailed upon it by the consequences arising from a contrary supposition; which supposition could only have been upheld, through past ages, by reason of the ignorance which pervaded the human race upon those all-important subjects.

No such change, however, as that which I propose can be established unless borne out by the sanction of a majority of the reflecting part of the population.

I therefore thus address you, that you may at leisure consider the principles upon which the proposed change is founded, and that all who may deem themselves interested in opposing that change, or its principles, may have an opportunity of bringing forward their objections with the least delay. I say with the least delay, because the sufferings of a large part of the industrious classes in Great Britain and Ireland are now almost greater than they can submit to, without seeking a remedy for themselves, unaided by the non-producing classes; and because, while the existing moral, political, and commercial system shall continue, these sufferings must unavoidably increase.

Jan. 11

ADDRESS TO THE IMPERIAL PARLIAMENT OF GREAT BRITAIN

The population of the British empire is oppressed by a superabundance of wealth, and by an excess of poverty.

It seeks the means of relief from both these evils. Other civilized nations are beginning to experience the same effects from similar causes; and the most enlightened individuals in these countries look to the wisdom of your Councils for a remedy.

All who reflect, now perceive that the immediate cause of these is an excess of production, unaccompanied by a knowledge of the means by which that excess may be advantageously distributed.

These evils were first experienced in the year 1810, when a new æra commenced with regard to supply and demand.

Up to that period the supply never equalled the demand; it was therefore the chief business of political economists and others to devise and point out the best means of increasing the supply.

The introduction, within the last 50 years, of machinery into the manufactures of Great Britain, overcame this difficulty; and in the year 1810 the period of a deficient supply was passed for the first time in the history of nations.

It was passed, too, in the midst of a long, general, and most wasteful war; proving that the powers of production were become not only ample for a period of peace, but were also more than sufficient to meet the exigencies of the most wide-spread warfare, simultaneously carried on by the most powerful nations of the world.

Since that eventful year, the distress which has arisen in Great Britain, in the United States of North America, and in many of the civilized countries, has uniformly arisen from an excess, continually increasing, of supply over demand.

In consequence a necessity at that period commenced for a change in the commercial policy of society; that necessity daily increased, producing periodical distress among the industrious classes, until at length its severity in 1816 became such, that the proceeds of a large public subscription were inadequate to afford relief to the extent required. Under these circumstances, a public Meeting was held in London, to consider the cause of the evil, and of its remedy.[a]

At this Meeting a Committee was appointed to investigate the subject,

[a] See *The Times*, no. 9900 (30 July 1816), p. 3.

composed generally of the most respected public-spirited Statesmen, political economists, and others, and the late Archbishop of Canterbury[a] was selected to preside over its deliberations.

It appeared inexplicable to the Members of this Committee how such general and alarming distress could arise among the agricultural labourers and manufacturing operatives, while there was at that moment, through Great Britain and Ireland, a greater superfluity of productions, both agricultural and manufacturing, than had existed at any former period.

At the first meeting of this Committee various conjectures were offered by different Members as explanations of this singular anomaly; but none were deemed satisfactory. The writer, who was supposed to have some useful practical knowledge upon the subject, was requested by the Chairman and others to state his view of the case; which he did, but probably in a very imperfect manner, as he was then unaccustomed to public speaking.

He attributed the difficulties, the cause and remedy of which they were met to consider, to the rapid extension of machinery and other scientific inventions and discoveries, which had been introduced during the late war, and which had superseded the necessity for so much manual labour as had formerly been called into action. Thus a large surplus of all kinds of productions was created, and a diminished supply became unavoidable: the newly acquired scientific power produced more economically than did manual labour; manual labour was, in consequence, dismissed from employment, and machinery was retained.

The Committee considered that this statement contained a reasonable and satisfactory explanation of the subject, and the writer was requested to draw up a Report on the existing state of the working classes, and to propose a remedy for the evils under which they were suffering.

He accordingly, in the Spring of 1817, presented to the Committee a detailed Report upon these subjects.[b]

The distress of the working classes had become so general, and pauperism had in consequence increased to such an alarming extent, that your Lower House was induced to appoint a numerous and highly-respectable Committee, under the title a 'Committee on the Poor Laws,' to trace the subject to its source, and through all its ramifications.

When the writer presented his Report to the General Committee, of which the then Archbishop of Canterbury was Chairman, the subject was deemed by them too important to be passed slightly over; and they recommended that the Reports should be submitted to the Committee of the House of Commons on the Poor Laws, which was then sitting.

---

[a] Richard Reardon (1737–1824): Archbishop 1802–24.

[b] See Owen, *Report to the Committee of the Association for the Relief of the Manufacturing and Labouring Poor* (1817), *infra*, vol. 1, pp. 143–55.

It was presented, accompanied by drawings explanatory of the practical arrangements proposed; and the writer offered to be fully examined as to the cause of the evils under which the country was suffering; the principles on which he proposed to apply a remedy; and as to the detail of the practice which he recommended.

The Report, the plans, and the offer of examination, were under the consideration of the Committee, with closed doors, for two days; at the termination of which, the writer was officially informed by one of the Members, that the Committee, after a long and interesting debate, had come to the resolution not to receive the Report, or to examine the writer upon the subject.[a]

The Committee judged wisely. The public had not then been sufficiently prepared by commercial difficulties, or by distress among the lower orders, to believe that a change so extensive as the one proposed was necessary, nor indeed would become at no distant period unavoidable.

The Report and detailed reasoning thereon were, however, at that time extensively published in the newspapers, to prepare the public for the adoption of the principles and the plan when the further extension of mechanic and other scientific producing powers should compel all classes to seek relief from the overwhelming effects of over-production, and of competition between scientific power and manual labour, and when the increased knowledge of the people should have convinced them of the necessity of changing the policy of the empire, in order to apply this new power in aid of, instead of being, as it now is, opposed to human industry, and the general prosperity of the British dominions.

In proof of the benefit arising from the practical adoption of his plan, the writer now begs leave to refer to the experiment commenced in 1818, in the Netherlands, under the sanction of the Government and the auspices of the Royal Family; when some of the principles, and much of the detail, were put to the test of experience.[b] That experience, during a period of nearly 12 years, has now abundantly proved these eminently calculated to diminish pauperism, and to improve generally the habits and condition of the industrious classes.

The principles and practice recommended in the Report to the House of Commons are no longer hypothetical, it having been proved that they have raised the condition of 30,000 ignorant, and therefore generally vicious and useless persons, from a state of burdensome dependence upon the producing classes of the community, to become industrious and useful, to earn their own support, and to acquire good and orderly habits; and these favourable results were produced, too, in a country where knowledge was less diffused than in

---

[a] See *infra*, vol. 4, pp. 209–10.

[b] See the description of the Dutch pauper colony at Fredericks-oord, in *The Philanthropist*, no. 1 (1829), pp. 67–76.

Great Britain, and where the Colonies were, to their pecuniary disadvantage, without the aid of modern improved machinery. Still they have produced a surplus, which will repay the original capital expended upon each establishment, and all the interest accruing thereon.

When the Committee of the House of Commons on the Poor Laws rejected in 1817 the Report and the plan presented to them by the writer, circumstances justified their decision; but these circumstances no longer exist, and have been replaced by others of a different character.

The machinery of the kingdom has been nearly, if not fully, doubled since that period, and in consequence distress now not only overwhelms the operative manufacturers and agricultural labourers, but pervades the smaller farmers, and a large portion of the master manufacturers, and threatens continually to advance upwards until the sufferings of the majority of the population will become greater than they can endure; and this by means of a power, which, under a wise direction, is capable of securing permanent prosperity, not only to those born within the British dominions, but to the subjects of every State brought under its influence, when aided by a national system of education, founded on a knowledge of the general laws of human nature.

The writer, therefore, now in the most earnest manner recommends the full consideration of these all-important subjects to the Members of the Imperial Parliament, as individuals and as constituents of that Government to which all nations are looking for direction, in the adoption of measures for the relief of their respective populations from poverty, vice, and misery.

Jan. 12

ADDRESS TO THE PROPRIETORS AND EDITORS OF THE PRESS IN GREAT BRITAIN AND IRELAND

Public opinion governs the world: and the public opinion of Great Britain influences, to a great extent, the public opinion of all civilized nations.

You, gentlemen, form, or might form, the public opinion of Great Britain; and you thus become agents in effecting the greatest amount of mischief or benefit among mankind.

Such is the importance which the present circumstances of the world give to your position; and such the magnitude of the good or evil which you may accomplish for the civilized world.

Were you intelligent, and at the same time independent in your circumstances, it would be unnecessary to add one sentence more, for in this case your direct and obvious interest would lead you aright. But, under the vicious circumstances in which you have been trained, and are compelled to act, it is impossible that you should possess intelligence, or acquire an independence.

Under the circumstances which have existed, you could not arrive at a knowledge of your nature, without which knowledge no man can be intelligent. You could not, by the acquirement of any amount sterling, obtain, at all times, a full supply of the best of every thing for your nature; and until arrangements shall be formed which will secure these objects, no one can be thoroughly independent in mind or circumstances.

It is now, however, in your power, by creating a right public opinion, mainly to assist in procuring these advantages for yourselves and for all your fellow-creatures; and to be the chief instruments in effecting this important change in the condition of the civilized world is, perhaps, the highest privilege that can be conferred upon any individuals.

But in order that you may be successful in speedily giving a right direction to public opinion, it is necessary that you should cordially and honestly unite your efforts, and that you should aid each other with as much zeal as is incumbent on those who have the same interest and object in view.

Before, however, that any general or permanent union can be effected among you, it is indispensable that each should acquire a knowledge of the great principle of union in human nature.

You have all been thoroughly trained in the notion, and been subjected from infancy to the mass of injurious consequences which follow from the supposition of its truth, that you possess, by nature, the power to feel and think as you please. And while your conviction in the truth of this notion remains, you cannot avoid being displeased or angry with those who cannot, or, as you suppose, will not, feel or think in accordance with your feelings and thoughts, – never suspecting that your thoughts and feelings, as well as theirs, are formed for each without your being aware of the means by which they are so formed.

It is this error alone which has hitherto prevented, and which now prevents, the existence of a cordial and sincere union among the human race. Let but this error, by instilling into the minds of men a correct knowledge of the laws of human nature, be withdrawn from the world, and universal union, peace, and kindness, must, and will prevail among all nations, people and individuals.

The simple task, then, which you have to perform, in order to create a right public opinion, and one which would be invaluable in its effects, is to stimulate all to examine the facts from which the great truth that 'man does not possess the power to feel and to think as he pleases,' has been deduced.

Make this fundamental law of our nature familiar to all – enable to trace the beneficial effects which a knowledge of it would produce among society in general, and the rising generation in particular; and a public opinion would thereby be formed, which would speedily remove the vicious circumstances which have hitherto created all the irrationality, disunion, and evil passions, now prevalent among mankind.

Do this with the industry and energy which you have been accustomed to exercise in the cause of party, of faction, and of sectarianism, or for the acquirement of common commercial gain, and you will become the instruments of removing for ever from the world the cause of ignorance and of poverty, of vice, and of misery.

Why should you, then, for the limited and inferior advantages which you obtain, longer lend yourselves to faction, sect, or party, when the means of obtaining the most ample permanent benefits that human nature can enjoy, are, by a noble straightforward course, so easy of attainment?

Abandon party – abandon faction – abandon sectarianism – and, above all, abandon that fundamental error which has engendered every human ill; and you will discover that science now offers the most certain and the most delightful means of creating unlimited wealth for all, and of giving to the coming generations, physically, mentally, and morally, a character greatly superior to any that has hitherto been formed for man.

This is the race which is now set before you; and by a prompt and decisive conduct, you will obtain the inestimable reward which is affixed to its completion. The press will then no longer be made instrumental in the creation of error, disunion, or malignant feelings; and, by becoming under your hands a powerful engine of good, will prove itself to be one of the greatest blessings that knowledge has yet discovered for the use of man.

Remember that man feels and thinks as he has been compelled by his nature to feel and think; and that to be displeased or angry with him for his thoughts and feelings, is a demonstrative proof that the individual thus displeased or angry has not yet been made rational in his feelings, thoughts, or actions.

Jan. 13

ADDRESS TO THE MERCHANTS AND TO THE WHOLESALE AND RETAIL TRADERS IN GREAT BRITAIN

The business in which you are engaged, is, fortunately for yourselves and society, rapidly drawing to a termination.

The genuine British merchant is already scarcely to be found in any part of the world, and the wholesale and retail trade of the kingdom will soon be absorbed by a few great houses, such as Morrison and Co., Leaf and Co., Ellis, etc[a] which principle of trade will continue to obtain until the whole business

[a] Morrison & Co., merchants of Crown Court; Leaf Son & Coles, wholesale haberdashers of Cheapside; probably Ellis & Co., merchants, wholesale grocers and tea-dealers of Bishopsgate.

shall be taken up by banking bazaars, which will supersede banking, and every other more expensive and hazardous mode of representing and distributing throughout society the wealth of the producers.

It is, doubtless, under existing circumstances, unpleasant to our feelings, to be obliged to alter our established habits, and to seek subsistence by a different direction of our faculties to that we have been accustomed; but such a change as that which is about to become unavoidable on your part, will, instead of being productive of injurious results, be ultimately highly beneficial to yourselves and to the public.

It is evident to every one that you do not create a particle of wealth for society; but that, without any adequate compensation to it, or real benefit to yourselves, you consume, in the support of useless, showy establishments, a large portion of that wealth which others produce.

The real utility to the public of all your industry lies in the distribution you make of the wealth produced by the industrious classes; but this your system effects, only at an enormous waste of that wealth, and at a cost of, perhaps 99 per cent. beyond what would be necessary, under a rational arrangement of society, to produce and to distribute in the best manner.

You are, however, blameless; you have acted under a system which you did not comprehend – which you could not direct; but which, on the contrary, has controlled you. You would run much less risk, you would be engaged in occupations greatly more favourable to health and intelligence, and be less liable to deteriorating mental and moral influences, were many of you to become producers of wealth, under proper arrangements, instead of being distributors of it, under the very unfavourable circumstances in which you have hitherto been placed.

The interest and happiness of yourselves and families require that you should, as speedily as possible, be relieved from the injurious position in which a most irrational state of society has placed you; making you almost a dead weight upon society, and rendering you by the fanciful, expensive establishments you have thought it beneficial to form, useless and extravagant consumers of wealth, instead of being active and intelligent producers of it, which wealth would have been made to add greatly to your own comfort, and to the riches of the public.

It is clearly, then, for the interest of the British empire, that there should be, among its population, the greatest number of intelligent producers, and the fewest distributors of wealth.

I, therefore, thus address you, to prepare you for a change of this description – a change, which the increase of knowledge renders necessary and unavoidable, and which will contribute, more than could any occurrence, however favourable under the existing system of society, to the attainment by your class of permanent prosperity and happiness.

The superior faculties of your nature can never be called forth under a system which makes it appear to be your interest to endeavour to buy as cheap, and to sell as dear as possible. While men are involved in such practices, it is idle to talk of virtue; as, under a system which is technically termed fair trading, they do but endeavour to obtain advantages one over the other – the more acute or intelligent prevailing over the more ignorant or simple.

In a rational state of society, were you to be as successful in obtaining wealth, as you are, under this system, generally the reverse, your employment would yet be deemed useless and degrading. It is a system of vicious competition, for the purpose of procuring for each family the greatest amount, directly or indirectly, of the hard earnings of the industrious classes. It is a wretched arrangement of society, productive of little good to any, and of much evil to all.

That such a system should be brought to a speedy termination, your interest and your happiness clearly require; and therefore it is expedient that you should afford all the aid in your power to effect the proposed change with the least possible delay.

Jan. 18

ADDRESS TO THE RELIGIOUS OF EVERY DENOMINATION

Brethren, – I am intimately acquainted with your feelings and thoughts, and with their origin; and I therefore know that many of you most conscientiously entertain the opinions and feelings which you have been made to possess; and that under your present convictions there are many who would prefer death rather than be compelled, by any other human power than the force of a stronger conviction, to deny what they now deem the fundamental truths of their respective religions. This conscientious character has been formed equally all over the world, – for the Jew, the Christian, the Mahomedan, the Hindoo, and the Pagan. And by it you have been made to view each other as irrational beings, and to act most irrationally, both as individuals and as members of the particular sect, by whatever name that sect may be called, to which you have respectively been trained to belong.

You have desired to be superlatively wise and good; and many of you imagine you have become so by the choice of the religion which you think that by your own decision you have adopted, and therefore expect unspeakable rewards in some future state of existence.

I regret the necessity, even when it may be for their ultimate benefit, to give to any of my fellow-beings even momentary pain; but the highest duty that can be performed for man is to remove error from his mind, and to enable him to see those great truths, upon which his own permanent well-being and the happiness of his race depend.

My friends, it now becomes, therefore, my duty to inform you that one and all have been in error; that you have been deceived by your education, and that you have been made ready to sacrifice your lives in support of a fallacious supposition, which is the real origin of evil, and to oppose a principle which would produce the greatest permanent good to yourselves and to all mankind.

The character of man, as it is exhibited in the particular character belonging to each individual, is an effect of the circumstances in which he has been placed, modified by the original organization or constitution which he may have received at birth. We have all, therefore, been made to be as we are; and we have been compelled, from our infancy, to believe that we possess the power to feel and to think as we please; on which basis alone has been formed the whole fabric of human society. This supposition is the sole foundation of all the religions which have ever been invented – of all Governments, of all codes of laws, and of all institutions, which have ever existed in any country. Yet, strange as it may appear to you, there never has existed one single fact to prove the truth of this supposition: on the contrary, all facts connected with the subject show it to be one of those popular errors received, without investigation, into the human mind, which it has required the experience of all past ages to detect, unveil, and remove.

Contrary, though I well know it to be, to your present strongest conviction, it is nevertheless true that the greatest of all evils to man would be for him to discover that he is capable of feeling and thinking as he pleases, did he make no better use of his power than he has hitherto done.

Fortunately, however, for all, it is now ascertained by facts equally free to the examination of every one that man has not been created with the power to feel and to think as he pleases and consequently the direct road to the attainment of the highest virtues, and of a very superior state of earthly existence, is opened, and may be securely travelled by all of the human race, without their experiencing any of the innumerable evils which the contrary supposition entails, and particularly that arising from a diversity of religious opinions.

You desire to introduce into practice universal charity and kindness, and to hasten the period when peace and good will shall pervade the population of the world and when truth, being freed from error, shall be made to extend its dominion over every part of the habitable globe. These results can only be secured when all shall be taught, from infancy, to understand the laws of their nature; and, especially, to trace the causes which demonstrate that man has been formed to feel in obedience to the impressions which are made upon him; and to think in obedience to the strongest conviction which is made upon his mind.

If you desire that a state of society should be brought about, such as you have been taught to expect the Millenium to be, then you should endeavour to examine these subjects without prejudice; because, if you succeed in doing so, you will discover that the supposition that man has been organized with the power to feel and to think as he pleases is directly opposed to the attainment of such an object, while the contrary supposition would tend in every way to promote it.

And as to the future state of existence, about which you now trouble yourselves so much in vain, it is sure to arrive to all material things: but no one, with our present knowledge, can ascertain what this change will be. We may feel certain, however, that the best preparation for it here is a life replete with good feelings and kind actions, which the knowledge that man is not formed to think and to feel as he pleases will infallibly create in every human being.

You, therefore, brethren, of all men, are the most deeply interested in having the truth or error of this important position ascertained, that the proposed change of circumstances throughout society may be speedily introduced, and thus all be relieved from the demoralizing effects of poverty, ignorance, and hypocrisy.

Your minds, through the influence of the belief that you are capable of feeling and thinking as you please, have hitherto been kept in a state of irritation or anger towards each other, and towards those whom you deem irreligious. But a correct knowledge upon this subject will exhibit to you the error by which these irrational feelings are engendered; it will calm your minds, destroy within you the seeds of anger, and fill you with that pure and genuine charity which will create in you good and kind feelings only for every child of man.

That you may be thus blessed is the sincere desire of your friend and servant.

Jan. 19

ADDRESS TO THE BANKERS OF GREAT BRITAIN AND IRELAND

GENTLEMEN – You have amassed enormous sums of money, by means of a system which has reduced the real producers of wealth to the lowest state of misery. You are, however, blameless, having acted as all other men would have done under like circumstances. And many of you are, I know, sincerely anxious to remedy the evils which the system under which you have acted has produced. You are too intelligent not to understand, that every shilling which you have acquired has been circuitously drawn from the hard earnings of the agricultural labourer, or from the skill and industry of the operative manufacturer.

The industrious classes have thus paid dearly for the representation of their wealth, with which you have supplied them. You have given to them a shadow, and have received from them their substance.[a] Had they possessed sufficient knowledge, they would have created for themselves another representative of the wealth which they produced; one which they might have obtained for a small commission, without risk or the payment of additional interest, by which to exchange their commodities and services; and thus would have been spared that enormous loss, sustained by them, in upholding banking establishments and their proprietors, to the real benefit of none, and to the injury of all. Had this knowledge not been hidden from the industrious classes, by reason of the ignorance in which they were involved, they would have discovered, that to possess the requisites of a sound or correct representation, it must be one which should increase as their real wealth increased; and diminish as their wealth diminished; and which was unchangeable in its value; and thus your bank notes would be rendered valueless, and your gold and silver held in less estimation than iron and steel.

Existing circumstances have permitted you to acquire the artificial wealth you now possess, but others are about to arise, which will reduce that wealth again to its intrinsic value. By all your proceedings, you have not created one pennyworth of real wealth; but you have abundantly consumed that which the working classes produced; of which, however, by a legerdemain in society, they have been prevented consuming but a very small portion.

What is now to be done? How is justice to be awarded, and yet none injured? Let some of the surplus artifical sums which you possess be applied, while the circumstances of society give them currency, to create new arrangements, under new knowledge, which will secure for yourselves and your children permanent advantages, a hundred fold more beneficial for you and them than can be experienced under the miserable system of deception in which you and the whole world are now involved, and in which you are compelled to act the part of irrational beings, to your own incalculable loss and grievous injury.

The principles on which those new circumstances will be formed, have been developed, and submitted to the consideration of the British Cabinet; but no government can change the fundamental principles on which human society has been based, without the aid of an enlightened and influential public opinion.

Your early accession to the measures proposed will benefit yourselves, and

---

[a] See for example Ecclesiastes 8:13.

the community, in an essential manner; and will be the best compensation you can make to those classes upon whose wealth and ignorance you have hitherto subsisted.

Jan. 22

ADDRESS TO THE AGRICULTURALISTS AND MANUFACTURERS OF GREAT BRITAIN

Fellow Countrymen. – I have been for some time waiting to see if the stimulus erected by your downward progress in society, through your own competition, or the misery, which, by that progress, you are obliged to inflict upon the labourers and operatives whom you employ, would enable you to discover the hopeless prospect before you, while the system which renders that competition necessary shall continue to govern your transactions. But it seems the distress which you have experienced, or your desire to accumulate individual gain by an increased competition with those who bring forward similar productions with your own, has hitherto prevented you from detecting the uselessness of your contest, or from perceiving the degrading and injurious character of the system in which you are involved.

You invest large capitals in your business; you employ all the producers of wealth in Great Britain and Ireland; you use much skill, and apply great personal industry in your operations, and yet, very generally, your capital is depreciated; you are obliged to reduce the wages of labour; and then, after your utmost toil, and being subject to the most corroding anxieties, you frequently experience an entire loss of your property, and are reduced to poverty, without any hopes for the future.

This is your present situation; while you, and those whom you employ, are the producers of all the wealth which is annually consumed in the kingdom. You can create a superfluity of wealth for the non-producers in society; you can overstock all the markets in the world open to you, not only with useful, but with the most useless productions; and yet you cannot prevent yourselves and those whom you employ, from sinking in the scale of society, or from often experiencing an actual want of the common necessaries of life. Surely these results are sufficient to call your attention to the system itself, in which you are involved; to those perpetually recurring circumstances which proceed from it, and which disappoint all your skill, exertion, and perseverance.

Does the thought never occur to any of you, why is it that we can and do bring forward an overwhelming amount of wealth, which we annually increase, and yet that we are compelled, by an irresistible necessity, to use less and less of it ourselves?

Why, my friends, if you could be enabled to look out of the confused and perplexing system in which you are involved, and calmly examine the cause of such absurd anomaly, you would discover that you are troubling yourselves in vain; and that there is no real necessity for any risk of capital for so much toil, or for any anxiety whatever.

You have it now in your power, without any of these evils, to produce – first, abundantly for yourselves and families, and then, abundantly also for all those for whom, beyond your own supply, there is any necessity you should produce.

You, and the labourers and operatives whom you employ, now create all the wealth which the whole population annually consumes; while a very large part of your capital, skill, and industry, is most injudiciously or injuriously employed. Produce for yourselves; and exchange your respective commodities and services for equal labour in other commodities, or for equal services, and you will perpetually superabound in all things that the human heart can desire. And such proceedings, were you once trained in the practice of them, would be simplicity itself, compared with the involved and perplexed transactions, in which, under the existing system, you are hourly engaged.

Those whom you employ are now the slaves of the non-producing classes in society; and you are no better, under this system, than mere slave-drivers; with this difference upon the part of your slaves, compared with those I have seen in the West Indies,[a] and in the Southern States of North America, that your slaves have no legal claim upon you, when you do not require their services, for houses, food, clothes, medicine, and medical advice, when necessary; all of which coloured slaves have, and are, therefore, free from the excess of anxiety and corroding care with which your white slaves are overwhelmed.

But there is in this case, as in every other, a sufficient cause for the irrational state in which, apparently without hope of relief, you are now entangled.

You exist in the midst of circumstances the most irrational, and, therefore, the most opposed to your well-being, and to the happiness of the whole community, in which are a few individuals for whom you toil so unremittingly, without adequate remuneration for your skill, industry, and capital.

Your expectations of happiness are continually blasted by a system, the foundation of which is an error the most lamentable that can afflict the human race.

It is in consequence of this error, that you are unable to relieve yourselves from the difficulties which surround you on every side; that you are compelled to continue the wretched practice of an overstrained attempt to buy cheap and to sell dear; while the sole efect of such efforts is to compel you to sell every thing at the cheapest rate to the non-producers, and to buy every thing from them, in return, at the dearest possible rate; whereby you do not, in reality, obtain one per cent. in return for your capital, skill, and industry.

---

[a] Owen visited Jamaica in October 1828, on his way to Mexico.

Through this error you are made too irrational to perceive or to pursue your real interest. You are made to imagine that it lies in one course, when it is to be found only in an opposite direction. And, until this error shall be removed, your condition must remain as hopeless as that error has made it.

No parties, therefore, have a greater interest in detecting and removing that error than you, and those whom you employ.

For, while this error shall be suffered to remain, to compel, as it does, all men to feel, to think, and to act irrationally, you cannot unite in feelings, thoughts, or actions, with sufficient sincerity and honesty to attain the relief you require, or the prosperity which your ample means would otherwise secure to you. Without a union of purpose and of action, your case is hopeless; and there can be no honest union of purpose or of action among any portion of the human race while they shall live under a system founded on an error so directly opposed to the well-being and the happiness of the human race as that on which the whole system of society, in all countries and at all times, has been established.

You will naturally enquire what is this error, the consequences of which are so calamitous to ourselves and to the human race? It is the supposition, '*that man has been formed by Nature to feel as he likes, and to think as he pleases*;' on which supposition alone all the religion, governments, codes of laws, and institutions in the world, have been founded; and from which supposition alone all the circumstances in human society, of man's formation, have arisen. Hence the disunion, vices, misery, and irrationality, with which those circumstances have afflicted the human race.

Detecting this error, and understanding all the direful consequences which follow in its train, it is for you to break this spell of iniquity; for it is you, and those whom you employ, who are the first and greatest sufferers from these consequences. You coin the wealth and keep the purse strings of society; and, therefore, you possess the power now to say to Ignorance and to Poverty, and to the innumerable afflicting evils which they generate – 'Thus far have you advanced; but your race is run, your origin is detected, and you shall proceed no farther.'[a]

For, henceforward, the foundation of society shall be laid deep in real knowledge; and, in consequence, its practice will be alone truth, sincerity, union, charity, and kindness.

The motives to induce any to buy cheap, to sell dear, or to obtain any advantage whatever over their fellows, will cease to exist, and will be for ever extinguished. All such irrational motives will give place to those which are rational; or, correctly speaking, to those only which are strictly virtuous, or in accordance with nature.

[a] See for example Hebrews 12:1.

If you were in possession of the requisite knowledge to direct your conduct, you would have the power to effect this great change for the benefit of the whole population, in a shorter period, and more effectually, than any other class.

Truth is always simple; and the knowledge of it, when honestly stated, is easily acquired by any portion of the human race. You have, therefore, but to examine the facts, which will be given to the public on these important subjects. You will find them all in unison one with another; for, when you discover inconsistency of any description in what is placed before you, there must be an error somewhere. And fortunately, there is a *certain criterion*, both of *truth* and *error*; the former being always consistent with every other fact in the universe, while the latter is opposed to some, or many, or all of them.

By this criterion we know that man has not been made to feel as he likes, and to think as he pleases; and that every system, founded on the supposition that he possesses the power to do otherwise, must lead to endless errors in human conduct, deception of every kind, and, consequently, disunion; to continual irritation and to every kind of misery.

That you may acquire moral courage, sufficient to examine these subjects fairly and honestly, and thus be enabled to relieve yourselves from the difficulties which now oppress you, is the sincere wish of your friend.

Jan. 26

ADDRESS TO THE OPERATIVE MANUFACTURERS AND AGRICULTURAL LABOURERS IN GREAT BRITAIN AND IRELAND

INDUSTRY, properly directed, is the foundation of wealth in human society; or, in other words, knowledge and industry are the sources of all wealth, except that which the earth spontaneously produces. You have now more persevering industry than is to be found, probably, among any other portion of the human race. You obtain less wealth, and are subject to more care and anxiety, than any other class. It follows that you are deficient in knowledge, or these effects could not exist. Your skill and industry, rightly directed, are sufficient to produce more wealth than you could beneficially use, and to enable you to have your children educated to make them superior, physically and mentally, to any of the present generation.

But, to direct your skill and industry aright, you require knowledge of a superior description to any that has yet been given to you; and, above all things, you should endeavour to obtain this knowledge, for it will enable you to discover the necessity for union of mind and action to relieve you from the difficulties by which you are surrounded. And it will also discover to you the impossibility of being united in mind and action, while you shall be compelled to live under a system, the foundation of which is an error, forced from infancy into the minds of the whole population, in direct opposition to every known fact. In consequence of this error, you have been trained in a system of deception, and in bad or inferior habits; and thus have been made the lower class in society, although you are the actual producers of all the wealth which is consumed in the British empire, and much that is consumed by the population in many other districts, in distant parts of the world; and yet by this system you are prevented from producing more than a very small part, probably not one-tenth, of the real wealth which your present skill and industry, rightly directed, would enable you to bring into existence.

Such, then, is the necessity for you to acquire knowledge, to relieve you from the system which has placed you under such unfavourable circumstances, and which has afflicted you with so many calamities. You, and the existing population of the world, have been compelled to become irrational in your thoughts and actions, and hence the misery and vicious character, not only of your class, but of the human race. This irrational character has been created by all receiving the impressions from infancy that they possess the power to feel and to think as they please, although, as soon as an unprejudiced judgment can be applied to the subject, it becomes evident that there never existed one single fact to prove the supposition thus formed and steadily maintained in the human mind through all ages which have passed. It is this error which has created universal disunion among the human race. It is this error which now keeps you in bondage to your employers; to the non-producing classes; and to all the vicious circumstances which have necessarily arisen from the system of society founded on this error.

Try to feel differently from what you are forced to feel, try to think differently from the conviction which you are compelled to receive, and the impossibility of effecting either will break the spell produced by this most calamitous of all errors. Your mental chain will be snapped asunder, you will commence a new existence, and the road to the highest virtues and most permanent happiness will be straight before you, and most easy of attainment. Acquire the knowledge which this simple experiment will give, and you will soon attain moral courage sufficient to enable you to look with pity upon those who, through the effects of this error, have been compelled to oppress you, even upon those who may be engaged at this moment in active measures to endeavour to rivet more securely those chains by which they suppose you are held in bondage to them. The invaluable knowledge which you will thus acquire will destroy all germs of anger and desire of revenge, and it will fill you with compassion for your oppressors and opponents. You will at once perceive the cause of the malady which urges them on to the destruction of their own happiness and the well-being of all their fellows; and you will have no other feeling but a desire to remove the cause of their malady, and to do them all the good in your power. But you will have no merit for this conduct, because the knowledge which you will acquire, by the means recommended, will compel you thus to feel, to think, and to act.

A new day will arise upon you, in which there will be no desire on the part of any to oppress or offend; and every one will be, of necessity, filled with charity and kindness for all his race.

Be not afraid that this change in human affairs will not be now accomplished; for there are none to oppose its progress, except for a little time, because it will be discovered to be for the interest of all that it should be now effected. It will benefit every one from the highest to the lowest; nor is there now any power in man, whatever inclination may exist, to stay its course, except for a short period.

Truth will, henceforward, take the place which error has occupied in directing the transactions of the world; sincerity will supersede deception, virtue vice, and happiness misery.

Acquire this knowledge of the laws of your nature; spread it widely among your class; teach it to your children; wait calmly and patiently; but be of good courage, and you will see what great things will be accomplished without force or violence, for you and all mankind.

Jan. 1830

TO THE POLITICAL ECONOMISTS AND UTILITARIANS

Fellow-Labourers in the Cause of Human Improvement. You have long occupied yourselves in attempts to elicit the principles on the practice of which society is to be rendered wealthy and happy.

Upon these points, however, you have not yet satisfied yourselves or others; but your search for truth on these important subjects is, nevertheless, continued with unabated energy and interest. That your pursuits are highly important and praiseworthy all must readily acknowledge; yet, from causes which may now be rendered obvious, you have hitherto laboured in vain; for with much learning, great ingenuity, and extraordinary acuteness of certain intellectual faculties, you have, through many words, made that which is plain and simple in itself a most involved and perplexed theory, unintelligible to those who desire to obtain knowledge from facts, and to apply that knowledge to practise for the general benefit of society.

One party desires that wealth may superabound; and the other that the greatest amount of happiness shall be secured to the greatest number. The latter includes the former; but the former does not necessarily include the latter; for there may be, and often is, a superfluity of riches, which tends to produce partial happiness only for the few, and misery for the many. The Utilitarians,[a] therefore, aim at the highest object, and at that which most deserves the attention of rational beings; for the investigation of the means by which to produce the greatest amount of happiness for the greatest number, is a subject which must ever deeply interest the best and most intelligent of the human race. By taking a somewhat different view to that which you have hitherto done of the means by which wealth and happiness are to be produced, it will now, perhaps, be possible for you to discover how these may be obtained and permanently secured to all; for until all shall be made to possess them, it will be impracticable for the few permanently to enjoy either.

The direct road to the attainment of wealth and happiness is only to be found through a correct knowledge of the fundamental laws of human nature; of the conditions which are necessary for its happiness, of the best means by which these conditions can be obtained, and permanently secured to all. The most important fundamental laws of human nature, and the conditions essential to its happiness, are annexed. From a consideration of these laws and conditions in connection with each other, it is evident that there is but one mode by which mankind can secure for themselves a permanent sufficiency of wealth and a full enjoyment of happiness. It consists in creating a new arrangement of circumstances, which shall form for each individual a character so superior, physically, mentally, and morally, that a due exercise of all his faculties alone will be sufficient to obtain for him, in a rational state of existence, a full supply of those things which are essential to the happiness of human nature. In a development of the means by which this new arrangement of circumstances can be formed, a knowledge of the science of the influence of circumstances will be found indispensable; for this science it is which explains the origin of good and evil; and which exhibits the means by which evil may henceforward be extracted from human society, and good alone retained.

For as the circumstances in which human nature is placed are of a vicious or virtuous, or of a rational or irrational character, so will be the general character of all the population placed within those circumstances, varied only in the character of each individual by the difference at birth in the organization of each, united to the difference of time and place, when and

[a] In this period, mainly adherents to Jeremy Bentham's doctrine that 'the greatest happiness of he greatest number' should be the defining principle of moral judgement and activity. Owen dopted utilitarian language and psychology on occasion. But the Benthamites were free traders, nd hence he opposed their economic ideas.

where the impressions of those circumstances are received, and the order and strength by which they are made to act upon the individual.

A first Essay to direct the application of these principles to practice has been made in an *exposé*, which has been submitted to the consideration of the British Cabinet; but, perhaps, your learning, ingenuity, acuteness, and practical knowledge, may enable you to suggest a better mode of applying these principles to practice than the outlines proposed in that *exposé*. In this case, you cannot perform a greater service to your fellow-beings, than by giving the result of that knowledge to the public; and, if it shall appear to be founded on reason, and of a practical nature, no one will more sincerely rejoice, or be more willing to aid, to the full extent of his abilities, in its reduction to practice, than your friend and servant.

Jan. 29

FUNDAMENTAL LAWS OF HUMAN NATURE

1st. That human nature, in the aggregate, is a compound, consisting of animal propensities, intellectual faculties, and moral qualities.

2d. That these propensities, faculties, and qualities, are united in different proportion in each individual.

3d. That this difference in the proportion of the same general propensities, faculties, and qualities, constitutes the original difference between one individual and another.

4th. That this difference in each is made by a power unknown to the individual, and therefore, without his knowledge or consent.

5th. That each individual comes into existence within certain external circumstances, and that these, acting upon his peculiar original organisation, during the early period of his life, impress their general character upon him; and that thus the local and national character of each individual is formed independently of himself.

6th. That the influence of these general external circumstances is modified in a particular manner, by the peculiar organisation of each individual: and that thus the distinctive character of each is formed and maintained through life.

7th. That no infant has the power of deciding at what period of time or in what part of the world he shall come into existence; of what parents he shall be born, in what particular religion he shall be trained, or by what other external circumstances he shall be surrounded, from birth to death.

8th. That each individual is so organised, that, when young, he may be made to receive, either true ideas, derived from a knowledge of facts, or to receive false notions, derived from the imagination, unsupported by, or in opposition to facts.

9th. That each individual is so organised, that he must necessarily become irrational, when he is made from infancy to receive, as truths, false notions; and can only become rational when he shall be made, from infancy, to receive true ideas, unaccompanied by any of an opposite character.

10th. That each individual is so organised, that, when young, he may be trained to acquire injurious habits only, or beneficial habits only; or that he may be made to acquire a mixture of both.

11th. That each individual is so organised that he must believe according to the strongest conviction that is made upon his mind; and that this conviction cannot be given to him by his will; but that the will is generally formed by the conviction which he is compelled to receive.

12th. That each individual is so organised that he must like that which is pleasant to him, or, in other words, that which produces upon him agreeable sensations; and dislike that which is unpleasant to him, or in other words, that which produces in him disagreeable sensations; and that he cannot know, previous to experience, what particular sensations new objects will produce in him.

13th. That each individual is so organised that his will is formed for him by the effect, either immediately or more remote, which circumstances produce on his individual organisation.

14th. That each individual is so organised that not only his *will*, his *feelings*, and his *thoughts*, are formed *for him* by the effect of the impressions which circumstances produce upon his individual organisation; *But that his whole character, physical, mental, and moral, is also thus formed independently of himself.*

15th. That each individual is so organised that impressions which, at their commencement, and for a limited time, produce agreeable sensations, will, if continued without intermission, beyond a certain period, become, first, indifferent, then disagreeable, and ultimately painful.

16th. That each individual is so organised that when, beyond a certain degree of rapidity, impressions succeed each other, the effect produced is to dissipate, weaken, and otherwise injure his physical, mental, or moral powers, and to diminish his enjoyment.

17th. That each individual is so organised, that his highest health, his greatest progressive improvement, and his permanent happiness, depend upon the due cultivation of all his physical, intellectual, and moral faculties and powers; upon all these constituent parts of his nature being called into action at a proper period of life; and upon their being afterwards temperately exercised, according to the strength and capacity of the individual.

18th. That each individual is so organised that he is made to receive a vicious, unhappy, or what is commonly called a bad character, when he has been created at birth with an unfavourable proportion of the general propensities, faculties, and qualities, of our common nature; and that, when so unfortunately organised, he has been placed, from birth, amidst the most unfavourable circumstances.

19th. That each individual is so organised that he is made to receive what is called a medium character when he has been created at birth with a favourable proportion of the general propensities, faculties, and qualities, of our common nature, and when the external circumstances which surround him from birth are such as to produce continued vicious or unfavourable impressions.

Or, when he has been created with an unfavourable proportion of these propensities, faculties, and qualities, and when the external circumstances in which he is placed are of a character to impress him with favourable sensations only:

Or, when he has been created with a favourable proportion of some of these propensities, faculties, and qualities, and an unfavourable proportion of others; and when the individual has been placed, through life, in varied external circumstances which make on him impressions which produce some good and some evil sensations. This last compound has hitherto been the general lot of mankind.

20th. That each individual is so organised that he is made to receive a superior character when his original organisation is such as to contain the best proportion of the propensities, faculties, and qualities, of which human nature is formed, and when the circumstances which surround the individual from birth are of a character to make impressions upon him which produce superior sensations only; or, in other words, when the circumstances or laws, institutions, and customs, under which he lives, are all in unison with the laws of his nature.

CONDITIONS ESSENTIAL TO HUMAN HAPPINESS

1st. The possession of a good organisation, physical, mental, and moral.

2d. The power of procuring, at pleasure, whatever is necessary to keep the organisation in the best state of health.

3d. That an education shall be given to the whole population, which shall cultivate in the best manner, from infancy to maturity, their physical, intellectual, and moral powers.

4th. The inclination and the means of promoting the happiness of our fellow-beings.

5th. The inclination and the means of continually increasing our stock of knowledge.

6th. The means of enjoying a superior society; and, more especially, the power of associating, at pleasure, with those for whom we cannot avoid feeling the most regard and the greatest affection.

7th. The means of travelling at pleasure.

8th. A release from superstition, from supernatural fears, and from the dread of death.

9th. That the origin of evil shall be removed from society; that is, the supposition that man has been so constituted as to have the power of feeling and thinking as he pleases, and that in consequence of the removal of this erroneous supposition, that all shall be enabled to speak only what they feel and think.

10th. That all the laws, institutions, and arrangements of society shall be in accordance with the laws of human nature.

ADDRESS TO THE INFANT SCHOOL SOCIETIES, AND TO THE PATRONS OF INFANT SCHOOLS

You have seen the effects of Infant Schools, as they have been introduced into practice, in various parts of the kingdom; and that practice, imperfect as it is, has been sufficient to induce you to encourage the extension of them throughout the British dominions. But Infant Schools, upon the principles from which they originated and were first introduced into practice, do not belong to the system of society in which you, in common with the whole human race are involved.

The Infant School, from which all modern Infant Schools in Europe and America have emanated, belongs, altogether to another system of society; to one the reverse in all respects of that by which the world has been hitherto governed.[a] This Infant School was established as the first practical step in a system intended to supersede that which has ever pervaded savage and civilised life. It was an experiment to ascertain how the practice of this new system would be received by those educated under the principles of the old; and the result has been most satisfactory.

But these Infant Schools are an anomaly in the system in which you and the inhabitants of the world have been trained to feel, to think, and to act; and, assuredly, those Schools, on the principles on which the first was established, or the system which the world now supports, must be abandoned; for they are in direct opposition to each other. The existing system of the world (and there

[a] Owen's school at New Lanark. See *infra*, vol. 1, pp. 120–42.

never has been any other known to the present race of man) has been founded altogether on the supposition that each individual is born with the power to feel and to think as he pleases.

The Infant School was founded in order to exhibit to the world the fallacy of this supposition; in order to prove that the nature of man has not been understood by our ancestors; and that the laws of human nature have been, hitherto, an enigma even to the intelligent of the past and present time. It was founded, first, to demonstrate to the learned and the unlearned, that man does not possess the power to feel and to think as he likes, or to form his own character. Secondly, to prove that the human race has been, through all past time up to the present hour, irrational, and that every individual may, hereafter, be trained from infancy to become a rational or consistent being in his feelings, thoughts, and actions. Thirdly, to prove that all the inferior passions, vices, and miseries of mankind, proceed from the supposition that each individual has the power, within himself, to feel and to think as he pleases; and that from the knowledge that he has not this power will emanate universal charity and kind feelings, and that a very superior character will be formed for the whole human race. Fourthly, to prove that all the nations of the earth are, at this moment, under a mental delusion with regard to themselves, and the means of attaining a superior character and happiness; and, consequently, that a rational Infant School and the present system of society cannot co-exist.

A right system of education has never yet been seen in practice, as one possessing that character could not exist under the system which has been alone known in the world. The prejudices which this system has forced all to receive from infancy have been an insurmountable obstacle to the formation of an establishment to educate human beings to become rational.

All seminaries of learning have been founded to instil the notions of man's responsibility, under the supposition that he is so organised as to possess the power to feel and to think as he pleases; and consequently they have been established, without one exception, to destroy, in the most effectual manner, the rational and superior faculties of the human race. None of these seminaries, therefore, deserve notice, when the foundation of a rational system of instruction for the rising generation from infancy is under consideration.

The rational Infant School, which was established at New Lanark, and opened on the 1st of January, 1816, by a public discourse, explanatory of the principles on which it was founded, and of the consequences which were expected to result from its establishment,[a] emanated from a knowledge of human nature, derived from a calm and attentive consideration of the facts relative to its organisation manifested at the birth of an infant, and of the formation of its character during its growth to maturity. From an accurate

[a] See *Address Delivered to the Inhabitants of New Lanark* (1816) (*infra*, vol. 1, pp. 120–42).

attention to those facts it became obvious that the whole character of every infant, child, and man, is formed *for* him; that in every instance, at every instant of time, it is created by a union of the original organisation of the infant with the impressions made upon it by the general and particular circumstances in which the individual is placed from birth to death; and that the character of every human being is, without an exception, an effect necessarily proceeding from these united causes.

Consequently all that man can do for man is to adopt the most efficient measures to improve the future organisation of all individuals of his race, and to surround them by those circumstances only which experience may prove to be the most effectual to create the best or most superior character in each of them. To attempt to establish a system of training and instruction for the human race, upon any principles than those developed by nature will continue to make man an ignorant, imbecile, vicious, irrational, and miserable being, inferior to many of the animals in health, consistency, and enjoyment, and superior to them only by his powers of speech and invention.

If, therefore, you desire to encourage the introduction of rational Infant Schools throughout society, you must acquire a knowledge of the principles on which they are founded, and the practice which is necessary to their success. And more, if you wish the children and the public to derive permanent benefit from them, you must establish other schools on the same principles, in which to receive the children who shall have passed through the course of education which will be given to them, in the rational Infant Schools. And in these seminaries of instruction, in which none but rational circumstances should be permitted to exist, the character of each individual should be matured; and then, and then only, will the saying be verified, that 'train up a child in the way he should go, and when he is old he will not depart from it.'[a]

But, perhaps, you will now ask, where is there a rational Infant School to be seen as a specimen, that we might adopt its practice? None exists; none can exist under your present system of belief, respecting the power of man to feel and think as he pleases. The nearest approximation that has yet been made was the New Lanark Infant School, as it existed from the year 1822 to 1824, when it approached as near to a rational Infant School as the prejudices of the proprietors and of the public would bear, and children were then seen to enjoy a slight foretaste of what a rational system of society will give to mankind.

The Infant School, on its original principles, has ceased to exist for some years at New Lanark. The schools for the older children at this establishment are, however, excellent schools under the old system for children of the working classes. Mr Charles Walker,[b] who now superintends the establishment, does

[a] See Peter 22:6.

[b] Charles Walker (b. 1798): the son of Owen's friend and partner, John Walker. For an account of New Lanark under Walker, see *New Moral World*, vol. 5, no. 25 (13 April 1839), pp. 385–8.

great justice to this department, in which he has retained, to the full extent, as much of the new and rational system as the conscientious scruples of his partners and the system of the Society of Friends will admit.

Before, however, you can establish a rational Infant School, the ignorance of society, with regard to the fundamental laws of human nature must be removed, and especially it must be generally known, acknowledged, and felt, that man has not the power to think and feel as he pleases; and the circumstances which now exist in opposition to this fact must be removed, so that all in unison with it must be introduced, to replace the former, and then, and not before, the inestimable and innumerable advantages of a rational education may be witnessed and enjoyed.

The present Infant Schools which you support and patronise, are evidences of your good intentions, and also of the vicious circumstances in which you are involved. They are, in very many instances, a mockery or caricature of the original school, and have no pretensions to be considered, as that school was intended to be, the first practical step towards a rational system of education; or, in other words, a new arrangement of circumstances in which to place children, as nearly approximating to virtuous and rational circumstances as the ignorance of the present vicious system will admit. And these new arrangements were so formed in consequence of the founder of the rational system of society seeing the children of the operatives at New Lanark, and in other manufacturing districts, surrounded from their birth with so many *unfavourable* and *vicious* circumstances. Your aid, therefore, to remove more and more of the existing vicious circumstances from around all children, and to create those of a superior character, with which to replace the vicious circumstances, will confer a practical benefit upon the human race, such as at present it knows not how to estimate.

Jan. 30

ADDRESS TO THE MEMBERS OF THE LEARNED, NAVAL, AND MILITARY PROFESSIONS

Gentlemen – you have been trained and placed, by the circumstances of the society in which you have lived, in professions by which to gain a livelihood or distinction. No one who is rational can attach blame to you on this account. Your professions have arisen from two suppositions – first, that it is impracticable to form arrangements to produce wealth to satisfy all; and secondly, that man is capable of feeling and thinking, and consequently, of acting as he pleases. The time, however, has arrived when by a new power unknown to our ancestors, more real wealth can be easily created than the inhabitants of the world can advantageously use; or than they will ever desire to possess. And the late progress of knowlege has been such that it is become publicly known that it does not belong to the nature of man to feel or to think as he pleases; but that he is compelled to feel and to think, according to laws of his nature, made without his knowledge or consent.

In consequence of these changes in society, your professions have become not only unnecessary, but most injurious to yourselves, and to every individual of the human race. It becomes, therefore, your duty to yourselves and to your fellow men, to aid in creating other arrangements, to supersede all necessity for the longer continuance of your professions; and your duty in this case will be found to be in strict accordance with your interest and your happiness.

A priesthood will be no longer necessary in the world, because, when the change of circumstances proposed shall be effected (and the knowledge now existing will effect it), each child will be so taught, trained, and placed, that he will be, of necessity, honest, sincere, and intelligent, and will possess unlimited charity and kindness for his fellow-beings, the practice of which virtues will constitute that pure and genuine religion which can alone be of any real utility to God or man.

The profession of law will be no longer necessary; for individual riches under the new arrangements will give place to a superfluity of public wealth, which will by a rational application of manual, mental, and scientific power, be annually produced, to an amount greatly beyond the wants or wishes of all. No one will then be required by law to think, or to say that he thinks, contrary to his conviction; or to feel, or say that he feels, in opposition to his impressions; for all will speak only what they are obliged to think and to feel, and they will act accordingly. Under these rational circumstances, law, or the ingenuity of lawyers, will not be required. All differences, if it be possible for differences to arise in a rational state of society, will be speedily adjusted by the prompt decision of individuals, formed by a rational education to be honest and intelligent, and who would be duly appointed to perform these friendly offices for society.

Physicians will be no longer necessary, for every child will acquire sufficient knowledge of the anatomy and physiology of the human frame to understand the nature of his own organisation and particular constitution, and thus be enabled to adopt proper measures for the prevention or speedy cure of any disease; for, as each individual must possess a more intimate acquaintance with his own constitution than any physician is likely to obtain, each will regulate his food and exercise as his feelings may dictate. Good air, proper exercise, temperance in all things, and the absence of corroding anxieties, together with the enjoyment of full liberty to speak whatever they may feel and think, will tend to keep all individuals in the best state of health and spirits.

Surgeons may be occasionally useful, but accidents or diseases, requiring surgical operations, are not likely to be frequent, when all shall be trained from infancy to be rational; and when, in order to produce this character, all must necessarily be surrounded, through life, with rational circumstances only.

Your professions have been generally filled by individuals, who, under the old irrational notions of society, were supposed to possess by nature superior intellectual powers, when compared with the other members of the family from which they were selected.

In the improved society that will arise, when all shall be trained in rational circumstances only, the individuals naturally possessing superior intellectual faculties will become members of a new profession, in which their powers will be applied to the most valuable, instead of the most injurious purposes. They will be taught to acquire a correct knowledge of the influence of circumstances, in giving a superior or an inferior direction to the human faculties, and will thus become 'Professors of the Science of the Formation of Character;' which science will soon be discovered to be, beyond all comparison, more valuable to themselves and their fellow-beings than all other sciences hitherto discovered. The practice of this new profession will become, in a rational state of existence, the most important of all occupations; and, therefore, the first department in every society.

In this new state of existence, when men shall be taught from infancy to understand the laws of their nature, and the conditions necessary for its happiness, no motive will arise to render it necessary that men should be united for the purpose of destroying each other's lives, their productions and all the means of human happiness. They will discover that all such proceedings, through the past ages of the world, have been the very essence of irrationality.

The energies and faculties necessary to conduct war, or in other words, to destroy upon a large scale, and to inflict misery upon nations, will, under the change which knowledge will speedily produce, be applied to create real wealth; to preserve and to distribute it; and thus to promote the happiness of the community, to which those valuable powers belong. And the immense waste of human labour, now sustained in the creation and support of the naval and military professions, will also, under the change about to commence, be applied to the preservation and improvement of society, in order to secure to every one the greatest amount of enjoyment of which his organisation is susceptible; and of the nature and extent of this enjoyment no one yet can form a just estimate. No one portion of society will feel the magnitude and importance of this change in a higher degree than those individuals who by their professions are compelled to murder some of the most noble and generous of their fellow-beings; and to render void the labour of others who have been occupied in producing for the public the necessaries, comforts, and luxuries of life. It is not possible, irrational as men have hitherto been forced to become, for a member of the naval or military profession to reflect upon his occupation without feeling deeply conscious of the misery which it inflicts upon the human race.

Under the change proposed, those individuals who have hitherto been compelled to be the destroyers of the human race, would become the most active promoters of its happiness. In hastening the proposed change – a change under which the world will be governed by knowledge and not by ignorance, Priests, Lawyers, Physicians, and members of the naval and military professions, have all an immediate and deep interest.

Permit me, therefore, to request your best attention to the consideration of the principles on which this change is proposed to be made; and of the consequences which these principles will produce in practice.

TO THE LITERARY MEMBERS OF THE BRITISH POPULATION

The great object of your ambition is to acquire knowledge, but, while you are ignorant of the laws of your nature, what knowledge can you be supposed to attain, capable of being applied to any useful or important purposes?

It has been said that knowledge is power; and it may be added with equal truth that knowledge is happiness. You wish for both, but possess neither, excepting to a very limited extent. The reason is obvious; the knowledge you have obtained has been that of useless or inferior objects; your acquaintance with these has been limited, and the facts you have discovered have been united with errors of such magnitude, as to depreciate, and to render useless or injurious, much of the knowledge which has been acquired, and upon which, therefore, you set a most erroneous estimate.

How little real benefit or happiness do the public derive from all your literary pursuits, and from all the establishments for the acquisition of learning, when compared with the time therein consumed, and with the expenditure, national and individual, which they involve! It is sufficient, however, that the inutility of such pursuits has at length become obvious; and that a different direction is about to be given to mental investigation, by means of which man will obtain a knowledge of his own nature; and thus be enabled to make a right, and therefore beneficent use, of all the less useful or unimportant knowledge now in his possession, or which he may hereafter acquire.

For the errors of the past, no one, who has, by acquiring a knowledge of the laws of human nature, been rendered rational, will ever consider you as blameable. These errors have been the necessary, the unavoidable results of the unfavourable and vicious circumstances in which all have been trained, and under which you have hitherto been compelled to live. In giving a new direction to the pursuits of many of your number, and in re-modelling, and thus rendering efficient for the prosecution of future important designs, the greater proportion of your establishments, your best interests would be consulted; for, by this proceeding, the greatest amount of real happiness would be afforded and permanently secured to all. If it be a truth (and such all known facts prove it to be), that man never possessed the power of feeling and thinking as he pleases, but that he feels and thinks in obedience to the laws of his nature, then do your theological studies, your law investigations, your moral systems, and your theories of government, rest upon an error which is indefensible, and which can no longer be upheld in opposition to public opinion.

By this single, simple, and now almost the best ascertained and most obvious of all abstract truths, it being in the power of every one to demonstrate it for himself, your learned treatises on divinity, law, morals, and government are rendered, not only of no avail, but are proved to be a positive evil to the world, in consequence of their filling the mind with confused and fanciful images and notions, which perplex, confound, and ultimately destroy all the rational faculties which belong to human nature.

The training which man has thus received through past ages has made him a weak, imbecile, and miserable animal, instead of a superior, intelligent, and rational being; a character which each individual is destined to acquire, as soon as society shall obtain a knowledge of human nature, and shall live under circumstances in unison with its laws.

In the promotion of this great change, all the powers of your mind may, most advantageously for yourselves, and others, now be called into requisition. A new religion, a new code of laws, a new moral system, a new theory of government, and a new science of education, will shortly be found indispensable.

Rational books of instruction for the rising generation, and a complete collection of the most useful real objects, or the best representations of these, with correct explanations of each, will also be immediately required.

The history of past ages too, in order to answer any useful purpose, must be entirely re-written.

But in assisting to render perfect the science of the formation of human character, by a full development of the influence of circumstances in producing vice or virtue, misery or happiness, among the human race, your services will be found the most important.

The change, then, which, in consequence of a knowledge of the laws of human nature being obtained, is now about to become general, will be highly favourable to the advancement of your future views and proceedings.

Every thing must, of necessity, assume a new character; but the whole arrangement of circumstances proposed being in strict accordance with nature, the change must unavoidably produce universal satisfaction and happiness.

Feb. 1

TO THE ARISTOCRACY OF GREAT BRITAIN

My Lords and Gentlemen, – Circumstances of former times, existing without your knowledge, have placed you, in the present day, in a situation in society, most injurious to yourselves and the population of the empire.

In consequence of your artificial condition from birth, you acquire feelings and sentiments which force you to become most irrational; and to believe, that the world was formed solely to administer to your gratification. Habits of luxury and of self-importance, destructive to your health and real enjoyment, are thus formed; and these involve a most useless and unreasonable waste of human labour; and absorb the means by which, if rightly directed, the general happiness of the community might be permanently secured.

In consequence of this combination of unnatural and vicious circumstances, you are encouraged to think, that the mass of the people exists only that you may employ them to promote your own views, and to provide for your real, or for your still more numerous imaginary wants.

By these means, an aritificial state of society has been created, which gives you an apparent interest, in direct opposition to that of the remainder of the British population, of which you form but a very small portion. I say an apparent interest, for such it is not in reality; there is but one true interest among the whole human race; which is, that every individual shall possess the means of obtaining the best of every thing for his nature, be trained to know what these things are, and to enjoy them rationally.

Your class is a formidable obstacle to the attainment of these objects; and it is now requisite that this obstacle should be removed; but you have rights of happiness, which require attention, as much as those of any other portion of the community.

Your habits of thinking and of acting have been formed for you; and your happiness depends upon being free to retain these habits or not, according to your pleasure; but arrangements may be made by which, without inconvenience or disadvantage to either party, your interest and happiness, as well as that of the public, would be permanently secured.

It is possible for you to retain such habits as custom may have rendered necessary to your enjoyment of life, and yet, essentially to aid in the promotion of a change, in which the happiness of your own posterity, and of all your fellow-beings, is equally involved.

You have hitherto made the laws, and generally controlled the Government of the British Empire. You have formed the one, and directed the other, to give and to secure peculiar privileges to your order, in opposition to the superior interests of at least nine-tenths of the whole population.

Experience has fully proved what effects these privileges have produced upon the members of your order, and upon the public, it must now be evident to yourselves, that under those privileges, you cannot possess, individually or collectively, one in a hundred of the superior advantages, which another state of society will afford you.

Modern discoveries in physical science, and of the real nature of man, have produced a new æra in the history of our race. The discoveries in physical science may now be made to aid in the creation of more wealth than the population of the world will desire to consume; and the discoveries which have been made of the laws of human nature have developed the means by which, without awarding particular privileges to any class, the permanent happiness of all may be effectually secured.

The discoveries in physical science have already placed, at the disposal of the British Government a power, for the production of wealth greater than could be created without them, by three times the present number of the producing classes throughout the world; and this power – enormous as it may appear, is but in its infancy – it is advancing in a continually increasing ratio, and to its further progress there can be no assignable limit.

Wealth and power, therefore, the chief objects of desire to your order, will, with the exception of a dominion over your fellow beings, which hereafter will belong to no party whatever, be fully secured to you as individuals, under the changes about to arise in society.

The knowledge that has been acquired of the laws of human nature, not only developes the cause of all the evil that has ever existed in the world, and the means of removing the cause of that evil; but it discovers a new mode for the government of the human race, which will render contest and competition unnecessary, and will effectually destroy in man all desire to domineer over his fellows. For he will clearly perceive that the path of happiness is to be found in another, and a very different course; and the real object of all being to secure happiness, that course alone will be invariably followed.

Were it possible for you to mistake your interest so far, as to attempt to oppose this change, you would discover that no efforts of yours can arrest its progress; but you may, on the other hand, essentially promote it, by employing some of your surplus funds, for which you would obtain an advantageous return, to assist in the creation of a new arrangement of circumstances, in conformity to the laws of our nature, by means of which a superior character, and an independence, would be insured to all who shall hereafter be born.

You are even, under the existing notions of society, too enlightened not to perceive that the old system of the world is worn out; that it is now producing, among the labouring class, the miseries arising from poverty or the fear of poverty; among the middle classes, the miseries arising from competition and contest; and, among the upper classes, as well as among the two former, the miseries arising from universal hypocrisy, the practice of which the very nature of the system necessarily engenders.

I therefore recommend to your most serious attention, the study of the principles on which it is proposed to effect a change in the moral, political, and commercial policy of the British empire, and to create a new arrangement of circumstances, in accordance with the new moral and scientific knowledge which every where pervades the population of the British dominions; in order that Great Britain may now take the lead in saving the world from the most overwhelming evils, moral and physical, with which it has ever yet been threatened.

That you may assist in effecting this change, in proportion to the influence which you possess in the empire, is the earnest desire of, &c.

February 4

TO THE CONDUCTORS OF THE LONDON PRESS

GENTLEMEN, – Having finished the addresses which appeared to me necessary to arouse public attention to the lamentable errors and consequent evils of the present system, previous to the development of the cause of, and remedy for, the existing distresses within the British dominions; permit me to return you my best thanks, for the liberal manner in which you have met my request, in publishing them to the world.

I am aware, that in so doing, you have run the risk of immediate pecuniary loss, in consequence of the principles which my feelings of duty compel me to advocate being directly opposed to the most deep-rooted prejudices and apparent interest of your subscribers. In no instance however, have I ever made an open and honest appeal to any public body of men, without being responded to by feelings of kindness and generosity; proving to me, that human nature, whenever it shall have justice done to it, by being placed in circumstances congenial with, and not opposed to it, will always exhibit every kind of excellence, as well as its capability of attaining in this life a high state of rational enjoyment.

February 4

[illegible]

[illegible]

Adieu.

TO THE [illegible] OF THE [illegible]

[illegible]

[illegible]

[illegible]

THE NEW RELIGION;

OR,

Religion founded on the immutable Laws of the Universe, *contrasted* with all Religions founded on Human Testimony,

AS DEVELOPED IN

A PUBLIC LECTURE,

DELIVERED BY

MR. OWEN,

At the London Tavern, October 20, 1830,

"To take into consideration the Advantages and Disadvantages of Religion, *as it has been hitherto taught*, in forming the Character of Man, and in Governing the World."

For modes of Faith let graceless zealots fight;
His can't be wrong whose life is in the right.
POPE.

Take advice, my good friends, go the Quaker's broad way,
'Tis free, without turnpikes, so nothing to pay.
GREEN'S *Poem of the Spleen.*

LONDON:

Published by J. BROOKS, 421, Oxford-street; C. STRANGE, 21, Paternoster-Row; J. WATSON, 33, Windmill-street, Finsbury-square; the Co-operative Bazaar, 19, Greville-street, and to be had of all the Booksellers.

Price 1½d. or 8s. per hundred to Individuals who intend them for gratuitous distribution.

Printed by J. Brooks, 421, Oxford-street.

Epigraphs:

Alexander Pope, *An Essay on Man* (1767), p. 81.

See Matthew Green, *The Spleen. An Epistle (in Verse) Inscribed to His Particular Friend* (1737).

THE NEW RELIGION
1830

The Meeting was called by Mr Owen, and was respectably and numerously attended, there being upwards of 1000 persons assembled. At one o'clock Mr Owen took the Chair, and proceeded to address the Meeting as follows:[a]

Under the new circumstances of general political excitement, which have lately arisen throughout the civilized part of the globe,[b] not one practical step can be wisely taken, in the improvement of society, upon a firm and permanent base, until it shall be calmly and temperately decided, whether the foundation of all new arrangements to ameliorate the condition of the human race shall be religion, and what religion; or facts derived from all the past and present experience of mankind.

This is now a vital question of paramount interest to the human race, and must be decided, not by angry feelings, or the violence of passion, or the errors of country, or by prejudices of any kind, but by facts which cannot deceive, and by self-evident deductions from those facts.

In the examination of this subject, so deeply involving the highest interests of humanity, I will endeavour to avoid hurting the feelings of any of my fellow-beings as much as truth will admit, and I trust every speaker to-day will also endeavour to keep in mind, that we do not meet here for personal contest, but to elicit, if possible, high and important truths that may be applied to practice for the permanent benefit of all.

Hitherto the character of man has been formed, and the world has been governed, under the direct influence of what is called religion; and facts to-day prove what that character has been formed to be, and how the nations of the earth have been governed.

All will admit that the character of man is no where what it ought to be; and

[a] First delivered as a lecture at the London Tavern, 20 October 1830. Many of the themes addressed here were developed in Owen's *Six Lectures on Charity* (1833).

[b] Revolution broke out in France in July 1830 after a coalition of liberal monarchists and republicans rebelled against the Crown. After three days' fighting by workers, Charles X was driven into exile and Louis-Philippe, Duc d'Orléans (1773–1850) became King of France until 1848.

also that no country has yet been rationally governed to promote permanently the general advantage of its population.

It is, therefore, a legitimate object of enquiry to ascertain the real cause of these errors and evils.

Under the arrangements which have hitherto existed for educating and governing man, four general characters have been produced among the human race.

These four classes of characters appear to be formed, under the past and present arrangements of society, from four different original organizations at birth, which may be numbered one, two, three, and four.

No. 1 May be termed the conscientious religious in all countries.

No. 2 Unbelievers in the truth of any religion, but who strenuously support the religion of their country, under the conviction that, although religion is not necessary to insure their own good conduct, it is eminently required to compel others to act right.

No. 3 Unbelievers who openly avow their disbelief in the truth of any religion, such as Deists, Atheists, Sceptics, etc but who do not perceive the laws of nature relative to man as an individual, or when united in a social state.

No. 4 Disbelievers in all past and present religions, but believers in the eternal unchanging laws of the universe, as developed by facts derived from all past experience; and who, by a careful study of these facts, deduce from them the religion of nature.

Class No. 1 is formed, under certain circumstances, from those original organizations which possess at birth strong moral and weak intellectual faculties. They usually become amiable, honest according to the religious notions they receive, good-natured, and what are called in the present defective state of the human character, the good members of society. They very seldom govern any class, sect, party, or country, as individuals, but they have considerable influence when acting in a body as a party, for they are numerous in all civilized countries.

Class No. 2 is composed of those individuals who by nature possess a smaller quantity of moral, and a larger quantity of intellectual, faculty. Of those who have sufficient intellect to discover the most glaring inconsistencies between all religious and undisputed facts, and therefore are compelled to disbelieve the truth of any religion, but who are deficient, under existing circumstances, in intellectual capacity to proceed further in the investigation of the laws of nature, and without sufficient moral faculty to declare their disbelief in the truth of religion. They have also too little intellectual faculty to discover the incongruity of their own opinions or notions; that, although conscientious belief in religion is not necessary to make them good and useful members of society, yet it is absolutely requisite to make other men honest.

They are therefore unavoidably hypocrites upon almost all occasions, or act from thoughts and feelings not publicly expressed. Usually these men, who are endowed with much cunning, called worldly wisdom, and with physical activity, are, under the existing system of the world, at the head of every class, sect, profession, party, and country; and from it, in all nations, the aristocracies are generally formed. The number of this original constitution of mind is considerable, perhaps equal to No. 1.

Class No. 3 is composed of men of strong moral and moderate intellectual faculty; of men who possess as much intellectual faculty as enables them to perceive the discordance between all the religions of the world and the general facts around them; also to discover that if religion is not necessary to make them honest, it is not required to make others conscientious: having at the same time as much moral faculty as to induce them, in opposition to their worldly interest, to express their conscientious convictions in opposition to the religious notions or dogmas of the country they inhabit; but yet without sufficient intellect, educated and placed as they have been, to investigate sufficiently for practice the laws of human nature and of society.

These characters are much abused by classes Nos 1 and 2, and have hitherto suffered all manner of injustice from them, owing to their superiority of intellect to the first, and their superiority of intellect and moral faculty to the second. They are not very numerous, chiefly in consequence of the obstacles which the present system places in the way of moral honesty.

Class No. 4 comprises those who, by nature, possess a high degree of intellectual and moral faculty; who distinctly perceive the opposition which exists between the fundamental notions on which, alone, all religions rest, and the everlasting laws by which man is governed, from his earliest formation to his decomposition at death; who can trace in their minds the necessary results of these laws when they shall be applied in practice, and who can comprehend a highly improved state of human existence, formed in all its parts in unison and perfect accordance with those laws; who have also sufficient moral faculty to discover the vast superiority of truth over falsehood in the intercourse between man and man, and who possess moral courage sufficient to contend openly against what they are compelled to believe are the errors of antiquity. This class of natural minds, under the present ignorance relative to the improvement of human organization, is not numerous; it has, along with some of class No. 3, supplied the martyrs of former days, and they are always prepared to go to the stake if necessary, to promote the advance of general knowledge, and permanently to increase the happiness of the human race. When men shall learn real wisdom, through a rational education, and be taught to understand the laws of their nature, and to act upon them, the original organization of almost all human beings will be formed of these qualities.

We thus see, that as long as the character of man shall be formed under the influences of religion, as it has been hitherto taught to mankind, and as long as the world shall continue to be governed under these influences, the four preceding characters which have been described will, with endless and small varieties, be produced. And the necessary consequence of training the present varied organization of man to acquire these artificial characters is to degrade human nature, and to instil into the human race every conceivable crime, and to afflict it with every conceivable misery.

In the first class are produced not only many amiable weak men, as the modern evangelists[a] of this and other Christian countries, but also in cases where the physical powers are strong, the furious bigot equally conscientious with the former, but who keeps all around him in a continual state of ignorant excitement, which generates endless practical injustice to those who cannot think as he does. And as none of this class are ever permitted to investigate the laws of their nature, but are trained from infancy to believe and not to think, and to talk at random respecting the imaginary notions which they receive in their early years, there is not only a considerable shade of difference among themselves, but there is also a most injurious antipathy created in their minds to the members of the other three classes, but more especially to the 3d and 4th class, who have too strong a feeling of morality to become hypocrites, and express their assent to their irrational dogmas.

In the second class, religion, as it is now taught, implants not only hypocrisy, but the worst feelings and passions that unnatural restraints upon nature's laws can generate; and thus produces endless crimes and evils throughout society.

A disbelief in religion by those who possess by nature weak moral faculties engenders selfishness, jealousy, revenge, hatred, anger, cunning, and every human depravity. Upon this class of natural minds, it is calculated to create every possible variety of bad character, and they are found to be very numerous in every class, sect, and party, in all countries.

Nothing can be more melancholy than the effects which religion produces upon this class; it destroys all that can be called honest principles in them, makes them enemies and opponents to each other as well as to the other three classes, and they thus considerably contribute to keep all mankind at enmity, and prevent the existence of charity for the infinite diversity of opinion or feeling, which under the present system is unavoidable. It is from this class that the far greater part of the evils and miseries of human life proceed.

Upon the third class religion produces the most unfavourable impressions. The individuals of which it is composed cannot avoid detecting the inconsistent notions on which all religions are founded, and of tracing the endless errors to which they lead in practice. They are quite satisfied that of themselves, they cannot alter their convictions relative to these inconsistencies in principle and errors in practice; and their moral sense is too strong to admit of

---

[a] Religious revivalists, especially within the Church of England, associated with the Clapham Sect and William Wilberforce.

them becoming hypocrites, and saying, to please others, that they believe in the dogmas of religion when their convictions are directly opposed to them. They therefore feel that they are honest; and when the conscientious religious and those who have no conscientious religious feelings, but who pretend to have them, apply abusive personal epithets to these moral opponents of religion; and call them deists, atheists, sceptics, and endeavour to traduce their characters by every unfair and unjust device that they can invent, they instil hatred and anger, and every evil passion and feeling into these men, who naturally are thus taught to consider all pretensions to religion to be hypocrisy, and that religion itself is a monster of cruelty and injustice. Thus, instead of kind feelings and genuine affection being engendered between man and man, through which dispositions alone the world can ever be reformed and rendered happy, both parties are regularly trained to become not only the secret, but the open enemies of each other; keeping the world in a state of perpetual discord, and affording no hope of its termination. Were it not for the irrational feelings and conduct of the classes Nos 1 and 2 with respect to this class, the latter would always become honest, well disposed and comparatively intelligent members of society. As it is, the mass of the unthinking part of every population is in direct hostility to them, and consequently they are opposed to this mass, and the worst passions and feelings of human nature are thus made to be the every day practice of mankind.

Upon the 4th class religion produces the deepest commiseration for the ignorance, poverty, weakness, and crime, which it inflicts upon the human race. They cannot avoid seeing the regular steps by which it is made to disorganize and disease the moral sense and intellectual faculties of all who are subject to its influence. They are compelled to discover the gradations by which it generates anger and discord throughout society, and perverts all the superior qualities of our nature into curses instead of blessings. They are penetrated with the keenest regret to perceive the earth, which might be, with ease and pleasure to every one, made a terrestrial paradise, remaining a vast, a wild, and a desert, solely for the want of cultivation; and its inhabitants generally, which might be formed into beings of a far superior order to any hitherto known in the history of the human race, poor, weak, irrational creatures, asking for bread, while they are surrounded by the most ample means, if properly used, to supply an inexhaustible store of every good thing that the heart of man could require, and while he himself, with equal ease and gratification, may be formed into a being of high intelligence, possessing the finest moral sense, filled with the purest affection and most genuine charity for all of his kind, and with perfect good feelings for all that has life in the universe.

It is therefore impossible for this class to know and witness this desolation of the earth, and this degradation of their fellows, and not to feel an irresistible umpulse to forego every private feeling and consideration, that they may assist the nations of the world to emancipate themselves from the depth of error in which they are now involved, and from the crimes and misery with which, in consequence of this thick mental and moral darkness, they are now overwhelmed.

It is solely for these purposes that we now, in the face of all nations, and in the centre of this great metropolis, hold these public meetings, to which we invite all those who have moral courage sufficient openly to meet error, under whatever specious name it may possess, or whatever garb of disguise it may assume.

We are well aware of the hold which what is called religion, varied and opposed as it is to itself over the whole earth, has upon the confiding and upon the unthinking part of the population of the world. We know that for numberless years men of the second class of mind, who have hitherto governed mankind in all their affairs, have adopted every device they could conceive to make men not to think, but implicitly to confide in their *ipse dixit* upon the most important questions connected with their intellectual improvement and happiness, and especially upon the subject of religion.

We cannot therefore be unconscious of the difficulties which we have to encounter, even at the threshold of our proceedings, in placing before the public the real advantages and disadvantages of religion, as it has been hitherto taught, in forming the character of man, and in governing the world.

I have endeavoured to explain the general effects produced by religion on the four most prominent divisions of our natural organization at birth, namely–

1st. The weak of intellect, with a strong moral sense, which religion makes amiable and conscientiously honest in their belief and dealings, as far as the inconsistencies of a weak intellect, rendered still more weak by religious mysteries, will permit.

2d. Those with higher intellectual faculties, but having a weaker moral sense, these religion makes into moral hypocrites, into selfish and designing men, whose business through life is to take advantage of the intellectual weakness and moral sense of class No. 1 and to make them their tools or instruments by which they oppress the members of all classes, but especially those of No. 3, who have been always most unjustly treated by this class for their opinions, when honestly and openly expressed.

3d. Those who have a moderate share of intellect, and a large proportion of moral sense. Upon these religion produces the most unfavourable results, by creating in them the greatest enmity to the conscientious religious, and to the pretenders to religion; and, in consequence, their lives are usually passed in endless and fruitless contests with those in their families and neighbourhood, who belong to classes Nos 1 and 2. Finding that they are most unjustly abused for expressing the convictions which they are compelled to entertain, and that they are grossly ill-treated for being conscientiously honest, the worst feelings of our nature are engendered within them; they imagine the whole human race to be their enemies, and that every man's hand is against them. They are almost always reduced to poverty, and, by a continuation of unjust and merciless oppressions, they are goaded on from irritation to irritation, until their opposition to the professors of religion and the institutions of society knows no bounds. A state of society is thus created most unfavourable to an honest enquiry after truth, and to a condition of charity and kindness between man and man, and nation and nation; and endless cruelties are devised and practised for the insane purpose of attempting to make men think alike upon imaginary notions in opposition to facts, and to the evidence of our senses. By this irrational conduct, engendered solely by religion as it has been hitherto taught, men have been educated, from infancy to become open or covert enemies to each other, and thus the millions are made to fall and remain an easy prey to a few, otherwise most weak, oppressors.

4th. Those who have a large share of intellect, and whose moral sense is strong. Upon this class of men, as soon as their faculties are sufficiently ripe to observe, compare, reflect, and to judge with accuracy, religion produces many painful conflicts in their minds. They ardently and sincerely wish to retain the belief forced upon them in childhood, in the divine origin and untainted truth of the religion which they have been compelled to receive before their minds could comprehend any part of it. – They begin to investigate its principles or dogmas, and are forced, by the facts around them, and with the strength of their intellectual faculties, to compare these dogmas with the facts around them, and with the laws of their own nature which they feel within them; and to their grief and dismay, they can discover no connection whatever between the dogmas of any religion, and the facts around them, or with the feelings of their own nature. They shrink from these first impressions of doubt as though they were committing the most henious of all crimes; yet they cannot, by any effort they can make, prevent their recurrence. As their intellectual powers and moral sense increase with their years and experience, the discordance between the doctrines of religion and facts, or the laws of nature, become daily more and more evident. Their first fears subside, their moral courage gradually increases, by degrees they investigate the foundation on which all religions rest; they compare these with the unchanging laws of human nature, and to their utter surprise and astonishment, they are obliged most reluctantly to come to the conclusion, that there is not only no agreement between them, but that they are in direct opposition to each other. They are therefore compelled to entertain the conviction, that the facts of nature as they are presented to our senses, are not facts but delusions; and that all the religions in the world, as hitherto taught, are the inventions of human creatures before they had acquired sufficient knowledge from experience to govern man except by the hopes and fears of future endless happiness or misery: devices which they formed before they had discovered that man could be far better trained and governed by real knowledge than by inconsistent notions invented by men weak, but cunning, to keep the mass of mankind in the very infancy of ignorance, and to retain them in mental helplessness.

Ascertaining these important results, the men possessing by nature strong intellectual faculties and a high moral sense, cannot avoid feeling an irresistible desire to set their fellows free from the mental bondage which enslaves all their superior faculties and feelings, while their inferior mental qualities and their worst passions are cultivated most successfully. These men therefore look around in every direction to ascertain in what manner they must commence their task.

With their knowledge of human nature and of the laws which govern it, they cannot have any hostile or unkind feeling for any portion of mankind; they therefore desire to perform their task with the greatest mildness and gentleness that will permit them to accomplish the great and good objects which they have in view.

But after every attempt not to wound the feelings of their weak brethren, they discover that while the imaginary notions relative to religion shall be forced into the infant mind, they can make little or no progress; and however unwilling they may be to hurt the artificial conscience which has been formed in their fellow-creatures by the dogmas taught to children in all countries, they find that it is utterly impracticable to benefit the human race without destroying all the errors of all the religions in the world.

This difficult but most important task must be effected to enable them to lay a solid and permanent foundation for that knowledge which can alone train man to have genuine charity and pure affection for all mankind. They know it is not only an easy but a delightful employment to teach the human race truth, without any error from infancy. But they also know, from all past experience, that it is the most difficult and dangerous of all tasks in which man can engage, to attempt to unlearn or disabuse the adult mind of those errors and prejudices on the subject of religion, which have been with the greatest care and industry taught to them from their birth.

We are now prepared to enquire what are the advantages of religion, as it has been hitherto taught, upon the four classes of original organization. But first it is necessary to state what religion is, as it has been hitherto taught under all the various sectarian names and forms, which the priesthood in different countries have given to it.

Religion then, as it has been hitherto taught, is an attempt to force mankind to think against the evidence of their senses and of all facts, that there is merit of the highest order in believing what the priests say their votaries ought to believe, and the deepest of all demerits in not believing these dogmas, which they one and all, whatever may be the name and form which they support, agree to call divine truths. And also in a similar attempt to compel mankind to believe, against the evidence of their senses and of all facts, that there is equal merit in loving real and imaginary beings and things, such as they recommend to love, and in hating real and imaginary beings and things, such as they recommend to be hated; and likewise, that their votaries, whatever name they may bear, shall be eternally rewarded or punished for so believing or disbelieving, and for so loving or hating.

Whatever sectarians may say to the contrary, this is the religion, stripped of all mystery, which alone has ever yet been taught to the inhabitants of the earth.

It is the religion, in all its naked deformity, which is, at this day, alone, taught in every country in the world where any religion is known. It is against this religion I have contended, and it is probable I shall contend against it to the last hour of my life.

Now when the eyes of men shall be opened, when they shall acquire the power to investigate facts, to observe with accuracy, cause, and effect, and to see all things within the range of their senses as they really are; all well know that this religion could not originate with a wise and good power, but that it must proceed from an ignorant and malevolent power.

Because each of these notions have necessarily a most demoralizing influence over the four general classes of organization which are given to mankind at birth, under the present neglect of forming a superior organization for the human race.

Upon the class of minds No. 1, this religion has a direct tendency to weaken the intellectual faculties; and it often does so to an extent which reduces the rational part of those faculties to the lowest state – sometimes, indeed, to their utter destruction. Experience teaches us that religion, in all countries, is one of the most common causes of insanity. But religion upon this class of minds also perverts the moral sense, and instead of forming it to become tenacious or conscientious in supporting real virtue, it is made by it to countenance many of the worst vices under the specious name of virtue. They are forced by it to love those who have been taught to believe the same errors which they have been made to imbibe, and to dislike or hate those who have been compelled to believe some other dogmas different from their own, or perhaps even truths free from all error. They are by this religion trained and educated to believe almost every thing in opposition to the evidence of their own senses, and at the same time to have their reasoning faculties so far destroyed as to be wholly unconscious of the existence of any incongruity between facts and their belief. They are very generally formed by it to become irrational conscientious beings, which is the least injurious character that superstition is capable of producing out of the four great divisions of human organization.

Upon the class of minds No. 2, religion, as it has been hitherto taught, produces the most mischievous results in forming their character. It gives the worst possible direction to their intellectual faculties by preventing them from acquiring a knowledge of truth, and receiving ideas only from facts, and all therefore consistent with each other; to the acquisition of a species of false knowledge known by the term cunning, which in all situations in life enables them to take advantage of the honest or conscientious class No. 1 and, through their ignorance and simplicity, to overwhelm with injustice and every kind of abuse class No. 3, and to make a formidable stand even to the open, disinterested, and magnanimous proceedings of class No. 4. Witness the persecutions, and punishments, and often violent deaths, of many of the greatest minds that the world has produced through all the past ages. In consequence of this class of mind being thus trained to become cunning, instead of being rationally educated, as it might be, under other arrangements, and made to become truly wise, and to possess real knowledge, valuable for a superior practice among mankind, the world is governed by the most intricate and crooked policy. The government of all nations is therefore unavoidably under the direction of cunning and craft, instead of sound wisdom or real knowledge; and this must continue, until some minds possessing a large portion of intellect and a high moral sense, shall unite their efforts, and by a generous enthusiasm in the cause of universal humanity, shall induce the governments of the most civilized nations also to unite their efforts to adopt decisive practical measures to change this wretched state of human existence for one governed under rational institutions. Were this change to be effected, the class of minds No. 2, now under consideration, would not only have its intellectual faculties greatly improved by proper cultivation, but its naturally weak moral sense daily rendered weaker under the present irrational Institutions of Society, would be continually strengthened and enlarged, until, at matured age, it would be equal to every useful practical purpose, and become greatly superior to any immoral temptations that could exist under the proposed change of principle in governing the affairs of mankind.

While this delusion, under the name of religion, produces over the whole world these melancholy results upon the class of minds of Nos 1 and 2, it has a most unfavourable influence upon class No. 3, who, under a rational system for the moral government of mankind, would become very valuable members of society. Having a strong moral sense of right and wrong, having sufficient intellect by nature to perceive many of the inconsistencies of what men call religion, and being by their nature strongly impelled to act right, according to their best conceptions of it, they honestly avow their disbelief in religion, and, by so doing, they make themselves most obnoxious to their fellow-beings belonging to classes Nos 1 and 2. For those of class No. 1, being trained to be conscientious believers in the religion which they have received from their infancy, and being taught that all those who do not believe as they do, upon what they call the fundamentals of religion, are dreadfully wicked, dangerous, and bad men, they shun those of class No. 3 as though they were a pestilence. The necessary result of such treatment is not only to injure the moral sense of No. 1, but also to stifle and pervert all the natural good qualities of class No.

3, and to create within them feelings of the strongest hatred and dislike to every one that possesses any religion, all of whom they deem hypocrites and bad men; and they usually make very little distinction in these respects between classes No. 1 and No. 2. But their real persecutors are very seldom of class No. 1, who are not only sincere in their belief, but often really kind and amiable in their manners, dispositions, and general conduct. But class No. 2, who are necessarily hypocrites, and who almost always appear to be the greatest sticklers for, and the most violent and boisterous in support of, the forms and ceremonies of what may happen to be the religion of the country in which they live, are the greatest enemies of class No. 3; for not being restrained in consequence of their weak moral sense from committing acts of injustice when custom and law support them, and believing that all men ought to think and act as they do in sustaining all old institutions, they devise all manner of vexatious proceedings by which to injure and torment their hitherto unfortunate neighbours, No. 3. – In this manner does religion render the lives of these poor oppressed and depressed individuals an existence of continued misery, making them, through their sufferings, detest the very name of religion, as well as its votaries. These hostile feelings act and re-act upon the respective classes, until they lose all feeling of affection and charity for each other, as much as though they did not belong to the same but to opposite species of beings; and thus is hatred, crime, and misery made to pervade those minds, which, if formed under rational institutions, would be free from crime, full of charity and love, and unacquainted with misery of any kind.

Religion as it has been hitherto taught to class No. 4, inflicts upon them, in the early part of their lives, great evils of another description. As they possess by nature superior intellectual faculties and moral sense, they are forced to receive certain doctrines taught in the country in which they are born, and live, as divine truths; and in all cases they ardently desire to think and act most conscientiously in accordance with those supposed heavenly instructions for which they are fully prepared by their strong natural moral feelings. As soon, however, as they are put in possession of a certain number of these said to be divine truths, their intellectual faculties cannot avoid comparing them, first, with each other, and then with the facts which their senses have made known to them. This natural and necessary progress of their minds compells them to perceive the glaring incongruities between these so called divine truths, one with another, and between all these divine truths, and all the ascertained facts and known laws of nature. These oppositions and contradictions alarm their moral feelings – they dread unbelief in divine truths – they compare and examine again and again – they investigate with all the order and honesty natural to such minds; but the farther they extend their inquiries after real truth, the greater [the] distance they are compelled to discover is, between it and what they have been educated to call – divine truths.

Their minds are then perplexed; they become full of alarming anxieties about what has been called the soul, and while they remain in this state of doubt and darkness their misery is great indeed.

But as their intellectual faculties increase towards maturity – as their moral sense becomes more enlarged and tenacious of what is true and right, and as their knowledge of undisputed facts, or their experience advances day by day, they, at length, acquire sufficient moral courage to ask themselves what is truth, and where is it to be found free from error? They become conscious that there can be no discrepancy in truth; that one truth, of necessity, can never be opposed to another truth. That it is a necessary law of nature that each individual truth must be in harmony, and in strict accordance, with every other truth in the universe. That, consequently, the universe is one great truth, and that every single fact is a part, and a necessary part, to form that one great truth, which is alone the essence of all power and knowledge. When the minds of this class have advanced thus far, they distinctly perceive the intensity of the darkness in which the intellectual faculties of men have been enveloped. That they have been, as it were, confined within an impenetrable shell of ignorance, and they become filled with an irresistible desire to break that shell, and to burst forth into the full light of intellectual and moral day, and enjoy all the advantages of its vivifying influence. They desire knowledge for their fellow-beings; they desire superior dispositions and habits for them; they desire their permanent happiness. They discover the means by which this knowledge, these dispositions and habits, and this happiness may be given and secured to them. They occupy themselves in preparations to aid their fellow-beings in acquiring these advantages; and they speedily find that religion, which, in their infancy and childhood, they were forced to receive as divine truth, and which had nearly perverted all their rational faculties, and given a false direction to their moral sense, is now, *alone*, the obstacle which stands in their way to prevent their making one step in practice, in a rational course, to accomplish these objects. They wish not to offend any of their weak brethren who remain conscientious in the superstitions of their forefathers. They know they are not just subjects for blame or punishment, but for commiseration and pity. These men of the 4th class cannot, however, allow their feelings of sympathy and pity for a small part of the present population of the world to arrest their efforts for a good of all their fellow beings who are now alive, and for those who shall exist through future generations. No, they are deeply impressed with the magnitude and importance of the duty which they have to perform. They know that it is utterly impracticable that truth and error can be advantageously intermixed; that one or the other of them must now, under some new form, prevail and direct the future proceedings of mankind.

They are convinced, that whatever attempts may now be made to compel men to remain in their present ignorance will be unsuccessful, and that the time is at hand when error must give place to truth. They therefore deem it best for the real interest of all parties, now to come forward and meet error openly in the field of reason and fair argument. And meet it, too, with kind feelings; that the changes, which to them appear inevitable, may be effected beneficially for all parties; and that the spirit of anger and violence, which ignorance alone generates on account of a difference of opinion and of feeling, should be allowed to die a natural death, and be for ever allayed. Religion, therefore, as it has been hitherto taught, materially injures the intellectual faculties of this class during their childhood and youth, and would effectually destroy them for all superior or rational purposes, were it not for their strong moral sense, which, united with a daily growing intellectual faculty, enables them to overcome all the obstacles, which religion places in their way; and in defiance of it, they become, in their matured age, the conscientious open advocates of truth without any admixture of error.

Thus have I endeavoured to explain without prejudice or passion the real effects unavoidably produced by religion, as it has been hitherto taught, upon the four great general divisions of human nature, or of man's organization at birth.

The reflecting and intelligent in all countries know, that man from the hour of his birth becomes materially the creature of the external circumstances which are allowed to act upon his organization, and that the religion of his district is the most material of all those circumstances, in influencing the formation of his matured character.

I have fairly and honestly stated to you my most deliberate and conscientious convictions relative to the advantages and disadvantages, which religion, as it has been hitherto taught, has had in forming the past and present character of the human race under its chief divisions. Let me not, however, be misunderstood, as though there were no apparent exceptions to these general results.

The natural variety in the individual character of man is so infinite, as well as the varied circumstances under which each one is placed from birth, that no general principle can be stated upon this subject, that will not admit of a few apparent exceptions; but, I may add, if all the circumstances forming the original organization, and if all the external influences acting upon it were known, these few apparent exceptions could be easily explained, in conformity to the general principles stated. – For the principles of natural things, or, in other words, the laws of nature, never change for man, or for any earthly affairs or proceedings whatever.

Now, when the effects of religion, as it has been hitherto taught, and impressed upon the human race, shall be followed through all their ramifications, it will be discovered that the religion of the world is the sole cause now of all the disunion, hatred, uncharitableness, and crime, which pervade the population of the earth; and that, as long as this ignorant and worldly religion shall be taught to mankind, it will be utterly impracticable to train men to love one another, or to have common charity for each other. And all who reflect, know, that until practical measures shall be devised to make them love each other in reality, and to have pure and genuine charity, without any unkindness in their dispositions for the whole family of mankind, there will be no hope on which to rest for the general permanent amelioration of the condition of our species. No: the happiness of man never can be secured, until he shall be trained from infancy in a knowledge of true religion, derived from the everlasting and unchanging laws of nature, undefiled by any errors opposed to those laws, which, when understood, and honestly acted upon, will be sure to produce universal love, charity, and harmony throughout the population of the world.

Do you ask me the source of this true and undefiled religion, from which these all-important practical benefits are to arise? – I reply, – from the daily and hourly declaration of all those facts around us which announce the never to be misunderstood laws of that Power at present hidden from our senses, but which our intellectual faculties assure us pervade and govern all the movements of the universe.

These facts declare that man is not formed to decide upon his own individual convictions or his feelings; that these ever have been, and from his nature, ever must be formed for him; that it is an error of the most lamentable description, involving the human race in unceasing perplexities and contradictions, and which engender all manner of injustice and crimes, to attempt to make him in any degree accountable for the one or the other; and that any institutions founded on notions opposed to these eternal facts, can lead only to the destruction of the rational faculties of the human race, and fill them, as they are at this day, with every evil thought and feeling, and stimulate them to the most perverse and injurious actions.

But are there no advantages derived from the religion which has been hitherto taught to the world to counterbalance these disadvantages?

I have been ardently engaged in searching for these advantages; I have been most conscientiously desirous of discovering where they could be found, and in what manner they act upon the human race. My search however for this purpose has been fruitless, for the more I have investigated the subject, the greater are the number of its disadvantages, and the advantages perpetually diminish; and these convictions, facts, compel me to receive contrary to my will and wishes.

All the advantages which I am enabled to discover from this religion in any part of the world are, that after it has confounded and perplexed the intellectual and moral faculties of the human race as I have described, and sown the germs of every evil thought and bad feeling, and injurious action, it does, by its artificial present rewards and punishments; by its promises to weak minds, of eternal rewards and punishments, which none but the most ignorant and simple can be made to believe; it does, I say, in some slight degree, counteract a part of the dire effects which the hatred, jealousy, revenge, malice, and every evil passion which it engenders, would otherwise make absolutely insupportable;

and destroy even the desire for the continuance of life among any portion of mankind.

It first of all creates evil of an incalculable magnitude, but which we will suppose to be represented by a million; this having been found by experience too much for human nature to sustain, it has been relieved by rewards and punishments, threats and promises, to make the practice of the system it generates in some degree bearable; and these effect a counteracting relief which may be in comparison of the million denoting the extent of the evils which it brings upon mankind, be fairly estimated by a number considerably under one hundred.

Man, from want of the means of acquiring real knowledge from infancy, instead of spurious and false notions, is unconscious of the incalculable extent of his degradation, or of the miseries which he is condemned to endure.

And yet, my friends, neither priesthood or laity, patrician or plebeian, ignorant or learned, poor or wealthy, or even the governors of the world, are benefitted by this wretched state of human existence! Yes, my friends, one and all are abject slaves to a false and artificial system of ignorance, imbecility, rapacity, and crime.

Let us NOW, for ever, put an end to it, by reason and firmness and moral courage, directed by justice and untireing kindness to all who have the misfortune to be made our opponents.

I have thus very briefly, considering the nature of the subject, endeavoured to explain to the meanest capacity the advantages and disadvantages of religion, as it has been hitherto taught, in forming the character of man – as an individual, as one of a congregated mass, as one who is not, but who ought to be, a member of the great family of mankind, having a sincere affection for each of its members, and a pure and genuine charity for every variety of thought and feeling which nature and education have forced them to receive.

I ought now to explain to you the advantages and disadvantages of religion, as it has been hitherto taught, in governing the world; for the world has been governed under the direct influences of the religion which I have described. But your time upon this occasion will not admit of entering upon this also highly important part of the subject. It shall be entered upon at the first convenient season. Now for the application of these principles to practice.

You have been often told, my friends, that my views of human nature, and of human society, are visionary and impracticable, but you have been always told so by men who have been trained from infancy solely in imaginary notions, and who know nothing about the practice, beyond the common individual proceedings of domestic life, or some favourite theory regarding it, of some inexperienced modern political economist, who himself knows little of practice, beyond his books and his closet, and the immense store of useless, and very often mischievous, learning which his library possesses.

On the contrary, my life has been a life of continued practice directed by principles derived from, or formed by, extensive practice. I attend, therefore, to the sayings of these men, many of whom are learned and well intentioned, as I would to those of a man born blind, who had been taught to believe he could give valuable knowledge respecting shades of colour to those possessing the full use of their eyes.

Those who are truly intelligent, practical men, know that the population of the world is woefully deficient in arrangements to give the rising generation a useful or good education, to give them beneficial employment, or to create sincere affection and pure charity among them. Until those who profess to be your teachers shall instruct you in the knowledge of the principles and practice by which you can attain these – the first and most important objects of human existence – they are not prepared to be your instructors; they only waste your time and talents in giving you much useless lore respecting antiquity, or some modern absurdities directly opposed to the every day experience of every reflecting practical man.

They think it practicable to well educate a human being, while, from infancy, they endeavour to force him to believe that he must think, feel, and act, contrary to his nature; that if he does not so think, feel, and act, he becomes an IMMORAL being, and that he will be ETERNALLY punished if he will not become an UNNATURAL BEING. This, my friends, is a sure and certain mode of compelling man to become an inconsistent irrational being, and they thus admirably succeed in making him to think and act from birth to death most irrationally.

And this is the high-sounding term EDUCATION which is now given, at the most enlightened era of the world as it is called, to all of human kind, or they are allowed to remain without any but BRUTE education. And as to the employment of the human race, under the direction of modern wisdom, allowing, as they term it, every individual to act right in his own eyes, while each one is well trained in ignorance, and no man has any real freedom of speaking his thoughts, or acting as he feels and knows would be beneficial for all, he is irresistibly carried forward in the midst of the irrational circumstances in which he is placed, to aid in making the already too rich more wealthy, and sinking the already too poor into a lower state of poverty.

These enlightened men of modern days, who say to the rich public (who, if they were really well-informed, could immediately, and beneficially to themselves, put an end to the poverty, or fear of it, which exists), leave human affairs alone; they will, sometime or other, right themselves; every thing is going on well; the wealthy are enjoying themselves, and are becoming daily more wealthy by the improved powers with which new mechanism aids the producer to toil for them, and at the same time to render it less necessary for the labourer to be paid as much as he had before for his labour. It is true that many of the producers will be starved to death for a few centuries under this system, and all of them will have continually increasing difficulties to encounter;

but never mind that, the rich will always be doing well, and in due time every thing will find its level.

Yes, my friends, these economists are right, every thing will find its own level by wise measures or by violence. And their principles, if much longer continued, will indeed find their level, for they will be sure to lead to violence; while the principles and practices which I recommend for your adoption will remove all cause for, and therefore fear of, violence.

The absurdity of the manner in which the people of the United Kingdom are now employed, can be equalled only by the absurdity of the folly which is forced into the minds of the population of the world from infancy, under the name of some sect or other of religion.

Then, my friends, we have been told through thousands of generations, and truly told, that the world will never be at peace, or in a rational state of existence, until the means shall be discovered and introduced into general practice, to make men love one another, and to have charity for one another.

I ask you, my friends, whether you think men have more charity and love for each other now than they had four, five, or six thousand years ago?

For my own conscientious belief is that they have much less. Two days ago I was told in company of some very respectable conscientious religious persons, and a clergyman of the Evangelical persuasion or sect, and by a very good, humane, and worthy Christian, who I am sure felt a deep interest in my conversion to his faith, that if I did not believe as he did, or if I continued to believe, as I publicly declare to all men I do believe, that I should be eternally burned in hell flames, and for ever tormented by the devil and his angels.

So, I thought, this is Christian knowledge and Christian charity in the nineteenth century. A pretty specimen this, truly, of credulity, imbecility, and inconsistency. To imagine, for one moment, that an Existence, said to be infinitely wise, good, and powerful, should create a being called man, and give him an organization which compels him to believe according to the strongest conviction made upon his faculties, and which belief he, of himself, has no power to change; and yet, for that belief, and this all wise, all good, and all powerful Existence, who gives belief and disbelief, shall punish the work of his own hands by torments which shall have no end!!

Yet, my friends, while from my inmost feelings I pitied the mental weakness of my host, I loved the man the more for the warmth and honesty of his expression, and for the deep interest which he evidently felt in my welfare and eternal happiness.

This party were of the class of minds, No. 1: they are amiable, possess the best intentions, will make many sacrifices to do good in their own way, and are what are called the best moral men in society; and this is the highest and best character that religion, as it has been hitherto taught, can create for man. And yet, my friends, you see it is full of the most glaring defects.

Now, if it be possible to make men love one another as they love themselves, and to imbue them from infancy with real charity, pure and genuine as it ought to exist in every created being, it must be effected through very different principles, and by a very different practice from any which the world has yet seen or known.

These heavenly results can be attained only through a knowledge of the religion of nature, the only religion that ever has been or can be true. And this religion, when it shall be developed to the world, and when it shall be fully understood, and when it shall be fairly and honestly applied to practice, will be found competent to make every man love his neighbour as himself, and to have like charity for others that he feels others, to be just, ought to have for him!!

When this religion of high intellegence and perfect purity, shall be introduced, and not before, there will be 'peace on earth and good-will to man;'[a] then shall the lion lie down with the lamb,[b] and war and famine and pestilence and poverty and evil speaking among men shall be known no more![c]

When next we meet, I will explain to you this religion of consistent principle and practice, that all men may fully understand it, and understanding its principles, may, without delay, introduce it into universal practice for the well being and happiness of the whole human race.

Mr Owen then proposed the following Resolutions; after which some persons, and particularly Mr Osgood, attempted to address the Meeting against the reasoning of Mr Owen, but it was impossible for them to obtain a hearing:

RESOLUTIONS

1. That the thoughts and feelings of all men are by their organization, or human constitution, formed for them.

2. That the thoughts and feelings of all men create their will, and that the union of their thoughts, feelings, and will, in all cases, stimulate to action and form the moral character and conduct of every individual.

3. That consequently, it does not belong to the constitution of man, or the original nature of his constitution, that there can be merit or demerit in the opinions or feelings of a single human being.

4. That to force a belief of an opposite character, or that there is merit or demerit in the individual for his opinions or his feelings, is directly calculated to produce disorder and confusion over the world; to engender all manner of crime, and especially to render it impracticable to produce love and charity among the human race.

5. That therefore true principles in accordance with human nature, and all nature, are now imperatively demanded to relieve the world from ignorance

[a] See Luke 2:14.
[b] See for example Isaiah 11:6.
[c] See for example Ezekiel 36:29.

and crime, and violent feelings of hatred and anger, threatening to exterminate those who hold opposing opinions in religion and policy.

6. That these principles declare that full and perfect liberty of conscience is the birthright by nature of every human being.

7. That consequently moral truth consists alone in the plain undisguised expressions of our real thoughts and feelings.

8. That moral truths, however, or the conscientious convictions of individuals, and the everlasting truths of nature, have no necessary connexion with each other, but are now generally opposed to each other.

9. That this opposition between the moral truth of individuals and the everlasting truths of nature, necessarily produce an irrational state of human existence.

10. That the unavoidable condition of this state of society is to disorganize all the rational faculties of human nature, and to convert them into wild and discordant imaginations.

11. That, in consequence, the human race is, at this moment, over all the earth, involved in universal perplexities, contradictions, and feelings directly hostile to their well-being and happiness.

12. That, every where, poverty, or an excess of injurious wealth abounds. – That ignorance and selfishness form the chief qualities in the character of every individual; and misery pervades the earth.

13. That this is the true state of society, which these fundamental errors have produced in all countries deemed the most civilized.

14. That, at this moment, this is the true state of the British Empire.

15. That there is no possibility of changing this lamentable condition of the human race, except by the discovery of the means by which moral truth, or the conscientious convictions that men are now compelled to receive from their birth, shall be, in every instance, made in full accordance with all the everlasting truths of nature.

16. That as moral truth is now in almost every instance directly opposed to all ascertained facts or real knowledge, the progress of the knowledge of facts, lately made by scientific men, will now enable us to unite all moral with all the everlasting truths of nature, and thus, out of mental and moral chaos, produce mental and moral order and harmony, and thereby obtain and secure, for the human race, that genuine charity, pure affection, and permanent happiness which the comparatively wise and good, in all ages, have darkly foreseen and foretold, would, at some future period, be the condition of mankind.

SECOND LECTURE

ON

THE NEW RELIGION;

OR,

Religion founded on the immutable Laws of the Universe, *contrasted* with all Religions founded on Human Testimony,

AS DEVELOPED IN

A PUBLIC LECTURE,

DELIVERED BY

MR. OWEN,

At the Freemasons' Hall, Dec. 15, 1830.

LONDON:

Published by J. BROOKS, 421, Oxford-street; W. STRANGE, 21, Paternoster-Row; J. WATSON, 33, Windmill-street, Finsbury-square; the Co-operative Bazaar, 19, Greville-street, and to be had of all the Booksellers.

Price One Penny.

Printed by J. Brooks, 421, Oxford-street.

THE NEW RELIGION[a]
1830

At an adjourned meeting, to take into consideration the advantages and disadvantages of religion, as it has been hitherto taught in forming the character of man, and in governing the world, Mr Owen spoke thus:

At the former meeting I explained the outlines of the advantages and disadvantages of religion as it has been hitherto taught in forming the character of man. I have now to develope the advantages and disadvantages of religion as it has been hitherto taught in governing the world: it will be recollected that I then endeavoured to shew in what manner the religions of the world have influenced the four general classes of original minds in forming their matured character; and that I explained, at some length, the varied injuries experienced by each class. I then also stated that all the religions of the world were founded on the self-same fundamental suppositions, taught to the multitude as divine truths; but which suppositions, real knowledge has now demonstrated to be gross errors, productive of the most mischievous results to the whole of the human race. These suppositions are, 1st. That there is an absolute necessity for all to believe what the priests say, true believers ought to believe. 2dly. That there is the deepest of all demerits, or the blackest of all crimes, in not believing their dogmas, which, however opposed the dogmas taught in one country may be to those taught in another, the priests all over the world, agree to call divine truths. 3dly. That there is the same necessity for loving what the priests say ought to be loved, and for hating what they say ought to be hated; and the same demerit in not thus loving and hating. 4thly. That for believing or disbelieving, for loving or hating, contrary to the opinions of the priests, all men shall be eternally rewarded or punished. I further stated, that whatever Jews, Hindoos, Mahomedans, or Christians, may say to the contrary, this is the real religion of all the sects in the world when stripped of its mystery; and that this is the only religion which has ever yet been taught to mankind. It is the sole religion, this day, of the people of England, Scotland, and Ireland, and of all the nations upon earth.

[a] First delivered as a lecture at the Freemasons' Hall, 15 December 1830. Reprinted 1991.

You thus perceive, my friends, that when religion is stripped of the mysteries with which the priests of all times and countries have invested it, and when such is explained in terms sufficiently simple that the common mind can fully comprehend it, without fear or alarm from a misguided imagination, all its divinity vanishes; its errors become palpable; and it stands before the astonished world in all its naked deformity of vice, hypocricy, and imbecility. If, indeed, religion, as it has been hitherto taught, has emanated from a divinity, it must have been from one possessing the most dire hatred to mankind; one, who well knew how the most effectually to destroy, in the bud, the finest qualities of human nature, and the highest enjoyments of every individual.

For all these fundamental suppositions on which the religion of the world alone rests are destructive of the well-being and happiness of the human race, each of them being in direct opposition to every fact of which man has hitherto acquired any accurate knowledge.

In consequence of this discovery, all testimony handed down to us from our remote and ignorant ancestors, by tradition, writing, or printing, when opposed to facts, or the unchanging laws of Nature, will not hereafter be received into any superior or intelligent mind. Such will be aware, that, of necessity, the universe must be one great truth, composed of all the facts which it contains, and that, from the same necessity, each fact must be in perfect harmony with every other fact, throughout the whole of this aggregate of facts; and that any tradition or testimony attempting to contravene these eternal truths must be errors of the imagination, or wilful falsehoods.

The past religions of the world being thus opposed to the eternal laws of Nature, will henceforth cease to disorganize the rational faculties of the human race, and to torment man from his birth to his grave. Even the governments of the world will now soon be made, by the progress of truth, to discover that religion will henceforth not serve their purpose to keep the people in ignorance, or much longer to give a divine sanction to imbecility and hypocrisy. No: the period for thus deceiving the human faculties is rapidly passing away; and the religion which has hitherto made the earth a Pandemonium, will now die a natural death.

Religion having until now controlled, to a very great extent, all the governments of the earth, the rulers of nations are, at this day, more or less compelled to form their laws and institutions under its direct or indirect influence. Rapid and extensive as the advance of science has latterly been, an advance, which makes the opposition to this religion of Nature the more glaring, the individuals composing the most enlightened of modern governments, have not yet deemed it safe to attempt to unshackle themselves from the restraints which an artificial religion has hitherto put upon all their proceedings. Even the Imperial Parliament of Great Britain carries on all its deliberations under the perpetual fear of this overwhelming influence.

I shall now endeavour to explain the advantages and disadvantages which all governments experience by submitting longer to be forced to govern under this influence.

In order to govern through the influence of the religion which has been described, it becomes absolutely necessary, first to make the people mental slaves, and to devise institutions, by which their rational faculties shall be perverted or destroyed from infancy. – This effect could only be produced by the influence of measures, acting perpetually upon their senses, which shall counteract the continual efforts of the mind to perceive facts, to compare them with each other; and to deduce from them natural and just conclusions. The measures so employed have been church services, conducted under an expensive and complicated church government. Nothing short of some such enormous power, applied without ceasing to the subversion of the reasoning faculties of the human race, could so long have kept mankind in the state of ignorance, poverty, imbecility, crime, and misery, in which they are at this day.

To support this enormous stultifying power, it has been necessary for the governments of all countries to render each of their institutions subservient to that power; and, in consequence, the great departments of the secular administration of all nations, have been established upon principles in conformity to the religion which has thus been employed to enslave the minds of the people.

It is therefore the church that governs in all countries in which a national church exists; or in which the minds of the population have been previously enslaved by the dogmas of some national church, or of some sect, or sects, emanating from it.

Now no church having such control over the people, through their ignorant religious prejudices, will suffer the national government to adopt any legislative measures calculated to give real knowledge to the people, or to instruct them in those principles on which their permanent prosperity and happiness depend. No! their codes of laws, their notions of morality and immorality, and the education of the rising generation must be, and are, all devised to promote belief in their mysterious and stultifying creeds; and to destroy, in the bud, the rational faculties of the human race.

In consequence man has been wretchedly ill-governed throughout all past ages. He has been forced into the most unnatural and artificial state that human ingenuity, under the direction of this false and artificial religion, could devise: his virtues have been perverted into vices; his superior reasoning faculties have been debased to the pursuit of every species of folly and absurdity, while all his powers of high enjoyment have been converted into the means of his most exquisite torments.

To cultivate the best faculties in man, physical, intellectual, and moral, to the greatest degree that his nature is capable of attaining, requires only an honest, straight-forward conduct on the part of those who govern society. It is simply this: to teach man truth from his infancy; to enable him to acquire an accurate knowledge of facts; to permit him to draw the necessary deductions from these facts; and to surround him from birth to death with circumstances which are in strict accordance with his organization; at the same time allowing him to act entirely in conformity to his nature.

This rational mode of proceeding is all that is requisite to ensure a superior state of human existence.

But religion, as it has been erroneously taught to man, compels him to receive lies from his birth; to shut his eyes to facts, or to refuse all accurate reasoning respecting them; and thus, to submit to the lowest possible degradation his intellectual and moral faculties. He is then, with all his qualities perverted from their natural state, trained to acknowledge that he is depraved by nature, although, by a strange inconsistency, he is taught at the same time to say that he is the work of an infinite wise and benevolent being. He is surrounded from his birth by the most vicious and injurious circumstances, eminently calculated to render him bad, and to become the most irrational and miserable animal upon earth; while, by the simple and natural mode of proceeding which I have described, he might easily be rendered the most rational and the happiest of created beings.

As, therefore, the errors and evils of society arise from man's nature being entirely misunderstood, on account of which he has been made to receive the grossest falsehoods for truths from his birth, and to have all his thoughts and his feelings misdirected, the first step to be adopted by the people of all countries, who desire permanently to improve their condition, is to aid their governments to emancipate themselves from the thraldom of that religon which has brought man into this wretched state of physical and mental degradation. Without this being effected, as a preliminary measure, no government can possess the power to benefit the population, whose interests are committed to its care. And until it shall be rendered practicable for men to be honest, and to give utterance to their genuine thoughts and feelings, at the same time that they lie under no fear of being deemed irreligious when they do so express those thoughts and feelings, it will be vain to expect that the members of any government can benefit either themselves or the people over whom they rule.

The reason is obvious: not one really useful institution can be established, or one rational law passed, until governments and people shall stand in a natural relation towards each other. To effect this, the people, as I have said, must delegate to their governments power to emancipate them from the greatest of all evils, with which they could be afflicted, viz. – the influence of artificial religion. With the people must the measure originate which will alone enable their rulers to lay the foundation of a good or rational government. Let public opinion pronounce the verdict, and who will gainsay or resist its overwhelming authority?

The religion of the world is founded on the supposition that man has the power, by nature, to think and to feel as he pleases. Now, as I have before sufficiently demonstrated, no superstructure of religion, raised upon such a basis, can produce aught except folly and misery. It follows that all codes of laws, founded on the same error, must partake, in a like degree, of absurdity and gross injustice. And as all governments devise their institutions in conformity with the religion and the laws which that religion directly, or indirectly, compels the government to adopt, the acts and proceedings of all governments must, of necessity, be a compound of the folly and injustice which the nature of its fundamental principles thus imposes upon it; there is no escape from the misery, which so much error in its consequences, cannot fail to inflict. It will also be readily perceived that the education, or the forming of the character of every individual, must be in accordance with this religion, the code of laws emanating from it, and of the government, the result of both; and that any education proceeding from such a source can only train the population of any country to be inconsistent animals, without reason or judgment, on those subjects on which their permanent well-being and happiness depend. It is also evident that any education, given either in schools or universities, under these circumstances, would be more injurious than beneficial, as it would train the mind to error, and imbue it with the most horrid and absurd prejudices. These the human being is taught to hold sacred, and to consider worthy of being defended with his life. Hence religious contests, wars, and massacres; and the universal disunion and want of affection and charity among mankind.

No one who is competent, accurately to trace cause and effect, can now mistake the source of all the professions now practised in the civilized world; they are necessary to the support of religion, and to extract the labour from the industrious without any solid equivalent.

Thus has religion made the world one great theatre of folly and hypocrisy, or perhaps, more correctly speaking, one great lunatic asylum, in which each individual to his own deep injury, is endeavouring to deceive his neighbour; and thus all are grossly deceived.

The spell is about to be broken: the reign of satan,[a] or of ignorance and hypocrisy, is rapidly approaching its termination: truth will now speedily govern the world; and all governments will be constrained to remodel their institutions on that base alone, or they will be forcibly remodelled by those whom they will no longer attempt in vain to govern through a system of deception and falsehood.

If any of the governing powers expect to escape this change they will be deceived, as Charles X[b] has been, to the abstraction of himself and his family from the government and throne of France.

[a] See for example Matthew 4:10.

[b] Charles-Philippe, Comte d'Artois (1757–1836), King of France 1824–30.

The most powerful governments are to-day paralyzed in all their measures by, as they imagine, three days fighting in Paris.[a] They may, indeed, be paralyzed; for every step they take upon the old notions of the world, will involve them in more inextricable difficulties. The three days of contest in Paris, with the old system, was but the spark which has set the public mind over the world in a flame that cannot be again quenched, until the religions of the world and its utter abominations shall be utterly consumed, to give place to the religion of nature, and to make way for the commencement, in practice, of a superior state of society continually increasing in real knowledge and in general happiness.

What has become of the armies of the world? They are vanished; and will no more exist, but as conservators of peace, and creators of valuable wealth, for the general benefit; instead of being horrid murderers of their fellow beings, and the devastators and destroyers of their hard-earned property. No! the time for man to murder man, in order to gratify the whim or caprice of some furious bigot, or half-idiot, is passing, and will soon be passed. Truth, with all its high attributes, union, industry, wealth, charity, and affection, not for this sect, or for that country, but for all mankind, will henceforward alone reign upon earth, directing men to all that is good, and teaching them to avoid all that is evil.

Why is the government of France now at fault? Why does it not proceed in unison with the feelings and knowledge of the people? Because those who administer it have too much of the old leaven; because, with all the power at their control, they know not how to lay the foundation for the new order of things, being stultified by old laws and precedents, and prejudices, generated by religion, for its support; not perceiving that these are, now, mere lumber of no value whatever, and that, root and branch, they must be consumed by the revolution.

It is not a change of men that is now deserving a moment's consideration: it is an entire breaking up of the false fundamental notions, on which alone the world has been hitherto governed. It is the total annihilation of all old errors, and their consequent practice, for true principles and a new practice, which only can now satisfy the population of France, and of the civilized world.

Let not the governments of Europe and America blame any one for the present feelings and conduct of those whom they govern; for in the year 1818 they were distinctly apprised of the great causes which were then in active and extensive progress, to produce the existing results; they were then told, that these results were inevitable, and the reasons were explained, at length, why they were inevitable, unless remedies to avoid the evils were immediately adopted.[b] These remedies were neglected at the proper period; and measures of

[a] Repressive legislation provoked the revolution in Paris in July 1830.
[b] See Owen, *Two Memorials on Behalf of the Working Class* (1818) (*infra*, vol. 1, pp. 253–67).

fraud and force were preferred. The present state of Europe proves the error of the choice then made by the advisers of crowned heads.

May what has passed prove valuable experiences to all statesmen for the future! But, my friends, what is the government of this country to do, in the altered and changing state of men's minds? Is it to be left at sea, to be tossed about in the whirlwind of men's prejudices and passions; and, perhaps, stranded, or wrecked, by being forced into a civil war? No! it is the duty and interest of all men to lend their best aid, to enable the government to extricate itself from the difficulties, by which, on all sides, it is now surrounded. For who will gain by a civil war, or by the success of any faction, attaining its end through violence? Not one single individual.

All that is really good, can be best attained by knowledge, union, and moral courage. These are the only legitimate weapons of the new state of society, about to become universal. And when a sufficient number of men shall know what is true, and shall perseveringly place that truth in plain language before the public, all error must give way before them, and no government can resist their influence. It is now solely owing to the ignorance of the mass, that poverty and misery exists; and it is solely owing to religion, as it has been hitherto taught over the world, that a single human being is, at this moment, in ignorance.

Let us, then, enable those who govern these kingdoms, to adopt decisive and effectual measures to educate the rising generation, in all the truths which prove themselves to be such, by their undeviating consistency with all known facts; while error, the parent of evil and misery, will be for ever withdrawn from among the whole population.

Let us, also, aid our rulers in forming measures to create general habits of healthy and beneficial industry; in giving, universally, good dispositions, or a right direction to the feelings of the people; and in devising a new arrangement of circumstances, all in unison with the laws of our nature, to supersede the existing injurious, vicious, and unnatural circumstances, which alone surround the population of this, and all other countries. Let us do this in earnest and in good faith, and not ignorantly arouse those irrational prejudices and passions, which the religious instruction of this country has compelled the people to receive; and when they can be made to understand the necessity for, and the benefits of this change, they will adopt it; and all parties will be benefited.

Nor, let any one fear that this result will not soon be obtained; for the advocates of truth, pure, unmingled truth, possess a moral power which sets all physical force at naught; a power which, until this day, has been unknown to the world, except by anticipation. The deeply reflecting, through past ages, have had it impressed upon their minds that the time would, at some future period, arrive, when truth should obtain the victory over error; or, when the religion of a distorted imagination, should be made to give place to the religion of nature; and, when nature's laws should prevail over the unnatural laws, which a false religion has compelled man to adopt.

This period, my friends, if it has not already arrived, is immediately at hand; and no human power can now arrest its progress. We are prepared openly to oppose all error, and to contend against every injurious prejudice; and all prejudices are injurious. Further: we are prepared to render all the benefits in our power to all our fellow-beings, who have been made the victims of those prejudices and of those errors.

Having now shown the disadvantages of religion, in governing the world, it is requisite, according to the terms by which this meeting was called, to consider what are the advantages to be desired, by governing the world under the influence of the only religion which has yet been taught to mankind.

The real object of this religion has been to keep man ignorant of himself, and of his nature, that men may be governed in the mass, by the few, with the least trouble and hazard to those few. And as long as it has been possible to keep a knowledge of facts from men, or to prevent them from comparing one fact with another, and reflecting upon the consequences which necessarily follow from those comparisons, religion, as it has been hitherto taught, did aid and assist the governing few, to keep the many in as much order as the ignorance of the many would admit. Their imaginary hopes and fears, from the promised rewards and threatened punishments, through all eternity, bowed the neck of the multitude to the yoke of the directing few; however galling that yoke was made by the priests of the respective sects or parties into which those professing a belief in religion are divided.

This is the sole good, if good it may be termed, that religion, as it has been taught, has effected for mankind; in exchange for all the crimes which it has engendered, and for the endless miseries with which, since its invention, it has afflicted the human race. And this period has continued during all the ages of which we have received any account, however imperfect, of the proceedings of our ignorant and abused ancestors. Its evils have been, and are beyond the power of numbers to estimate; its benefits will be more than expressed by the lowest terms that can be applied to them.

Let us, then, act like men who have detected, not some common errors, in common society, but who have discovered the fundamental errors of human laws and institutions, the very cause of all the evils of human life. Let us act upon the knowledge of these new and superior circumstances, as men attaining such high privileges are called upon to act. Let every minor feeling and consideration give way to those noble and enlarged sentiments; while our conduct is that, which belongs alone, to the advocates of truth and of real knowledge.

Let us, then, place truth and knowledge in the most conspicuous manner before the world. Let us address his Majesty, and petition both Houses of Parliament to take these high and important subjects into their immediate consideration; that a new order of society may be, without delay, established throughout the whole of the British dominions.

Let us, then, now address his Majesty,[a] and petition the new Parliament[b] to take into consideration the advantages and disadvantages of religion, as it has been hitherto taught, in forming the character of man, and in governing the world. And that, if, upon such investigation, it shall appear palpable to all who can reflect, that the disadvantages exceed, beyond all estimate, the advantages, that the religion of truth and nature shall be immediately substituted for this false and unnatural religion, which has heretofore destroyed the rational faculties of man, and the happiness of the human race.

I, therefore, move, that this meeting address his Majesty, and petition both Houses of Parliament, to take into consideration the advantages and disadvantages of religion, as it has been taught in forming the character of man, and in governing the world; and that, if the disadvantages shall be found to exceed the advantages, that the religion of truth and nature shall be immediately introduced throughout the British dominion, in order to supersede the present unnatural religion of the world. And, also, that the teachers of the present unnatural religion shall receive double the encouragement, to instruct the people in the natural and true religion, that they have, heretofore, enjoyed, for opposing its progress.

THE ADDRESS TO HIS MAJESTY

SIRE: –

We are deeply impressed with the conviction, that your Majesty has a sincere desire to aid your subjects, throughout the whole of the British dominions, in improving their condition.

We believe, that it is not possible, by any device of man, to improve the condition of this population, more effectually, than by changing the unnatural religion in which they have unfortunately been educated, from infancy, for the religion of truth and of nature, which may now, for the first time in the history of mankind, be taught to them, without danger, or more evil, than a very temporary inconvenience.

We, therefore, entreat your Majesty, to afford all the aid and assistance of your high station, to induce your Ministers, to take into their immediate consideration, the advantages and disadvantages of religion, as it has been hitherto taught, in forming the character of man, and in governing the world. And, by thus attending to our wishes, you will acquire higher, and more lasting glory, than all the Monarchs who have preceded you, in the past history of the world.

[a] William IV (1765–1837).

[b] The Whigs had a large majority after the 1832 election.

THE PETITION TO BOTH HOUSES OF PARLIAMENT

HUMBLY SHEWETH: –
That your petitioners desire that the amelioration in the condition of the people of this country, now rendered so necessary, as to be no longer, with safety to the State, withheld from them, should be effected through the wisdom of the new Parliament, now assembled, aided by the cordial assistance of his Majesty.

That your petitioners are convinced, from all past experience, that no effectual permanent improvement can be made in the condition of the people of this country, so long as they shall be forced to receive, from childhood, the unnatural doctrines of the religion of the world, which, heretofore, all children have been compelled to receive; to the almost entire destruction of their rational faculties and moral feelings.

That your petitioners being most deeply impressed with the paramount importance of this subject, over every other that can come before the Imperial Parliament, pray your Honourable, (or Right Honourable,) House, to take into your immediate consideration the subject of religion, as it has been hitherto taught in these realms, as to all mankind; and that you will devise measures to relieve the population of Great Britain and Ireland, and the British dominions abroad, from the incalculable evils which that religion has accumulated upon them, through so many past ages of misery.

And your petitioners shall ever pray, etc

I have now to propose measures of deep interest to the public: – It does not appear to me to be practicable for the legislature of this country to effect such a reform, under the present state of public opinion, as will admit of any other representation in the House of Commons than of wealth and of long established errors, on subjects the most vitally important to the well-doing, and well-being, of the people and of the permanent prosperity of the state.

It is perhaps not desirable that a universal representation of the people should take place, until they shall be better educated and more correctly informed; but it is most desirable, that measures should be immediately adopted to better educate – and more correctly inform the great mass of the people – upon those subjects on which permanent prosperity and happiness depend.

To effect these objects in a manner constitutional and beneficial to all classes, I propose that public meetings shall be occasionally held in this metropolis; meetings that shall cover their expenses, and yet be open to the public; meetings at which the interests of the producing classes shall be calmly and temperately investigated; meetings that shall aid the authorities of the country to effect, without producing evil to any class, such changes as the progress of knowledge render necessary; meetings in which the most valuable truths hidden, during past ages, from the public mind shall be brought to light, not factiously, but to inform all, for the permanent benefit of all; meetings, in short, to remove the cause of the irritations and anger which now divide mankind, and prevent the creation of that charity for the unavoidable convictions and feelings of their fellows, which can alone establish among the population of the world, the peace and good will which Christians have been taught to expect will some day pervade all nations.

To accomplish these most important objects, it has occurred to me that the best mode will be to hold a public meeting as often as may be found convenient, and that an arrangement shall be made to cover the expenses, and yet to admit a certain portion of the public free of charge; and that every shilling received shall be applied, by a committee appointed for that purpose, to pay the rent, printing, and advertisements; and that no individual connected with these proceedings, receive from this fund any emolument whatever.

It appears to me, that public meetings of this character offer the best mode of enlightening the public, peaceably and satisfactorily to all parties, upon those subjects in which all now require to be well informed, I say well informed, because, heretofore, there has been no real knowledge given to the public upon these subjects on the right understanding of which, the permanent well-doing of the people, and the prosperity of nations depend. Hitherto the most valuable truths relative to the rational government of society have been most carefully hidden from the people of all countries; while this knowledge will prove to be the only real protection and safeguard, of those who now govern the nations of Europe: – All; yes I say all: producers and non-producers, rich and poor, governors and governed, will owe their relief from existing difficulties and their progressive improvement and safety to the rapid spread of this invaluable knowledge. Well do I know – concluded Mr Owen – that all men of the old system of the world would be, for a short season offended, because of my public proceedings. Knowing the source of their feelings, their offence will not offend me; but the time cannot be far off, when they will discover, that so far from being offended at my perseverance, in so long advocating a system for governing mankind, of a character altogether different from any that has ever yet existed, that I shall, sooner or later, receive their lasting and highest commendation. My intention is to benefit every one, and injure no one. These meetings will therefore be held to remove error, in principle and practice from the public; and to establish truth and the most consistent practice in perfect accordance with it.

The Address, Petitions, and concluding Proposal were carried by acclamation. Notice will be given of the Public Meeting.

OUTLINE OF THE RATIONAL SYSTEM OF SOCIETY

FOUNDED ON DEMONSTRABLE FACTS DEVELOPING THE CONSTITUTION AND LAWS OF HUMAN NATURE BEING THE ONLY EFFECTUAL REMEDY FOR THE EVILS EXPERIENCED BY THE POPULATION OF THE WORLD THE IMMEDIATE ADOPTION OF WHICH WOULD TRANQUILIZE THE PRESENT AGITATED STATE OF SOCIETY, AND RELIEVE IT FROM MORAL AND PHYSICAL EVIL BY REMOVING THE CAUSES WHICH PRODUCE THEM.[a]

1830

THE FUNDAMENTAL FACTS ON WHICH THE RATIONAL SYSTEM OF SOCIETY IS FOUNDED

1st. That man is a *compound being*, whose character is formed of his constitution or organization at birth, and of the effects of external circumstances upon it, from birth to death; such original organization and external influences continually acting and re-acting each upon the other.

2nd. That man is compelled by his original constitution to receive his *feelings* and his *convictions* independent of his *will*.

3rd. That his *feelings*, or his *convictions*, or both of them united, create the motive to action called the *will*, which stimulates him to act, and decides his actions.

4th. That the organization of no two human beings is ever precisely similar at birth; nor can art subsequently form any two individuals, from infancy to maturity, to be the same.

5th. That nevertheless the constitution of every infant, except in case of organic disease, is capable of being formed or matured, either into a *very*

[a] New edns in ?1836, 1838, 1839, 1840, 1841, 1842, 1851; Welsh trans. 1841; French trans. 1837 and (n.d.). Reprinted in *The Crisis*, vol. 1, no. 10 (26 May 1832), pp. 37–40, vol. 3, no. 24 (8 February 1834), pp. 193–5, *New Moral World*, vol. 7, no. 21 (29 February 1840), p. 1143, *Social Hymns* (Leeds, 1840), pp. 2–24, A *Development of the Principles and Plans* (1841), Appendix 4, pp. 22–31, and in *Robert Owen's Congress of Advanced Minds* (1857).

inferior, or a *very superior* being, according to the qualities of the external circumstances allowed to influence that constitution from birth.

THE CONSTITUTION AND LAWS OF HUMAN NATURE, OR MORAL SCIENCE OF MAN

I. Human nature is a compound of animal propensities, intellectual faculties, and moral qualities, or the germs of them.

II. These propensities, faculties, and qualities, are united in different proportions in each individual.

III. This diversity constitutes the original difference between one individual and another.

IV. These elements of his nature, and their proportions, are made by a power unknown to the individual, and consequently without his consent.

V. Each individual comes into existence within certain external circumstances, which act upon his peculiar original organization, during the early period of his life, and by impressing their general character upon him, form his local and national character.

VI. The influence of these general external circumstances is modified in a particular manner, by the peculiar organization of each individual: and thus the distinctive character of each is formed and maintained through life.

VII. No infant has the power of deciding at what period of time, or in what part of the world he shall come into existence; of what parents he shall be born, in what religion he shall be trained, what manners, customs, or habits shall be given to him, or by what other external circumstances he shall be surrounded, from birth to death.

VIII. Each individual is so organized, that, when young, he may be made to receive either true ideas, derived from a knowledge of facts; or false notions, derived from the imagination, and in opposition to facts.

IX. Each individual is so organized, that he must necessarily become irrational, when he is made from infancy to receive, as truths, false notions; and can only become rational when he shall be made, from infancy to receive true ideas, without any admixture of error.

X. Each individual is so organized that, when young, he may be trained to acquire injurious habits only, or beneficial habits only; or a mixture of both.

XI. Each individual is so organized that he must believe according to the strongest conviction that is made upon his mind; which conviction cannot be given to him by his will; nor be withheld by it.

XII. Each individual is so organized that he must like that which is pleasant to him, or which, in other words, produces agreeable sensations in him; and dislike that which is unpleasant to him, or which, in other words, produces in him disagreeable sensations; and he cannot know, previous to experience, what particular sensations new objects will produce on any one of his senses.

XIII. Each individual is so organized that his *feelings*, and his convictions, are formed *for him* by the impressions which circumstances produce upon his individual organization.

XIV. Each individual is so organized that his will is formed for him by his feelings or convictions, or both; *and thus his whole character, physical, mental, and moral, is formed independently of himself.*

XV. Each individual is so organized that impressions which, at their commencement, and for a limited time, produce agreeable sensations, will, if continued without intermission, beyond a certain period, become indifferent, disagreeable, and ultimately painful.

XVI. Each individual is so organized that when, beyond a certain degree of rapidity, impressions succeed each other, they dissipate, weaken, and otherwise injure his physical, mental, or moral powers, and diminish his enjoyment.

XVII. Each individual is so organized that his highest health, his greatest progressive improvement and his permanent happiness, depend upon the due cultivation of all his physical, intellectual, and moral faculties, or elements of his nature; upon their being called into action at a proper period of life: and being afterwards temperately exercised, according to his strength and capacity.

XVIII. Each individual is so organized that he is made to receive what is commonly called a bad character, when he has been created with an unfavourable proportion of the elements of his nature; and has been placed, from birth, amidst the most unfavourable circumstances.

XIX. Each individual is so organized that he is made to receive a medium character, when he has been created with a favourable proportion of the elements of his nature, and has been placed from birth amidst unfavourable circumstances.

Or, when he has been created with an unfavourable proportion of these elements, and when the external circumstances, in which he is placed, are of a character to impress him with favourable sensations only.

Or, when he has been created with a favourable proportion of some of these elements, and an unfavourable proportion of others; and has been placed, through life, in varied external circumstances producing some good and some evil sensations. This compound has hitherto been the general lot of mankind.

XX. Each individual is so organized that he is made to receive a superior character, when his original constitution contains the best proportion of the elements of human nature, and when the circumstances which surround him from birth, and through life, are of a character to produce superior sensations only; or, in other words, when the laws, institutions, and customs under which he lives, are all in unison with the laws of his nature.

THE CONDITIONS REQUISITE FOR HUMAN HAPPINESS

I. The possession of a good organization, physical, mental, and moral.

II. The power of procuring, at pleasure, whatever is necessary to preserve the organization in the best state of health.

III. The best education from infancy to maturity, of the physical, intellectual, and moral power of all the population.

IV. The inclination and means of promoting, continually, the happiness of our fellow beings.

V. The inclination and means of increasing, continually, our stock of knowledge.

VI. The power of enjoying the best society; and more particularly of associating, at pleasure, with those, for whom we feel the most regard, and the greatest affection.

VII. The means of travelling at pleasure.

VIII. The absence of superstition, supernatural fears, and from the fear of death.

IX. The full liberty of expressing our thoughts upon all subjects.

X. The utmost individual freedom of action compatible with the permanent good of society.

XI. To have the character formed for us to express the truth only upon all occasions, and to have pure charity for the feelings, thoughts, and conduct of all mankind, and to have a sincere good will to every individual of the human race.

XII. To reside in a society whose laws, institutions, and arrangements, well organized and well governed, shall all be in unison with the laws of human nature.

THE SCIENCE OF SOCIETY, OR SOCIAL STATE OF MAN

I. A knowledge of the laws of human nature derived from demonstrable facts, and which prove man to be a social being.

II. A practical knowledge of the best mode of *producing*, in abundance, the most beneficial necessaries and comforts, for the support and enjoyment of human life.

III. A practical knowledge of the best mode of *distributing* these productions, most advantageously for all.

IV. A practical knowledge of the principles and practice, by which to form the new combination of circumstances, for training the infant to become the best matured human being.

V. A knowledge of the principles and practice by which to govern man under these new arrangements, in the best manner, as a member of the great family of mankind.

VI. A knowledge of the principles and practice, for uniting in one general system, in their due proportions, the five preceding branches of the SCIENCE of SOCIETY; to effect and secure, in the best manner for all, the greatest amount of permanent benefits and enjoyments with the fewest disadvantages.

CREED AND DUTIES OF THE RELIGION OF THE SYSTEM

ARTICLES

I. That all facts yet known to man indicate, that there is an external or internal cause of all existences by the fact of their existence; that this All-pervading cause of motion and change in the universe, is the Power which the nations of the world have called God, Jehovah, Lord, etc; but that the facts are yet unknown to man, which define what that power is.

II. That all ceremonial worship by man of this cause, whose qualities are yet so little known, proceeds from ignorance of his own nature, and can be of no real utility in practice; and that it is impossible to train men to become rational in their feelings, thoughts, or actions, until all such forms shall cease.

III. That it is man's highest duty to himself and his fellowmen, to acquire an accurate knowledge of those circumstances which produce EVIL to the human race, and of those which produce GOOD; to exert all his powers to remove the former from society, and to create around it the latter only.

IV. That this invaluable practical knowledge can be acquired solely through an extensive search after truth, by an acurate, patient, and unprejudiced enquiry into facts, as developed by Nature.

V. That man can never attain to a state of superior and permanent happiness, until he shall be surrounded by those external circumstances which will train him, from birth, to feel pure charity and sincere affection towards the whole of his species; to speak the truth only on all occasions, and to regard with a merciful disposition all that has life.

VI. That such superior principles and feelings can never be given to man under those Institutions of Society, which have been founded on the mistaken supposition, that man forms his *feelings* and *convictions* by his *will*, and is therefore responsible for them.

VII. That under Institutions, formed in accordance with the rational System of Society, these superior principles and dispositions may be given to the whole of the human race, without chance of failure, except in case of organic diease, and influenced only by the natural consequences of our actions.

A RATIONAL GOVERNMENT WILL ATTEND SOLELY TO THE HAPPINESS OF THE GOVERNED

It will ascertain what human nature is; what are the laws of its organization, and of its existence, from birth to death; what is necessary for the happiness of a being so formed and matured; what are the best means by which to attain those requisites, and to secure them permanently for all the governed.

It will devise and execute the arrangements, by which the conditions essential to human happiness shall be fully and permanently obtained for all the governed; and its laws will be few, easily to be understood by all the governed, and perfectly in unison with the laws of human nature.

A GENERAL CONSTITUTION OF GOVERNMENT, AND UNIVERSAL CODE OF LAWS, DERIVED FROM THE CONSTITUTION AND LAWS OF HUMAN NATURE ON THE LIBERTY OF MIND OR CONSCIENCE

I. All shall have equal and full liberty to express the dictates of their conscience.

II. No one shall have any other power than fair argument, to control the opinions or belief of another.

III. No praise or blame, no merit or demerit, no reward or punishment, shall be awarded for any faith whatever.

IV. All shall have equal right to express their opinion respecting a FIRST CAUSE; and to worship it under any form or in any manner agreeable to their consciences, not interfering with equal rights in others.

ON THE IRRESPONSIBILITY OF MAN

V. No one shall be responsible for his physical, intellectual, or moral organization.

VI. No one shall be responsible for the sensations made on his organization, by external circumstances.

VII. No one shall be responsible for the feelings and convictions within him, and which are to him the truth, while they continue.

ON PROVIDING FOR, AND EDUCATING THE POPULATION

VIII. Every one shall be equally provided through life, with the best of every thing for human nature, by public arrangements; which arrangements shall give the best known direction to the industry and talents of every individual.

IX. All shall be educated from infancy to maturity, in the best manner known at the time.

X. All shall pass through the same general routine of education, domestic teaching, and employment.

XI. All Children, from their birth, shall be under the especial care of the community in which they are born; but their parents shall have free access to them at all times.

XII. All the Children shall be trained and educated together as children of the same family; and shall be early taught a knowledge of the laws of their Nature.

XIII. Every individual shall be encouraged to express his feelings and convictions only, – or, in other words, to speak the truth solely upon all occasions.

XIV. Both sexes shall have equal education, rights, privileges, and personal liberty; their associations will arise from the general sympathies of their nature, uninfluenced by artificial distinctions.

ON THE GENERAL ARRANGEMENTS FOR THE POPULATION

XV. Under the Rational System of Society, after the children shall have been trained to acquire new habits and new feelings, derived from the laws of human nature; there shall be no useless private property.

XVI. As soon as the members of these communities shall have been educated from infancy in a knowledge of the laws of their nature; trained to act in obedience to them; and surrounded by circumstances all in unison with them; there shall be no individual punishment or reward.

XVII. Society shall not be composed, as at present, of single families, but of communities or associations of men, women, and children, in the usual proportions, from three hundred to two thousand, as local circumstances determine.

XVIII. As these new communities increase in number, a union of them shall be formed for local and general purposes, in tens, hundreds, thousands, etc, according to the less or more extended objects and interests, which shall require their consideration and direction.

XIX. Each of these communities shall possess around it, land sufficient for the support, for ever, of all its members, even when it shall contain the maximum in number.

XX. These communities shall be so arranged as to give to all the members in each of them, as nearly as possible, the same advantages, and to afford the most easy communication with each other.

ON THE GOVERNMENT OF THE POPULATION, AND DUTIES OF THE COUNCIL

XXI. Each community shall be governed by a general council, composed of all its members between the ages of thirty-five and forty-five, and each department shall be under the immediate direction of a committee, formed of members of the general council; chosen by the latter, in the order to be determined upon.

XXII. After all the members of the community shall be rendered capable of taking their full share of the duties in the general council of government, there shall be no selection or election of any individuals to office.

XXIII. All the members at thirty-five years of age, who shall have been trained from infancy in the communities, shall be officially called upon to undertake their full share of the duties of management; and at forty-five, they shall be excused from officially performing them.

XXIV. The duties of the general council shall be, to govern all the circumstances within the boundaries of its community; to organize the various departments of production, distribution, and formation of character, to remove all those circumstances which are least favourable to happiness, and to replace them with the best that can be devised among themselves, or of which they can obtain a knowledge from other communities; to regulate and assist in the establishment of new associations composed of the surplus population of the community, and to send delegates to the circles of communities to which they shall be attached.

XXV. The general council shall have full power of government in *all things appertaining to the community under its direction*, as long as it shall act in unison with the laws of human nature, which shall be its sole guidance upon all occasions.

XXVI. All individuals trained, educated, and placed in conformity to the laws of their nature, must, of necessity, at all times, think and act rationally, except they shall become physically, intellectually, or morally diseased; in which case the council shall remove them into the Hospital for bodily, mental, or moral invalids, where they shall remain until they shall be recovered by the mildest treatment that can effect their cure.

XXVII. The council, whenever it shall be necessary, shall call to its aid the practical abilities and advice of any of the members not in the council.

ON THE ADJUSTMENT OF DIFFERENCES

XXVIII. If the general council shall ever attempt to contravene the laws of human nature, which is scarcely possible, the elders of the community, who have passed the council, shall call a general meeting of all the members of the association, above sixteen years of age, who have been trained from infancy within it. This meeting shall calmly and patiently investigate the conduct of the general council; and if a majority shall determine, that it has acted, or attempted to act in opposition to these laws, the general government shall devolve upon the members of the community who have passed the council, and who are under fifty years of age, united with those who have not entered the council, and are above thirty years of age.

XXIX. All other differences, of every description, if indeed it be possible for any to exist in these communities, shall be immediately determined and amicably adjusted between the parties, by the decision of a majority of the three senior members of the council; except when the difference shall exist between members of the council, – when it shall be, in like manner, decided by the three members who have last passed the council.

CONCLUSIONS DEDUCED FROM THE FACTS, CREEDS, DUTIES, AND, PRINCIPLES, CONSIDERED IN REFERENCE TO THE PRESENT EXCITED AND UNSATISFACTORY STATE OF THE CIVILIZED WORLD

I. That the period for introducing the rational system for remodelling the character of man, and for governing the population of the earth, in unity, peace, progressive improvement, and happiness, is near at hand; and that no human power can resist the change.

II. That the governments of the world will soon be compelled, in their own defence, to adopt this superior system; to prevent their being involved in factions, anarchy, war, and ruin.

III. That this change will root up and utterly destroy the old vicious and miserable system of ignorance and poverty; individual competition and contest; and of national wars thoughout the world; and introduce, in place thereof, the rational System of Society, in which competition, strife, and wars, will cease for ever, and all will be trained, from infancy, solely to promote each other's happiness.

IV. That this system can be best commenced by convincing governments of the truth of the principles on which it is founded. There must be also a sufficient number of individuals imbued with its spirit of genuine charity, affection, and philanthropy, and instructed in the best mode of applying it to practice; they must likewise possess patience and perseverance to overcome all the obstacles which prejudice will oppose to their progress; and above all, they must be united, have full confidence in each other, and be directed by one heart and one mind.

CONCLUDING REMARKS

Under the past and present irrational system of the world, devised in opposition to Nature, 19 out of 20, or perhaps, more truly, 99 out of 100 of the external circumstances formed by man around society, are of an inferior and vicious character; but under the Rational System of Society now proposed to be formed in accordance with Nature, all the circumstances under human control, will be of a superior and virtuous character.

Under the existing religious, political, commercial, and domestic arrangements of Great Britain, 250 individuals cannot be supported in comfort on a square mile of land; while under the proposed System, with much less labour and capital than are now employed, 500 may be immediately supported in abundance, and in a few years after the new arrangements shall have been matured, 1000, 1500, and probably, without any additional new discoveries, 2000 individuals may be so supported upon every square mile of an average quality of soil.

Such is the difference between a Rational System formed in accordance with Nature, and one founded in opposition to it.

A Work developing the whole Science of the Rational System of Society, of which this paper is a Synopsis, is now preparing for press, and due notice will be given of its publication.

ROBERT OWEN'S

REPLY TO THE QUESTION

"WHAT WOULD YOU DO, IF YOU WERE PRIME MINISTER OF ENGLAND?"

Price One Penny. [2ND EDITION.]

ROBERT OWEN'S REPLY TO THE QUESTION 'WHAT WOULD YOU DO, IF YOU WERE PRIME MINISTER OF ENGLAND?'[a]

?1832

An intelligent friend, who has long studied, with deep interest, the system which I recommend for general investigation, and who approves of it, to the extent to which it has been explained, lately suggested the great utility that would arise to the public, from supposing myself invested with full power to administer the affairs of this country, and stating the measures which, in that case, I would adopt to obtain and secure the permanent prosperity and happiness of the people.

And as many of my disciples, in this and in other countries, have, at various times, expressed a similar wish; and as the continuance of life, especially at my age, is uncertain, I now feel it a duty incumbent upon me to comply with the request.

But, to perform this task as it ought to be executed, it is requisite that I should take into consideration the existing prejudices, customs, and practices of the lower, middle, and higher orders; the present state of parties, religious, political, and commercial; the new position in which late events have placed the two Houses of Parliament, with respect to each other and to the country;[b] the condition of Ireland, as it bears upon the general interests of England, and of the empire; and our present foreign relations.

Under the supposition, then, that I was appointed by the Crown, with the consent of the People, to effect for them the greatest amount of advantages, in the shortest time, and with the fewest evils to individuals, the question is, What course would I adopt, and what are the practical measures which I would recommend?

My answer to these questions is, that I would change all the existing low, inferior, and vicious circumstances, for others of a very superior character. I would therefore, commence my administration by informing all foreign states

[a] 2nd edn, Stockport, 1832. Reprinted in the *New Moral World*, vol. 1, no. 45 (5 September 1835), pp. 356–9.

[b] E.g., after the 1832 Reform Act.

that the British Government was about to change its national proceedings, both domestic and foreign; – that it was going to effect this change in consequence of having detected the source of the errors on which all governments have been hitherto founded and governed, and from which, in fact, all laws and institutions have emanated; and because it had discovered the principles on which society ought now to be based, and upon which all laws and institutions ought now to be established, for the general benefit of all nations; – that the whole extent of the change should be fully explained to them, and their aid and cordial co-operation solicited to carry it into effect, without injury to individuals or nations; – that the old mode of conducting the diplomacy between nations, should, on the part of Great Britain, be abandoned: and, instead thereof, the plain, simple language of truth should be used, and no attempt should be made to deceive any party, or to take advantage of their ignorance or weakness; but, on the contrary, that Great Britain would exert all her power and energies to promote the improvement and happiness of all nations.

I would also inform them, that, while this change from wrong to right principles and practices was in progress, Great Britain would adopt, and maintain, an attitude of national power, that would render all attacks upon her from without so hopeless of success, that none would be attempted. While, on the other hand, all nations would become conscious that the new principles which she had adopted would prevent, on her part, any aggression or injustice of any kind.

Great Britain would, by these means, acquire the confidence and friendship of all nations and people, and soon terminate the necessity for the continuance of the present extravagant and injurious system of diplomacy, with all its absurd and unmeaning phraseology.

I would next make arrangements to give, after proper preparation for the purpose, political freedom to all our dependencies in the four quarters of the world, and to enable them to govern themselves; but I would, as at present protect them from foreign attack or subjugation. These colonies should, also, as long as it was necessary, receive every aid from the mother country to improve their character and condition, and increase their wealth.

I would also institute measures to induce all nations to adopt a common language, in addition to their own, to facilitate the communication between the most distant parts of the world, and, by degrees, to make all men of one nation, with one language and one interest.

Simultaneously with these proceedings relative to foreign nations and our colonies, I would announce to the population of the British empire the change of the fundamental principles which was about to commence, for the benefit of all persons, of every rank, and of their posterity through endless ages. And, to calm the minds of those who now hold private property, and possess exclusive privileges, it should be declared, and so arranged, that none should be deprived of the one or the other, or disturbed in their present position, until their increased intelligence should induce them to desire the change.

I would then inform the population that the existing laws, customs, and institutions should remain in force, until new arrangements could be made to supersede them, without any violent or sudden change; but that the evils arising from the present order of things should be prevented, by removing, as rapidly as the national means would admit, the causes which produce them: and the causes being the mal-arrangements of society, formed under the most mistaken notions of human nature, and a total ignorance of the mode of adjusting the affairs of life, new and very superior arrangements should be adopted for educating, employing, and governing the whole population.

All who can observe and reason, now know '*That man is the creature of the circumstances in which he is placed*;' therefore the vicious and inferior circumstances, which the want of better knowledge and more experience in our ancestors has allowed to grow up to their present complication of error, should be made gradually to yield to new and improved arrangements, in which the superior natural qualities of man might be called into full action, and in which he should obtain all the advantages of a wise association of his powers with those of his fellow-men, for their highest mutual advantage.

And this is, really, all that is now required, to change the present most cruel and irrational condition of the human race, into a state of terrestrial paradise. Ignorance has produced the one; while wisdom, which includes knowledge and goodness, will produce the other.

I would then have explained to all parties the following great and everlasting truths, on which, alone, universal charity and affection can be established, and applied in practice to the daily and hourly transactions of every individual: viz. –

'That man is not a being formed by nature to deserve individual reward or punishment; but a being so totally different, that he may be educated from his birth, by the arrangements of others, to become good in all his relations in life; highly useful to himself, and beneficial to his fellows; rational and wise in all his conduct, so as to insure happiness to himself and others. Or, with the same certainty, he may be educated to have his faculties so neglected, or erroneously cultivated, that he shall be made to acquire the worst qualities that can be given to human nature, and to become, to himself and others, through his life, the cause of much misery.'

As all who consider themselves in a comparatively better situation than the great mass of the people, are unwilling to risk any great change, and would, therefore, oppose every thing that indicated the introduction of an entirely new system, – I would calm their fears, by showing them the change of character and condition which I would make first on those who now the most require to have them changed; that is, upon the ignorant, the vicious, and miserable. And I would convince all of the practicability of this change, by creating new circumstances for these individuals, which should gradually turn their ignorance into intelligence, their viciousness into real goodness, and their misery into happiness.

From this alteration in the minds, manners, and conduct of these *now poor*, unfortunate, because neglected, beings, all should be satisfied of the overwhelming power of the influence of external circumstances. Of the full extent of this power, all parties are yet without knowledge: it is unlimitable, and competent to make man, angel or devil.

By these preliminary proceedings, all would be convinced, by occular demonstration, that a due cultivation and wise exercise of all our natural powers – physical, intellectual, and moral, are absolutely necessary to give a high degree of happiness to each individual; and that the over-employed and under-employed, the uncultivated and ill-cultivated, are necessarily imperfect and unhappy beings.

These preliminary proceedings would also prove to the world, that the necessity for poverty, or the fear of it, has ceased, through the discoveries in various sciences; for these discoveries should be so applied, under our new arrangements, that, with their aid, every portion of the population should be enabled, with light labour, or rather with necessary and pleasant exercise, to produce more of all the necessaries, comforts, and beneficial luxuries, than the same population would desire to use or consume; and thus real wealth would be continually upon the increase in every part of the British dominions, and, soon, in every other part of the world.

I would effect this change without adding any new burdens to the people. The funds which are now wasted, in what is called supporting the poor and bringing criminals to justice, as the poor and criminals would rapidly be diminished, would be ample to defray the expense of the great change proposed; and by the creation of these new arrangements, the annual wealth produced would be very speedily doubled, then trebled, and quadrupled. It is a great want of a knowledge of facts, which prevents parties from discovering how easily wealth may be produced by every population, greatly beyond the most extravagant wants of that population.

I would raise the funds requisite for the objects to be attained, by making the poor national, and collecting an equitable rate from all parishes; which rate would be speedily diminished below the average parish-rate now collected, and then it would be gradually reduced to nothing. As long as there shall be one shilling raised for poor-rate in Great Britain; that is, as long as a system shall be allowed to continue, which permits one British subject to be in poverty or in idleness, or in the most distant fear of poverty, Great Britain will be ignorantly governed. And as long as there shall be one person in the British dominions allowed to grow up in ignorance, vice, and bad habits of any kind, Great Britain will be ignorantly and viciously governed; for both of these evils may now, by good government, be easily avoided.

To prevent these enormous national evils, I would make immediate arrangements to employ every person willing to be, and capable of being, employed in creating the new circumstances, in which the present unemployed and ignorant should find useful work and instruction, at all times, suitable to the age and capacity of the individual: and within these arrangements young, middle-aged, and old should immediately be instructed in the most useful knowledge.

To attain these objects, I would make arrangements to purchase, at a fair price; all such estates, proper for the purpose, as were offered for sale in England, Ireland, and Scotland. On these estates, the new superior circumstances should be created, that should gradually render the continuance of the present inferior and vicious circumstances unnecessary and impossible.

These new superior circumstances would consist in a different disposition and better cultivation of the land; in a different disposition and internal arrangement of the domestic dwellings and public buildings for instruction and recreation; in a different disposition and better arrangement of manufactures and trades, and for distributing the various productions among the population upon these estates, and for exchanging them with more distant populations, in other countries.

By these changes it might be expected that, before the expiration of four or five years at the most, two millions per day of additional substantial valuable wealth would be produced in Great Britain and Ireland, and that there would be, what to the ignorant would appear a miraculous change in the character, condition, and happiness of the population of these islands.

There is now no one obstacle to this change being immediately commenced, and to a great progress being made in it annually, but the want of knowledge on the part of those individuals who influence the measures of our government.

And the change may be effected by the most plain, simple, straight-forward, practical measures; such as farmers, gardeners, manufacturers, tradesmen, teachers of youth, sea-faring persons, and practical statesmen, could readily comprehend, and, by direction, put into practice. And these changes would naturally arise from acting, consistently, upon a few fundamental principles, now admitted by all well educated, reflecting persons, and upon facts well known to all scientific and intelligent practical men.

I would thus, as director of the administration of this country –

First, Obtain for Great Britain the confidence and friendship of all foreign nations and people, by so decidedly deserving both that they could not be withheld.

Second, The same confidence and friendship should be, on the same principles, secured from all our present dependencies.

Third, Arrangements would be thus made to remove the cause of poverty, or the fear of it, in one year, from the British dominions, and to make it evident to the least experienced in the production of wealth, that we possess, in our mineral productions, in our surface soil, in our climate, in our peculiar native physical and mental energies, in the already acquired skill and habits of industry of the people, in the national and private capital, in the domestic and foreign political or national power of the population, in the knowledge of the principles by which these may now be united to effect the most gigantic and mighty purposes; a mine of inexhaustable materials, affording the most ample means that can be desired to create wealth so rapidly, abundantly, and permanently, that, as soon as all the private property shall be purchased, by the nation or government, from individuals, at a full price, which it soon may be, all will perceive the gross folly or madness, in the inhabitants of this, or of any country, hereafter misdirecting their invaluable faculties, in degrading, demoralizing, useless contests for individual possessions or private wealth of any kind; those faculties which might be employed for the attainment of excellence in all knowledge, and for the enjoyment of high happiness in the due cultivation and temperate exercise of each of those faculties. Were it not for the overwhelming influence of early impressions, continually repeated, from external circumstances, the folly and madness of all people and governments, relative to the creation, distribution, and enjoyment of wealth, would appear so glaringly absurd, that children, rationally trained and educated, would, at a very early age, be astounded at the gross inconsistencies of the present nations of the earth, – but more especially of the people and government of this country, who have unlimited means of increasing their powers to produce wealth beyond the possible wants or use of rational creatures.

Fourth, Arrangements would also be thus made to arrest, at once, the flood of ignorance which is daily over-spreading the land, flowing from those appointed to instruct the people in kindness, justice, and charity; which knowledge they have been trained to mistake, and, instead thereof, to be employed most actively in teaching the principles and practices of superstition, oppression, and uncharitableness. These unwise – may we not say, insane? – proceedings, would be superseded by decisive practical measures to prevent one British or Irish child being allowed to remain in ignorance, or permitted to acquire any superstitious or unjust notions, or any uncharitable feeling towards one human being. But, on the contrary, every British and Irish child should have all the faculties of his nature cultivated in their due proportions, and called forth into regular healthy exercise, in such a manner that the individual and society should be the most permanently benefited by them.

Fifth, Arrangements would be thus made to supersede, as speedily as possible, all the present inferior, vicious, and insane circumstances, within which so large a portion of the British and Irish people are now involved. These evil circumstances would be superseded by a new creation of good circumstances, through the irresistible influences of which, these same individuals would have their persons, minds, and morals so changed and improved that they would not, in a comparatively short period, be deemed, by those who had not witnessed the progress of the change, and were uninformed respecting the means applied to effect it, to belong to the same species: the one would be thought to be the irrational, while the other would be deemed the rational beings, of the same genus.

These are the changes, or the new circumstances, which, as Prime Minister, or Adviser of the Crown and People, I would immediately begin to form; and in less than twelve months, the population of this country could be made to think, feel, and act so differently, that their characters should be the reverse of what they now are, or have ever yet been: anxiety would be unknown amongst them, and confidence, arising from the perpetual practice of truth and sincerity, would pervade all, from the oldest to the youngest.

Were these measures adopted with decision, throughout the British dominions, they would also soon change the condition of other nations; for those who have been trained in erroneous principles only, and have never seen any other practices than those which have emanated from erroneous principles, can form no adequate conception of the rapidity with which the human character, in the mass, may be changed, and improvements of every kind made to advance, as soon as public opinion and the public institutions shall be based upon true fundamental principles, and public measures shall proceed in strict accordance with them.

It is upon this part of the subject that the world is in such complete darkness. It has hitherto known error only in principle and practice; it has found itself involved, by these errors, in continual difficulties, and has met with never-ceasing obstacles to its progress towards excellence and happiness; and it has imagined that evils, and their innumerable obstructions, were to keep man in the bondage of ignorance and of the inferior passions, which ignorance alone engenders, for ever. The world could have no belief in the statements which affirmed that the cause of these errors and miseries was known, and could be removed; and that the earth, with less human labour than is now required, and without anxiety, could be made a paradise.

The immediate conversion of men and women from an irreligious to a religious state of mind and feelings, has been often known. But truth, without mystery or mixture of error, being publicly taught from authority, and enforced with the powers of eloquence, which would then be eager to enlist under its banners, could be made by the existing governments to banish all error, and falsehood, and deception, in a period so short, that the regeneration of the public mind would, at first, be considered as the most extraordinary of all the miracles of past times. And it would be so considered, until it should be made manifest by the fact, that the laws of nature, when understood, are capable of effecting more extensive and wonderful changes, than any of the petty local proceedings, even supposing them to have been true, that have been recorded as miracles in any of the religious or other writings of the ancients.

Let the British government now adopt these principles, and act decisively upon them, and all the governments of Europe and America would be induced, or irresistibly, impelled, for their own safety, interest, and happiness to follow her example; and thus would the more civilized portion of the earth be relieved from the oppressions and bondage of ignorance, and of all the inferior and vile passions which it cultivates in man, and human society would become the abode of high intelligence, under the perpetual influence of the kindest and finest sympathies of our nature; and thus would knowledge, charity, and love fill the minds and hearts of men, and pervade all the transactions of the human race. What a glorious position is now held by the present administration of the British government, if it had knowledge and firmness to make the best use of it!

The most intelligent and best disposed of the Tories, Whigs, and Radicals, and the most enlightened of all parties in church and state, are conscious that a revolution, such as history has not recorded, is now taking place in the human mind; and they must desire that it should proceed and be completed without violence, and, if possible without evil of any kind.

Let the present administration, then, communicate frankly and freely with these individuals; explain to them the necessity for union among them to direct this great change in the destiny of mankind, and the incalculable benefits which one and all may be made immediately to derive from it.

Let them, at the same time, invite the people to turn their attention from their present petty, useless political and religious squabbles about folly and inanity, for they produce only a total absence of justice, charity, and kindness, – and encourage them to give their whole powers to understand the new order of things which this revolution in public opinion will effect; and then truly may it be said, that the great change from evil to good will come 'like a thief in the night,'[a] and be produced by a Power, which no man knows 'whence it cometh, or whither it goeth.'[b]

Thus, by the most simple and natural means, might the present administration speedily remove ignorance and poverty, or the fear of it, and all uncharitableness and unkindness, from the British dominions, and speedily from all other nations, for ever; and thus might they effect, at once, that great reform, to which, if they had had foresight, they might have been sure the reform of the Commons' House of Parliament would ultimately lead. The deed is done, and it cannot be undone! The decree has gone forth that 'the mind (of man) shall be born again, the world shall be regenerated, a new heaven and a new earth shall arise, and sin and misery shall be known no more!'[c]

ROBERT OWEN

[a] See Job 24:14.
[b] See for example Psalms 121:1.
[c] See for example John 3:3, 5.

Extract from Robert Owen's Address to the Electors of Great Britain and Ireland

'It is for you, by the members whom you elect, to convince the world that you have advanced beyond the narrow and most injurious views of mere party and personal considerations; – that you desire, as speedily as possible, to terminate class legislation and obtain the rights of humanity for yourselves and your children, that you may no longer remain the slaves of an ignorant system which is most injurious to all classes.

'To secure these rights and gradually to prepare society to abandon class legislation, or the oppression of wealth over poverty, the following measures are necessary; –

1. *A graduated Property Tax, equal to the necessary National Expenditure.*
2. *The abolition of all other taxes.*
3. *Free Trade with all the World.*
4. *National Education for all who desire it.*
5. *National Employment for all who require it.*
6. *Liberty of speaking and writing on all subjects, civil, religious, and political.*
7. *Full and complete Freedom of Religion for Christians, Jews, Mahomedans, Hindoos, and every other form, under every name by which men may call themselves.*'

THE ADDRESS OF ROBERT OWEN

AT THE GREAT PUBLIC MEETING, HELD AT THE NATIONAL EQUITABLE LABOUR EXCHANGE, CHARLOTTE-STREET, FITZROY-SQUARE [LONDON] ON THE 1ST OF MAY, 1833, DENOUNCING THE OLD SYSTEM OF THE WORLD, AND ANNOUNCING THE COMMENCEMENT OF THE NEW[a]

1833

The existing condition of mankind makes it evident to those who can reflect, and who have been formed with minds capable of generalizing the ideas acquired from the past and present history of the human race, that the associations of men, from their commencement, have been founded upon a false basis, and that, in consequence, man has been found to be the creature of error and deception, of sin and of misery.

All associations have been based on the supposition that man possesses the power to believe and to feel according to the bidding of others; and that virtue consists in thus believing and feeling, and vice in refusing so to believe and feel. And by analyzing the complex proceedings of mankind, it has been discovered that the system of forming the human character, and of governing the human race, derived from these notions, is the only system that has ever been known in any part of the world, and consequently is the only one that has yet been practised.

The experience of the past, the only valuable knowledge which man has acquired, proves that this system continually generates, and effectually cultivates, all the inferior animal passions – is opposed to the progress of real knowledge, to natural sincerity, to all the higher moral virtues, and to the finest and best feelings of our nature. Also, that as long as this system shall be supported, ignorance, poverty, and of necessity, sin and misery, must

[a] The original manuscript is held in the Brougham Collection, University College, London. Owen termed this address, which was reprinted the following week in *The Crisis* (vol. 2, no. 11, 11 May 1833, pp. 210–14), 'the Magna Charta of social regeneration' (*The Crisis*, vol. 2, no. 18, 11 May 1833, p. 144). Reprinted in 1969. On the context of this meeting, see R. W. Postgate, *The Builders' History* (Labour Publishing Company, 1923), pp. 95–8, and G. D. H. Cole, *Attempts at General Union: A Study in British Trade Union History, 1818–1834* (Macmillan, 1953).

continually pervade all the associations of men; while pure charity and affection must remain as hitherto, unknown and unpractised.

Clearly perceiving this wretched state of human existence, and knowing that all governments are blind to its errors, inconsistencies, and wickedness, I have decided, after the most calm and deliberate reflection, to renounce on this day, thus publicly, in what may be justly called the metropolis of the civilized world, for myself and my disciples, the entire of this old system, and to declare my conviction that to countenance it any longer will be the grossest act of folly and the greatest of all crimes.

I also thus announce my determination henceforward to advocate thus openly and fairly another system, founded upon opposite principles, and leading to a totally different practice.

It is also my determination to recommend to all who think with me, to adopt the same course, and now to put these principles into full practice, and to assert the natural right of all men to act conscientiously, according to their convictions, as long as their conduct shall be beneficial to the public and not injurious to others.

If the existing laws of this country cannot protect the people in this moral and only really virtuous line of conduct, it is evident a despotism exists over the public mind which ought now to cease, and that the constitution of this and other countries ought to be changed to meet the improved intelligence of the age.

It is now the time to try the moral courage of men, and to ascertain who possesses virtue and knowledge sufficient to abandon falsehood for truth, folly for wisdom; yes, the period has arrived when the moral courage of man will be put to the test, and it will be proved who are prepared to overcome the mental bondage, in which, hitherto, all have been held from their infancy.

Do you feel desirous to ask me what we of the 'New World' now mean to relinquish, and what to adopt?

That none may misunderstand our proceedings, or falsify our intentions, I now thus openly, before the world, declare, that: – 1. We abandon all the false religions that have been forced upon the human race, founded on the superstition that man, by his will, has the power to believe or feel as he likes, or to believe contrary to his convictions, or feel contrary to his nature, at the bidding of others.

2. We now adopt the only religion which can be true, because it is derived immediately from the unchangeable and everlasting laws of nature, which never lie, or deceive the human race. The basis of this Religion of Truth, the only one which ever can conduct man to the practice of pure charity and real virtue, and to the enjoyment of unalloyed happiness, is the knowledge that the laws of nature have given the power to adult man, so to control the mental faculties and physical powers of his infant, as to force it to receive error, however absurd and inconsistent, or to imbibe truth only, known to be truth

by its undeviating consistency with the ascertained laws of nature; and to acquire the most wretchedly vicious and injurious, or the most highly virtuous and beneficial habits through life: and thus, through our new religion, we attain the invaluable knowledge of the certain mode by which, without individual reward, or punishment, or responsibility, to make the whole human race morally, intellectually, and physically, either inferior or superior, good or bad, miserable or happy; and yet no two of them is likely ever to be formed to be without various desirable physical and mental differences.

3. Our future practice will be in conformity with this new religion, as far as the rapidly expiring errors of the old system shall be removed to admit its adoption, and the evils necessarily emanating from this old system we shall now adopt every means to make manifest to the human race.

4. We shall be opposed to no men, but solely to the old errors, which in the period of their mental weakness they have been compelled to receive.

5. In conformity with the principles of the new religion of demonstrable truth, we shall adore in admiring silence, as alone becomes man, that, to us at present, Incomprehensible Power, which acts in and through all nature, everlastingly composing, decomposing and recomposing the materials of the universe, producing the endless variety of life, of mind, and of organized form.

6. We will not degrade, blaspheme, or merely humanize this power, so far beyond man's present knowledge as to attribute to it the human form and passions, or any of the qualities of our limited senses and vague imaginations.

7. Neither will we attempt to force others to receive or acknowledge our impressions upon this subject, seeing that up to this hour similar attempts have confounded and perplexed the human mind, making every man in every district of the world a degraded mental slave, irrational and miserable. On the contrary, we shall patiently wait until an evident accurate knowledge of this power shall be made manifest to all mankind, who will then, by the law of their nature, be compelled to admire and to love it, in proportion to the extent and the goodness of the qualities which it shall be discovered to possess.

By this course of proceeding, dictated by common sense, or plain right reasoning from self-evident facts, all injurious differences of opinions respecting religion will cease from among men; charity unlimited will take the place of presumption and violence; anger, ill-will, and irritation of all kinds will cease, and in place thereof pure love and affection, through a superior education, will be made to pervade and direct all the proceedings of mankind.

8. Directed by this knowledge and these feelings, we will, as soon as it shall be practicable, form arrangements to create New Institutions to new form the general character of the rising generation, and to regenerate the existing adult population; for the period is near at hand when the minds of men must be born

again; when they shall no longer see as through a glass darkly,[a] but face to face, and know each other even as they know themselves.

To effect this change, other arrangements, very different from those which now exist, will be formed to insure a superior education from birth, such as will give a new and very superior character to all children; arrangements that will preclude any child, free from mental disease or bodily defects, from acquiring physical, intellectual or moral injurious habits or qualities; and that will render the succeeding generations a superior order of beings compared with those who have hitherto lived.

9. As a knowledge of facts has now disclosed to us that, liking or disliking, or loving or hating, depend not upon the will of man, but upon the manner in which his organization is affected by the every-varying qualities of external objects, none will be required to perjure themselves, as they are compelled to do under the old system of the world, before they can legally enjoy the natural rights of the sexes, by solemnly declaring that they will love to the end of life a being who is liable to perpetual change, and whom they may be forced to dislike or hate before the year expires. No! instead of this blasphemy against the laws of nature, other arrangements dictated by common sense, or right reason, will be formed to insure all the good that can be derived, and to avoid all the vice and evil that has been experienced from the social converse between the sexes. All will then be fully conscious, and will openly acknowledge, that pure chastity consists in forming this connexion only when affection exists between the parties, and that it is a vile, abominable, and injurious prostitution to form or continue this connexion when there is no affection between the parties, even when they are what is called legally bound to each other. The union between the sexes will be, in consequence, always pure and chaste; it will be a union of affection only – it will continue as long as that affection can be maintained, and cease only, under well-devised public forms and regulations, when the affection between the parties can no longer be made to exist. And the experience of the world has proved that affection is more disinterested, pure, and durable, without than with these legal bonds. In order to prevent confusion or any evil whatever by these changes, other arrangements, very different from the existing family arrangements, will be made, in conformity with this superior union between the sexes, and the superior national education to be provided for the children.

10. We shall abandon the present degrading and demoralizing mode of distributing wealth by the ordinary method in practice, of buying cheap and selling dear, through the medium of the common money of the old system of the world. Arrangements will be made, as speedily as possible, to effect an equitable exchange of labour for equal value of labour throughout society, by

[a] See 1 Corinthians 13:12.

the intervention of the *labour note*,[a] the most perfect money in all respects ever yet introduced into society. But this method of transacting the business of life will be an intermediate and temporary arrangement only, and will be continued no longer than till permanent arrangements can be formed to re-constitute society upon the scientific principles, giving to each separate division of society, in practice, the due proportion of the producing, distributing, educating, and governing principles, so combined and organized that more of all kinds of wealth, possessing intrinsic value, may be, with advantage to all parties, so easily created, that those made to be the most penurious or avaricious will cease to desire any individual accumulation of it; and all contests, private or public, for the possession of wealth will terminate for ever. And then all the human powers and faculties will be directed, to promote in a straightforward manner, to the exclusion of all private interests, the general happiness of the whole of society.

11. Conscious of the unlimited powers possessed by the British nation when wisely united in its operations, to produce wealth through all future time, far beyond the wants or desires of its population, we renounce the principle of individual competition in the production and distribution of wealth, as being, in its immediate and remote consequences, not only the most demoralizing principle on which man can now act and govern his affairs, but as being, also, the greatest obstacle, in practice, to the beneficial production and distribution of wealth, to the formation of a superior individual and national character, and to the well-ordering and good government of the people.

12. We shall, therefore, as soon as the means can be obtained, exchange the principle of competition, and of mistaken individual interest, for the principle of unlimited union and of undivided national interests. And by this change in conducting the affairs of this empire, we know that more and better wealth can be produced in one day than is now produced in one week; that this greater amount and better quality of wealth can be more advantageously distributed for the whole population, by one day's occupation of those at present employed to distribute wealth, than is now effected by them under the existing competitive system of distribution in one month: that by this change, with less labour and capital than are now applied to the task the individual and national character can be formed to be many hundred-fold superior to that which has been, is, or can be found under the competition system, and that by the abandonment of the principle of division of interests, the empire will be more easily and far better governed than it ever has been under the old system, with one per cent. of the capital and labour which are now required.

[a] From 1820, Owen proposed exchanging goods on the basis of their labour value and materials costs, using notes to represent the former to replace existing money. These notes were used in several labour exchanges in the early 1830s. The best account of their operations remains W. H. Oliver, 'The Labour Exchange Phase of the Co-operative Movement', *Oxford Economic Papers*, 10 (1958), pp. 354–67.

13. As the false basis upon which the moral part of the old system has been founded, united with the principle of competition, when applied to practice, form together the sole cause which renders law, or codes of law, necessary in society, we, of the new world, renounce all law proceedings in our transactions with each other, and we will form arrangements to adjust whatever differences may arise between individuals, or associations of individuals, by the decision of three persons selected for their superior knowledge and experience in the new principles, and their known love of justice; these individuals to be annually chosen by the elders of their district.

Courts of law, and all the paraphernalia and folly of law, with its animosities and ruinous expense, cannot be found in a rational state of society and will, therefore, not be found among the children of the new world.

14. As the principles on which this new system is based will immediately check, and effectually prevent the growth of anger and ill will, and speedily remove all the causes of dislike from among the children trained from infancy in the new world, war will be discountenanced, and ultimately abrogated as a practice, the most grossly ignorant and vicious that a well ordered or rational mind can conceive; a practice contrary to our new religion, and to be followed only by those who have been made irrational from their birth or by wholesale murderers and robbers.

Charity, peace, and good-will to the whole family of mankind, without regard to any of the petty aritificial or irrational causes of division now existing between them, will be the inevitable, and, therefore, uniform practice of all the children of the new world; and one of their chief offices, until the ignorance which causes the evil shall be removed, will be to reconcile man to man, and nation to nation, throughout the world, and to enable all to understand that they have but one interest, which is, to insure the permanent happiness of each and all, to promote which, by every means that the aggregate of knowledge and power can devise, will be the great business of human life, and then will be seen how easy and straightforward is the true path to real virtue and the most refined enjoyments.

15. But although the private and public warfare and contests, with their endless train of unavoidable crime and misery, will be unknown among the children of the new world, effeminacy, with its train of evil, will also be discountenanced and discarded. The new mode of forming the character of the children of the new world will cultivate, and bring forth to maturity and perfection, all the physical, intellectual, and moral faculties and powers which have been given to human nature. Arrangements will be formed to admit and encourage the due exercise of each of these faculties and powers up to the point of temperance, for it is only by all of them being called into action at the period designed by nature, that man can feel satisfied, contented, and happy. Anxiety is the natural feeling which arises when any one of these propensities or qualities is not duly exercised. The physical powers will, therefore, be better

cultivated than they were in the best days of Greece and Rome, and a far superior form of body and expression of mind, and a duly regulated activity of both will be obtained for all the future generations.

In consequence, celibacy, in either sex, beyond the period designed by nature, will no longer be considered a virtue, but, on the contrary, it will be known to be, as it is, a great crime against nature, causing other unnatural crimes, all of which produce disease of body and mind, giving a false direction to both thoughts and feelings, and thereby making the human race the most artificial, unnatural and criminal beings in existence. The earth is yet a wilderness for want of people to drain its marshes and cultivate its soil, nor does it yet produce one thousandth part of the excellence and enjoyment which it is capable of bringing forth and permanently sustaining. Upon this, and almost all other important subjects, the world is in gross darkness, because it has hitherto been instructed and governed, or rather uninstructed and misgoverned, by men trained to possess only the most feeble and puny knowledge of themselves, of nature, and of wise and good government.

16. We now also renounce the separate interests which have been created by the errors of the old world; and we will adopt another mode of carrying on the general business of society. Originally many and various occupations were performed by one individual; but as population increased in particular places, the variety of employments practised by one person gradually diminished, until they are now become so much divided, that many individuals have their time and attention taken up and occupied in making a small part of a common pin,[a] a needle, or of thread, to the destruction of their health, their mental faculties, and all the higher enjoyments of a rational existence. Experience has now developed the means by which the union and division of labour may be combined to secure the peculiar advantages of both, without the evils of either. The science of society, so totally unknown in the old world, has disclosed the necessity for, and the benefits of, uniting a due proportion of agriculture, manufactures, commerce, education, and government, in every separate association, for carrying on the business of life; and in the new world all these individualised and opposing interests will become one, and each part thus united, will essentially aid and promote all the others. The communities of the new world, when the public shall acquire any rational notions respecting them, will be found to be nothing less than a combination of all these interests, so united as to insure to every individual living within them, the greatest amount of advantages, and the highest degree of individual freedom and happiness that human nature, in its present state of knowledge, is capable of enjoying. Thus will man, as a member of an association formed purposely for his benefit, experience the utmost share of

[a] See Adam Smith, *Wealth of Nations*, Bk 1, ch. 1.

individual freedom that is compatible with the still higher privileges of a social state of existence.

17. We consequently abandon all the arrangements to which these separate interests have given birth; such as large cities, towns, villages, and universities, as well as the existing arrangements for carrying on the business of agriculture, detached from manufactures, education, and commerce. These accidental individual circumstances, formed without knowledge or foresight, are not such as can ever form man into a rational being, or insure to him more than a very small portion of the wealth, health, and happiness, which his nature may be made to enjoy.

18. We also abandon, to the irrationality of the old system of the world, all places for ceremonial worship of an unknown Power, and with them all mysteries in every department of life, as being much worse than useless. In like manner, we abandon to the same system all places of punishment and confinement, such as Prisons, Penitentiaries, Houses of Correction, and Workhouses; and all charitable institutions, as they are called, as being prominent and magnificent monuments of the utter incapacity of the rulers of human affairs, to form arrangements to insure a superior character, wealth, and health of body and mind, to the respective populations which they have governed or do now attempt to govern.

19. We abandon also all individual ambition, and desire for personal distinction, knowing we possess nothing but what we have received, and that these personal distinctions cannot benefit mankind but are, in themselves, the cause of endless errors, crimes, and miseries, and tend to keep men in perpetual ignorance of themselves, and to make them highly irrational.

20. We also dismiss, for similar reasons, all envy and jealousy from the new world, in which all will partake of the advantages derived from the excellencies of each; all will, therefore, feel their happiness to be increased in proportion as each excels in all superior qualifications, and in consequence all will aid to enable each individual to acquire and enjoy them. Thus will unity of design, of duty, of interest, and of sympathy, among the human race, supersede the division, competition, and opposition of man to man, and nation to nation, and remove the causes of all the envy and jealousy which instigate to crime, make man a demon, and the earth a pandemonium.

I therefore now proclaim to the world the commencement, on this day, of the promised millenium, founded on rational principles and consistent practice.

ADDRESS TO THE TRADES' UNIONS, AND TO ALL THE PRODUCERS OF WEALTH AND KNOWLEDGE THROUGHOUT GREAT BRITAIN AND IRELAND[a] 1834

You now appear before the world to assert the rights of industry, in opposition to the assumed power of idleness and uselessness over your property, lives, and happiness. Your enemies are alarmed at the position you have taken; your friends are afraid you have scarcely sufficient experience and wisdom to assert these rights in a proper spirit, and to maintain them, without throwing society into confusion.

Your enemies are the friends of ignorance, corruption, and human misery, and well may they be alarmed; the days of their power are numbered, and discovered to be few; while your friends have been preparing themselves calmly and quietly to come to your aid as soon as they shall ascertain that you have received the true spirit of forbearance, charity, and kindness for your opponents, knowing that until this spirit in all its genuineness of purity shall be imbibed, you cannot adopt wise measures to obtain your emancipation from the ignorant and vicious system by which your opponents have so long oppressed you.

This spirit has been introduced among you, it has taken root, has been nurtured, and is about to produce fruit a hundred-fold. This, then, is the day of your salvation, the time for you to arouse yourselves to effect the great and glorious change that is before you.

In this conflict, between the industrious and useful and the idle and useless, many errors will be at first committed by the former, for the want of that experience so long possessed by the latter; limited views will be at first adopted, as they have been; but now is the time for these limited views to give place to sound principles, and a more extended field of action.

The operatives have formed their Trades' Unions, and confined them at first to partial numbers in the respective branches of a general trade or manufacture. They have latterly been extended to several branches of the same general

[a] First published in *The Crisis*, vol. 3, no. 20 (11 January 1834), pp. 156–7.

business or calling; they now require to be further extended to all the branches of each general trade, manufacture, or employment, and that these also should be united by one common bond of interest among all the producers of wealth and of real knowledge.

This union is to be perfected by considering all the producers of every thing of real value as members of one body, having but one interest; and by uniting these producers in well devised practical measures, to give efficiency to their proceedings.

The shortest, easiest, and most certain mode by which to accomplish this union, is first to unite the masters and men: producers of all that is useful and necessary for happiness. They are, in fact, one and the same body, the masters having gradually arisen out of the mass of workmen.

It is true that some of these masters are ignorant of their own real interests, and therefore act the tyrant, being cruel, unjust, and illiberal. They exact severe labour from, and pay low wages to, all those whom they employ; but not so with many other masters. They know that those who, by their daily toil, produce wealth for them, are their best friends, and their interests never can be separated without the most grievous evils resulting to both. It becomes the interests, therefore, of the operatives to aid the good masters to obtain the rights of industry for both, and to form arrangements to render it incumbent on those masters who are not at present so well disposed to become such as the superior and best disposed now are.

This, Sir, is the real object of the Society for Promoting National Regeneration;[a] and surely it is necessary that a thorough regeneration of the ignorant and vicious system by which the world has been so long misgoverned should now be commenced.

The promoters of this change in human affairs are not the disturbers of peace, but real conservatives. They desire to remove grievous evils, not by violence or anger, which generate other, and sometimes worse, evils than those intended to be removed, but by practical measures equal to the task devised by reason and experience, and which must produce in a short period unmixed good to the whole of society.

They, therefore, recommend that the intelligent and well-disposed among the masters in each trade, manufacture, and beneficial occupation should unite and form a Masters' Union, as a majority of the master manufactures in the Potteries have already done;[b] that these masters encourage the intelligent, temperate, and well-disposed of the operatives whom they employ to form union among themselves; that both parties elect from their union properly chosen persons to be delegates to form a union of friendly communication

---

[a] Short-lived reform organisation set up by Owen and John Fielden (1784–1839) in 1833–4, aiming at the eight-hour workday.

[b] See for example *The Crisis*, vol. 3, no. 5 (5 October 1833), p. 36.

between them, and by which all differences of opinion may be amicably adjusted each week as they may arise; and thus that spirit of opposition, discontent, and, I fear too often, hatred, which has been engendered and cultivated by the ignorance of both employer and employed, will be changed for one of mutual confidence and kindness, and a sincere desire to promote each other's interest and happiness. By this union of masters of men, producers of wealth and knowledge, the following benefits will result:

1. The operatives, or actual producers of wealth, will be employed a reasonable time per day in producing wealth for society, and afterwards in acquiring the most useful knowledge for themselves, and in recruiting their health and spirits, by rational recreation and social enjoyment, that they may be usefully and happily occupied during their lives.

2. For producing this wealth for society, they require in justice to have, and will obtain, a good living for themselves and families, and a sound practical education for their children.

3. The master manufacturers, or employers of the operatives, will obtain a fair remuneration for their capital, the wear and tear of their establishments, and an average of ten per cent. profit upon the productions of British industry, for their own skill and labour, or for the skill and labour of those who direct the general operations of their establishments; and lastly, the public will have good, honest productions, instead of the articles of deception with which all markets now superabound.

This union of the producers, employers and employed, will therefore permanently improve the condition of the working men and of their families; of the employers and their families; and of the public generally, both at home and abroad; of a public now cheated, deceived, and injured in almost every possible way, and for no other reason that can be discovered except to bolster up a little longer the gross absurdities, in contradiction to all known facts, of the most visionary imaginations of men and women – of men and women, too, who are totally ignorant of all national practice, and of the extraordinary beneficial results which may be attained by our national power wisely directed.

These incongruous and contradictory imaginings they have dignified with the name of *political economy*, while they have not yet discovered the data on which the science of political economy can be alone founded.

It is these imaginations which have been put forth in every popular form and shape, in newspapers, periodicals and pamphlets for the last twenty-five years, that have confounded the intellects of what are called learned men, and of all their readers. Were a correct judgment formed of modern learning by their publications, it would be fully proved that no two things could be more removed from each other than modern learning and real knowledge; they appear to be the very antipodes of each other, and hence alone the disorganised state of British society; for the very lowest of the people, as soon as they began to think at all, discovered that they were governed by those who opposed their vain imaginations to facts – who would support the most destructive theories, although they daily witnessed the most appalling miseries which they created to the people – miseries created solely by those theories being forced into practice, and which have been persevered in so long that the population has lost all confidence in the wisdom and humanity of those who ought to lead and govern them. In consequence, the most valuable portion of the people – that is, the useful, or the producers of real wealth and knowledge, from dire necessity have been compelled to take their own affairs into their own hands, to prevent their utter degradation, to stay the downward progress of demoralization and poverty, to prevent that power which might be, and which might easily be made to be, the greatest blessing to the population of the world, from being a curse to the productive classes of the British empire, and through their unnatural and most ruinous competition with all the other industrious portions of the earth, the greatest of all curses to them also, and to their posterity.

Let, therefore, all anger, ill-will, and dissention cease among all the producers, both employers and employed, of real wealth and knowledge throughout Great Britain and Ireland, and let them now adopt practical measures, founded on experience, to insure a good living to themselves and families, and a good quality of all articles for the public, and make no more of any thing than the public will pay a fair remunerating price for; and let all who wish to produce useful wealth be constantly employed a reasonable period daily; but let not any over-work themselves, or be half their time idle, from want of employment being found for them, while others are compelled to be altogether without occupation, because the first class named are required by their ignorant employers to over-exert all their powers and faculties.

Therefore, before all things, as the most important step that can now be taken to emancipate the population from gross ignorance, I recommend a cordial union of all the producers of real wealth and knowledge, both employers and employed, and that this senseless warfare, carried on between the masters and operatives, solely for the gain and advantage of those who neither produce wealth, knowledge, or any thing really useful and beneficial for any portion of mankind, should now cease, and their interests hereafter be for ever united.

I am, your friend,

ROBERT OWEN

PROPOSALS FOR A CHANGE OF SYSTEM IN THE BRITISH EMPIRE, SUBMITTED TO THE CONSIDERATION OF THE BRITISH GOVERNMENT[a]

Propositions demonstrating the necessity of a general change.

1. That the late progress made in the mechanical arts, in chemistry, and in various other sciences, has rendered manual labour less necessary, and therefore, less valuable, in a commercial point of view, than formerly.

2. That manual labour being, as society is now constituted, the only medium through which the industrious class can obtain the means of support for themselves and their families, the reduction in the commercial value of labour has necessarily produced among them the great and general distress at present prevailing.

3. That the commercial value of manual labour, in agriculture, and in many branches of manufacture, having in many cases sunk to its minimum, while the extension of scientific power still continues rapidly on the increase, commercial difficulties are consequently speedily advancing to a crisis, the approach of which, is viewed by the middle and working classes (a number comprising two-thirds of the whole population) with feelings of the utmost anxiety and alarm.

4. That, under the existing commercial system, it is impossible that manual labour should ever again compete with the powers of science.

5. That the working classes, as the only practicable mode of ameliorating their condition, will be compelled to adopt a system of mutual exchange of labour, and thereby render themselves at once independent of the *non*-producing classes.

6. That this measure, if generally adopted by the working class, would create great confusion and misery among the *non*-producing classes, as their wealth would thus lose the adventitious value which it now possesses.

7. That although this system, if adopted by the working classes alone, would be attended by the injurious consequences above-mentioned, yet that, if carried into effect by the aid of the higher classes, and under the sanction of

[a] First published in *The Crisis*, vol. 3, no. 23 (1 February 1834), pp. 180–6.

government, the introduction of the measure would produce the most beneficial permanent results to the whole population.

8. That the physical and mental, as well as the scientific powers of society, are now so mis-directed that enormous evils, moral, political, and commercial, are entailed upon all classes.

9. That those evils are such as to excite among a large portion of the community an ardent desire for an entire change in the system of society.

Propositions demonstrating the fitness of the present period for the introduction of a change

1. That experience has now developed the origin of evil among mankind, and the means of its removal.

2. That the state of the world has never hitherto been such as to admit of moral truth being taught to the rising generation, nor therefore of the introduction of a system founded upon consistent and rational principles.

3. That the extraordinary political events which have lately occurred, and the general progress made in scientific and in moral knowledge among the population in the leading states of Europe and America, have in a remarkable manner prepared all classes in these countries to expect some great moral, political, and commercial changes.

4. That the commencement of this change is, at this time more particularly, looked for in the British empire, in consequence of its surplus powers for the production of wealth being superabundant for all purposes, yet continually on the increase; while, under the existing moral, political and commercial notions of society, those powers must continually more and more oppress, instead of ameliorate the condition of the people; and because there is sufficient stability in the government and knowledge in the population to introduce and control the progress of such a change most advantageously for the British dominions, and for the world.

Propositions demonstrating the necessity of a moral change.

1. That the moral system of the world has hitherto been founded on the supposition that man is so constituted as to have the power of creating his own opinions and feelings, and consequently of forming his individual character.

2. That facts have now proved this supposition to be an error fatal to all

genuine moral truth, and therefore fatal to the well-being and happiness of society.

3. That man is forced to think in obedience to the strongest conviction that is made at any moment upon his mind, and to feel in obedience to the particular impression which any object is fitted to produce upon his individual organization; that his character is entirely formed FOR *him* by the action of external circumstances upon his own peculiar original organization.

4. That the erroneous supposition that man had the power to think and to feel as he pleased, and the character of each individual is formed BY himself, is the origin of evil among mankind, and has created all the misery which has been ever produced in human society.

5. That the whole nature of man is decidedly opposed to all the doctrines which this erroneous supposition involves; yet that the religious and political power of the world has compelled him to submit to the effects of these doctrines, and that he has been forced to become an ignorant hypocrite, and thereby fitted with every motive to the commission of vice and crime.

6. That, while the doctrines which necessarily arise from this erroneous supposition shall continue to be taught to the rising generation, the most superior character that can be formed will still be a compound of imbecility, deceit, selfishness, and distrust, accompanied, at the same time, with a strong but unavailing desire to counteract these lamentable defects.

7. That while human beings shall be compelled to receive an unnatural character, it will be impossible for them to become rational, or to be generally united in opinions, feelings, or actions.

8. That, until the principles which can effect a general union among mankind shall be universally disseminated, which can only be done by instilling into every mind, from birth, a correct knowledge of human nature, it will be in vain to expect that permanent prosperity and happiness shall ever be found among any portion of the human race.

Propositions demonstrating the beneficial effects necessarily arising from the adoption of a new Moral System, founded upon the knowledge that man has neither the power to THINK *nor to* FEEL *as he pleases, nor to form his own character.*

1. That, in consequence of men being trained from their infancy in these principles, they will acquire a knowledge of human nature, and thereby unavoidably become sincere, intelligent, and rational, and be filled with kindness alone for the entire family of mankind.

2. That they will receive natural impressions, and therefore right feelings from that power, whatever experience may ultimately prove it to be, whence all the movements of the universe originate.

3. That individual responsibility being thus withdrawn, no motive can exist to generate anger, nor any of the inferior passions which are now so prevalent and injurious throughout society.

4. That all individuals being thus trained from infancy to be rational beings, no motive to whim or caprice could be formed in any mind, but that every one would be consistent in thought, word, and action.

5. That a character of this consistent nature, combined with the best dispositions, habits, and manners, and the most valuable knowledge, will be secured to every one by a science as certain in its laws and results as those of any of the fixed sciences now known.

Propositions demonstrating the necessity of a political change

1. That all governments having necessarily been founded upon the same erroneous notions from which the spurious morality of the world has originated, their code of laws has been opposed to nature, complicated and unjust, and their practice therefore has been of necessity deceit, contention, and war.

2. That, under this error each government has been compelled, in its own defence, to pursue the same course, or otherwise to fall victim to some other power, superior in force or in these arts of deception.

3. That all nations, having been forced by this error into a miserable and irrational state of existence, governments have been compelled, for their own support and security, to oppress the governed, and to keep them, as much as possible, in ignorance of the motives on which they have acted.

4. That, under the present system, all being ignorant of the fundamental laws of human nature, no good government can exist, nor can any be devised which would mutually benefit the governing and governed.

5. That, under this error, armies and navies have been necessarily created, to govern human nature by force instead of by reason.

6. That a government of force requires for its support a very large proportion of the labour and best faculties of the population, and necessarily entails innumerable other evils upon both the governing and the governed.

7. That war, under this error, is unavoidable, and that, although incidentally it has been productive of some partial advantages, it is yet, almost without exception, the cause of the most grievous evils to both the victors and the vanquished.

8. That, under this error, the whole system of government has necessarily made irrationality and folly of every conceivable description the high fashion among the leading parties of all nations, and that, in consequence, the most valuable powers, national and individual, have been applied to produce the most useless or injurious results.

Proposals demonstrating the beneficial effects necessarily arising from the adoption of a political system, founded on the foregoing new Moral System.

1. That, under the new Moral System of truth and sincerity, which would arise from an accurate knowledge of human nature, no motives could exist to tempt governments to pursue any other course than that which would be most conducive to the public good, and that they would then clearly perceive how to direct all their proceedings for the mutual permanent benefit of themselves and the governed.

2. That, in consequence, no contest could arise between the government and the people; and that, as both parties would evidently have but one common interest, all men would engage in promoting it with more zeal, satisfaction, and pleasure, than they now engage in the schemes of individual interest, ambition, or sensual gratification.

3. That, under this system, no cause can ever arise to disturb the confidence or weaken the good feelings which will naturally subsist between the government and the people; and that a union of mind and action, proceeding from a correct knowledge of the best means of promoting the permanent happiness of both, will necessarily pervade all their transactions.

4. That governments would no longer be a mystery to the people nor an object of contest between individuals or parties, nor be maintained by a counteraction of interests; because all their transactions would be made solely with a view to the public good, and be made familiar to all.

Propositions demonstrating the necessity of a commercial change.

1. That the interchange of commodities, and the practices of commerce, as hitherto carried on, have arisen from the same erroneous notions of human nature as those that have created the false morality and mistaken policy of all countries.

2. That, in consequence, trade, commerce, and manufactures, which ought to be productive of unmixed good, are now almost an unmixed evil, producing falsehood, cunning, competition, and opposition of feeling, between buyers and sellers individually, oppression and poverty among the community at large, and counteraction, contest, and war between nations.

3. That as these departments of life are now conducted, they are instruments by which the weaker part of society is imposed upon by the stronger, or, in other words, by those who possess greater capital, influence, or cunning; and

by means of which men are trained to endeavour, through their lives, to take advantage one of another.

4. That all, from the highest to the lowest, are now engaged, in one form or other, in this universal traffic of deception.

5. That the effects which necessarily arise from conducting commercial affairs on these erroneous notions are, first, to excite a most mischievous desire on the part of all for individual gain; a desire, which, in its consequences, deteriorates the finest feelings and best faculties of the human race; and secondly, to deprive all of the real advantages which belong to a rational interchange of both commodities and of the productions of the human faculties.

6. That the human race is thus made to live, contrary to its interest and happiness, in perpetual contest, and in the constant fear of poverty, and to have all the highest faculties of the mind perverted by the universal practice of buying cheap and of selling dear.

7. That this universal desire, as now applied to practice, so blinds the understanding or judgment of all, that they cannot perceive that they are thereby, as all are doing at this moment, compelled to sell cheap and to buy dear; for that now, in this supposed enlightened age of commerce, the productive physical and mental powers of all human beings are sold at one per cent. of their real value.

8. That this enormous loss in the real value of the productive powers, both physical and mental, of human nature, is an unavoidable result of men being, through ignorance of the laws of their nature, so placed, that they must prey upon one another, in order to support themselves, and are thus compelled to live by contest instead of by union.

Propositions demonstrating the beneficial effects necessarily arising from the adoption of a Commercial System, founded on the foregoing new Moral and Political Systems.

1. That, as no motive could exist for deception of any kind, nor any arise to induce one man to counteract another in any pursuit, the physical and mental powers of all will be brought to an equitable market, one in which, without any bargaining, each will obtain full value in exchange for the productions of those powers.

2. That, by this moral and equitable mode of interchange, each will receive a full supply of every thing most beneficial for human nature, or, in other words, of every thing that can contribute to the improvement of men, and to his highest enjoyment of life.

3. That these results will be secured without contest or competition between

individuals or nations, except as to which among them shall be the instrument of producing the greatest amount of happiness to the greatest number.

4. That this great change in the commercial transactions of society is, only to be brought about by giving an entirely new direction to the latterly discovered scientific powers of production, which could only be effected under the new Moral System, out of which no thought or practice but of good can ever arise.

5. That these powers of production are now so unwisely directed as to deprive a large proportion of the working classes of the means of existence, and grievously to oppress the whole of them; and that, in consequence, the time must soon arrive when the prosperity of the *non*-producing classes will be equally endangered; while, by the proposed change of system, these new powers will be applied to *aid* the labour of the producing classes, and thereby secure incalculable advantages to all individuals of every rank and condition.

Outline of the mode by which this beneficial change may be effected in the British Empire.

The most direct and the most effectual mode of producing this great change is, to create a new public opinion. A right public opinion upon these subjects will, perhaps, be best formed by the truths included in them being published in the most plain and simple manner, in all newspapers and periodicals which may be under the influence of government, or of individuals who may be made to feel the importance of the measure.

Public meetings in London and in the principal cities and towns in the empire, if properly conducted, may also be made a powerful means of aiding the press in producing this change in public opinion; and as religion, under the new Moral System, will consist in *truth*, in *sincerity*, in *universal charity* and *kindness*, and in *good actions, only from each to every other human being*; and as this character will be secured to every individual by the new mode of education recommended, all cathedrals, churches, chapels, meeting-houses, synagogues, mosques, pagodas, temples, and every other description of buildings now dedicated to mistaken notions of the utility of senseless forms and ceremonies, may be appropriated to the daily instruction of the population of every country in which Great Britain has, or may acquire, sufficient influence, in a knowledge of the laws of human nature, and in the ultimate good effects which will arise from the introduction into practice of the new Moral, Political, and Commercial System, founded on these laws. And all should be taught, especially, to understand that TRUTH, when undefiled by error or inconsistency of any kind, is alone pure religion; for that moral truth and genuine religion are synonymous terms.

And as moral truth, when unmixed with error, can be readily taught to the human mind, all may be made to comprehend it.

By these means, aided by the hearty co-operation of the clergy of all denominations, whose situation it is intended, by the practical arrangements to be proposed, shall be greatly changed for the better, the population of the British dominions may be so enlightened in an incredibly short period, that they will be enabled to ascertain whatever is true or false, in moral or religious principle that may be presented to them. Because that, by their superior instruction, they will soon perceive that truth is always consistent with itself, that, consequently, each separate truth is in unison with every other truth in the universe, and that, therefore, wherever there is inconsistency there must be error.

By these means pure and genuine religion, or moral truth, or, in figurative language, 'the knowledge of the Lord,'[a] will be made speedily 'to cover the earth as the waters cover the sea.'[b]

While the means of disseminating moral truth, or pure and genuine religion, shall be in full operation, some of the enormous surplus capital, skill, and labour, which now overwhelm and oppress the British population may be rationally employed, under the sanction of government, to create, for all classes, new moral, political, and commercial arrangements, to supersede the vicious circumstances by which, in every department of life, individuals are now surrounded; all of which circumstances are, more or less, calculated to produce, as they now actually do, vice, and crime, and misery, throughout the British dominions.

The experience of past ages has elicited the preceding facts, and proved them to be the only sure guide to instruct man in a knowledge of his nature, and in the means to insure his happiness as an individual, and as a member of society; it also proved that, in consequence of the ignorance of these facts, the nature of man has not been properly understood, that he has been surrounded, from infancy, with circumstances uncongenial to, or in opposition to his nature, and thereby made a vicious, inconsistent, irrational, miserable being.

From the writings of our ancestors therefore, no useful knowledge can be derived, except that of simple facts. The past history of our race, as known to us, is no more than a development of a period of human existence, when, under the influence of an immoral system, generating universal disunion of mind and feeling, counteraction, wars, and massacres, human beings were rendered irrational. Under the new Moral System, none of these evils could have place; but the past will be an everlasting memento of human sufferings, which, by comparison, will always add to the enjoyment of the new state of

[a] See for example Daniel 1:17.
[b] See Genesis 6:17.

existence, in which these sufferings will be wholly unknown, except as a matter of history.

The new preliminary arrangements intended for the existing division of classes in society, consist of a new combination of circumstances, calculated to change them gradually, from the irrational state in which they now are, to become, with the least loss of time, comparatively superior beings, and to enjoy, as much as their respective habits will admit, the yet unknown pleasures of a rational existence.

To prepare mankind for a superior state of existence, they must be educated, from infancy, in the knowledge, dispositions, and habits which would be given to them in the new Moral System; for the present generation, therefore, preliminary or compromising arrangements will be the best suited for the three classes into which society is now divided. These arrangements, however, may be so formed as to secure, without too great a change of their present habits, the means of continued improvement, and much enjoyment for the adults and the best education for the children. Until the overwhelming effects of an education founded on a knowledge of the laws of human nature, shall be witnessed, the public will be incompetent to judge of the practicability of forming permanent arrangements to secure to all individually the best of every thing.

Proposed preliminary arrangements necessary to effect a general *change throughout the British Empire.*

Towns to be formed of sufficient extent to admit of a population composed of a due proportion of the higher, middle, and lower classes, and the buildings to be arranged in the manner most convenient for each class, according to its present habits.

The towns to be of sufficient extent, and the buildings to be so arranged, as to give the inhabitants the united advantages of a metropolis, an university, and of a country residence, without the disadvantages of either, which, under the whole combination of circumstances proposed, will be practicable. Schools to be established in each town, for the purpose of educating the children of the population in a very superior manner, compared with any past or existing mode of education; that is, by training the children, by placing them under proper circumstances from infancy, to become rational beings.

A sufficient quantity of land to be around each town to allow of the formation of a superior agricultural establishment, that the inhabitants may, by means of their capital, knowledge, skill, and industry, obtain a perpetual supply of the best of every thing for the three classes respectively, according to their present wants and habits. A portion of the land to be laid out as gardens and pleasure-grounds, to combine, as far as might be practicable, the useful and the beautiful.

Manufactories, on a superior plan, to be established at a convenient distance from the town, of sufficient extent to furnish the inhabitants with such productions as they may require; and to create a surplus, to give in exchange to the inhabitants of other towns for a similar amount of such of their productions as may be necessary to keep up a continual supply for all in the stores and granaries, and to enable them to procure the best of every thing generally for human nature.

Each town to be furnished with libraries, laboratories, lectures, artists, music, and assembly-rooms, for the improvement and amusement of the population; as well as with the means of engaging in field-sports, and other exercises, according to the respective habits of the three classes.

No class to interfere with the amusements or exercises of the other, except by mutual consent.

The children of the whole population to be educated together as one class, and trained to live afterwards on an equality, within much superior arrangements to any which can now be formed. For the enjoyment of this higher order of society, they will be prepared through a rational education from infancy, by which they will receive superior knowledge, dispositions, and feelings, literally be formed into perfect beings, compared with any of the known past or present inhabitants of the world.

The population of each town to be limited to the number most convenient to be governed, educated, employed, supplied, and amused under one general arrangement.

In each town, every new improvement and discovery in machinery, in manufactures, and in agriculture, in chemistry, and in the arts and sciences generally, to be introduced and acted upon, by means of which labour may be diminished, and the happiness of the whole population promoted; and when each individual shall be scientifically educated, theoretically as well as practically, from childhood, and when all shall be trained to delight in the most useful application of their powers, mental and physical, surrounded, as they will be, by means for the most beneficial exercise of both, the general progress that society will make, cannot be estimated by those so irrationally educated and placed as all of the present generation have been.

The respective classes in each town to be governed by a committee of twelve persons, chosen by ballot, by the members of each class who are between 35 and 45 years of age. Three members to be renewed annually.

The general establishment to be governed by a committee of nine persons, chosen by ballot by the class committees, three from each class; three new members to be elected every third year; in both cases the retiring members to be eligible for re-election, after one period of absence.

All differences between the inhabitants to be adjusted by the division of a majority of three persons, one chosen from each class committee by ballot; one member to be renewed annually, but always eligible, after one year, for re-election.

Pure morality to be taught in the schools of each town, by training each child to speak the truth only, without fear, by forming him to be perfectly sincere in look, word, and action; to have real charity and kind feelings for every individual of his race, and to receive his highest pleasures from the performance of kind offices and beneficial services for all, without exception, with whom he may come in contact. Each child to be educated to become his own priest, physician, and lawyer; which, under this new moral, political, and commercial system, will be easy of attainment.

The capital to be furnished by the upper classes, for which they are to receive an equitable return from the middle and working classes, by obtaining, in proportion to the capital advanced, a supply of the best of every thing for human nature. That which is best for human nature, to be agreed upon at the formation of the establishment. It is presumed that, by means of this arrangement, the capital of the upper classes will obtain for them at least double the number of advantages which they now derive from their present mode of expenditure.

The general rules and regulations for conducting the affairs of each establishment to be as much in accordance with the fundamental laws of human nature, and the conditions necessary for its happiness, as the present habits of man will admit.

Under this new combination of comparatively rational circumstances, the habits, views, and conduct of the parties might be confidently expected daily to approach a state of rationality.

This arrangement would unite the interest of the whole population; for it would at once relieve all from the fear of poverty, and from sinking in the scale of society; it would speedily remove ignorance and all inferior habits, and gradually introduce a better understanding and kindly feeling between all classes, than ever exist, under the present irrational system of universal disunion and counteraction.

It would be discovered, with surprise and pleasure, how rapidly, in proper circumstances, formed under a knowledge of the laws of human nature, each individual would acquire a character in all respects superior to any that has hitherto been formed for him. The change which these new circumstances would speedily create would appear to the ignorant as a miraculous new birth, or regeneration; and such, no doubt, is the change which the ancients anticipated would take place as soon as their descendants should acquire a knowledge of the laws of human nature, and live under circumstances in unison with them.

The general principles now recommended, if applied to Ireland, would be the means of relieving it from its present distresses; for under this arrangement its population and revenues might be advantageously doubled, trebled, and quadrupled.

Or, the middle and working-classes, both in Great Britain and Ireland, might be united, under similar arrangements to those recommended; the establishments being formed upon a less expensive scale by dispensing with that part of the arrangements extended for the general accommodation of the upper classes. Or the system might, in the first instance, be applied to the relief of the working-classes and to the relief of pauperism, under an arrangement possessing somewhat of the following character.

Plan for the Relief of the Working Classes, and for the Gradual Diminution and Future Prevention of Pauperism.

A population composed of the usual proportion of men, women, and children, to be congregated in such numbers as will be more conveniently governed, educated, supplied, and rendered happy in the best manner for themselves and the public. To ascertain this number is the first problem to be solved in the science of political economy; for without a solution of this problem, no correct knowledge on the subject can be obtained. The present miserable condition of the working-classes may shortly perhaps force this valuable discovery upon society. It is probable that the number most convenient for these combined purposes is from 500 to 2000 as a minimum and a maximum, and from 800 to 1200 as the best general aggregate, were it advantageous to make permanent arrangements for a number less then 2000, which perhaps is not the case.

A population of from 500 to 2000 would, if properly educated, comprise within itself all the elements of a superior independent association; and it is probable that it would be highly advantageous to each individual and to the public that society should never consist of a greater or less number in one congregated mass.

That the nucleus of society should be formed upon associations such as are recommended, instead of the isolated families of which it now consists, is rendered apparent by the fact that the division of society into single families continually generates selfishness, vice, and misery, and will keep man, as long as it shall exist, in an immoral state of great degradation and universal disunion. It is a state of society which has been framed in ignorance of the laws of human nature, and of the conditions necessary to its happiness, and one which is calculated to render man perpetually deceitful, weak, dependent, ignorant, and irrational.

Arrangements to be therefore formed, at the commencement of each establishment, to admit advantageously of a gradual increase of population, from 500 to 2000.

In choosing the first members to form the nucleus of each establishment, a due proportion of trades and physical and mental occupations, requisite to supply the wants of the population, to be selected.

Each village to be laid out, at its commencement, with a view to the health, convenience, and comfort of the population, when it shall have attained its maximum, as well as during the period of its gradual increase.

Around this village to be as much land as will be sufficient to secure to the whole population, when at its maximum, by means of its own well-directed industry, a full supply of the necessaries and comforts of life.

Schools to be established, in which to train all the children, from infancy to maturity, in the best manner, physically, mentally, and morally.

Manufactories, of the most useful descriptions, well arranged, to be established, at a convenient distance from each village, sufficient, together with agriculture and gardening, to occupy as much of the time as may be found to be beneficial of the whole population capable of being advantageously employed.

The village arrangements to be under the general direction, for a certain period, of a board of commissioners, composed of experienced and intelligent individuals, familiar with the general practical business of life, and consisting of such a number as would most conveniently direct measures of so much magnitude and importance. The members of this board of commissioners to be chosen by the government or the parliament.

Each village to be directed in all its internal affairs by a committee, under the general direction, for a limited time, of the board of commissioners. The committee to be chosen by all the inhabitants of the village, who may be between thirty-five and forty-five years of age, and to consist of twelve members.

The business of each village to be divided into the six departments of education: agriculture, building, manufactures, police, and external and internal exchanges, or commercial transactions; and each of these departments to be under the control of a sub-committee, appointed by the general village committee.

Differences of every description that may arise between the villages to be speedily and finally adjusted by the decision of a majority of three persons, chosen by a majority of the inhabitants between 35 and 45 years of age; one new member to be elected annually, to replace one of the former members, who, at the expiration of a year will be eligible for re-election.

As long as the present inferior habits in which all have been trained shall render any individual exchanges beneficial or necessary, all exchanges of commodities, as well as those of services, to be made on the principle of labour for equal labour, at a bazaar to be established in each village, and so arranged that every commodity may be conveniently exchanged, without loss of time or morals to the producers, or to those who have personal services to dispose of. The value of all kinds of labour, as well as that of personal services, to be estimated by the sub-committee for external and internal exchanges. No money to be circulated among the members of the same village, except labour-notes of time and an account of all business transactions between the individual members and between the members of the village bazaar to be kept in days and hours, reckoning ten hours to the day.

The external exchanges between the associated villagers to be made in time-notes; but between the villagers and common or general society, in the currency of the country, to be obtained in exchange by the time-note, at a par of exchange which will be always regulated by the punctuality of the bazaar payments. No principle to be inculcated which will lead the members to desire to buy cheap from, and to sell dear to, any one; and the sub-committee of exchanges never to attempt to take the slightest advantage, in any of their transactions, of the members of their own village, of other villages, or of any individual or parties in common or general society. By these arrangements, the necessity for all the immense machinery now employed in the prevention of fraud, and in the production of inferior or useless articles, would be superseded. The articles of the greatest necessity and utility to be first made at and in these villages, and afterwards the less useful, or the merely ornamental, to be gradually introduced, as the knowledge and powers of the inhabitants increase. Each village might be made, by means of its superior fundamental arrangement, by the just proportion of each part to the whole, in the architecture of the dwelling-houses and manufactories, in the arrangement of the gardens or pleasure-grounds, and in the general order and cleanliness of the establishment and its population, an object of great interest, and of high ornament to the country. The funds to purchase the land, erect the buildings and machinery, to stock the farm, to purchase the first supply of raw materials, and the means of supply for one year, for the inhabitants, to be borrowed by the Government upon the best terms on which money can now be procured. The funds so vested under the control of government, to bear the same interest as charged to government, with the addition of a sinking fund to pay off the capital in twenty years. When the interest shall be paid, and the original capital repaid, the property in its improved state, to belong to the inhabitants; government until then holding sufficient security over the services of the inhabitants jointly and severally.

Until the whole capital and interest shall be paid, the board of commissioners to be empowered to inspect at all times, each establishment, in order to ascertain if the buildings are in good repair, the lands under efficient cultivation, and the whole arrangement of the establishment properly conducted.

Reasons for the adoption, at the present period, of one or more of the preceding plans

Great Britain can no longer command a foreign commercial monopoly, nor is the command of it at all necessary for her own prosperity and happiness. It is therefore requisite that another foundation should be laid on which to erect her future permanent security, and to establish a new moral influence with the leading powers of the world.

In the internal strength of the islands of Great Britain and Ireland, their best security for the obtainment of these desirable results will be found. These islands can be made to maintain a certain population, all in the highest state of enjoyment that human nature can experience. The precise number cannot now be ascertained, but it may probably exceed that of ten times its present population. The real strength of the British dominions must at all times depend upon the *number* and *character* of the population, and more especially upon the number and character of that portion of it which shall occupy the islands of Great Britain and Ireland.

That plan, therefore, will be the best for Great Britain, by which the greatest amount of population can be supported in the greatest degree of comfort, and by which the best individual and national character would be secured.

A greater number of persons can be maintained in these islands, under an arrangement which will secure a comfortable support, and a superior moral and general character, to the whole population, than when any part of it is allowed to exist in poverty, or to be viciously or defectively trained.

A much larger population can be supported in comfort, and be furnished with the advantages of a superior education, when the greatest number of the industrious class is employed in *producing real wealth*, and when the smallest number is employed in *distributing only*, or in the *production* of *useless wealth*.

A much larger population can also be maintained in comfort, and be made to receive a superior character, in a country in which public opinion shall be in favour of that part of the population whose physical and mental faculties are beneficially employed for themselves and the public, than in a country in which public opinion is in favour of the individual whose physical and mental powers are uselessly or viciously employed.

Those arrangements, therefore, are the most to be desired which will admit of the greatest amount of the population being employed in producing the most useful wealth, and which will require the fewest persons to be employed as distributors of it; which will create a public opinion in favour of the useful and the superior ornamental occupations, over those which are vicious, or which merely consume time without producing any beneficial result.

That country in which pure and genuine religion shall form the essential part of every character, will have an incalculable advantage over all countries in which religion is made to consist in mysteries, miracles, and in useless forms and ceremonies.

It is reason itself which proves that religion consists not in these, but in a real charity for the opinions, feelings, and conduct of mankind, without any exception whatever; in the absence of every feeling of anger for, or any desire to injure, a single individual; in an inclination evidently displayed throughout the whole conduct, to benefit our fellow-creatures to the utmost extent of our power; in not unnecessarily giving pain, but, on the contrary, in promoting the happiness of all. This religion is only to be secured by openly opposing with reason and argument whatever tends to keep man in ignorance and poverty, under oppression, or in subjugation to a false system of religion, which necessarily forms his character to hypocrisy and all manner of deceit. Such arrangements, therefore, as will, by rendering this false religion unnecessary, gradually remove it for ever from society, and in the place thereof shall establish pure religion in the heart of every one, will be found, beyond all estimate, more beneficial for every country than the existing systems of deception, which unavoidably lead to all kinds of error and crime.

It is also true economy to *produce, manufacture,* and *use* only the *best of every thing for human nature* that the existing state of the arts and sciences, and general knowledge, will enable the population of any country to procure. Those arrangements, therefore, which will train all to acquire the knowledge, and give them the inclination, to produce the best of every thing in every department of life, are greatly to be preferred.

Arrangements that will destroy the motives which generate all the inferior passions and bad feelings that now pervade the human race, are evidently more to be desired than those circumstances which generate the motives that create all the inferior passions and bad feelings which, through error, are now made to exist among mankind.

The same may also be said of those arrangements which will gradually remove the circumstances that create poverty, and the fear of a deficiency in any of the necessaries, comforts, and advantages of life, opposed to those arrangements which have a contrary tendency. Those arrangements, in short, which will secure the means of a due exercise of all the physical, mental, and moral powers of human nature, by the due exercise of which man can alone become a rational and permanently happy being, are beyond all comparison, more to be desired than a continuance of those circumstances which a general ignorance of the laws of human nature, and of the conditions necessary for its happiness, has rendered universally prevalent.

It is believed that either the general or the partial plan now proposed, when it shall be fully investigated, will be discovered to contain the foundation of all the arrangements requisite for the attainment of all the beneficial results now enumerated, by exhibiting the means of gradually removing all the vicious circumstances, which now surround men from their birth to their death, rendering them irrational, and, consequently, miserable; and by the removal of which a race would, in the second, or, at the latest, in the third generation from the commencement of the change, be formed far superior in character to any thing we can now conceive. Nor would the beneficial effects of such a change of system end here. The character of each generation would be an improvement on the preceding, while the daily accession of real knowledge would perpetually keep the minds of all in a continued state of joyous activity.

To conclude: it is believed by the proposer of these plans, that the happiness of each individual can never be secured until all individuals shall have a superior character formed for them from infancy, and until all shall be made independent in their condition; and further, that, by the adoption of these plans, both these results may, without injury to any class, be gradually obtained for the whole human race.

THE CHARTER OF THE RIGHTS OF HUMANITY[a] 1834

Passed at a great Public Meeting of the Producers of Wealth and Knowledge, held in the Metropolis on Wednesday, February 12, 1834.

The Period has arrived when the Producers of Wealth and Knowledge have decided that they will not waste any more of their Time or Labour on Objects of minor Importance, which, if obtained, could effect no permanently beneficial Change in their Condition; but that, overlooking the local Advantages of Class, and considering only the general and permanent Interest of Humanity, they will henceforth devote all their Energies to the attainment of those superior Objects and Advantages developed in this their Charter.

1. A *graduated property-tax, equal in amount to the full exigencies of government, when wisely administered.*

Because property acquired ought to pay for its security and the means afforded for its enjoyment.

Because large properties in single possessions are injurious to the possessors and to the public.

Because none ought to be taxed who are producing wealth for society by industry, physical or mental.

Because a graduated property tax is the most just and economical mode of raising national supplies.

Because the national prosperity would advance much more rapidly under this equitable mode of paying its expenses than under any other, and a less amount of taxation would be required.

2. An *abolition of all other customs, duties, and taxes, national, county, and parochial.*

Because all these modes of raising revenue create immorality and crime, and withdraw large numbers from being made, useful producers of wealth or

[a] First published in *The Crisis*, vol. 3, no. 24 (8 February 1834), p. 200, and read by Owen at a public lecture in March 1834 (see *The Crisis*, vol. 3, no. 27, 1 March 1834, p. 219).

knowledge, to become useless collectors of the wealth of others, under circumstances most unfavourable to good feelings, morals, and happiness of the payers and receivers; and because it would be more economical to have but one complete and superior arrangement for all the national receipts and expenditure.

3. *Free and protected ingress and egress for all persons into and out of all countries; and the free interchange of all improvements and commodities between all nations.*

Because it is for the interest of the human race, and of every individual member of it, that there should be the most free intercourse between all nations, and an unlimited interchange of knowledge and commodities among the individuals of all countries.

Because, by an open, honest and general intercourse of nations, the wealth, the knowledge, and the happiness of the world will be increased to an incalculable extent; and because all people would derive permanent substantial advantages from unrestricted ingress and egress.

4. *Wars to cease; and all differences between nations to be adjusted by an annual congress, to be held in rotation in each of the different states.*

Because wars are now in direct opposition to all the best interest of the human race.

Because they are grossly cruel and immoral.

Because they change producers into wasteful consumers, and turn the creators of wealth into wholesale destroyers of the most valuable property.

Because they generate anger, violence, crime, poverty, and misery.

Because they train man to murder man, and to have a pleasure and a supposed duty and interest in so doing.

Because they tend to detain the human race in their present ignorant and irrational condition, and to encourage the growth of all the inferior passions and qualities that can be given to human beings; and because, while wars shall be permitted to decide national differences, nations must suffer; for national differences will be devised for the supposed benefit of rulers, and man will be compelled to continue to act as heretofore, – more irrationally than any other species of animals.

5. *Liberty of expression of conscientious opinions, upon all subjects, without limitation.*

Because truth and sincerity cannot be established without perfect freedom of expression upon every subject; and because it is the natural right of all to speak fearlessly what they are compelled, by the laws of their organization and the mode of their education, to think and to feel.

6. *No dominant religion to exist, nor any one to be encouraged by any worldly temptations whatever; but all persons to be equally protected in the rights of conscience.*

Because there is no merit or demerit in belief of any kind, whether relating to immaterial essences, or to material objects or beings; and because no particular religious belief has ever yet produced in practice among its votaries truth, charity, knowledge, kindness, or happiness. But, as so large a portion of the human race have been compelled by their education, or the society surrounding them, to receive notions respecting some religion, which notions they cannot of themselves relinquish, all have an equal right to express their opinions respecting their faith, and to support these by fair and friendly arguments, but in no other manner.

7. *National, scientific, physical, intellectual, and moral education for all, who from any cause cannot be otherwise well trained and cultured in all these respects.*

Because society has a direct interest in the right formation of the character of every child that comes into existence. A child uneducated or ill-educated may be trained by the inferior and vicious circumstances which now every where improperly abound, to create extensive misery to his neighbourhood, to his country, and even to many nations. Society has, therefore, a much greater stake, a far deeper interest, in the formation of the character of each of its members than the parents of the children, and it has a far more legitimate right to train and educate them; and to obtain a well-devised superior national education ought to be, and when men become wise, will be considered, the first and highest duty of every government.

Because all infants may have a superior or an inferior character, a useful or a useless one, formed by the supreme power of the state; and no inferior power in any country can have the same command over the national arrangements which are necessary to well-form the character of all the children of the state.

8. *National employment for all who cannot otherwise find productive or beneficial occupation, that thereby the greatest amount of wealth may be produced for every individual.*

Because it is contrary to common sense that those who desire to create wealth for themselves, and a surplus for others, should not have the means provided to enable them to do so; and yet more contrary to it, that they should be compelled, for want of proper national arrangements, to live in idle wretchedness, and be thereby daily tempted to acquire the worst habits, and to commit every kind of crime.

9. *The children of all classes, without any exception, to be trained and employed, physically or mentally, to produce for society as much as they require* from *society.*

Because the general happiness of society ought to be the ruling principle by which to govern the proceedings of all the numbers of it; and as every child born within any state is the child of the state, its powers and capacities ought in every single instance to be made so far available for the general happiness, that it shall be trained and educated, and afterwards employed to produce, physically or mentally, as much *for* society as it requires to receive *from* society for its full enjoyment. Under wise arrangements, this may be accomplished greatly for the permanent advantage of every individual in every country, in whatsoever rank, station, or condition the individual may be born or placed.

10. *National measures to set the poor and unemployed immediately to beneficial employments, under arrangements which shall reform their feelings and habits, and secure their comfort and happiness.*

Because, to improve society on rational principles, the lowest in the scale of habits and knowledge should be first put in a condition in which useful and valuable knowledge, superior habits, and better feelings and dispositions may be given to them; and without a due proportion of employment, this change cannot be effected.

Because it is the palpable interest of the whole of society that not one of its industrious members should now be kept in idleness or discomfort.

11. *National arrangements to distribute the new wealth, created by the national employment of the poor and unemployed, beneficially for them and the nation.*

Because the new wealth created by the employment of the now idle poor, will, under the existing irrational arrangements for producing and distributing wealth, interfere with the profitable disposal of the wealth now produced by the present industrious classes, and will effect what is called 'a glut in the market.' Other arrangements are, therefore, required to dispose advantageously of the new wealth thus to be created.

12. *Unlimited freedom for the production and interchange of all commodities and riches, until more wealth shall be produced than is necessary for the happiness of the population of every country.*

Because the happiness of all requires that there should be no artificial limits to the production of real wealth or to the freedom of exchange,[a] that no capital

[a] A concern to avoid 'artificial' limits to production was a prominent feature in John Gray's later books, in contrast to the more stoic, puritan and agrarian bias of some Owenites. See for example Gray's *The Social System: A Treatise on the System of Exchange* (1831), and Gregory Claeys, *Machinery, Money and the Millennium. From Moral Economy to Socialism, 1815–1860* (Princeton: Princeton University Press, 1987), pp. 188–95.

or time should be wasted or misapplied, that all may be the more speedily secured in a full supply of the necessaries and comforts of life. Any restrictions upon the interchange of commodities or services is an unnecessary waste of labour and power, both of body and mind, to some portion of society.

13. *A change of the vicious and degrading circumstances by which the productive classes are now surrounded, for others possessing a virtuous and superior character.*

Because the circumstances in which the productive classes are now obliged to exist are unhealthy, and calculated to produce vice and misery, and not such as producers of the wealth of society ought to have around them, nor such as any human beings ought to be placed within.

Because the industry of the productive classes, if wisely directed, is capable of creating, in a short time, circumstances greatly superior for themselves and for the whole of society.

Because it is the direct interest of society that none of the inferior circumstances in which the industrious classes now are should longer exist; and because society has the full power and most ample means to remove them speedily, and replace them by others of a much better and more virtuous description: and man ever has been, is, and must be, the creature of the circumstances in which he lives, whether they shall be permitted to be bad and indifferent, or be made good and superior.

14. *The present property of all individuals, acquired and possessed by the usages and practices of old society, to be held sacred until the possessors shall discover that it can no longer be of any use or exchangeable value, from the facility with which a surplus of wealth will be produced for all; thus destroying the* motive *to accumulate individual wealth, as the* motive *to accumulate water where it is in abundance has been destroyed, although it is the most intrinsically valuable of all our wealth*

Because the present possessors of individual property are the creatures of their circumstances, and are really blameless for possessing it.

Because it will be easy to create more new property than the world will require.

Because it will require less time, and be far better for all, that new property should be created, than that a contest should arise, or a scramble be made, for the possession of the wealth now in existence. This old wealth had far better be peacefully and wisely used, than be destroyed by violence; for charity and kindness could not be created under any harsh or violent proceedings.

15. *The just rights of both sexes to be universally established.*

Because, to produce general prosperity and happiness, it has become necessary, by the progress of events, that individual dependence should terminate between human beings for ever; that a new state of society should arise, in which the arts and sciences should become the slaves and servants of the human race.

Because men and women will become superior beings, and attain a much higher state of happiness, when they shall become individually independent of each other in all respects, except that pleasing dependence upon each other which will arise from their natural sympathies, when all shall be innocently and honestly trained and educated in a knowledge of themselves from their birth.

16. *The congress of nations to determine on some one language, which shall be taught to all the children of each state, in addition to their mother tongue.*

Because it would be a great permanent advantage to all individuals, in every part of the world, that they should be taught but one language; and that language should be devised to be as simple and perfect as language can be made.

Because no one nation or people can have an interest in the continuance of a variety of languages, which tend to separate man from man, and to create and maintain contests and wars throughout society.

17. *Arrangements to be adopted, as soon as practicable, to put an end to individual and national competition and contest, now unnecessary and producing innumerable grievous evils to all classes.*

Because individual and national competition and contest create innumerable vices and evils throughout all the nations of the world.

Because they are no longer necessary as stimuli to human invention and industry.

Because they greatly limit the production of wealth and the means of enjoyment, and prevent the most important benefits that could be now obtained and secured for all people and nations by a union of interests.

And because, as long as the system of individual and national competition and contest shall be encouraged, or permitted to exist, the world must continue in all manner of deception, vice, and wretchedness, and remain devoid of real knowledge, charity, and kindness.

LECTURES

ON THE

MARRIAGES OF THE PRIESTHOOD

OF THE

OLD IMMORAL WORLD,

DELIVERED IN THE YEAR 1835,

BEFORE THE PASSING OF THE NEW MARRIAGE ACT.

By Robert Owen.

FOURTH EDITION.

WITH AN APPENDIX,

CONTAINING THE

MARRIAGE SYSTEM OF THE NEW MORAL WORLD;

And proving that the Author never entertained the sentiments attributed to him by the opponents of Socialism.

LEEDS:
PRINTED AND PUBLISHED BY J. HOBSON, MARKET STREET, BRIGGATE;
SOLD BY ABEL HEYWOOD, OLDHAM STREET, MANCHESTER;
AND J. CLEAVE, SHOE LANE, FLEET STREET, LONDON.

1840.

LECTURE ON THE MARRIAGES OF THE PRIESTHOOD OF THE OLD IMMORAL WORLD 1835[a]

PREFATORY REMARKS[b]

In consequence of the frequent gross misapprehension of Mr OWEN's views on the subject of Marriage, the Editor, in offering to the public the present edition of these lectures, deems it expedient, for the sake of truth, to prefix the following remarks.

It has been imagined that Mr OWEN desires to abrogate *all* Marriage. That this is a gross error is evident from the fact, that so long ago as 1830, in a course of Lectures he then delivered in London, he published the laws by which he proposes that Marriages should be regulated in the New State of Society;[c] which laws were again published in 1833 in the 'Charter of the Rights of Humanity;'[d] and subsequently, in an address to his disciples, (*see 'New Moral World,' page* 443,)[e] he most explicitly stated that marriage regulations ought, on no account to be abandoned, and that it is his opinion, they must ever exist – improved as society advances in knowledge and goodness.

All reasonable persons must admit that it is a grievous evil for man or woman to be induced to become, or compelled to continue, united in marriage to an individual for whom they cannot feel a sincere affection; and none but

[a] 2nd edn, Leeds, 1838, entitled *The Marriage System of the New Moral World; with a faint outline of the present very irrational system, as developed in a Course of Ten Lectures*; 3rd edn, Leeds, 1839; 4th edn, 1840, entitled *Lectures on the Marriages of the Priesthood . . . with an Appendix containing the Marriage System of the New Moral World* (reprinted here). The lectures themselves were delivered in late 1834 and early 1835 in London, and first published in *New Moral World*, vol. 1, no. 6 (6 December 1834) – no. 16 (14 February 1835), pp. 41–5, 51, 57–60, 65–8, 81–3, 89–91, 97–9, 105–8, 113–15, 121–3. French trans., 1841.

[b] The Prefatory remarks were first added c. 1839–40.

[c] See *The Addresses of Robert Owen* (1830), p. 37 (*infra*, vol. 2, p. 155).

[d] See *The Charter of the Rights of Humanity* (1834) (above, pp. 257–8).

[e] See *New Moral World*, vol. 5, no. 28 (4 May 1839), p. 443.

the most irrational can consider it otherwise than a most gross and lamentable error to call such marriages virtuous, or to imagine that the sanction of legal or religious ceremonies, so called, can render them other than most vicious, demoralizing, and wretched. It is needless to expatiate on this point: few are so utterly stultified that their feelings will not respond to the truth of these remarks. Any person who reads Mr OWEN's writings with but a moderate degree of attention and candour, will at once perceive that it is *these* Marriages, with their innumerable evil consequences, which he desires to put an end to, by introducing arrangements and regulations dictated by common sense, or right reason, to insure all the happiness that can be derived, and avoid all the vice and evil that have hitherto been experienced, from the social converse of man or woman.

Nor can it, with any pretension to truth, be asserted that it is the object of Mr OWEN to lessen conjugal fidelity, or the permanence of marriage; for he expressly states in these Lectures that 'the unions of the New Moral World will be the result of affection; and therefore, in the very great majority of cases, will be of a permanent nature;' and in the Manchester Lectures he says, 'under the arrangements of this new state of human existence, the affections will receive every aid that can be devised to induce them to be permanent; and there can be no doubt they will be far more durable, and produce far more pleasure and enjoyment to the parties, and far less injury to society, than has ever yet been experienced.'[a] In a word, a candid attention to the true tendency of Mr OWEN's writings must convince all but the most superficial or obtuse, that this single object, as regards the social converse of man and woman, is to promote, to the greatest possible extent, true purity, delicacy, virtue, and happiness, now most lamentably deficient, through the false notions of society on these subjects, and the vicious customs and institutions which have emanated from those notions.

LECTURE FIRST

MR OWEN commenced his Lecture, by stating that in that morning's Discussion a lady had brought forward three questions, which were put by the celebrated Chateaubriand[b] in a work he had written, but which was not to be published until after his death. The questions showed the anxiety in the minds of the Statesmen of the world about the present state of society, which they were satisfied could not much longer be bolstered up.

[a] See Owen, *Six Lectures Delivered in Manchester* (Manchester, 1837), pp. 76–7.
[b] Francois René Chateaubriand (1768–1848).

The first question asked is: 'What shall be the *new* state of society?' What! does one of the leading ministers of France, and a high Tory – does he ask such a question as this; and a question, too, that shows that he and his friends have made up their minds that a change must take place? Without entering further into the subject now, I will merely say, that the new state of society will be entirely different from the present state, and will be based on principles totally distinct. I hope our friends, in investigating our plans, will make no attempt to unite the two states of society. I have said again and again, that they never can amalgamate in any proportion, and it will, therefore, be useless to draw inferences on the new system from any thing we see around us.

The second question is, 'How shall women arrive at legal emancipation? Up to the present day, society has proceeded upon the principle of classes, bodies or corporations, and of distinct families.' The third is: 'What *appearance* will society present when these regulations shall *no longer exist*, and women become INDIVIDUAL, as is the TENDENCY that they should become?'

I rejoice that these questions have been put, and that too by so eminent and intelligent an individual; they go to confirm my own impressions on the subject.

In my previous lectures[a] I have stated, that the chief of the Satanic institutions over the world, though somewhat varied in name and form, are the priesthood; the lawyers and magistrates; the military; the unnatural and artificial union of the sexes; individual and national competition and contest; and the single-family, or universally disuniting arrangements of society; and the metal, or any other medium liable to change in value, for the circulation of wealth. And I then hastily glanced at some of the leading evils necessarily arising from the priesthood, the laws and magistracy, and the military. I now proceed to notice, in the same hasty manner, some of the remainder of these Satanic institutions, or institutions of moral evil; and first of the unnatural or artificial union of the sexes. It seems that many of the readers of the NEW MORAL WORLD,[b] many of my usual audience, as well as a large portion of the public, are much opposed to any thing being said openly, to a mixed assembly, on the subject of marriage, because, say they, we are none of us prepared to enter upon the consideration of this delicate subject. The disciples of our system say: 'We readily acknowledge the truth of the three fundamental errors of moral evil, and the three fundamental principles of moral good. We fully understand the facts whence they are derived, and consider the developement of them, in this plain intelligible form, the greatest boon that man has yet acquired from his intellectual faculties. To know the cause of evil and of good

[a] See *New Moral World*, vol. 1, no. 5 (29 November 1834), pp. 33–5.

[b] Main journal of the Owenite movement in this period, from 1834–45, initially edited by Owen, later mainly by George Alexander Fleming, whose love life was of great interest to opponents of Owen's marriage doctrines.

among the human race is the most valuable knowledge that can be given to man; it is to know the *cause of misery and of happiness*: in fact, it is to learn how to make the earth a pandemonium or a paradise.' All this the disciples of the system readily admit; but they add: 'What has all this to do with the present marriages of the world, seeing that the prejudices of the human race are so deeply rooted in favour of their continuance?'

When I hear these sentiments repeated time after time, by many who have long professed themselves disciples of our system, and some who are esteemed the most intelligent among them, I am obliged to say, as I have often done, greatly to the annoyance of those who deemed themselves sufficiently advanced in a knowledge of the new system to be the experienced instructors of others: 'You really know nothing yet about the system which you are teaching to others.' And upon this occasion, as we are now about to lay a solid foundation in the minds of those who are to take an active part in our future proceedings, it is incumbent on me to declare to you, that no parties can be considered to understand correctly or practically any part of the system which I contemplate, unless they know how to apply the third fundamental principle of moral good, and to trace the third fundamental error of moral evil to practice, and also to carry them out through all their ramifications into the domestic and public arrangements of society, and to trace the endless train of moral evil, and consequent misery, which the present marriage system in all countries necessarily engenders.

Surely none of you can imagine that I decided upon relinquishing a situation, which was perhaps the most enviable that man could hold under the existing vicious system of the world, bringing me in, at the same time, many thousands a-year, merely that I might instruct my suffering fellow men in a few theoretical truths, which of themselves could never be applied to useful practice, much less to emancipate the human race from ignorance, sin and misery? Or that I gave up a situation in which I could effect much practical good, to teach *some truths*, and *refrain from teaching others*; to flatter the prejudices of any man, woman, or child; when the latter truths were essential to effect the great good intended, and which could never be attained until all ancient prejudices were removed? Or do any of you imagine that I meet you here to pander to your prejudices upon important subjects, in which your permanent happiness is involved? No, my friends; I have made the sacrifice of extensive wealth; of an extraordinary personal consideration among the great and good ones of the earth, as they are now called; that, being freed from all such shackles, I might attain the highest elevation and the most enviable condition to which a human being can aspire; that is, to be at full liberty to speak to the world a new language of truth, unmixed with error, upon subjects of the most vital interest to all of human kind, and to send forth these truths, without fear of man, to the great ones of the earth; to emperors and kings, and to the learned and wise, as they are called, until they shall attend to them, become conscious of their truth and high value, and shall willingly adopt them.

Think you that I am to be withheld from this course because a few or many of my readers or hearers are alarmed at new, and to them astounding truths? truths essential to be known and publicly acted upon for the eternal well-being and happiness of the human race.

Those who have imbibed these impressions little indeed know the early determinations of my mind, and the thoughts which have long been within me. I tell you now, I am not teaching in the midst of the metropolis of the British Empire to please my hearers, flatter their prejudices, and live upon their ignorance. I am purposely come among you to oppose all your oldest, strongest, and most inveterate prejudices; to stir them up from their *lowest foundations*, and to withdraw them, root and branch, out of your constitutions, or to sacrifice all that man holds dear in the attempt.

You are prepared, you say, to give up some of your old errors and prejudices; but you wish I would not touch upon others, and especially upon the present married state.

What would you think of the wisdom of those who were afflicted with some dreadful disorder, hitherto deemed incurable, saying to a physician, who had happily discovered a certain and effectual cure for it: 'We are indeed diseased from head to foot; we feel the malady most excruciating from morning to night and from night to morning, but, pray, dear good doctor, do not touch this sad and incurable disorder, it is too bad to be interfered with; but you may, if you please, cure our toothache, or one of our little fingers that occasionally gives us some pain!'

Such is your state and condition; and knowing what different beings you will be when you shall be restored to sound health, I shall disregard your sickly or feverish complainings, and proceed to effect your cure.

And I now tell you, and, through you, the population of all the nations of the earth, that the present marriages of the world, under the system of moral evil in which they have been devised and are now contracted, are the sole cause of all the prostitution, of all its incalculable grievous evils, and of more than one half of all the vilest and most degrading crimes known to society. And that, until you put away from among you and your children for ever, *this accursed thing*, you will never be in a condition to become chaste or virtuous in your thoughts and feelings, or to know what real happiness is. For now almost all who are in the married state are daily and hourly practising the deepest deception, and living in the grossest prostitution of body and mind; and misery is multiplied by it beyond any of your feeble powers, in your present irrational state, to estimate; for it extends directly and indirectly through all the ramifications of life. Yes! your fathers, mothers, brothers, sisters, husbands, wives, and children, are one and all suffering most grievously from this opposition to nature; from this ignorance of your own organization; from this unnatural crime; which destroys the finest feelings and best powers of the species, by changing sincerity, kindness, affection, sympathy and pure love, into deception, envy, jealousy, hatred and revenge. It is a Satanic device of the Priesthood to place and keep mankind within their slavish superstitions, and to render them subservient to all their purposes; and until you can acquire fortitude and moral courage to look this subject fairly in the face and meet it fully on the ground of common sense and right reason, and can show it to be, as it is, in direct opposition to the laws of your organization, it is eminently calculated, to make you, in the greatest extreme, ignorantly selfish, wretchedly vicious, and most unhappy. And while this evil is suffered to remain you cannot reasonably expect to advance one single step in practice in the right road to real virtue and happiness. There is, therefore, no hope whatever, for you until you acquire sufficient strength of mind to overcome this evil, and openly denounce it both in principle and practice. It is now ascertained that you have not been organized to feel or not to feel at your pleasure. You, therefore, commit a crime against the everlasting laws of your nature when you say that you will 'love and cherish' what your organization may compel you to dislike and to loathe, even in a few hours. Away then with this eminently false delicacy and sickly appetite for truths which are the most essential to the progressive improvement and permanent happiness of our species!

The species, man, as approaching towards a rational nature, is yet in its cradle; and if we do not soon remove it from this infant condition it will be rocked too long, and the reasoning powers of man will be not only of no benefit to him, but a grievous evil, and place him, relatively to the enjoyment of happiness, greatly below the majority of terrestrial animals.

Not speak of the present marriage state and its endless crimes: why what absurdity yet remains in the public mind! Not to speak and expose the greatest of the practical sources of vice and misery! As well may we at once close our eyes and put a seal upon our lips, that we may not see or speak of the greatest deceptions, the most abandoned wickedness, and the cause of the most extended calamities known to the human race. The time is now past for those who have a desire to ameliorate the condition of the human race upon everlasting principles of truth, to pander to the prejudices of any portion of mankind; much less to this prejudice in favour of artificial marriage and unnatural union of the sexes: of a prejudice which is one of the deepest seated in human society, and the most fatal to the happiness of men and women from their birth to their death.

Under this baneful crime against nature, man must continually degenerate in his physical, mental, and moral powers, as he has done during many past ages, in proportion as this crime has been extended, and made, through the influence of increasing wealth and superstition, more and more unnatural and artificial. The inhabitants of the British Empire, said to be the most advanced of modern nations, although, through the progress of science, the most powerful in all the means requisite to insure the highest physical, intellectual and moral qualities to every member of its extensive and widely-spread population, are greatly inferior, individually, in all these respects, to the individuals of former times, who possessed greater physical powers, more intellectual strength and vigour, and more exalted notions of public virtue, and of truth and sincerity, than are to be found in modern times. When we look at the ancient inhabitants of Greece and Rome, and compare the present race of men to them, we find the comparison greatly to the disadvantage of ourselves. It is true we have scientific powers which they had not; but on these we are accustomed to place too much reliance. We, the said-to-be-envied of the world, have gradually degenerated, through all ranks and degrees, into mere pedlars and panderers for money gains, or some tom-foolery of name or personal distinction, which makes the individual appear only the more conspicuously irrational to those who understand the nature and real character of man. And instead of natural connexions being formed between those whose sympathies or qualities of mind and body are in harmony with each other, wealth, family, titles, or privileges of some kind, have been the artificial uniting motive, in opposition to natural desires or pure and chaste feelings.

It is full time that this increasing degeneration of the species, bodily and mental, should cease, and that the natural association of the sexes should be resumed, but improved by all the experience of the past.

Previous to the great change which we have ultimately in view, relative to the new position in which the sexes will be placed, many highly necessary arrangements and provisions must be made, to render these changes practicable and beneficial. For in the present irrational condition of the human race relative to the association of the sexes and to the single-family arrangements, to mix the two most opposing principles and practices together, would be to make the present confusion of ideas and feelings and conduct ten times more perplexed and irrational.

Many of our friends have, perhaps naturally, with their very limited views of the great changes which must be made in passing from a state of moral evil to moral good, supposed that the principles and practices of the one state were intended or could be made to assimilate or amalgamate with the other. Yet, had they any clear conception of these two systems, they would, at once, discover that the greatest of all impossibilities will be to unite the practice of the one with any part of the practice of the other. We have now the pure unadulterated system of moral evil, both in principle and in practice, producing a perfect terrestrial pandemonium. Were any of our friends to attempt, individually, to introduce any of our principles and practices of moral good into this pandemonium of single-family feuds and mal-arrangements, they would increase, ten-fold, the evils which now reign triumphant throughout almost all the families of mankind. But this now most interesting of all questions, at this crisis of our proceedings, must not longer be left in doubt or mystery, or in a state liable to be misunderstood by the friends and of moral good.

Therefore, *let it now be known to all*, that when the mind of man shall be regenerated, and he shall enter upon the state of moral good, in an association of sufficient numbers to support and protect itself, and its rising generation, against the ignorance and consequent prejudices of moral evil; that CELIBACY, beyond the period plainly indicated for its termination by nature, (although esteemed a high virtue under the reign of moral evil,) will be known to be a great crime, necessarily leading to disease of body and mind, and to unnatural thoughts, feelings, and conduct, and to every kind of falsification of our real impressions, sympathies and sensations, all of which are of nature's most wise creation, in perfect accordance with the superior organization which it has given to man over the inferior animals.

Also, in the present state of moral evil, it is esteemed a high and superior virtue to be chaste, according to the unnatural notions and imaginations of a most degraded order of men, called the Priesthood, who, in various parts of the world, have taken upon themselves to direct the opinions and feelings of the human race, as though they were themselves divinities, and could by their fiat of absurdities and almost ceaseless irrational ravings, reverse the laws of earthly things, and change the everlasting decrees of that universal and hitherto incomprehensible power which 'directs the atom and controls the aggregate of nature.' This order of men, to whose oppressions of mind and body no rational being will longer submit, have chosen to make chastity to consist in having sexual intercourse in accordance only with *their* most fantastic whims and unnatural notions; and whom they thus discordantly join '*let*' say they '*no man put asunder*!'[a] This human decree of the Priesthood is the origin of all prostitution, and of all its endless crimes, evils, and sufferings; of all impure and unchaste thoughts and desires, and of all the known and unknown, and almost unimagined multiplied crimes and miseries of the present married life; and has been the most unnatural grievous misconception of all the crudities which the various insanities of the Priesthood have engendered. They have ever been totally ignorant of the laws of man's organization, and they have been governed in all their proceedings by the imbecility of infancy or the ravings of a disordered intellect or distempered imagination.

Had they not been thus ignorant, they never would have supposed that pure and undefiled chastity consisted in men and women abiding by *their* bidding. Chastity is a feeling and sympathy mysteriously implanted in human nature, and exists only between the sexes when in their intercourse they feel a sincere and genuine affection for each other: and this delightful union of heart and mind the Priesthood never gave by their unhallowed and grossly absurd ceremonies,

[a] See Matthew 19:6.

which they have invented for their gain, and called marriages; nor do they yet know how to create these pure affections, or to retain them when created.

Real genuine chastity is a sentiment and a feeling far too elevated and refined for their ignorant and gross conceptions, or they could never have artificially tied bodies in their bonds of wedlock, and then said: 'Be you united, mind and body, for life; or be miserable in this world and everlastingly dammed in the next.' What a sacrilege of the best and finest sympathies of our nature! What ignorance of the organization of man and woman! What horrid sacrifice of the happiness of the human life!

In the New Moral World no such destruction of common sense; of our most refined and best feelings; of our just and natural rights and privileges; of our open-hearted sincerity; and of our highest enjoyment and purest happiness, will ever be required or permitted. No; for the unerring laws of our nature, that guide which, when referred to, never deceives us, will alone direct the mode by which the association of the sexes shall be maintained, as well as every other arrangement for the well ordering and conducting the whole business of human life; but, assuredly, the present marriages of the Priesthood of the world, the source of so much crime and misery, will form no part of it.

Celibacy is a virtue of the Priesthood of the world, but it is a vice against Nature; and, I ask, shall Nature or the Priesthood prevail?

When you and the public shall have had time to digest this highly important and deeply interesting subject, I will return to it, and expose, in detail, more of its unnumerable crimes and miseries.

In the meantime let no one misunderstand me. The present system of society over the world is founded on notions of unmixed falsehood, leading, of necessity, to every absurdity and evil in practice; a perfect unmixed system in principle and practice of moral evil, most admirably calculated to give a false direction to all the higher qualities and best feelings of our nature, and to render the whole mass of the population of the world a compound of ignorant selfishness, of folly and absurdity, of counteraction and division, of vice and crime, and of sickening disappointment to all superior minds, and of grievous misery to all: and that the New Moral system is the reverse of it in all these particulars, and so opposite in principle and practice that it will be for ever utterly impossible to bend or blend the one to conform to the other. The world must have the whole of the one or of the other.

Now, my friends, I have just placed before you the last obstacle in our way, and the most difficult to be overcome. In 1818, I proclaimed that ignorance and error, crime and folly, had their source in the different religions of the world. I was at that time, perhaps, the most popular man in the world.[a] No

[a] Probably a reference to Owen's August 1817 meetings at the City of London Tavern. See *Address Delivered at the City of London Tavern, on Thursday, August 21st* (1817) (*infra*, vol. 1, p. 201–10, and vol. 4, pp. 211–17).

daily newspaper then refused to publish, however long, the addresses delivered by me in London. I well knew I was opposing all the stronger prejudices of the world; and that when I stated what I did on the subject of religion, I was casting away from me all the popularity which I then possessed; but which I considered then, and I consider it now, not worth one straw, except when expressed in favour of truth.

I was then preparing the public mind for the principles I advocated; and it has taken me ever since, a period of seventeen years, to prepare it sufficiently for the introduction of the subject of the present evening's lecture. We are now fairly and fully before the world, and we must keep our position. I now denounce the priestly marriages of the old world, as I then denounced religions.

Do not mistake me, my friends. Were you to attempt to unite any parts of the two systems, you would be sure to fail. When you go into the world, tell your friends and neighbours, of all I have said; but tell them also that we shall reserve the practice of these principles till we are so situated, in the New Moral World, as to have a society of our own, when, and not till then, we shall be prepared to put on the marriage garment.

Can you go away, knowing all this, and not try to change the existing state of things? We are now forming an association to effect this change soon, and which, I hope, will spread over the world. I care not what some individuals may think of our little nucleus here; I hope we shall soon show them that we are the grain of mustard-seed,[a] which shall flourish and spread until it covers the whole world.

LECTURE SECOND

In my lecture on Sunday evening last I denounced the present unnatural and artificial marriages of the world, and stated them to be a cunningly devised fable of the priesthood to keep the population of all countries subservient to them, and to the unnatural and artificial laws of the governments of all countries.

These proceedings of the priesthood and governments some parties contend, were necessary while men were savages, or in a partial state of civilization; that they were then necessary to control their brutality or mere intellectual animal violence; but they admit that now they may be advantageously abrogated, and that better arrangements for society may be in this enlightened age, most beneficially introduced.

I will not now occupy time in discussing the question with these parties

[a] See Matthew 17:20.

whether real knowledge and straightforward truth would not have civilized society much more speedily than the devious course of error, mystery, and superstition; because I am satisfied with the admission which they have made, that the time is come when man may be instructed and treated as a rational animal.

But I am desirous of proving to all classes, that the marriage state, as devised and supported by the priesthood of the world, and the single-family arrangements necessary thereon, are calculated to produce, and have produced, a most ignorant, selfish, vicious character for man and woman, and a disunited miserable state of human existence: and that while the marriages devised by the priesthood and the single-family arrangements shall be permitted to continue under the protection and sanction of governments, this inferior character of man will be formed and this miserable condition of the human race will increase daily, and hypocrisy and wickedness will more and more abound; that in fact, there can be no wise legislation, or government, or virtue and happiness for the people, while these errors in principle and practice shall be supported by the governments, or by public opinion.

The evil of these institutions is not confined to any sex, age, or class, for all classes and ages of both sexes, suffer grievously from this unnatural malarrangement of society. Unnatural, as well as most absurd and farcical, because two persons of different sexes are induced to make solemn engagements to live together during life, and to love each other, without reference to the changes which may arise in the appearance, qualities, and character of the parties. Now as men and women have not been formed with power to create their own feelings, or to love or hate at their own pleasure, but are on the contrary, compelled to receive such feelings as the influence of external objects produce in their organization, it is blasphemy, if any thing is blasphemy, against the laws of their nature, for man or woman to make any promises or engagements relative to their future feelings of affection or hatred, or of liking or disliking, for each other. These feelings are neither to be promised nor bartered away with impunity, for nature will have her course, and her course is a wise one; and nature declares that man and woman shall associate together without evil only when they shall have a real affection for each other; and that affection will be strong and durable in proportion to the extent of the good and superior qualities which shall have been cultivated in each from infancy. Man, with the present immoral and irrational character which has been formed for him – immoral, because irrational – can form no adequate conception of the altered state of mind and condition in which he will be when he shall be taught truth only, and shall be trained to be truly good and virtuous; for his mind will be born again, and all his thoughts, desires, and affections will be regenerated, and man will no longer see man as through a glass darkly,[a] but face to face; and

[a] See 1 Corinthians 13:12.

he will know others as he knows himself, and as others shall know him; and there will be no secrets or mysteries or hiding of the thoughts or feelings among men. These thoughts and feelings will be known to be nature's thoughts and feelings, and not of man's creation; and nature can do no wrong. The secrets of nature will be therefore no longer unwisely hidden, and man and woman will acquire more knowledge of themselves and of human nature in one day, than they have hitherto attained in a hundred years.

The marriages devised by the priests have been the chief cause of this long night of ignorance and supersition, of mystery and secrecy. Man and woman in an artificial and unnatural bond of wedlock, could be only hypocrites to each other and to the world. And the more they became acquainted with the facts from which the general laws of nature are deduced, the greater would be their hypocrisy relative to the most obvious laws of their nature, and the greater would be their sufferings; for hypocrisy and suffering advance together, for deception always produces misery.

Now the present artificial marriage state is most injurious in all its consequences to the husband, wife, and children of both sexes and all ages, to society, and to human nature.

It is my intention to enter more fully on these subjects in my lecture on Sunday next; for it is now necessary that all the disciples of the System should make themselves well acquainted with every part of this all-important subject. In fact they must understand it thoroughly in principle, and how it should be applied in practice, before they can become members of any rational community.

LECTURE THIRD[a]

In my lecture on Sunday last I stated that the marriages of the world, devised by the priesthood, placing the whole of society in the most artificial and vicious state, were the most injurious in their consequences to the husband, to the wife, to the children of both sexes and of all ages, to society, and to human nature.

And first, it is most injurious to the husband, who has been trained from infancy by the priesthood, to believe that he has the power to feel or not to feel at his pleasure. This is the foundation on which the priesthood and governments form his character. With this impression deeply made on his mind, we

[a] At the beginning of this lecture, Owen 'cautioned his audience that he did not intend his views on marriage to be adopted in the present state of society: it was totally impossible that this could be done; the systems were so entirely distinct' (*New Moral World*, vol. 1, no. 8, 20 December 1834, p. 57). He repeated these comments at the end of the lecture (p. 61).

will suppose him in the ordinary circumstances attending these irrational unions; and that he is about to form a marriage of affection, and of affection, too, on both sides. He supposes, as he has been taught naturally to believe, that the delightful feelings of affection which he entertains for his wife on the day in which they are made by the priests and the government, to engage to be *one* during their lives and to love each other until death, will remain, and that he shall have no difficulty in permanently retaining those feelings. Nothing, according to his previous instruction, can be more easy than to love or hate whom he pleases, and for as long or short a time as he pleases. He had been told 'that to be good, he must love his neighbour as himself.'[a] He therefore naturally concludes there can be no difficulty in loving the selected most favourite object of his choice with the most sincere and ardent affection so long as they both may live. The solemn engagement is therefore entered into, and the promise unhesitatingly given by the 'happy pair,' as they are usually denominated by their relatives and neighbours, and the ceremony concludes by the parties discovering, in one short hour, that they are inseparably bound for life.

Little are most men aware of the new and altogether altered position in which they stand immediately after marriage, from that in which they were immediately before the ceremony was performed. They are in this short space taken out of all their old accustomed bachelor circumstances, and placed within others altogether new to them; and they find themselves as it were by magic (and *it is* a legerdemain trick,) linked to a being of whose nature, as well as their own, they have, from infancy, been not only ignorant, but of which they have been continually misinformed, kept in the dark, and totally deceived. The husband has thus been taught to consider his wife a being possessing powers and capacities altogether different from those which nature has given her.

To this being of whom he is thus made ignorant, he now, for the first time, feels and knows that he is, in a mysterious manner, bound for life; that he is hers and she is his, for better and for worse; and both have placed themselves in a state of bondage to each other, not for any limited term, to ascertain if it increased or diminished their happiness, but until the one or the other shall die. Such is the wisdom of the engagement, sacred and solemn as the priests and the law know how to make it!

The single independent man now becomes the husband, and he is at once placed in a condition in which, from morning to night, and from night to morning, he is acted upon by an overwhelming new circumstance of untried influence – one which, in most cases must increase or diminish his pleasurable sensations. It is barely possible, but not very probable, that it will do neither,

[a] See Mark 12:33.

but keep then in *statu quo*. When this case occurs, it is the exception to the general rule. Now, the two parties which are thus joined for life, are very complicated, compound beings, each possessing a natural and acquired character, consisting of a great variety of faculties and qualities, physical, intellectual, and moral; and some of these faculties and qualities are in constant action while in each other's presence or thoughts, the qualities of the one continually influencing the feelings, thoughts, and actions of the other. Previous to this continued influence from the *wife*, the husband could form no correct conception of the effects which it would have upon him, that is, upon the physical, intellectual, and moral parts of his nature. We say wife, because the feelings, thoughts and actions which a *wife* produced on the husband, are almost always very different from the feelings, thoughts and actions, which the wooed maiden calls into existence. The day after marriage both husband and wife are placed in such new circumstances, that they become almost new persons in the eyes and to the feelings of each other; and not only to each other, but it is no uncommon occurrence to see new married persons exhibit a character and conduct sometimes for the better, and oft times for the worse, the reverse of that which their relatives, friends and neighbours, previous to the union, had anticipated from both. This change of character has not been the result of the will of the parties, or of any premeditated design, but it has arisen from one organization perpetually acting upon the other, and imperceptibly changing both through the natural influence of these new impressions, and of the other new circumstances of a married life, so different from their former state.

When the husband is the wooer, his will was in abeyance to the will of his beloved object; but usually when the wooer becomes the husband, the reverse takes place, and the wife is *expected* to be obedient to her husband. They are now placed, as they have been trained, in a false and most vicious position; one well calculated to commence a life of misery. Living, as they do continually, together from morning to night, and from night to morning, one or other must become the leader or master-mind; and in the struggle for this superiority the affections generally begin to abate in fervour – and then once lost or weakened they are often difficult to renew – and then painful sensations take the place, more or less gradually, of those highly enjoyed pleasurable ones which were experienced previous to the marriage bond; and of these painful sensations the husband begins to feel daily more and more; and they necessarily become more distressing from the sickening knowledge that relief from them cannot be obtained, without loss of character and consideration in the circle in which his habits and association of ideas have been formed; and in ninety-nine cases out of a hundred, as society is now constituted, the husband had better smother all the feelings which he is compelled to have, and play the hypocrite to his wife and to the world, than to openly avow the truth, and say: 'I married, expecting to increase my happiness; but the new influences of wedded life, of which, when I married, I was totally ignorant, have produced, and are producing, the most painful sensations, which are daily increasing; and, as the union I formed was under the expectation of adding to my happiness, surely it would be better and far wiser that my wife and I should not thus continue to destroy each other's well-being and comfort – it would be better that we should at once separate.' But no, this language is too natural and rational, and this mode of proceeding would be too near an approach to common sense – an approach which the cherished system of moral evil will not with impunity permit to any of its slaves or victims of the priesthood, and victims consequently, of hypocrisy and vice of every description.

The husband, thus finding his situation without remedy, as to change, tries to make the best of what he feels to be the worst bargain he ever made, producing day by day misery and the most vicious thraldom of both body and mind. But he finds, by living daily and hourly with a being who was trained in a family of its own peculiar notions and habits different from his own, that there is occasion for continual difference of opinion upon family matters of one kind or another; and, when there are children, relative to their treatment and management; and they are called upon, by their peculiar situation as heads of a single-family establishment, to coincide in numberless matters, more or less important, upon which a decision must be made; and thus a necessity is most unwisely created to render it unavoidable that the taste, feelings, and judgment of the one should be sacrificed to the other, to insure a life of even ordinary indifference.

Thus the husband day by day loses the delightful feelings of the lover; the affections daily diminish; indifference succeeds: and but too often, it is to be feared, when unsuspected by the world, dislike and hatred, and the most sickening hopeless misery is the consequence.

To be relieved for a short time from these dreadfully annoying feelings, he seeks alleviation by change of scene and person; he goes from home; he sees others properly or duly prepared to receive visitors, and, when it is a pleasure to the party, to communicate their thoughts and feelings without any family annoyances; and the husband thinks that he has made an unfortunate choice; that he could have escaped those dreadful differences of opinions and feelings which he suffers at home, if he had been more prudent, and thought more coolly and calmly before he had ventured upon this throw of the dice for life. He has not been taught to consider the very varied circumstances in which he is placed when disputing with his wife about pecuniary or other family matters, and when he is conversing with a person feeling himself independent, and bringing only her best feelings and most fascinating powers of look, language and manners into action. If the husband had been taught to know himself and the influence of circumstances upon human nature, he would become conscious that the pleasurable sensations which he experienced in the company of the person visited, and the painful ones inflicted upon him in the company of his wife, arose more frequently from the *difference of the circumstances* in which these parties were placed, than from the *difference of persons*. Were the wife, as she was the first choice of the husband, placed in the position of the visited female, and the latter within the circumstances of the wife, it is most probable that in nineteen cases out of twenty, the feelings respecting them would be reversed. This unfavourable effect of the married life arises naturally, and of necessity, from the impolicy of forcing two persons, dissimilarly trained, into daily and hourly unceasing communication with each other, under circumstances which are almost sure to create, sooner or later, many opposing opinions and feelings, or the frequent sacrifice of them by one party or the other. But the husband finds his home less and less competent to give him pleasurable sensations, and daily increasing in those unfavourable circumstances which are painful. He then, according to his class in life, seeks relief from his painful sensations, and naturally desires to exchange them for those which give him pleasure. He seeks his relief by some of the various roads which present themselves, in the higher, middle, or lower walks of life, to tempt or seduce men from their disagreeable homes. And thus, by degrees, the husband withdraws more and more from his wife and family, in which he can no longer feel healthy or pleasurable sensations; and he condemns the unfortunate step which he has taken in forming this engagement for life, without ever understanding that he has been made the unnecessary victim of a most irrational and ignorant convention among the human race, to make each other miserable. The husband, trained in the ignorant manner in which all human beings have been, naturally attributes this permanent destruction of his happiness to his wife; and she becomes, in his heart, whatever appearance to the contrary he may assume to her and the world, an object of disgust and hatred; and hence the bickering, quarrels, and fightings in the lower ranks, and the more-hidden differences among the middle classes, and separations in them and in the higher orders.

If such is the general sketch of the positions, change of habits and feelings of the husband, we shall find those of the wife equally, if not more unfortunate. Before marriage she is usually the idol of her lover; her will is a law to him; and he even attends to her whims, and anticipates her wishes. All is done by him from affection, and therefore it is done with alacrity and pleasure. On the day of her marriage she, all at once, feels conscious that some great change has taken place in her circumstances; she has now upon every occasion, another will to consult and obey instead of her own. This of itself is a new position, which, without experience, she could not know, but merely conjecture; but this new will is strange to her, for it had been heretofore in abeyance to hers; she has now to learn what kind of one it is, and she becomes perplexed often to divine what it may be under the new circumstances in which both find themselves. No human being ought to be thus most unfavourably placed: the great chance is, that now their permanent happiness may be ship-wrecked any hour. They know not whether their physical, their mental, or moral natures will assimilate or accord. It is experience only that can give them this knowledge, and we know how dearly this experience is often acquired. We know that both often sorely repent the union in a few months, not unfrequently in a few weeks, and too often, it is to be feared, in a few days! But the poor wife is most generally the most to be pitied of the two. If her expectations previous to marriage have been raised too high, which is most frequently the case with husband and wife, the disappointment is the greater when these delightful anticipations vanish like a dream, and the sad reality of misery take their place. Under these altered circumstances, as she is now her husband's by religion and law, she must have no will of her own, no opinions, nor any feelings, but in accordance with the will, perhaps a capricious one, of her lord and master.

As nature, however, has never once been consulted in all these proceedings of artifice, ceremony, and absurdity, and all her laws have been neglected or openly opposed, she interposes and insists upon having *her laws obeyed*; and the will, opinions, and feelings of the wife are consequently not the husband's, but nature's, and if he will insist upon that which it is not in the power of his wife to give to any one contrary to nature's laws, he forces her to learn hypocrisy and deceit, and to become an adept in hiding from him her will, her opinions, her feelings, and often her conduct. While to the wife the long life of deception becomes the most destructive of every ennobling and superior faculty, feeling, and quality of human nature, and she is necessarily forced to become a weak, cunning, deceptious, inferior being, whatever she may be considered by her husband and the world. The fault, however, is not hers; she is greatly to be pitied, as well as her husband; both are forced to become victims, through a wretchedly ignorant system of falsehood, to each other's duplicity. – There can scarcely be any real confidence between parties thus most unnaturally united to produce unnatural children, and to be placed under the most unnatural circumstances, that they may be trained, like their parents, to become most artificial and unnatural characters.

The highest happiness of human existence will be enjoyed when the men and women shall be so naturally and rationally placed, that they can and shall, upon all occasions, speak to each other the innocent language of truth alone; for the language of truth is the only innocent language that man can ever know. The present general converse of the world is the guilty language of falsehood, and there is, perhaps, now more deception expressed in look, manner and words, all forming language, between the husbands and wives, made such by the Priesthood of the world, than there is between any other parties throughout the whole of society, not even excepting the present buyers and sellers of goods or money for pecuniary profit. As soon as mankind shall acquire a small portion of common sense, or the mere elements of rational knowledge, this guilty language of falsehood will be made to terminate, and the innocent language of truth will be made universally to prevail. And then, and not till then, mankind will feel and know, for the first time in the history of their species, what is the true meaning of virtue or happiness, the terms being synonymous, for virtue is happiness, and happiness is virtue.

We have slightly sketched the outline of the ordinary married life, as devised by the priesthood of the world, when it is a marriage of mutual affection, as it affects the husband and wife. We refrain, as useless, from tracing the existence of those parties who unite for other motives than sincere affection; some of their usual results in every rank of life may be daily read in the police reports, and in the newspapers, of separations and trials for unfaithfulness, or the want of the chastity of the priesthood, on the part of the wife; while husbands are allowed unnoticed the full natural sexual animal freedom.

Hitherto, however, we have considered these unnatural marriages devised by the priesthood, as they affect husbands and wives personally. We have now to consider them in the character of parents of unnatural children, or children produced according to man's laws: unnatural, in contradistinction to natural children, or children produced according to nature's laws.

The first effect of these artificial marriages is to make it necessary for the new married couple to have a single-family establishment, varied in the detail, according to the class or rank of life of the parties. Within these new arrangements the husband and wife place themselves, to provide for their family, to the utmost extent of their powers and capacities to advance themselves and children towards the highest pinnacles of society, and thus they are at once placed in a direct or indirect contest with all other families having the same laudable object, as it is now termed, in view.

Now this single-family arrangement is one of the most unfortunate and vicious for the husband and wife, for the children, and for society, that could be devised. It is calculated, in the first place, to make the husband, wife, children, and the public most ignorantly selfish, and to make the greatest mistakes relative to their individual interest. It next places the husband and wife under such unfavourable circumstances relative to each other, that there are many, many, chances, considering the erroneous notions respecting themselves and human nature, which they have been forced from infancy to receive, that they will speedily create an unfavourable difference of feeling for each other, on account of some of these single-family arrangements, or daily and hourly transactions and proceedings. Then this mode of life is highly injurious for well training and educating of children. The family arrangements are made to be as convenient as the parties know how, for the adult part of it, and they thus become most inconvenient for the children. The whole furniture in the house of a single-family establishment, in all ranks of life, is itself a most vicious and unfavourable circumstance placed around the children from their birth; and within such arrangements one, two, three, or half-a-dozen children will require more care and attention to bring them up, and train them to become ignorant and vicious members of society, than would be necessary to well train and educate one hundred children, to ensure them to become, at maturity, superior, rational members of society, provided the children were placed within the arrangements which are alone calculated to give them health, good dispositions, good manners, useful and valuable acquirements, real knowledge, and a superior character as men and women to become members of the great family of mankind. It is worthy of remembrance, not only that the single-family arrangements are thus most opposed to the forming of good or desirable characters for children, but that parents are very generally the least competent, owing to the excess of their ignorant, selfish, animal attachment for them, to do them justice in forming their characters to become valuable, superior men and women.

And we are speaking now of those parents and single-family arrangements which are esteemed by the world as examples, recommended to be followed by others deemed in these respects greatly their inferiors. A rational being cannot be formed within the existing single-family arrangements of the world.

But as this subject is one of the most vital importance to the well-being of every member of society it is my intention to resume it where I now leave off on Sunday evening next; and when I shall have placed the whole of this subject before the public, the proper and highly necessary preparation will have been made for the rational discussion of it.

Up to the present period the world has been kept so ignorant of this subject, on a right knowledge of which the happiness of mankind mainly depends, and all were made so grossly irrational respecting it, that it was as useless to address the public, to attempt to enlighten it on this subject, as to speak to the most insane or mad of the inmates of Bedlam,[a] upon the subject matter which was the origin of their disease and madness.

LECTURE FOURTH

In my last lecture I stated, that as the subject of marriage is one of the most vital importance to the permanent well-being of society, I should resume it in my next lecture; and I now proceed to fulfil this promise.

It has been stated, in previous lectures, that the marriages of the priesthood of the world were the most injurious in their consequences to the husband, to the wife, to the children of both sexes of all ages, to society, and to human nature.

Already we have hastily sketched a few, and but a very few, of the injurious

[a] Mental asylum founded in 1747, and located in Southwark from 1815.

influences which this artificial and unnatural state of society inflicts upon the husband and wife individually. We will now consider, in like manner, some of the innumerable evils which these permanent single-family unions inflict upon the children of both sexes of all ages.

These unions are, in the first place, one of the chief causes of the great inequalities in the condition and wealth of individuals; and all who have studied the unavoidable influences of the extreme of wealth and poverty, upon any population, are aware that ignorance and slavery must be the general lot of extreme poverty, and that tyranny, injustice, and presumption must be the general characteristic of the possessors of great wealth. Most true is the saying, that 'It is easier for a camel to go through the eye of a needle, than for a rich man to enter the kingdom of heaven;'[a] or, in other words, riches blind the judgment, and give a false direction to all the best feelings of human nature.

The rich man *lives upon*, and *wastes, extravagantly, the labour of others*; while no man has a just right to the labour of any other man, *without giving equal labour or value in exchange for it*. This is a principle of such vital importance to the permanent well-being, well-doing, and happiness of mankind, that it is now high time the world generally should be enabled thoroughly to understand it, and to trace its practical influences, as they affect all ranks and conditions of men, through every stage of society.

But these most interesting developments relative to the effects of the inequality of property we shall leave to future Lectures, when they will come in their due and proper course; all we shall now say on this subject is, that after the most calm and deliberate consideration of the proceedings of human affairs, as now conducted, by all gradations, in all the countries we have had an opportunity of visiting; we are obliged to come to, or, more correctly speaking, to receive, the conviction, that no society can be just, honest, or virtuous, that admits of great inequalities of wealth, of condition, or of education. And that any individual, be he who he may, who is in the possession of great riches, in a country in which numbers of his industrious fellow-men have been reduced to a state of wretched poverty, and whose children, in consequence, are brought up in ignorance and vice, necessarily leading to the misery of the individuals, and to the general disorder of society; that that rich man is an enormous evil to his country and to the world; and that, while he retains those riches unemployed for the general benefit, IT IS UTTERLY IMPOSSIBLE THAT HE CAN BE A GOOD OR A JUST MAN.

Now the artificial union of the sexes as devised by the priesthood, requiring single-family arrangements, and generating single-family interests, is directly calculated to lay the foundation of this injurious inequality throughout society, and perpetually to increase it.

[a] See Matthew 19:24.

Some of these unions do not produce any children, others produce one or two only, while some of them produce many. All circumstances being supposed to be the same with these parties at their marriage; and the management of their domestic affairs, and of their business, profession, or pursuits in life being equal; the parties who have no children will become annually more and more wealthy than those who have large families or a numerous offspring; those with one or two children, will annually become less wealthy than the first, and more wealthy than the last. And the last will, in the lower walks of life, sink into poverty, and often into the extreme of vice and misery.

The same gradations of wealth take place in the middle and upper classes, and the increasing presumption of these who are rising into more wealth, and the growth of envy in those who are declining into less wealth, and especially into poverty, are the natural fruits of these unwise and unjust proceedings; – unwise, because any general measures which have a tendency to increase artificially the inequalities of society are injurious to the whole population, and destructive of the best feelings of human nature, as well as being obstacles in the way of attaining the best state of human existence; – unjust, because in these unions we have supposed all the parties to have been equally industrious, clever, and well-conducted; yet without any other qualification than incapacity to procreate or bear children, the barren pairs are rewarded with little care and much wealth; while the prolific pairs are burdened with an excess of parental care and trouble, and are further punished by annually increasing the inequality of condition between them and the barren pairs.

It is not supposed, at this *enlightened* period, as it is called, that any one will attribute merit to *barrenness*, and demerit to men and women for being *prolific*, except my friend, Mr Malthus, and his ardent, but inexperienced disciples; inexperienced in all the great principles of man's nature and of human society, or they would long since have abandoned notions which are in direct opposition to common sense and the everyday practice of every class of producers in town and country; notions which have so confounded and perplexed the mind of political economists, so called, that they cannot perceive any of the common transactions of human life in their natural and ordinary course, or understand the necessary consequences to which they lead.

Even our talented late Lord Chancellor[a] has been so bewildered by these unnatural and impracticable theories of Mr Malthus, that, when in office, with the greatest desire, no doubt, to benefit mankind, he could conceive no better method to have them well educated and employed, as all ought and now easily

[a] Henry Brougham (1778–1868): Whig lawyer, MP and friend of Owen's for nearly fifty years; Baron of Brougham and Vaux after becoming Lord Chancellor from November 1830 to November 1834, when he was succeeded by Lord Lyndhurst.

might be, than through the workhouses of his Poor Law Act,[a] – a measure that will prove the greatest mistake that a talented well-intentioned political economist could have imagined, with a view to relieve society from poverty and vice.

But these unions of the sexes, devised by the priests, still further tend to increase the inequality of wealth in society, by creating motives for wealth to unite in marriage with wealth; and for wealth thus to become the general bond of union between the sexes, instead of affection and suitability of the physical and mental qualities of the parties. These artificial unions are also the least likely to improve the organization or natural constitution of the children at birth; and all know how important it is to have the best materials to commence with, when we desire to form a superior character for mankind.

It has been discovered that it is practicable materially to change and improve the organization of many animals for particular purposes. The subject is so well understood that it is known by some men almost as a science; so accurately can they attain the points and qualities of the animal formation, which they desire to obtain. Now, it is much more important to the well-being and happiness of man that the human organization should be advanced and essentially improved, than that the organization of any of the inferior animals should be thus made more perfect. The improvements of the organization of man, however, have been neglected, and must be neglected, as long as the marriages devised by the priests and sanctioned by governments as a divine institution, and conducted on the principle of individual competition for individual wealth, shall remain the law of the land. While this irrational and truly impious practice shall be the law, and sanctioned by the public opinion of the most civilized, or rather, least barbarous states, the original constitution or organization of human nature will remain not only unimproved, but it must be annually deteriorated.

The effects of wealth, luxury, and marriages of ambition, upon the upper, and of the manufacturing system upon the lower orders, are now rapidly reducing the superior powers and qualities of the human organization in this country to a very low and inferior standard; and should these pernicious measures be permitted to continue, this inferior standard must, in every generation, yet become more and more defective physically, intellectually, and morally.

Thus do these marriages of the priesthood tend to injure all children at their birth, and to give society, which is the chief instrument in the forming of every individual character, an inferior material to work upon, and it is thus compelled to commence its most important occupation and chief business of life under

[a] The Poor Law Amendment Act of 1834 instituted a much harsher system of poor relief than previously, predicated on the principles that all relief should be inferior to the lowest-paid job available; that aid for the able-bodied should be available only in workhouses; and that a central authority should ensure uniformity of relief throughout the country.

great disadvantages; and instead of having a sound healthy subject, physical, intellectual, and moral, or a good material to work upon, it receives from the deteriorated, unnatural, and immoral parents, an infant organization, defective and diseased to a considerable extent in all its powers, bodily and mental.

In the next place, the children are grossly injured by coming into the world either in poverty or in a state of affluence, the result of individual competition, and derived from a system of gross injustice to the industrious portion of society. They are thus of necessity trained from the hour of their birth to become vicious and ignorant of themselves, of their fellows, and of human nature generally. They are unavoidably trained to acquire all the peculiar vices of poverty or of competitive riches, both of which are grievous and enormous evils; and necessarily, in different ways, deprive man of the health and enjoyment which all ought to possess, and which, in a state of society devised and governed by common sense, or a comparatively low degree of correct knowledge, all might be made to possess.

But should this inferior-organized being come into the world in what is called the middle walk in life, it is trained by its also trained-to-be irrational parents in another set of vices, equally injurious to itself and to society. It is not trained immediately to have the notions and feelings of a mere slave, to be obedient to the whims, caprices, and gross tyranny and injustice of an extravagant tyrant who revels in the wealth which he did not create, but which he most unjustly exacts from the over-exerted labour of the industrious poor, and of the helpless against wealth and power. No: the infant born in the middle ranks of life is not directly trained to be the one or the other of these deformities of human nature; but it is carefully educated in a system of the most ignorant and vile hypocrisy, which effectually destroys or perverts all the natural, good, and superior qualities of human nature, and admirably fits it, as it may rise or fall in the scale of society, to become the abject slave of the wealthy, or the oppressor of the poor and helpless. But should it remain through life within the usual range of the middle ranks, it is formed by the tuition and example of its parents, and those around it of the same class, to acquire the double extent of deception and of pious ignorance, to become either the slave of those above it in rank and wealth, or the petty tyrant of those unfortunates who may be below it in these respects.

That there are partial exceptions in all the different ranks of life is true, but they are few, and of small extent in their deviations from these general results; not more, certainly than to prove the almost universal results which have been stated.

Under these artificial marriages of the priesthood, and the governments, rendering the single-family arrangements a necessary appendage to them, the children in every walk of life are thus of necessity trained to beome what the world calls fools or knaves; the duped or the dupes. But, in fact, they are all trained by means of these unnatural unions of the sexes, and all the artificial arrangements requisite to render them at all bearable or suffered by mankind, to be dupes, from the highest to the lowest, of a grossly erroneous system. And whether trained by their condition at birth to become slaves or tyrants, or to be prepared to become either as circumstances may afterwards decide, not one child of the human race can, under the old immoral system, be trained physically, intellectually, or morally, as it ought to be; nor can any one of them be placed within those arrangements which may now be easily formed, to insure it the full enjoyment that those extraordinary powers, faculties, and qualities, are capable of being trained to receive by all the human race.

But it is now asked very confidently by those who have been trained from their birth to become ignorant and prejudiced upon every subject connected with their daily well-being and permanent happiness, 'Are not the parents of children the most fitting and the most competent by nature to bring up, train, and educate their own children?'

The true reply to this question of ignorance of human nature, and of inexperience in the general affairs and proceedings of mankind, is, that the facts which now offer themselves to our notice over the world, as well as the details of all past history, demonstrate that the immediate parents of children are generally the least competent, from their ignorance of human nature, and from their excess of animal affection for their offspring, to well and properly form the character of their own children. Nor, if the parents were *not* so greatly deficient in these respects, are the *external circumstances* within any of the single-family arrangements well calculated, or at all properly disposed, to promote a right training and good education of all children.

This subject, by far the most important to every individual of the human race, is perhaps less understood at this moment in the British Empire, among all classes, than it has long been among the superior tribes of North American Indians, who understand far better how to form a superior Indian character for the life which these tribes lead, than the parents, teachers, or professors of education know how to form a superior character for what is so ignorantly denominated civilized life.

Until nations shall understand the true principles and right application of them to practice, relative to the formation of the character which ought to be formed for man at maturity, all the religions, laws, and learning hitherto known in the world, will be of no avail in making known the means by which the adult man and woman can be formed into intelligent, good, rational, and happy beings.

But the single-family arrangements are hostile to cultivation in children of any of the superior and ennobling qualities of human nature. They are trained by them to acquire all the most mean and ignorant selfish feelings that can be generated in the human character. The children within those dens of selfishness and hypocrisy are taught to consider their own individual family their own world, and that it is the duty and interest of all within that little orb to do whatever they can to promote the advantages of all the legitimate members of it. With these persons, it is *my* house, *my* wife, *my* estate, *my* children, or *my* husband; *our* estate, and *our* children; or *my* brothers, *my* sisters; and *our* house and property. This family party is trained to consider it quite right, and a superior mode of acting, for each member of it to seek, by all fair means, as almost any means, except *direct* robbery, are termed, to increase the wealth, honour, and privileges of the family, and every individual member of it.

Now, all other families are so placed and taught that they also feel a similar desire to promote, by the same *fair* means, as they are called, the interest of every individual relative within their family circle.

And thus is every family made a little exclusive world seeking its own advantage, regardless of, and to a great extent in direct opposition to, all other families, having the same objects in view; and, consequently, there is a more or less direct competition between all families.

In this warfare for family advantages, all the inferior qualities, feelings and passions, which can be implanted in human nature, are cultivated with the greatest care and assiduity, and under such terms that the grossest ignorance is called high intelligence, and the worst vices are dignified with the terms of superior virtues. But deep hypocrisy and all-pervading deception are the general vices which are fostered with the greatest attention and perseverance, under the names of prudence and discretion, by which, they are to hide from all other families what the individuals really think and feel; or, in the language of plain truth, what by their nature, in the circumstances in which they are placed, they are compelled to think and feel.

How absurd then was the assertion of our ancestors that they intended to establish a state of society in which each individual should love his neighbour as himself! Why, my friends, every measure they have adopted has had a directly contrary effect. No arrangements could be better calculated to produce division and disunion in society than those now esteemed as of the greatest perfection.

In this manner, all the cunning deception and stratagem of a covert warfare are kept continually alive among these contending families, each one endeavouring, by all *fair* means within its power and control, to obtain advantages over all the others. And this conduct is pursued and ardently encouraged in public and in private instruction, we must suppose, that each may be taught 'to love his neighbour as himself,'[a] and to bring about that, hitherto, in vain, every-looked-for state of society, when 'peace and good-will shall universally prevail.'[b]

To bring about these divine results, this happy and natural state of human existence, by the present single-family arrangements, created in consequence

[a] See Mark 12:33.
[b] See Luke 2:14.

of the marriages devised by the priesthood, is just as probable as that an infant could drain the seas with a sieve.

The whole of these single-family proceedings, from their commencement to their dissolution by the death of the parent, are one continued compound of absurdity, folly, and wickedness, daily added to wickedness, absurdity, and folly. But, at the death of the head of these families, the property possessed by them at that period is to be divided in some manner among the children, most generally according to the will of the parents; the children know this, when there is property, from an early age; and, in consequence, they are not only opposers and covert enemies to other families contending with them for advantages of one kind or another, but the children of the same family are thus most unwisely made the rivals of each other for their parents' affections, and, in consequence, they often oppose each other with as much acrimony and virulence as they are taught to exhibit in their contests with the members of rival families.

Then, follow these children of the marriages of the priesthood, and of the consequent single-family arrangements, when they attend the reading of the will of their parents. Look then into their hearts; analyze their thoughts and feelings of and for each other, and say, whether in the great majority of cases, instead of disinterested brotherly and sisterly affection being permanently enthroned within them, – the feelings of envy and jealousy and the god Mammon, do not reign triumphant. It is not at all surprising that these latter results should prevail, – for the whole of the existing arrangements of society are admirably adapted to produce them, and most especially those which necessarily emanate from the marriages devised by the priests, and the consequent single-family arrangements founded on individual opposing interest.

LECTURE FIFTH

I have in my previous lectures stated a few of the innumerable evils which the artificial marriages, or unnatural unions of the sexes, formed by the priesthoods of the world, inflict upon the husband, wife, and children of these marriages.

I have now to explain the effects of these unnatural unions upon society.

Inasmuch as men and women are continually taught that these marriages constitute a necessary and virtuous bond of society, and that it is a duty of high importance for each pair sincerely to love each other until death, and that it is a crime not thus to love each other, the husband and wife are at their marriage put within new arrangement of external circumstances, daily influencing them to become bad, wicked, or irrational members of society.

The party thus put into matrimonial bondage, having been taught that they *must* love one another and not love others in a similar manner, and taught also that they can love or hate at their pleasure, are compelled, they know not how or why, to become daily more artificial in their conduct to each other, and to society.

Usually from the day of marriage they commence a regular practice of hiding a certain number of their thoughts and feelings *from* each other, which nature and education compel them to have for each other; and the number of thoughts and feelings thus withheld often gradually increase, until husband and wife know very little indeed of the real thoughts and feelings which they entertain for each other, or for many of their friends and acquaintances. By this artificial bondage nature is thwarted in her righteous course; and, in consequence, the intercourse between the married pairs, and their intercourse with other married pairs within their visiting circle, is usually one of deception, cunning, and counteraction of each other's happiness.

Instead of the intercourse of these parties being the honest genuine expression of the thoughts and feelings which nature compels every individual, by the law of their organization, to have independent of their will; the speech, look, and action, are generally studied, to prevent many of the parties knowing or forming any correct conception of what those thoughts and feelings really are. The conversation of a party of married persons is not the natural language of rational beings, but a conventional language, meaning little or nothing, for passing a few hours in each others' society in the most insipid, heartless, and unsatisfactory manner, except to afford the opportunity, when these married pairs return home, to have some new conversation relative to criticisms on the habits, manners, looks, dress, or language of those whom they met and left as friends and neighbours.

Thus do these marriages of the priests, or the notions on which they are formed, tend essentially to introduce falsehood, cunning, and deception upon a most extensive scale, into all circles of married persons, and gradually to form the character of each of the men and women to be a compound of artifice and heartlessness.

'But,' say the advocates for the permanency of these unnatural unions, 'were it not for our marriage laws, there would be no security for chastity among women; the bonds of society would be broken; the children would be uncared for; prostitution would be general, and a promiscuous intercourse would exist between the sexes; men would continually quarrel about the women, and utter confusion would pervade society.'

This is the present language and conviction of the so-called civilized world; but both are the result solely of the grossest ignorance and prejudice. They are an additional proof, if proof were wanting, that man is yet a mere irrational animal, without sufficient intelligence to discover what manner of being he is; that he has been for centuries, nay, for thousands of years, taught from his infancy to call virtue, vice; vice, virtue; good, evil; and evil, good.

The most advanced of the human race have been carefully trained to consider the priestly marriage-bond the bond of virtue, – the safeguard of chastity, – and the only security for the well-being and happiness of children; while a correct knowledge of the first elements of our nature, and of the nature of society, will demonstrate, from the never changing laws of human nature, that these artificial marriages and real virtue can never exist in the same society; and that such marriages are alone the real cause of prostitution, and of all the crimes and miseries with which it this day afflicts the best portion of the sons and daughters of man.

The marriages of the law and gospels united, or those of the law alone, where they obtain, *and create the necessity for single-family arrangements and interests*, drive pure and genuine chastity far from the abodes of men. This virtue is far better known and practised among all other tribes of animals, who are content, in this essential part of their nature, as well as in every other instinct, to be governed by the laws of their respective natures: while man, boasting of his reason, deems himself wiser than the power that gave him all his faculties and sympathies, and ignorant of them, he presumes to disobey, and unnaturally to counteract them.

And to insure the chastity of mankind, the whole of society is put into the most absurd and artificial condition, both of body and mind, by which the sound health of mind and body is destroyed, and men and women are forced to become diseased, and filled with every species of deception.

To carry on the farce of these priestly marriages, and the notions of the spurious chastity which the priests or other ignorant persons have introduced into the human mind, children of both sexes, who have no notions but those which are natural and innocent with respect to their own persons or the persons of others, have to be tutored from their infancy to become as they grow up, much more ignorant of their own nature than all animals are of their respective natures, and, in consequence, to form the most incorrect conceptions relative to the whole business of life, and especially in all their intercourse with the sex different to their own.

This trained ignorance of their own nature is the foundation of all the artifical feelings and deceptions which ultimately take place between the two sexes. Young persons are filled with a false shame relative to the best and most valuable sympathies of their nature, and respecting which each sex is continually deceiving the other.

Upon that subject, on which the plain and simple truth, without any disguise whatever, would be of the most essential importance in promoting and securing the happiness of both sexes, men and women are now compelled by the education forced upon them by society, to resort to every kind of deception to prevent the truth being known; instead of young persons being taught from their infancy a knowledge of the simple elements of their nature, and to know that the affection, sympathies, or feelings which they entertain for others are the natural result of the qualities, sympathies, and feelings, of those parties acting upon them, and that the feelings thus produced in them are as innocent as any of those feelings created in them from seeing, hearing, tasting, smelling, or feeling any objects in nature; and that there is the same necessity for speaking the truth relative to the former as to the latter.

A far greater benefit would accrue to society from the exact truth being told in all simplicity relative to the impressions made upon us by all whom we saw or with whom we conversed, than by expressing the feelings produced in us by the objects presented to any of our external senses.

Were we taught common sense from our infancy, instead of folly and deception, we should know that one of the strongest desires of human nature is the love of the approbation of the world, but especially of those with whom we live in daily intercourse; and that the most powerful incentive to the acquisition of every good and superior quality, would be to learn from our fellows, in our hourly intercourse with them, what are the exact impressions which the qualities we possess make upon every male and female of our acquaintance. It would be the most powerful circumstance that could be brought to act upon human nature to insure, in a short period, the greatest improvement among all classes in every country.

And until all the absurd notions relative to the necessity for falsifying our feelings to those of our own, or of the other sex, shall be altogether abandoned as the prejudice of ignorance, it will be vain to expect wisdom or virtue, or even common sense, to be found among mankind.

To make the human race rational it must be surrounded with those external circumstances which shall enable it, with the most strict propriety, to speak the truth only on every subject.

Men are now prevented by the most puerile notions from speaking the truth, and are compelled, contrary to their highest and best interest, to talk continually the language of falsehood: while *falsehood* is always injurious, and *truth* is always highly beneficial for all the permanent interests of mankind.

Who then will be the first to break through this bondage of falsehood, everlastingly producing sin and misery?

Having already offended the world to the extent which I have done, in declaring amidst assembled multitudes, truths the most opposed to the obvious prejudices of ignorant man; must I offend yet more, and publicly announce other strongly offensive truths to the artificially made minds of the present generation?

As others *dare not*, or *will not* thus offend; and as *all* shrink from doing that which must be done before man can be made rational and happy, LET THE TASK BE MINE! – *It shall be* ACHIEVED; and man shall be regenerated and born again. He shall no longer be compelled to see as through a glass darkly,[a] but he shall

[a] See 1 Corinthians 13:14.

be made to see and know all things necessary to his emancipation from sin and misery without fear, veil, or mystery.

Then I now tell you, and through you, the whole of the human race, that man and woman have been made perfect; that each part of them is an essential part of their existence; that nature never intended that they should remain always ignorant of each other; or that secrecy, or mystery, of any kind, should permanently exist between the two sexes: that the time is arrived when whatever secrecy and mystery have been engendered between the sexes, through ignorance of their real nature, should now terminate for ever; and that arrangements should be formed, as speedily as possible, to enable them to return, in all their ideas and feelings, to the innocency and simplicity of their original condition, in these respects, before the priesthood of the world introduced their ignorant mysteries, which created the real fall of man.

It was the introduction of these priestly mysteries relative to the nature of man and woman, that introduced a spurious shame and falsehood into the world, and by degrees removed truth from the intercourse between male and female, and which now renders the return to truth, in all the simplicity of our nature, so dangerous and difficult to effect.

The human race, combining both sexes, has been made perfect in its organization for what nature intended it should be. The male and female, form, together, human nature; separate and apart from each other they are but half of it. Both ought, from infancy, to be instructed in an accurate knowledge of themselves, as the ground-work necessary to form them to become rational beings. Nature made no one part or division of human nature to be esteemed more sacred or secret than another; nor did it intend that any portion of the human frame should be ever considered more or less excellent than another; or that any division of it should be made by artifice and priestly contrivance to excite any but the most innocent feelings necessary for the health and happiness of every individual of the species. The fall of man from innocency and from the plain and direct road to intelligence and happiness occurred when the priesthoods of the world induced some of our ignorant ancestors to feel ashamed of any part of their nature. That this feeling is altogether an artificial and false shame may be ascertained by observing how difficult it is to impress the necessity for it upon all children, and to notice the different habits respecting it which obtain among various nations and tribes, and how much the people of our country contemn the notions of others upon the practices which, in these respects, are national in various districts of the world.

Before we can have the slightest chance of making mankind really innocent, virtuous and happy, these false notions, generating the most corrupt and injurious feelings, must be overcome, and men and women in all the nations of the world, must be made to know themselves, to accurately understand in all simplicity what manner of beings they are, and then it will be utterly impossible that they should acquire feelings of false shame relative to any part of their own nature.

And will this change from gross ignorance to real knowledge, respecting ourselves and human nature, destroy true delicacy of feeling in man and woman, for themselves and for each other?

It is those only who have been made grossly irrational, that imagine this false shame is necessary to create true delicacy of feeling, or to insure a virtuous or healthy and happy intercourse between the sexes.

But why do I bring this subject now before the public? Because I know that, until it shall be properly understood, not one step can be taken to lay a solid and permanent foundation for a rational and happy state of human existence. The previous measure must be to remove every vestige of falsehood and deception in the training of the human race, and the false notions which the artificial marriages of the priests have introduced into the world relative to sexual feelings. These errors are now, and will remain (until they shall be removed by some great effort of moral courage,) insurmountable obstacles to the progress of virtue and happiness, and an utter bar to that state of innocency in which it is narrated that our first parents lived before they fell into a corrupt and immoral mode of life.

As long as any false notions relative to sexual differences between the sexes shall be allowed to remain to influence the feelings unnaturally, or to support institutions founded to create and perpetuate the notions of those differences, men and women must continue to be the artificial beings which these errors and institutions have made them; and as long as these false impressions shall be permitted to remain, it will be vain to attempt to form any association of men and women, who could think, feel, or act rationally, or in any manner to insure a continuance of a life that could be called the truth, a virtuous and happy condition of society.

LECTURE SIXTH

Mr Owen began his lecture by observing, that he had lately, in several lectures, introduced the subject of marriage, that the friends of the rational system might know how to proceed when they were prepared to adopt practical arrangements to carry out his principles. As long, said he, as the present inferior circumstances are allowed to exist around man, he must continue the grossly ignorant and irrational animal he now is; and until he becomes sensible of the causes of the evils which surround him, he can never successfully attempt to escape from them. I continue, therefore, the subject of marriage; for until this is fully understood, it will be quite useless to commence any efficient plans to benefit mankind.

The mass of the people in all countries receive, without thought or reflection, the impression made upon them by their predecessors, relative to the notions, forms, and ceremonies long established among them; and never inquire into the origin of them, or examine their consistency with existing facts, to ascertain their truth and wisdom.

In this loose and vague manner the people of the present generation have received the forms and ceremonies long established among their predecessors. And among other vague notions, the laws and customs of marriage, and of married life, have been handed down and received implicitly, without consideration of their origin, or reflection as to their immense influence in forming the character of male and female, and deciding and controlling the general arrangements of society, and, of course, the happiness or misery of the human race.

Our ancestors, no doubt, intended their priestly marriages for the general benefit of the population of their respective countries. But when they devised them, and established their rites and ceremonies, they were ignorant of the laws of their own nature, and inexperienced in the knowledge of all that was necessary to produce and maintain a wise, rational, or happy state of society. They were altogether ignorant of the facts requisite to enable them to conceive the arrangements which could alone, by being in accordance with the nature of man, create and secure these grand results for the human race. They did not know that human feelings were not the creation of voluntary power in man; and thus they erred, most egregiously, at the very outset of all their devices for forming the character and governing human beings, to enable them to attain the great objects of human existence, that is, excellence of individual character, and general social enjoyment.

Our ancestors, therefore, instead of forming their institutions and plans of government in accordance with the laws of human nature and to be consistent with general well-known facts, have formed them, from the beginning, on imaginary notions, conceived from the vague unexamined impressions of the first general appearances of the various objects around them. And this they did because they could do no better; they were without the knowledge requisite to carry them beyond the infant world of wonder and of the most wild and random conjectures.

It was in this manner, when the imaginations of men ranged unchecked by a knowledge of accurately-defined facts, into the wide field of fancy and conjecture, and began to try their infant experiments on human legislation, that priestly marriages were conceived and devised, and a spurious chastity in consequence made a virtue of the highest order among women, while it has been scarcely admitted as a virtue among men.

Never did man make so great a mistake, as to substitute this spurious chastity and virtue of human law for nature's law of chastity, and of real virtue. By this error the characters of men and women and children have been mystified to themselves, degraded in their own estimation, made unnatural in their general intercourse, and artificial to the greatest possible extent. It has given a wrong direction to the feelings, thoughts, and actions of all of human kind, and compelled them to become the most deceptious of the whole animal creation. It has created and extended the vices and miseries of prostitution, or the total want of real chastity, over the earth; and filled it with physical and mental diseases of the most cruel, degrading, and melancholy character; and deprived the human race of a superior virtue, which would have secured more peace of mind, more health, more benevolent feeling, and more innocent enjoyment than any of the virtues at present known or acknowledged as such by any portion of mankind.

It is said that the chastity of woman could not be secured without the legal bondage of marriage. It may with much greater truth be said, that it never can be secured with the legal bondage of marriage. Has this bondage hitherto secured it? Was there ever a period in the history of man when the vilest prostitution was so universal over the world as at present? And is there a single vice in the whole catalogue of crimes which so degrades the human character, or inflicts the same extent of misery on its votaries, and upon society in general, as prostitution? No: but the miseries engendered by prostitution, and suffered by individuals and their families, friends, and connections, are generally hidden from public gaze and inspection, and are covered by the darkness of night, or concealed in dens of wretchedness. No security for the chastity of woman! What blasphemy against nature, which has provided the most ample security in the innocent affections of the female and in the cultivated feelings of the male, whenever ignorant inexperienced man shall permit these virtues their free and natural course of action.

The pure and genuine chastity of nature is to have connection only with affection; and prostitution arises only when connection is induced or forced without affection; and it is always induced by artificial causes, or forced by some necessity of law or custom, when it takes place without affection. And now all married pairs, with a very few exceptions, are living in a state of the most degrading prostitution, enforced upon them by the human laws of marriage. Pure, genuine, unadulterated chastity will be known only when men and women shall form their unions through the sympathies of unbiassed affection, and when those feelings, given to us by our nature for our happiness, shall be openly and undisguisedly expressed in all the simplicity and innocency of truth, that all may know them, and, knowing them, that none may interfere.

This is the only mode by which the chastity of woman can be insured; for if men are not chaste, how is it possible for woman to be so? But, it is said, without legal or artificial marriages, the bonds of society would be broken, and utter confusion would pervade society.

So ignorant are the human race even now upon this subject, and so prejudiced are the minds of all by ancient customs, they cannot discover that there is no bond of society existing to be broken; that there is no order or harmony in society to be thrown into confusion.

Society is now, everywhere, a chaos of the most conflicting feelings, sentiments, and interests. It consists only of an ignorant, mistaken self or individual interest, opposed to the general interest of the whole of the human race. This strange association is, now, the only bond, or thread of the weakest texture, which feebly holds society together; and the sooner that this slight binding shall be broken assunder, the better it will be for mankind. For society will then be dissolved into its original elements, and may be easily united upon the laws of nature, instead of the laws of man, and be effectually cemented by the grand law of general, instead of private, interest; and this change will promote the happiness of every individual of the human race. But, it is also said, that the children would be uncared for, unless their immediate parents were compelled, by the marriage laws, to provide and take care for them.

This supposition is another error arising from the present infant state of the human mind. Children have never yet been well educated by parents in their single-family arrangements; nor is it possible that children should ever have a superior character formed by such parties under such arrangements.

A child is the most valuable product nature can give to man. When its natural capacities shall be known and wisely appreciated, it will be discovered that society may train it to become, at maturity, a being of incalculable worth, capable of returning to society many hundred-fold the capital expended, and labour bestowed, in nursing and rearing it to the attainment of its full powers; that it might be made to acquire a very superior character, capable of giving and receiving the highest degree of pleasure and enjoyment, and of adding to the general stock of the wealth and valuable possessions of the world. This result, however, cannot be effected by the immediate parents of the children; society alone can insure these blessings to mankind; and the first indication of Governments becoming rational will be, when they shall be discovered to be earnestly and sincerely engaged in devising a sound practical national education for the children of all their subjects; an education in which physical and mental employment of real utility and value to mankind, must, of necessity, become an essential part. Whatever may be the intentions of Tories, Whigs, or Radicals, of the religious or the irreligious members of the new House of Commons, if they do not bring forward this subject on the only solid foundation on which it can be placed, that is, to form a superior rational character for each individual, believe not in their wisdom or practical knowledge for legislators. Be assured they are mere talking members, without the requisite qualifications to lay the foundation on which to make useful laws or regulations for the government of the British Empire; and more especially to make them, at this important period, in the emergency of human affairs, when the nations of the earth are looking to the parliament and people of this country for a great and good example, an example, too, which all nations and people might with safety adopt, to insure, in peace, their future progress in all kinds of improvement, physical, mental, and moral; that their progressive prosperity and happiness might be rendered certain, without creating the envy or jealousy of any other portion of the human race.

The artificial marriages of the priests, therefore, are not only of no value, now, relative to the care and culture of children, but, in this respect, they are a positive nuisance, maintaining and enforcing a continuance of highly unfavourable circumstances around children in all the gradations of society, whatever may be the occupation, profession, or rank of the parents.

But, it is said, that without these marriages, prostitution would become general, and a promiscuous intercourse would exist between the sexes.

It has been already stated, that prostitution exists at this moment to the greatest extent;[a] that its results are the most degrading and lamentable to the human race, physically, intellectually, and morally; and that the misery produced by it is most extensive and appalling.

Were it solely to put an end to this daily increasing enormous evil, artificial marriages, which are the sole cause of this crime, ought now to be made to cease; for as long as they shall be suffered, much less maintained and enforced by the law and the church, they will inevitably engender this most vicious, and, by its consequences, melancholy derangement of the happiness of human life.

The poor, helpless, unpitied victims of this unnatural state of human feelings and affections, are the most unjustly and cruelly used of any portion of the population of the world; although it is most probable that generally they are capable of being trained and placed by society, rightly constituted, to contribute most largely and most innocently to the physical, mental, and moral happiness of the species. Oh! that men could see and feel the enormity of this evil, and compel the legislators, of what is falsely named the civilized world, to turn their attention to the atrocity of the laws, which, for man's unhallowed, low, and temporary gratification, dooms the finest portion of the human race to the most acute, cutting, and desperate desolation; lacerating the best feelings of our nature, and sinking them into utter despair!

Upon this part of the subject volumes might and ought to be written, to arouse every latent sense of stern justice and common equity; if feelings of mercy, commiseration, and generosity are dead in man, to stimulate him to a prompt, decisive, right course of action. But the great, and formidable, and, said to be, irresistible argument in favour of the continuance of these artificial marriages is, that without them, there would be a promiscuous intercourse between the sexes.

Now, this argument I mean to meet in my next lecture openly, fully, and fairly, as it ought to be met, for the satisfaction of the public. For the principles

[a] There were as many as 80,000 or more prostitutes in London in the mid-nineteenth century, out of a total population of about two and a half million (or one in every sixteen women including infants).

of the New Moral World shall be without spot or blemish; they shall be consistent throughout, and no error shall be found in them.

My friends, I have opened this subject, and proceeded in part to explain some of its evils as they exist in the old immoral world. I have no doubt these lectures confound and perplex the minds of many of my hearers. Wait, however, till the whole subject be fairly before you, and then you will be able to see the difference between the old and the new systems. Many of my friends are alarmed at my opening this subject at the present time, as they also were at the course I pursued in 1817.[a] They did not see my object then, any more than they do now. I then threw away from myself more solid popularity than was perhaps ever possessed by any other individual. But what is popularity to me? If I had allowed popularity to affect me, I should have done scarcely any thing that I have. I am now sixty-three years of age; and as in the course of nature I cannot remain long with you, I am anxious to push forward measures, in the best manner that my experience suggests, to lay a foundation for proceeding, with advantage to all parties, to show what our principles can effect in a new state of society, for securing the happiness of the whole human race.

LECTURE SEVENTH

I resume the subject of marriage because it is the source of more demoralization, crime, and misery, than any other single cause, with the exception of religion and private property; and these three together form the great trinity of causes of crime and immorality among mankind. I resume the subject also because it is the most unpopular, and the most difficult to meet in public; and because it stands prominently in the way, at the very threshold, of every real improvement in the general condition of the human race.

While the errors which have been impressed on the public mind relative to artificial marriages and the intercourse of the sexes shall be suffered to remain, it is utterly impossible that man or woman can feel, think, or act as rational beings. The natural strength of their character, physical, intellectual, and moral, is destroyed by the absurd notions and feelings which they are compelled to receive respecting their sexual natures from early childhood, and by the false training which, for this period, is forced upon both sexes. That which nature made the very simplicity of innocency, and the foundation for a refined and superior character, the priesthood has made the means by which to

[a] A reference to Owen's attack on religion in particular in the August 1817 meetings at the City of London Tavern.

introduce an artificial weakness of body and mind, false shame, loathsome disease, with crime and misery, to an incalculable extent.

And when the priesthood had produced these lamentable results throughout human society, it became necessary that the whole arrangements of public and private affairs should be made in accordance with these weaknesses and errors; and, in consequence, a combination of artificial thoughts, feelings, and actions has been engendered, and, from age to age, multiplied to such an extent, that, at this moment, the human race, viewed with the eye of sober reason, has attained to a condition of absurdity and folly that we shall seek for, in vain, among any other tribes of animals.

Were it not that we are accustomed, and thereby reconciled, to what is around us, and to the habits and practices of our friends, companions, and other persons within the circle of our experience, we should be impressed, in the most forcible manner, with the strange, inconsistent, and most extraordinary proceedings of the inhabitants of Great Britain and Ireland. It is a subject of great doubt whether there is any other congregated mass of human beings, any other nation, tribe, or people, termed civilized, barbarian, or savage, which at this day exhibits such gross incongruities, grave absurdities, and unjust and cruel conduct, as is now to be seen in the general conduct of the population of these two Islands, and to be seen too in all their various gradations, from the pauper expiring from famine, to the sovereign surrounded by his motley courtiers and fantastic puerile paraphernalia.

Nothing short of the effect of habit upon the human organization could close our perceptions to the extent of the gross folly, and utter irrationality of the people and government of this country.

We will endeavour to exhibit a mirror of truth,[a] which will reflect, at least, some part of the strange incongruities and cruelties of their character and conduct.

The government and people generally now profess that their object is to insure to themselves and others the greatest extent of the most permanent happiness.

And to effect this object, they teach that all should worship, in all sincerity, an infinitely wise, powerful, and good Being, who can do all things, and who, above all things, desires the happiness of his creatures.

They endeavour also to train their children to love this Being, and, as far as possible, to imitate his wisdom and goodness, and especially to love their fellow-creatures whom this all-wise Being has made, and who, they say, is the common parent of all of them, without exception.

This is the professed object of the people and government of the British empire at this day. And, to accomplish these results, their practice is the most

[a] *The Mirror of Truth* was the title of the first journal published by Owen, in 1817.

extraordinary, and certainly the most extravagantly insane, that the human mind can imagine. – 1st. They teach in words, that all must love their neighbour as themselves;[a] and, to effect this object, they devise arrangements and adopt measures which render it impossible that any one can acquire this feeling; arrangements and measures which, of necessity, train and force all to oppose, dislike, and hate, and many to murder, one another. And these feelings are engendered, not for the real benefit of a single individual of the human race, but to the lasting injury of all; and the conduct thus produced is in direct opposition to all the religious views which are daily taught to the people,

2nd. They teach, in words, that they should express the truth only, upon all occasions; while they adopt practices which induce each other to speak a language generally of gross falsehood, with scarcely any genuine truth mixed with it.

3rd. They teach, in words, that they should be honest in all their dealings and transactions with each other and all mankind; while, in deeds, they continually attempt to obtain advantages over all, and their thoughts are chiefly occupied in devising schemes for promoting their own individual interest in opposition to the interest of those immediately around them, or of others more remote.

4th. They teach, in words, that all should obtain equal justice; while the rich make laws and regulations which render it impossible that the poor should obtain justice in opposition to the man of wealth.

5th. They teach, in words, that heaven is to be desired above all things on earth; that it is impossible for a rich man to enter into the kingdom of heaven; and yet teachers and all, are daily exerting their best energies to obtain riches.

6th. They teach, in words, that idleness is a crime; and yet all are endeavouring to attain a state to enable them, and their children after them, through endless generations, to live continually in idleness upon the over-exerted industry of others.

7th. All are taught and trained to acquire the desire to become rich; while the far greater part are actively, but most blindly, engaged in measures which, to an incalculable extent, prevent the increase of the most valuable wealth, which, by the adoption of rational measures, might easily be made far more than sufficient to satisfy the utmost craving of all, even with riches exceeding their powers to enjoy them.

8th. They teach, in words, the principles and spirit of peace and good-will to mankind; while they practice openly, or covertly, all means to create disunion, unkind feelings, and often war, on the most extensive scale.

9th. They teach, in words, that wisdom and knowledge are most desirable

[a] See Mark 12:33.

for all; while those who thus teach, and who could materially assist to extend wisdom and knowledge to the whole people, are indirectly using all their influence and power to prevent the spread of these invaluable acquisitions.

10th. They teach, in words, temperance; while those who have the power, adopt the most effective indirect measures to insure the continuance and increase of gross intemperance among the mass of the people.

11th. They teach, in words, the duty and advantage of union among all; while, in practice, they adopt the most certain measures to disunite, and to keep disunited, the whole of the human race.

12th. They teach, in words, the great advantage of forming a superior good character for all individuals; while they actively and perseveringly pursue the most direct measures to force all to acquire an inferior and immoral character.

13th. They teach, in words, the high morality of all women being chaste; while they adopt all the most artificial and unnatural methods to force men and women to become prostitutes.

14th. They teach, in words, that above all things they should have pure and genuine charity for each other; while they have adopted every conceivable notion and measure to render it impracticable that they can entertain one particle of real charity for each other, or practice it in any part of their conduct.

And, lastly, the men, women, and children of the British islands are, at this day, with more means at their disposal to effect the most extensive benefits to mankind, than any congregated mass of human beings ever possessed, 'doing what they ought not to do, and leaving undone all they ought to do' for their own well-being and happiness. But there is no limit to the gross incongruities in the British isles. And it is under this complication of irrationality that these pretenders to virtue and right conduct say, that 'without the artificial marriages of the priesthood, prostitution would be general, and a promiscuous intercourse would exist between the sexes; men would continually quarrel about the women, and utter confusion would pervade society.'

Now, the plain matter of fact is, that prostitution *is* become general in married as well as single life; men *do* continually quarrel about the women; a promiscuous intercourse *does* exist, and utter confusion pervades society.

Our object is to prepare the way to bring these evils and disorders in society to an end, and to introduce measures to terminate them forever; and, as a first and most necessary step, to abolish over the earth the artificial marriages of the old immoral world.

We ask the men and women who have a knowledge of society as it now exists in practice, if the marriages of civilized nations, as they are most ignorantly termed, are calculated to produce real chastity between the sexes, or truth in their communications with each other? We fearlessly answer for them, no! for chastity and truth never can exist under such an unnatural arrangement. The unavoidable results of this complicated artifice of the priesthood are, an almost total want of real chastity, a general, vile, concealed, promiscuous intercourse of the most disastrous and degrading character; and, in addition, a general language and conduct of insincerity and deception among married and single, young and old. These are the present *wise* practices of the old immoral world, which no one must presume to condemn or attempt to change! There is not an honest and intelligent man or woman, who is acquainted with the general practices of society, who is not conscious of the accuracy of this statement, and who would not confirm it openly if they dare speak their thoughts and feelings freely and honestly, as will be done when men and women shall be permitted to be trained to be rational beings.

We ask, what has nature intended the intercourse between the sexes to be, natural or artificial? We enquire again, whether nature or man, ignorant as he has hitherto been of his nature, is the most likely to direct aright, and most beneficially for the objects intended by nature, the intercourse between the sexes? Does nature, for her wise purposes, intend that this intercourse should be restricted *through life* by the artificial union of one of each sex, as man, in some countries, has vainly endeavoured to decree? or between one male and several females, restricted by the law to that male, for life, as man has decided shall be the practice in other countries? or that it would be more in accordance with common sense, and the most delicate and virtuous course, for nature herself to direct her own proceedings and decide upon her own operation?

Is there any sexual crime or prostitution known among any other tribe of animals? Do they act wisely or viciously in their sexual intercourse? Is there more virtue among any race of animals in eating, drinking, and sleeping, than in continuing, by the same natural laws, the existence of their species? Does nature regulate this latter propensity in animals, as wisely as the former? Is it not probable that nature, if not interfered with by ignorant presumptuous man, would regulate and direct this propensity in the human race, as wisely for their good, as she regulates and directs it for all other races of animals? Who made the intercourse of the sexes in opposition to nature, among the human race, a virtue? Who made this intercourse in accordance with nature, a vice? Was it God, or the Devil; nature, or the priest? Is the intercourse of the sexes, devised, and now maintained by the priesthood, a virtue or a vice? Is the intercourse of the sexes, as ordained and directed by nature a virtue or a vice?

Let those who have knowledge and experience of the world, and who dare be honest, in opposition to gross ignorance and vulgar prejudice, now answer these questions.

But such is the debasement of the human intellect, such the enslavement of the natural feelings to the fear of the power of the priesthood, that to these most important questions the tongue of man must be mute; and whatever may be the response in the heart of the learned or the ignorant, the sovereign, or the beggar, all, all must restrain its utterance to the world, in deference to the priestly power which for so many centuries has ruled the destinies of man, making him an ignorant miserable bigot, when he might so easily be made an intelligent, rational, and happy being.

If the degenated sons of man are thus sunk below the condition of the brute creation, who fear not, at all times, to express their feelings, the sacred feelings of nature in them as they are also in man, we will now relieve the human race from their mental bondage; and, thus relieving them, we shall emancipate them from sin and misery.

We shall thus regenerate them and again make them the sons of God or nature, willing to adopt, and in future to abide by, the divine love of their parent, and to reject for ever the ignorant and wicked laws of the priesthood, or of the devil.

Behold! the period is arrived when one man, at least, dare publish the truth to the world; and this is a sure and certain sign that the time draweth nigh when the mind of man shall be born again,[a] and when truth, peace, and love shall reign for evermore.

My friends, I have asked some questions which ought now, for the benefit of the human race, to be answered simply and plainly. Who can answer them? Who dare answer them publicly? I have put them before you now; think of the answers which ought to be given to them. Next Sunday I will answer them myself, and we shall then see if our answers coincide. I shall then consider whether we are acting upon nature's or upon man's decrees, and what nature would produce if left to herself. Whether would nature's or man's decrees be the best to act upon? Many individuals have told me that they are afraid the minds of their friends are not yet prepared for the subject of marriage; but I must place it fairly before the world. I have opened the subject, and must continue it until I have rendered it as familiar to my hearers as it is to myself.

LECTURE EIGHTH

In my last discourse I have asked several questions necessary to be answered, relative to the natural state of man and woman, and also respecting their present artificial condition. And these questions were purposely asked, because they must be openly and honestly answered to the world, before the human race can stand any chance of being emancipated from ignorance, sin, and misery.

When these questions were asked I well knew there were none to answer them. But I have told you that the veil of mysteries is about to be rent asunder,

[a] See for example Romans 12:2.

and that you shall no longer see as through a glass darkly,[a] but that your minds shall be born again,[b] and that you shall see face to face, and know each other, even as you are known, or as you know yourselves.

The subjects to which these questions refer, are said, by the priests, to be too *sacred* for man's investigation; he must receive their dogmas implicitly as divine truths, too sacred to be doubted by mortals. Now it is deserving of everlasting remembrance, that what the nations of the earth have been taught by their priests to believe to be divine truths, too sacred for other *mortals* to examine, or to doubt, have been diabolical falsehoods, which were so contrary to known facts and common sense, that it became necessary to fence them round with the mysteries of their invented divinities, to prevent the grossness of their deception becoming glaringly evident through the increasing knowledge of the multitude. Therefore, in future, for divine truths read priestly falsehoods and gross and injurious deceptions.

It has been in this manner that the priests have contrived to call their marriages, which they have devised, a divine ordinance, and that all the ignorant mysticism between the sexes has been concocted and maintained for so many generations, even until many of the priests themselves really believe most conscientiously in the divinity of their own absurdities.

We must now unmask the ignorance and deception of all these proceedings; for in our New Moral World there must not be ignorance or deception of any kind, which our present knowledge of facts will enable us to remove; but especially there must be no avoidable mystery relative to the nature of man and woman, or to the right foundation on which to erect the new state of society, which is to give to human nature a new character and a new existence. For now man is indeed to be regenerated and born again, and raised to a life of intelligence and happiness, that is, to the innocency of paradise, united with the intelligence of all past experience.

And in this new world, to free it from sin and the cause of sin, there will be no marriages of the priest, or giving in marriage.

The reasons for this new condition of human life will be obvious when we shall answer the questions which were asked in our last discourse; and to this task we now proceed.

The first question asked was, 'Has Nature intended the intercouse between the sexes to be natural or artificial?'

The priests have made it artificial; and the priests rule and controul all things in all the so-called civilized nations of the earth. They have devised the marriage ceremonies of the various nations, and established the laws of marriage for all people. These proceedings they contrived and adopted when their power over the minds of the multitude was unlimited and uncontrolled; when

[a] See 1 Corinthians 13:12.
[b] See for example Romans 12:2.

they directed the actions of kings and princes more despotically than kings and princes can now command the services of ordinary men.

In the plenitude of their ignorant despotism, the priests, disregarding all Nature's divine and sacred laws, or being ignorant of them, substituted their own imaginations, called *them* divine inspirations, and then compelled the spell-bound fanatic to adopt them without investigation, as being *too sacred* for human reason, and, therefore, to be implicitly believed by faith alone, which they assert is superior to reason or sound common sense.

But the power of the priest is passing away; man is beginning to investigate the causes of the effects which now exist around him; he is approaching the confines of the rational period of his existence; he doubts the knowledge of the priesthood, and he doubts the sincerity of many of them. He is preparing himself to enquire, without superstitious fear or dread, into the origin of their authority, and into the wisdom of the laws and institutions which they have induced the world to receive from them, and especially into those laws, regulations, and institutions, relative to the intercourse of the sexes.

Having examined this subject to its foundation, as far as facts yet ascertained by man admit, we do not hesitate to say that the priests of the world, when they devised the various laws of marriage in different countries, were either totally ignorant of their own nature, and of human nature generally, or that they were hypocrites, and devised laws and ceremonies to keep the multitude in ignorance and in subjection to them. But whether they have acted from ignorance or through design, they have instituted the most immoral laws, leading to the most immoral, unhealthy, and miserable practices throughout society; instead of abiding by Nature's laws, which would have led to the most moral, healthy, and happy practices.

The artificial laws of the priesthood for regulating, by man's ignorance, the intercourse of the sexes, have at once destroyed truth among mankind, and made it unavoidable that falsehood should have uncontrolled dominion as long as those laws shall be allowed to remain to direct the conduct of the sexes, and as long as the priests possess the power to deceive mankind by the presumed sanctity and sacredness of their divine character.

It is now evident, from the crime and misery which the unnatural laws of marriage, forced upon society by the priesthood, have produced, and are at this hour producing, that Nature has ever intended that the intercourse of the sexes shall not be artificial, but natural; and that future generations shall bring forth superior natural children, in place of the inferior artificial children which the priests have caused to be brought among all the civilized nations of the earth; and, in consequence, the race is rapidly declining in natural powers. The answer, therefore, to the question, 'Has Nature intended the intercourse between the sexes to be natural or artificial?' is, that nature intends it shall be natural, as soon as man shall be trained to become rational.

The next question was, 'Whether Nature or man, ignorant as he has hitherto been of his nature, is the most likely to direct the intercourse of the sexes aright, and most beneficially for the objects ultimately intended by Nature, which are, evidently, the attainment of excellence and happiness among the whole family of mankind?'

Man, as is proved by his every-day practice, has never yet known the laws of his own organization: he has been kept totally ignorant of himself; and he has been living in a state of mental and moral blindness. His language, manners, and customs prove that he has totally mistaken the fact relative to the powers and capacities of his natural constitution, and that, in consequence, previous to this period, he has been incompetent to examine and comprehend the laws of his nature to a sufficient extent to enable him to apply them to practice in the daily business and affairs of life.

Nature, when left to herself, as is seen throughout the whole of the animal creation, directs every faculty and power of each creature wisely for the apparent objects to be attained by its peculiar nature; and, no doubt, she would direct man with still more wisdom, for her wise purposes, if from some cause or other, yet to be discovered, man did not interpose his inexperience to thwart her righteous course and his own permanent happiness. The present extraordinary excitement among the human race in the four quarters of the world is an indication that Nature is actively at work to overcome this ignorance, error, or defect in man, to teach him how to avoid the evils which he has hitherto experienced, and to secure the good and attain the happiness which his nature is so admirably fitted to enjoy. We are, therefore, compelled to conclude, that Nature can, and will, direct the intercourse between the sexes far more wisely to secure the permanent good and happiness of the human race, than man can ever comprehend while he remains so ignorant of the laws of his own nature, as he has proved himself to be by his past history, and is, even at the present period.

The next question in rotation is, 'Does Nature, for her wise purposes, intend that the intercourse between the sexes should be restricted, through life, by the artificial union of one of each sex, as man in some countries, has vainly endeavoured to decree? or, between one male and several females, restricted by human laws to that male for his life, as is now the custom over a large portion of the earth? or, that it would be more in accordance with common sense, and also the most delicate and virtuous course to adopt, for Nature herself to direct her own proceedings, and decide upon her own operations?'

Now we have had great experience of the two first artificial customs, and probably the population of the world is at present divided nearly equally between these two very opposite practices; and yet both modes are said, by their respective priests, to be of God's appointment. Whether they have been introduced by a good or malignant spirit, by wisdom or ignorance, they have served to give man, during many generations, a knowledge, through dear-bought experience, of the effects of both of these artificial unions of the sexes.

And certainly they have proved to be, to an enormous extent, vicious and unfavourable circumstances, which have tended more to weaken and degrade human nature than any other artificial institution invented by man.

The human law which binds one man to the same woman, and the woman to the man through life, whether or not they can retain an affection for each other, has produced more hatred, and destroyed more love between these parties than would otherwise have taken place, probably many thousand-fold. It has produced a general practice of the most gross as well as refined falsehood, and the deepest deception between these parties, and to the public. It has given rise to the most extensive jealousy and revenge, and severed those, for ever, from each other, who were compelled, by their natures, to entertain the strongest and most sincere mutual affection, competent by their union to create as much happiness as their forced separation produced misery. This permanent artificial union of a single pair for life has forced a system of promiscuous intercourse, in those countries in which this law prevails, most degrading and injurious to the physical, intellectual, and moral character and conduct of both sexes; and thereby produced an extent of injustice, cruelty, and misery, especially to the female, beyond the power of any written statement or mere wordy document to enable the present race of man to comprehend.

In fact, this forced continued union of a single pair of human beings through life, with or without affection, as it may happen to be, is calculated, in all its consequences, to the old, young, and middle-aged, to create an extensive ramification of the most immoral external circumstances. And through the natural effect of these vicious institutions of the priesthood, acting and re-acting continually upon human nature, they are also calculated, as well as if they were devised for the purpose, to constitute a weak, artificial, heartless, miserable condition of human society. This Christian custom cannot, therefore, be intended to be the practice of the human race when they shall acquire sufficient experience to become rational creatures.

Then the Eastern legal custom of one man having permission to have as many wives as he can maintain, although, perhaps, less injurious in some respects than the customs of Christians, and especially as it materially diminishes promiscuous intercourse, is, nevertheless, a most unfortunate device for mankind. It tends powerfully to make men and women weak, jealous, irrational beings. It destroys the confidence of man in woman, and woman in man; and makes woman a mere slave to man's sexual propensity; it tends to perpetuate woman in a state of mental childhood: it destroys the confidence of man in man relative to his converse with women, and creates an ignorant and most anti-social state of society, and retards the free communication of mind with mind without injurious artificial restraints; and it makes man, and a few women united with him, and their immediate offspring, isolated beings, knowing and caring little for the progress of useful science, or of the great truths relative to human nature; through which knowledge, alone, man can discover the only road to a superior mode of existence, and to permanent happiness.

We therefore, pronounce that neither of these modes of restricting the intercourse between the sexes, will ever produce a virtuous, intelligent, rational, or happy state of human society; and that it will be more in accordance with common sense and with virtue, for Nature, when man and woman shall be trained to be rational creatures, to direct her own proceedings, and to decide upon her own operations. But before this very superior state of existence can be obtained, new general external arrangements must be introduced, of a very different character to those which now exist throughout society, or have yet been devised, or, to our knowledge, ever been imagined, by ignorant, inexperienced, irrational man.

Our next question was, 'Is there any sexual crime, or prostitution known, or imagined by them to exist, among any tribe or species of animals, except man?' We reply, we know of no other animals who fancy there is any crime or vice whatever in continuing their species as their nature directs, or which do not follow the instinct of their nature, and no evil ensues. Do they thus act wisely or viciously in their sexual intercourse? Most wisely; and if they were to act otherwise, their conduct would soon become as unwise, and as vicious, and immoral, as the past and present conduct of the human race has been.

The next question that follows, is thus stated: 'Is there more virtue among any race of animals, in eating, drinking, and sleeping, according to the laws or propensities of their nature, than there is in continuing, by the same natural laws, the existence of their species?' We fearlessly say, no; there is quite as much common sense and rationality in the one case as in the other; they have all the same origin and character, and will for ever remain the same in character, whatever name or term the fancy of men, in their ignorance, may presumptuously give them.

The succeeding question is, 'Does Nature regulate the law or propensity for continuing the species in animals as wisely as she regulates the laws or propensities for eating, drinking, or sleeping?' We are convinced that Nature is as perfect in the one as in the other: nor can we believe, with the knowledge of facts now known to the world, that any reasonable being will ever entertain a doubt upon the subject. Why, therefore, do not the priests, as they presume to controul and regulate Nature in *one* of her wonderful operations, make their own artificial laws in opposition to Nature for all other feelings and senses which man professes, and decide upon one general law or rule, by which every individual shall eat, drink, and sleep, as respects quantity, quality, time etc? for there is quite as much wisdom in, and necessity for, the one as for the other. Let the priesthood answer this statement when they shall have reflected upon it.

We proceed to the next question, as it is intimately connected with the preceding. It is as follows: 'Is it not probable that Nature, if not interfered with or interrupted in her course by man in his present ignorant state, would regulate and direct the sexual intercourse of the human race as wisely for their good as she regulates and directs it for the benefit of all other races of animals?'

Upon this question we conclude, that no one, with common understanding, can have any doubt. The chief of animals would not, it is presumed, be left, in this important part of its nature, more uncared for and less protected than the inferior tribes. On the contrary, it is not reasonable to suppose that Nature would guide her chief work upon earth, in this essential part of the economy of its life, as much more perfectly as she has provided for all its other wants, and make it contribute, like all its other propensities, to the health and happiness of the species? Yet, in defiance of this most natural conclusion, the priesthood, in its ignorance, has made this propensity, which is necessary to our existence, health, and happiness, the source of disease and wretchedness. When man shall be permitted to attend to, and be governed by, the innocent laws of his nature – and all Nature's laws are innocent – he will discover how egregiously he has erred in this respect, and how much misery he has by that error inflicted, for so many ages, on the whole of his species. He will also discover that he has taken the greatest and most unnatural pains to render the finer and more delicate sympathies of our nature, the source of the most extended mental and physical diseases, and of the most acute and heartbreaking wretchedness; when, on the contrary, if these prime sources of man's most valuable enjoyments had been judiciously cultivated and wisely directed, they would, long ere this, have made him a very superior and happy being; a being filled with charity, benevolence, and affection for all of his species, and in secure possession of the highest enjoyments.

When man shall be placed within those external circumstances, practical arrangements, and wise institutions which are in accordance with human nature, and which can alone train him to become rational, and enable him to know what real virtue and happiness are, then will Nature not be interrupted in her wise course by man's inexperience and his consequent presumption, and the intercourse of the sexes will be solely under the guidance of Nature, and not of the priests' irrational devices and laws. And who can doubt that Nature will regulate and direct this propensity, which she has formed in man, as wisely for *his* happiness, immediate and remote, as she has ever regulated and directed the same kind of propensity also of her own creation, for that of *all other* races of animals?

The remaining most interesting questions we must now leave to be answered in our next discourse. These answers, with the consideration of the effects which the artificial marriages devised by the priests have upon human nature, will terminate our discourses on the effects of the artificial unions of the sexes under the institutions of the old immoral world.

When we shall have explained, in future lectures, the direful effects on human nature of the other two great sources of crime and misery in the old immoral world, viz, private property, and what the priesthood has heretofore called religion, we shall be prepared to lay the foundation and to build up the New Moral World; and then the minds of our hearers and readers will be somewhat better prepared than they are now to understand what ought to be, and what will be, the new position of man and woman in their rational state of existence; and they will also acquire some faint impressions of the *great and glorious change* which is about to take place in the condition of the human race in every part of the globe in which man can be found.

You are perhaps aware, my friends, that the subject of the marriages of the world, as devised by the priesthood, is one of the most unpopular and difficult to treat properly. The disciples of the new system themselves are, many of them, alarmed at its open discussion at the present time. They supposed we had sufficiently shocked the prejudices of the world in openly denouncing all other parts of the old immoral system; but were not aware that all the truth which we have previously spoken, is of little or no practical value without our entering fully and freely into the subject of marriage. There are many parties in the country waiting anxiously for our commencing operations; but it would be quite useless for us to begin, until the subject of marriage, private property, and religion be properly understood by those about to enter upon a rational state of society. Many persons conceive that nothing can be easier than to establish a community, and to carry the system into practice: but no community has yet been begun which did not consist of married couples. I have known from the first that no such practice could succeed, as the interest of private families is quite opposed to that of a number of equally free and intelligent individuals. Before such a community as I advocate can take place, our minds must be born again, and we must be possessed of a very different knowledge from that which we now have. The truths I have presented to you appear startling only when seen at a distance, and when they are new to the mind; as they become familiar, it will then be perceived that they are the farthest removed from morality, and that the only right course is to adopt the conduct now recommended; for it is truth only, unmixed with error or mystery, that can ever produce a virtuous state of society.

LECTURE NINTH

We have now to continue the subject of marriage from the point at which we left off on Sunday evening last. Of all the great and interesting subjects now before the public, not one appears to be so little understood in its extensive relations and consequences, throughout society, as marriage. No persons, perhaps, are aware of the totally different character which this single institution has given to the human race, from that which it would have acquired provided the association of the sexes had been in accordance with the natural laws of our organization; for in that case, the other great arrangements of human life would have been made consistent with it.

The institution of marriage has forced the populations of all countries to adopt a system of exclusion and mystery in all their domestic arrangements, and has made it unavoidable that they should acquire the most injurious habits of falsehood, secrecy, and deception in their general conduct to each other, and to the world at large. This institution has also rendered it a matter of necessity that the most extravagant and injurious external circumstances should be formed for the accommodation of each married pair and their offspring; and it has inflicted, morally, and physically, the direst calamities upon the human race. As men have never yet been taught to reflect and reason rationally, or universally, all their thoughts have been confined to considerations of self, sect, or party, and the great interests of the human race have been altogether neglected. The far greater advantages to be derived by every one from the adoption of unexclusive general principles in practice, are yet a dead letter with all who have been trained to acquire only individualizing feelings, notions, and interests; and all have been so trained. While these feelings, notions, and interests shall be inculcated, enforced, and induced, by the temptation of present gain, and the promise of future everlasting rewards, the race of man must remain ignorant and immoral; and confusion and misery, both public and private, will continue, as heretofore, to pervade all the nations of the earth. But we must proceed to unravel more of the principal causes of these evils, by replying to the remaining questions which were asked in our last discourse but one, and which were left unanswered in the discourse which we delivered here on Sunday evening last.

The questions to be answered in regular succession are the following: – 'Who made the intercourse of the sexes in opposition to Nature, among the human race, a virtue?' or, in other words, 'who made the observance of the laws of man, which are in opposition to the laws of Nature, a virtue; and the observance of the laws of Nature, which are in opposition to the laws of man, a vice? Was it God or the devil, Nature or the priest?'

Now these are questions of vital interest to the human race, for upon the truth of the reply to them, depends the possibility or practicability of giving a progressive happiness to all of human kind. If it be indeed virtue to oppose Nature, and vice to act in accordance with it, then is man doomed for ever to be a miserable being. We greatly rejoice to know that he has not been doomed always to remain in this wretched condition; although he has, to this period, been made by the priesthood so ignorant of himself and of human nature generally, that he has been forced by them, and by the other governors and directors of society, to refrain from the study of human nature, in some cases under the penalty of death, and at least of destitution. And thus, instead of pursuing this study, the only wise practice that man can adopt, he has been compelled to waste his most valuable powers and energies in the wilds of an over-excited imagination, and to occupy himself in the pursuit of mysticisms which none can explain, or of useless baubles, or for the attainment of silly additional names, called honours, and of privileges highly injurious to the best and permanent interests of mankind. Our greatest men, so called, are at this moment, thus uselessly or mischievously occupied; or they are engaged in a desperate political warfare, to ascertain which of two or three most ignorant parties shall obtain the power of the state: and to obtain this power, too, solely to enable the victorious idle or injuriously-occupied rich, the more effectually and safely to maltreat and oppress the industrious poor, by every kind of unjust device; for their contests, when stripped of all mystery and verbiage, are commenced and continued for no other purposes than for one section of those rich parties to gain greater facilities to effect these diabolical objects for the benefit of themselves, to the exclusion of others. Now the marriages devised by the church and law tend greatly to enable the priests and the rich to trample upon right and justice, and to set the most palpable and everlasting truths at open defiance. And to make a colourable pretence for these marriages, the priests and the rich and powerful, who deemed it to be for their interests thus to impose upon mankind, united to contrive an artificial conduct for the industrious and poor, and to call that conduct by high-sounding names, and expecially to *call* it *virtuous*. And thus, and thus only was the chastity of the priests and lawyers first made a virtue; and as these parties found the deception take with the multitude, and as the trick was a great gain to them, they have adopted most effectual measures to extend and continue the error and its evils through the succeeding generations, even to the present hour.

The priest's and the rich man's laws of chastity are very different to Nature's laws of chastity; and it becomes now of the highest importance to the men and women of all the nations in the world to understand the difference between *real* chastity, or the *chastity of Nature*, and the *spurious* chastity of the *church and law*. This difference should be made as obvious to the multitude as it has ever been to the select cunning few among those who have hitherto governed mankind.

The chastity of Nature then, or real charity – that chastity which alone is virtuous – consists in the intercourse of the sexes when there is a pure and genuine sympathy or sincere affection between the parties; when the physical, intellectual, and moral feelings of the one are in perfect accordance with those of the other; when, in fact, their natures are so happily blended, that together they form but one harmonious whole, and become, when thus united in heart and soul, or body and mind, one being, whose feelings and interests are identified, and who are thus made capable of enjoining these sympathies and affections so long as Nature has designed them to remain, and thus to experience the full happiness of their nature, or of a virtuous mode of existence. But as these sympathies and affections are the productions of Nature, and not of the individuals whose constitution Nature has formed, there will be no secrecy respecting them, but the same open frankness will take place in explaining and expressing them as now exists in relating the impressions made upon any of our other senses; for these sympathies have a right to be called a sense as much as our faculties of seeing, hearing, etc, have to be denominated senses. Our sympathies of affection for the other sex are as natural and as innocent as any one of our other natural feelings.

Now chastity made a virtue by the church and law is of a very different character. Regardless of Nature, priests and lawyers deemed it wise and practicable to bind affection by the restraints of ecclesiastical and civil laws, and by ceremonies, and an artificial public opinion, created by their influence, in opposition to Nature; and they decreed it to be chaste for men and women to be united, and to *remain united* by their bonds, when no natural sympathy or affection existed between the parties, or even when their natures forced them to feel a strong *repulsive*, instead of an *attractive* propensity for each other.

Thus they made their chastity to consist in a man and woman, by law, cohabiting together for life, whether they had a natural affection for each other or not. And when the parties were compelled, by their natural feelings, to entertain a great dislike, or even hatred of each other, and were thus made most miserable by their unnatural union, the priests called it chastity and a cardinal virtue for them thus to cohabit together, and destroy, for the gratification of the priests, the whole happiness of their lives.

Thus have men and women been duped to lead a life of open opposition to each other's feelings, or of consummate hypocrisy, that they might be called by the priests, solely for their (the priests') gain, chaste and virtuous, when, in fact, they have been living a life of prostitution and vice. There surely never has been a more bare-faced deception than this ever practised upon mankind, to rob them, by law, of their kindest and best sympathies, and of the most delightful feelings of their nature; of those feelings, which, when thwarted or repressed, so often produce mental derangement or severe bodily disease, creating the most heartbreaking sufferings and miseries, and too frequently premature death in the prime and pride of life.

But these afflictions, severe as they are, are yet, perhaps, less to be deplored than the crimes and wretchedness which this spurious chastity of the priests has engendered by introducing and maintaining a permanent sacrifice of the person, for mere mercenary considerations, when the affections are not interested; for a general promiscuous intercourse between the sexes is a natural consequence. How could it be expected to be otherwise, when no sympathy of the feelings or natural affections existed between the parties? Thus have the priests, by making a spurious chastity a virtue, in oppostion to Nature, filled the world with mercenary marriages, and with an endless catalogue of crimes and miseries; and thus they keep the human race in a low and degraded state, from which they cannot advance until they relinquish the marriages and chastity of the priests, and place men and women in their natural and rational position.

But this change, so necessary to all human improvement, cannot be effected until other great changes shall be made at the same time in other parts of the present system; in fact, not until this old immoral world shall be effectually regenerated by the abolition of the false religions, and of all the evils of private property, by the introduction of arrangements to establish a rational state of society, or, the new moral world. For the present laws of marriage are so intimately blended with the existing systems of religion and property, all of them being founded on the same false notions, that when one shall be destroyed the others shall perish also.

Nor can the virtue of real chastity be introduced under the present system of falsehood and deception. This virtue can only be known in a world of innocency and truth; qualities which the present world laugh at, and condemn as being impossible to exist in their state of society. In this conclusion the inhabitants of the old immoral world are correct, for innocency and truth have nothing to do in all their present proceedings. As real chastity cannot exist except in a society in which truth alone is the converse of all its members, and as truth cannot be the converse of the public in this old immoral world, it is in vain to except the introduction of real chastity into general society until the old immoral world shall be changed for the New Moral World.

These discourses on the marriages of the priests, are to prepare the way for this great change in the condition of mankind; and when we shall have explained the necessity for abolishing the whole system of private property, and all the old mysteries which the priesthood of the world has called religion, but which have been only an obstacle in all countries to the introduction of truth and virtue; we will then explain the principles on which to found the true association of the sexes to produce health, real chastity, and happiness, and make the association of the sexes what Nature evidently intended, a great good, instead of, as at present, a great evil.

There is one more lecture remaining to conclude this subject, which I will deliver next Sunday. I will then proceed to the examination of the subjects of private property and religion; for these three are so connected with each other that all the evils of society may be traced to them.[a]

---

[a] See *New Moral World*, vol. 1, nos 17–18, 24 (21–28 February, 11 April 1835), pp. 129–31, 137–40, 185–7.

LECTURE TENTH

We have now to enquire what effect the marriages devised by the priesthood, have had upon human nature: and this will for the present finish our course of lectures on these artificial marriages.

Human nature, as presented to man at the birth of each infant for man's own direct influence to be applied to it, is perhaps, the most delightful compound of physical, intellectual, and moral powers to be acted upon, to produce the highest degree of intelligence, goodness, and happiness, that the human mind is capable of comprehending.

We are not in possession of facts to enable us to say that these natural powers of human nature are, in any of their compounds, different now from what they were at any former period of man's existence. On the contrary, ancient history and representation of human beings leads us to conclude that the infant man is no way superior now to what he has ever been. But it is necessary to enquire why human nature, which has ever been capable of being trained to acquire so much physical, intellectual, and moral excellence, should have remained in the degraded condition in which we now find it in Great Britain and in other nations, deemed the most advanced in learning and civilization?

Why are such multitudes of the most useful parts of the population at this moment, suffering all the evils of neglect in the cultivation of these invaluable powers? Why are ignorance, poverty, and wretchedness, with every bad and irrational feeling, allowed to grow up with and pervade the character of so very large a portion of the human race? And why are *all* thus made far more inferior, and less happy, than any human being ought now to be?

The true reply to these questions, vitally important for man to know, is only now, for the first time perhaps in the history of the human race, to be honestly obtained.

The answer to these questions is, that these evils have been so long experienced, and are now endured, because man has been so formed as to be influenced in the infancy of his powers, most strongly by the first impressions made on his several senses, and because imaginary notions have been, and are, thus clearly impressed upon him, made to precede a knowledge of facts, accurate observation, reflection, and comparison; and thus, for a season, the *imagination* of the human race has maintained the mastery over the judgement, and in consequence, the imaginary notions of man have to the present period governed and directed the conduct of all individuals and of all associations of men. And hence the evils which have been and are now suffered, more or less, by all mankind.

The laws for human nature, for what reason no man yet knows, have been until this period, hidden from man; the cause of this, the discovery of new facts may perhaps, as science advances, disclose. We may then learn why the artificial or imaginative laws of man have preceded, for so many ages, an accurate useful knowledge of the laws of Nature; why man's imaginative laws in opposition to Nature's laws, produce so much error, evil, and misery; and why we now perceive that Nature's laws are capable of giving so much truth and good, or happiness to the human race, unalloyed with misery.

The discovery of Nature's laws in this our day, renders it a moral, or rather an irresistible obligation upon us to exert ourselves to the utmost to effect this great, and glorious, and happy change in the life, conduct, and condition of man; that ignorance, poverty, and distress of body and mind may cease, and be no more experienced by future generations, but that they may attain that new life, so long promised, when charity, peace and goodwill shall pervade the minds of all people in all lands,[a] and when the knowledge of truth, or of Nature, or of God, which ever term may be most acceptable to each individual, shall extend over and cover the earth, as the waters cover the sea.[b]

The period when this great change shall take place is now near at hand. The excitement and distress of all nations proclaim its approach; it is coming upon us from above and below, and from all sides, as an irresistible torrent, to sweep away from the earth all the laws, ceremonies, customs, and irrational arrangements of man which have produced this old immoral world, to make room for the laws of Nature, on which to found the New Moral World, with laws, customs, and arrangements, all in perfect accordance with Nature's laws.

The imaginative laws of the marriages of the priesthood must be among the first to be abolished, by reason of their extended injurious influence upon human nature, poisoning all the sources of the most valuable qualities which Nature has given to infant man. These marriages have dried up the fountain of truth in human nature; they perpetually insinuate that man can love and hate at his pleasure, and that to be virtuous he must love according to the dictates of the laws and ceremonies devised by the priesthood, that he must hate according to the same dictation, and that if he does not thus love and hate, he is vicious, and he will be eternally punished in another world; and as this eternal infliction will not be suffering sufficient for his disobedience to the laws of the priests, he must, also, be grievously punished by human laws, and by public opinion created by the priests and those leagued with them; leagued to enforce those laws, *through this life*, it might be supposed, as a necessary and just preparation to fit them for the torments of the damned for ever.

Could any proceeding be more grossly cruel and unjust, or have a worse

[a] See Luke 2:14.
[b] See Genesis 6:17.

influence upon human nature than this? The combination of error engendered by such a mass of absurdities, being continually enforced upon the young and weak imaginations of men, could not fail to produce the most severe conflict of fears for their temporal and eternal happiness; while the irresistible laws of their nature compelled them to love that which was the most agreeable, and to dislike that which was the most disagreeable to their nature; and these again, both as to persons and things, being often in direct violation of the dogmas of the priesthood, it ought not now to surprise us that all of the human race were forced to become irrational, and many insane or mad.

It is well known to those who superintend in lunatic asylums, that the disappointment of the affections is one main cause of lunacy; and experienced medical practitioners know, that both body and mind are liable to the most painful, acute, and dangerous disorders from this cause. So much so, indeed, that the most observant and intellectual of them know, that until this unnatural condition of human society shall be changed, they cannot expect to find 'a sound mind in a sound body' among any portion of the human race.

While men and women trained and educated as they have hitherto been in the old immoral world, shall be compelled, by the laws of man and the ceremonies and opinions of the priests, to live day and night together for their lives, after Nature has caused their love for each other to cease, it cannot be supposed that either the men and women themselves, their children, or the public, or human nature itself, as exhibited in their persons, can be otherwise than in an irrational degraded state of body and mind, or be better prepared for all manner of vagaries in their conduct, or can be put into a condition more likely to commit those actions, which now continually disturb the peace, the comfort, or the happiness of each other.

The strange notions engendered by the doctrines of the priests, on which they have founded their marriage rites and ceremonies, are, of themselves, sufficient to reduce human nature far below the conditions of the superior tribes of animals when permitted by man to enjoy their natural course of life. The animals in that state fulfil the intention of their creation by acting in accordance with the laws of their respective natures; and those laws insure to them health and content, which to them is happiness. But man, forced out of his nature by the imaginative laws of the priests, has his health of body and mind diminished and disordered, his nature most ignorantly, unjustly, and unwisely thwarted; and it is impossible that as long as he remains in this condition he can be content, or know what manner of being he is, or why he is so much more miserable than other animals, when they are governed solely by the laws of their nature.

The artificial laws of the priesthood have not only thus generally deteriorated and disordered human nature, but they have forced man to build up an entire artificial state of society, and to make all the arrangements for conducting and carrying on the business of domestic and public life in accordance with those foolish laws of their imagination, in opposition to Nature's wise and beneficial laws.

In consequence, the whole arrangements now existing over the world for educating children; for forming their characters as men and women; for providing for the physical wants of mankind; for acquiring new knowledge; and for uniting the human race in an interest beneficial to the whole, are in the greatest possible disorder and confusion. They have, in fact, more of the character of insanity, with the view to the attainment of the objects professed, than of any rational combination of the materials and circumstances at our control to obtain or secure the ends we seek, or the purposes which we desire to accomplish.

In short, the baneful influence of the laws of the marriages of the priesthood upon human nature, in the aggregate, as it is seen in the conduct of men, women, and children of every grade and class of society, is evidently destructive of all that is truly entitled to the character of rational or sane: and there can be no well-founded expectation that any of the wise and profound, as they are termed, of the political or commercial changes proposed to diminish public and private misery, can be of the least permanent benefit to mankind as long as the imaginative and artificial laws, ceremonies, customs, and public opinion invented and now maintained by the influence of the priests, shall be permitted to govern, or to have any considerable operation in directing the affairs of human life. And, consequently, the sooner the order of the priesthood shall be made to cease over the world, the sooner will the human race become prosperous and rational, or moral and happy.

We have now shown the certain and necessary effects of the marriages devised and continued by the acquired influence of a body of men called the priesthood, existing, with more or less power, in all so-called civilized nations, but which nations never can become really civilized, as long as the order of the priesthood shall exist with power to deceive the people, or disorder all their intellectual and moral faculties.

We have, although very slightly and imperfectly, traced the blighting effects of these marriages upon the husband, and wife, and the children, upon society, and upon human nature generally; and we have shown that in each of these characters and divisions of humanity, man has suffered and is now suffering the greatest evils, and that he is at this moment deprived, by these insane institutions, of the only means by which he can reach the highest excellence and the great extent of happiness which his nature, governed by the laws of Nature, is capable of attaining and enjoying.

Much, very much more may be said on this subject, which is the most important at the present moment to bring before the population of all countries. It is important on account of the wretched state of ignorance and prejudice which exists respecting the origin and consequences of these unnatural institutions, and of the extended ramifications of misery which they are inflicting upon all classes and conditions of men and women. For these are kept much more in the dark now respecting their own nature, and the right path to happiness, than their ancestors were in the earliest stages of human society. It may be reasonably doubted whether their ignorance upon this subject, is not greater now than it was at the earliest period of what the world calls civilization. To put an end to those evils, the amount of which is far beyond the present feeble powers of human comprehension to estimate, all who have a sincere desire to see man attain his proper station among organized beings; all who wish him to become a wise and good or a rational being; all who feel an interest in seeing him relieved from the degraded condition of prostituting his high intellectual faculties to pander for the possession of wealth which he did not assist to create; and all who would rejoice to see man no longer a mere slave to produce for others what he himself cannot enjoy, or to toil four-fold, or rather ten-fold, more than is necessary under wise arrangements, with the present surplus capital and powers of society, to saturate the world with whatever is best for him to possess and use, or enjoy; these all ought now to unite their energies to extend the light of this knowledge over every quarter of the globe, to remove the gross mental darkness with which all nations, tribes, and people have been so long overwhelmed, and to prepare all men in all countries to lend their immediate utmost aid to affect this great salvation from ignorance, poverty, sin, and misery for themselves and their posterity for ever.

APPENDIX[a]

The following extracts from Mr Owen's writings, place his views on the subject of *Marriage and Divorce* in a clear and indisputable light; and furnish a most complete reply and refutation to the mis-statements which have been so industriously circulated by means of garbled and disconnected quotations from his various publications,[b] and by the most filthy and unfounded assertions of parties either excessively ignorant of Mr Owen's real views, or determined, in defiance of morality and truth, to distort and misrepresent them. They also prove beyond the possibility of doubt, the total disregard of truth in those parties who have endeavoured to make it appear that Mr Owen's denunciations of the '*Marriages of the Priesthood,*' *Indissoluble Marriage,*' '*Marriages without affection,*' *etc,* were applied to ALL Marriage.

FIRST EXTRACT

From Mr Owen's Six Manchester Lectures, delivered in 1837. Shewing that the proposed arrangements of the New State of Society are formed with a view to promote the PERMANENCE *of Marriage, the happiness of the parties united, especially of the Female sex, and the general good order and virtue of Society.*

'Under this classification and consequent arrangement of society, every individual will be trained and educated, to have all his faculties and powers cultivated in the most superior manner known; cultivated too, under a new combination of external objects, purposely formed, to bring into constant exercise the best and most lovely qualities only of human nature. Each one will be thus well educated, physically, intellectually, and morally. Under this classification and consequent arrangement of these associated families, wealth, unrestrained in its production by any of the artifical absurdities now so common in all countries, will be most easily produced in superfluity; all will be

[a] An extract from Shelley's *Queen Mab* is pp. 87–91 of the 1838 Appendix, followed by 'The Five Fundamental Facts' and a brief description of 'The Religion of the New Moral World'.

[b] Pamphlets written against Owen's views on marriage included *Talk About Socialism* (n.d.); Edward Birch, *Remarks on Socialism* (?1839); Joseph Mather, *Socialism Exposed* (1839), all published by the Religious Tract Society; and Francis Morrison, *The Influence of the Present Marriage System* (Manchester, 1838).

secured in a full supply of the best of it, for all purposes that may be required. They will, therefore, all be equal in their education and condition, and no artificial distinction, or any distinction but that of age, will ever be known among them.

'There will be then, no motive or inducement for any parties to unite, except from pure affection arising from the most unreserved knowledge of each other's character, in all respects, as far as it can be known before the union takes place. There will be no artificial obstacles in the way of permanent happy unions of the sexes; for under the arrangements of this new state of human existence, the affections will receive every aid which can be devised to induce them to be permanent; and under these arrangements, there can be no doubt, that, as the parties will be placed as far as possible in the condition of lovers during their lives, the affections will be far more durable, and produce far more pleasure and enjoyment to the parties, and far less injury to society, than has ever yet been experienced, under any of the varied arrangements which have emanated from the imagined free-will agency of the human race.

'If however, these superior arrangements to produce happiness between the sexes, should fail in some partial instances, which it is possible may yet occur, measures will be introduced by which, without any severance of friendship between the parties, a separation may be made, the least injurious to them and the most beneficial to the interests of society.

'No immorality can exceed that which is sure to arise from society compelling individuals to live continually together, when they have been made, by the laws of their nature, to lose their affections for each other, and to entertain them for another object. How much dreadful misery has been inflicted upon the human race, through all past ages, from this single error! How much demoralization! How many murders! How much secret unspeakable suffering, especially to the female sex! How many evils are experienced over the world, at this moment, arising from this single error of the imaginery free-will system by which men have been so long, so ignorantly, and miserably governed!

'This portion of the subject, to do it full justice, would, alone, require a longer course than is now given to the development of the whole system under consideration; but this limited view must suffice at present, for a sketch or outline of what is in contemplation.' – *Pages*, 76, 77.

SECOND EXTRACT

From Mr Owen's Address, delivered at the Charlotte-street Institution, London, in 1833. Shewing the object of the proposed changes in the laws of Marriage and Divorce; and the regulations proposed. (This is divided into paragraphs, with headings, for the sake of perspicuity.)

Many persons grossly mistake our views on the subject of the union of the sexes. Our object is to remove the causes of the immense amount of sexual crime and misery, and consequent physical and mental disease which now exists. It is nature's laws, now disregarded, which we desire to discover and implicitly obey; there being none other which can produce virtue and happiness. In the present absence of real knowledge, derived from experience, and with the existing irregular feelings of the population of the world, created by a false education, we propose that the union and disunion of the sexes should take place under the following regulations:

MARRIAGE

Announcement. – 'Persons having an affection for each other, and being desirous of forming an union, first announce such intention publicly in our Sunday assemblies.

Preliminary Period. – 'If the intention remain at the end of *three months*, they make a second public declaration.

Marriage. – 'Which declarations being registered in the books of the Society will constitute their marriage.

OBJECT OF MARRIAGE

'Marriages will be solely formed to promote the happiness of the sexes; and if this end be not obtained, the object of the union is defeated.

DIVORCE

FIRST: WHEN BOTH PARTIES DESIRE TO SEPARATE

Announcement. – 'Should the parties, after the termination of *twelve months, at the soonest*, discover that their dispositions and habits are unsuited to each other, and that there is little or no prospect of happiness being derived from their union, they are to make a public declaration as before, to that effect.

Preliminary Period. – 'After which they return and live together *six months longer*; at the termination of which, if they still find their qualities discordant, and both parties unite in the declaration, they make a second declaration.

Divorce. – 'Both of which being duly registered and witnessed, will constitute their legal separation.

SECOND: WHEN ONE ONLY DESIRES A SEPARATION

Preliminary Period. – 'Should one alone come forward upon the last declaration, and the other object to the separation, they would be required to live together *another six months*, to try if their feelings and habits could be made to accord, so as to promote happiness.

Divorce. – 'But if at the end of *the second six months*, the objecting party shall remain of the same mind, the separation is then to be final.

POSITION OF THE PARTIES AFTER DIVORCE

'The parties may, without diminution of public opinion, form new unions more suited to their dispositions.

PROVISION FOR THE CHILDREN

'As all the children of the new world will be trained and educated under the superintendence and care of the Society, the separation of the parents will not produce any change in the condition of the rising generation.

CONCLUDING REMARKS

'Under these arrangements, we have no doubt, a much more virtuous and happy state of society will be enjoyed than any which has existed at any time in any part of the world.'

THIRD EXTRACT

From Mr Owen's Address, April 29, 1839. (see 'New Moral World,' page 443.)[a]
Shewing that it is not contemplated that MARRIAGE *should ever be annulled.*

'My present impressions are, that for ever there must be rationally devised Marriage, and Divorce, improved as society advances in knowledge and goodness.'

[a] See *New Moral World*, vol. 5, no. 28 (4 May 1839), p. 443.

FOURTH EXTRACT

From Mr Owen's Preface to his Manifesto, 1840. *On the present Laws of Marriage and Divorce in England.*

'Since the publication of my views upon the old system of "Marriage by the priesthood," the *form of Marriage*, by the new Marriage Act,[a] has been made exactly to meet my ideas and wishes; and all that I now desire is to see another law enacted, by which *Divorces*, under wise arrangements, and on principles of common sense, may be obtained equally for rich and poor; to remove the chief cause of so much existing deception, prostitution, promiscuous intercourse, and crime, and the dreadful evils which ncessarily flow from them to both sexes, but especially to the poor unprotected part of the female sex, whose extremity of suffering is so much hidden from the world. And this change in the law of Divorce is all that is now required to enable me, legally and immediately, to introduce to the world the most splendid practical arrangements, easy of introduction, for the emancipation of man from ignorance, poverty, division, and crime, that have ever yet been conceived, even in the most fervid and sanguine imaginations of poets, philosophers, and reformers, of past and present time.'

THE RATIONAL RELIGION

The Principles and Practice of the Rational Religion, as developed and promulgated by Robert Owen.

I

That all facts yet known to man indicate that there is an external or an internal Cause of all existences, by the fact of their existence; that this all-pervading Cause of motion and change in the universe is that Incomprehensible Power which the nations of the world have called God, Jehovah, Lord, etc: – but that the facts are yet unknown to man which define what that Incomprehensible Power is.

II

That it is a law of nature obvious to our senses, that the internal or external character of all that have life upon the earth, is formed *for* them and not *by*

[a] The Civil Marriage Act of 1836 regulated all marriages solemnized otherwise than in accordance with the rites of the Church of England.

them; that, in accordance with this law, the internal and external character of man is formed *for* him and not *by* him; and therefore he cannot have merit or demerit, or deserve praise or blame, or reward or punishment.

III

That the knowledge of this fact, with its all-important consequences, will necessarily create in every one a new, sublime, and pure spirit of charity for the convictions, feelings, and conduct of the human race, and dispose them to be kind to all that has life – seeing that this varied life is formed by the same Incomprehensible Power that has created human nature, and given man his peculiar faculties.

IV

That it is man's highest interest to acquire an accurate knowledge of those circumstances which produces EVIL to the human race, and of those which produce GOOD; and to exert all his powers to remove the former from society, and to create around it the latter only.

V

That this invaluable practical knowledge can be acquired solely through an extensive search after *truth*, by an accurate, patient, and unprejudiced enquiry into *facts*, as developed by Nature.

VI

That man can never attain to a state of superior and permanent happiness, until he shall be surrounded by those external circumstances which will train him, from birth, to feel pure charity and sincere affection towards the whole of his species, – to speak the truth only, on all occasions, – and to regard with a merciful and kind disposition all that has life.

VII

That such superior knowledge, and feelings can never be given to man under those institutions of society which have been founded on the mistaken supposition that man forms his *feelings* and *convictions* by his *will*, and, therefore, has merit or demerit, or deserves praise or blame, or reward or punishment for them.

VIII

That under institutions formed in accordance with the Rational System of Society, this superior knowledge and these superior dispositions may be given to the whole of the human race without chance of failure, except in cases of organic disease.

IX

That in consequence of this superior knowledge, and these superior dispositions, the contemplation of Nature will create in every mind, feelings of high adoration, too sublime and pure to be expressed in forms or words, for that Incomprehensible Power which acts in and through all Nature, everlastingly composing, decomposing, and recomposing the material of the universe, producing the endless variety of life, of mind, and of organized form.

X

That the Practice of the Rational Religion will therefore consist in promoting, to the utmost of our power, the well-being and happiness of every man, woman, and child, without regard to their sect, party, country, or colour; and its Worship, in those inexpressible feelings of wonder, admiration, and delight, which, when man is surrounded by superior circumstances only, will naturally arise from the contemplation of the Infinity of Space, of the Eternity of Duration, of the Order of the Universe, and of that Incomprehensible Power, by which the atom is moved, and the aggregate of Nature is governed.

THE

CATECHISM

OF

THE NEW MORAL WORLD.

BY ROBERT OWEN.

"Sacred to Truth without Mystery, Mixture of Error, or Fear of Man."

SECOND EDITION.

Leeds:

PRINTED BY J. HOBSON, 5, MARKET STREET, BRIGGATE.

1838.

THE CATECHISM OF THE NEW MORAL WORLD[a] 1838

QUESTION. What is man?

ANSWER. An organized being, or, an animal possessing certain physical, intellectual, and moral powers and faculties, and attractive and repulsive propensities.

Q. Wherein does he differ from other animals, or known organized beings?

A. By being endowed with higher intellectual and moral faculties than all other animals, and being thus enabled to obtain the mastery over them. He is, therefore, the chief of animals.

Q. How has man been produced?

A. Facts are not yet known to enable any of the human race to give a rational or satisfactory answer to the question. All that can be predicated with truth upon this, at present, useless enquiry is, that man has been generated by a power unknown to him, in like manner as all other organized substances have been generated; each of these organized substances being formed with its own propensities, or peculiar powers of attraction and repulsion, which are the laws of its nature, or the natural laws of each species; each one possessing the general and individual law of its species.

Q. What are the attractive propensities of man's nature?

A. They are, generally, the desire of pleasurable sensations; but particularly, the desire of food, and attachment to those who supply him with it when he is hungry or thirsty; the desire of sleep or rest when he is exhausted in body or mind; the desire of propagating his species according to the laws of his nature; the desire of the due exercise of all his faculties and powers, physical, intellectual, and moral, by which alone he can become healthy and happy; the desire always to speak the truth, to express all his sensations without guile; the desire to promote or extend to others the happiness or pleasurable sensations, which he himself enjoys; the desire always to experience pleasurable sensations, and therefore to change one sensation for another as soon as the first ceases to give pleasure; and the desire for full freedom of action.

---

[a] 2nd edn Leeds, 1838 (reproduced here); another edn, Manchester, 1840. Reprinted in *New Moral World*, vol. 1, no. 10 (3 January 1835), pp. 73–7.

Q. What are the repulsive propensities of man's nature?

A. Generally, aversion to whatever gives pain to the individual, physically, intellectually, or morally; but particularly, to whatever withholds his food, or prevents him, when hungry or thirsty, acquiring as much of it as satisfies his nature; aversion to whatever prevents him taking his natural rest or sleep; to whatever prevents him propagating his species when his organization naturally stimulates the desire; aversion to whatever prevents him the free use of his physical, intellectual, and moral powers and capacities, whenever his organization impels him to exercise them; aversion to whatever restrains him from freely expressing the convictions and feelings which his organization compels him to receive or experience; aversion to whatever prevents him receiving and enjoying pleasurable sensations; to whatever inflicts painful sensations on those who have not offended his organization, or that prevents them enjoying pleasurable sensations; and to whatever prevents his freedom of action according to the natural impulse of his organization.

Q. Did man form for himself all or any of these propensities?

Q. No: he is incapable of forming for himself the least part of any one of them.

Q. Can he be justly or beneficially praised or blamed, rewarded or punished, or in any manner made responsible to man, or to any other existence, for the formation of them, or for any of their peculiar qualities or powers?

A. No: the notion is most preposterous, and it has proved most pernicious in practice.

Q. Are these propensities of man's nature good or bad?

A. They are all in a high degree good, all of them being necessary to form an intellectual, rational, and happy being, and to continue the species in existence.

Q. In what does man's happiness consist?

A. In pleasurable sensations, or in all the wants of his nature being satisfied to the point of temperance.

Q. What practical measures are calculated to insure, through life, to all the individuals of the human race, the greatest amount of the most innocent or healthy pleasurable sensations?

A. Arrangements which shall call into healthy or innocent action, at the proper period of life, all the physical, intellectual, and moral powers and faculties of man's nature, and insure the regular temperate exercise of them, according to the organization or constitution of each individual; and which arrangements shall also preclude the desire to fall short of, or to exceed that point, because it is alone competent to give the highest active and permanent enjoyment to man.

Q. In what does man's misery consist?

A: In painful sensations, or in the wants of his physical, intellectual, or moral powers remaining unsatisfied.

Q. Under what conditions will man become a good or rational being?

A. When all the wants of his organization shall be regularly satisfied to the point of temperance.

Q. When does man become a wicked or irrational being?

A. When the wants of his nature or organization remain unsatisfied.

Q. Under what circumstances will man be the most easily governed?

A. Under arrangements that will enable him at all times to supply or satisfy the wants of his nature to the point of temperance.

Q. When is man the most difficult to govern?

A. When the wants of his organization, physical, intellectual, and moral, are the least satisfied.

Q. How can all the wants of man's nature be satisfied to the point of temperance, beneficially for the individual and for society?

A. By the governing powers among men, making general arrangements to effect these results.

Q. Can this great desideratum in human affairs be now attained in practice by the means under the control of the governments of the more civilized parts of the world?

A. Yes most beneficial for all men; and happiness will remain unknown to man until this grand result shall be attained.

Q. Has man ever been placed, in any country, by any government, under such circumstances as would admit of all the wants of his nature being regularly satisfied to the point of temperance?

A. No, never: nor in any degree approaching to such a rational state of society.

Q. Is it now practicable to place man under such circumstances as would admit him, beneficially for himself, as an individual, and also as a member of society, to have all the wants of his nature satisfied to the point of temperance?

A. Yes, for the most abundant means and materials exist to enable man to attain this happy state, and the concurrence of the public will is now alone the one thing needful to induce all governments, whatever may be their form, to begin, in right earnest, to effect this change in a peaceable and rational manner, beneficially for all individuals, and for all states.

Q. What are the obstacles which exist to prevent this change being now made in the public will, which, you say, can so speedily effect this great and glorious emancipation of mankind from ignorance, sin, and misery?

A. The most formidable obstacles are the fundamental errors by which the public will has been hitherto formed.

Q. What are those fundamental errors which thus so banefully stand in the way of universal improvement and happiness?

A. The fundamental errors from which all moral evil originates, and upon which all the institutions of all countries have been, and are now, based.

Q. What are these errors and institutions?

A. The errors and institutions which are now supported by the Priesthood and the Governments of all countries in which there are Priests and Governors.

Q. Are the Priests and Governors benefitted by these errors and institutions?

A. No, quite the reverse, for, as men, they lose all the superior advantages of their nature. But from their infancy they have been trained by society to believe that they are individually much benefitted by them, and that society could not be peaceably conducted without them, nor exist except in the greatest disorder and confusion.

Q. Has society then, the power to train the Population of this and other countries, to receive as truths gross errors, or to teach them from birth truths only?

A. Yes, and to compel such populations to receive, and retain through life, a strong impression in favour of error or of truth; but it would be much more easy to impress convictions of truth than of error, if the Priesthood did not direct the formation of the character of the people.

Q. What is society, whose opinion is thus all-powerful for good or evil?

A. It is a number of individuals of both sexes, formed into an association for their mutual support and comfort, and whose general sentiments, which constitute the public opinion, can effect, even suddenly, the most important changes.

Q. Is man, when acting individually and unsupported by his fellows, or when united in society, the most powerful to effect good and evil?

A. When he is united in society. Because, in this case, the powers of each member are greatly multiplied while the actions of each member can be effectually controlled and directed by society to produce far more of either good or evil.

Q. Can individual man do more to promote the happiness of the human race when his own interest is placed in opposition to society, or, when his whole interest is united and identified with society?

A. When the whole interest of the individual, and of society is identified as one family, whose powers, faculties, properties, and possessions shall be directly applied to promote the well-doing and happiness of each individual, without partiality, according to the peculiar constitution of each member of this large family.

Q. Is it then a proof of wisdom in mankind to adopt notions, and found institutions thereon, which of necessity place the interests of individuals and of society in direct hostility to each other?

A. No: for these notions, and all the institutions founded on the supposition of their truth, tend to perpetuate ignorance, poverty, and disunion, and to generate inferior feelings, and the worst passions human nature is capable of receiving. These erroneous notions and institutions must, therefore, produce far more evil then good, or many more painful than pleasurable sensations, to the whole of mankind, and by which the earth is made a Pandemonium, when it might now be most easily made a Paradise.

Q. Then all the errors from which the laws, institutions, and the practices emanating from them, which disunite the interest of mankind, and place the apparent interest of individuals in opposition to the public real interest of the human race, are calculated to give far more pain than pleasure through the life of every individual, male and female, whatever may be their rank, station, or condition?

A. Most certainly; there is no law of nature more fixed and unchangeable than the law which determines the superiority of united, to individual interest, to insure permanently, the vast superiority of the human race overall other terrestrial beings.

Q. Is it an evidence of sound wisdom, or of rationality in mankind, to adopt notions and found institutions to give pleasurable sensations only; or to adopt such as will create painful sensations through the lives of all human beings?

A. It is wise and rational to adopt principles and found institutions which can insure pleasurable sensations through life to all individuals. And it is most foolish and irrational to found institutions on imaginary notions, which are opposed to facts, and which must, of necessity, produce incalculably more painful than pleasurable sensations through the life of every individual.

Q. What are the institutions founded on erroneous notions which give the most pain to the human race?

A. The institutions which are derived from, and give support to the notions or imaginations that man is organized to be bad by nature: that he has the power to form his own convictions by his will, and to feel or not to feel at his pleasure, in opposition to the fixed laws of his organization, that is, to nature's laws, which compel him, regardless of his will or desire to the contrary, to believe in obedience to the strongest convictions made on his mind, and to feel as his individual nature compels him to feel.

Q. Can you more fully explain what these institutions are?

A. Yes: they are those which have been devised, and which are now supported, to teach the people the erroneous notions stated in the preceding article: and those devised to enforce, by what is called law, all the mischievous, unjust, and irrational practices, which necessarily emanate from those wild and absurd imaginations.

Q. Explain more particularly what are the institutions which emanate from these erroneous suppositions?

A. All the institutions for the support of the Priesthood, and their temples throughout the world: for the support of the Lawyers, Judges, and Magistrates, and their Courts throughout the world. All the extensive arrangements for the support of the standing Military powers of the world: for the support of the buying and selling system of the world for money, not directly and honestly representing real property, or which money is changeable in its value, when estimated by a fixed quantity and quality of the first necessaries of life. Also all the institutions which divide the interests and feelings of individuals; which tend to separate mankind into single families, into classes, sects, parties, and sectional divisions, called nations; which tend to oppose the apparent interests of individuals against the apparent interest of the public, when the real interests of both are eternally one and the same.

Q. Are there other institutions which give more pain than pleasure?

A. Yes, there are innumerable others, but they emanate directly or indirectly from some of the preceding, that is, from what is called religion, law, marriage, and private property, all founded in opposition to nature's laws.

Q. How does the Priesthood of the world produce more pain than pleasure?

A. By always attempting to oppose the natural attractive propensities of man, by ignorantly calling them vices, and by ignorantly supporting his repulsive propensities by calling them virtues; and thus compelling him to become irrational or wicked.

Q. Is it wise then longer to retain the Priesthood and its various institutions?

A. No: for the reasons just stated, it is the greatest of all errors to retain any part of it, or any of the collateral institutions by which it is now supported.

Q. How are the codes of laws prevalent throughout the world calculated to produce more pain than pleasure?

A. By the same general means; for they also have been made to oppose and prevent the action of the natural attractive propensities, and to support the natural repulsive propensities, or laws, of man's physical, intellectual, and moral nature. And man's attractive propensities are all good, and necessary to insure his health and happiness. Codes of laws devised and maintained in opposition to these attractive propensities are well calculated and are sure to make man irrational and wicked.

Q. Is it wise then longer to retain these codes of laws and institutions, and to support them?

A. No: for the reasons stated, it is most unwise to retain them, or longer to give them any kind of countenance.

Q. How are the Military or Naval institutions of the world calculated to produce more pain than pleasure?

A. By being devised and employed to compel man by physical force, to act and speak contrary to his convictions, and in opposition to his feelings and natural attractive propensities, and consequently to force him, against his nature, to become irrational and wicked.

Q. Is it wise then to continue to maintain permanent Military or Naval institutions?

A. No, most unwise; for while they are allowed to exist, the human race must remain in a state of slavery and misery. And these institutions are now useless, for it is not necessary to apply physical force to make man act in accordance with his natural propensities.

Q. How are the buying and selling of commodities, and the exchanging of artificial money, either metals or paper, for a monied profit, calculated to give more pain than pleasure?

A. By the highly injurious effects which continual bargaining for a money profit makes upon the disposition, mind, and conduct of each individual when so occupied, tending, as this practice does most powerfully, to lower the character and make hypocrites of buyers and sellers, and also to engender a perpetual covetous warfare among the whole of the human race, each one seeking to take advantage of the ignorance or weakness of others: and by giving all the advantages of human life to the idlers and worthless, and withdrawing them, in a greater proportion, from the industrious producers. And also by placing the most formidable obstacles in the way of increasing the most valuable wealth, by limiting the increase of it to the amount of the artificial circulating medium which the producers of wealth can obtain.

Q. How is the system of individual competition for the necessaries and comforts of life, and the arrangements of society requisite to maintain this competition, productive of more evil than good?

A. By it being now, whatever it might have effected formerly, well calculated to retard the progress of improvement to an incalculable extent; to extend deception and every evil passion throughout all the ramifications of society; by increasing the drudgery of human existence and the labour of man many hundred-fold; by forming man into an imagined cunning knave, when, at the same time, he is out-witting himself; by greatly diminishing his means of enjoyment; by deteriorating his intellectual and moral qualities, and by giving to each of these powers of his nature a false direction. It is also well calculated to train man from childhood to become both fool and knave, and to class him among the most irrational of animals. It is, in fact, with the existing materials for happiness among the human race, one of the great curses of the world; for it is the great waster and destroyer of wealth, the great obstacle to its increased production, and the great preventer of its enjoyment.

Q. What ought the people and the governments of the world now to do to remove the causes of pain or evil, and, to insure an everlasting progress in pleasure or good, without any retrogression through future ages?

A. To abandon all the fundamental errors, which produce moral evil, the source of all pain, and adopt the fundamental principles of moral good, the source of all pleasure. To allow the institutions established to maintain pain, or moral evil in the world, to die not a violent, but a gradual natural death, and immediately to form new institutions, to introduce and maintain pleasure, or moral good. That is, to form arrangements for all to preach and practice continually and in all sincerity, the principle of peace and truth, and that all shall cease to preach and practice the principles of violence and falsehood.

Q. Is it practicable to effect such a glorious change in human affairs, without throwing the whole of society into confusion and interminable disorder?

A. It is perfectly simple and easy to make this change; all the materials requisite to effect it, in the most ample manner in a short period, are now at the disposal of the Governments of Europe and America as well as of those in other more distant parts of the earth.

Q. Would Governments be injured by thus making use of these materials?

A. No, quite the contrary; they would be far more benefitted as individuals than they can be now by the utmost success of all the plans they have hitherto devised, or now wish to accomplish under the reign of moral evil.

Q. Why then do they not adopt immediately, measures to enable them to make the change without delay?

A. Because they do not sufficiently understand the principles, and much less the practices, which are alone competent to effect the change; and because if they knew both principles and practices, public opinion, which governs the world, has not been sufficiently enlightened to enable them, in opposition to it, to undertake so great a change in human affairs.

Q. Then the time for effecting this great change depends on public opinion?

A. Solely on public opinion.

Q. It then appears that the most important work in which man can be engaged, is to assist to create a new public opinion in favour of truth and in opposition to falsehood?

A. Most certainly this is now the great work which man has to perform, to remove the cause of all evil and to establish everlasting good among the human race.

Q. How is this new public opinion to be formed?

A. By the friends of truth, who have sufficient moral courage to contend against popular error and extensive prejudices, coming forward to support public meetings, public lectures, public discussions, and cheap publications advocating the cause of truth in opposition to error; and by becoming members of an Association now forming to extend truth unmixed with error over the whole world.

Q. How are those public proceedings to be promoted and carried on with sufficient vigour and perseverance to effect in a reasonable time the grand object now proposed to be attained?

A. By effective, active, vigorous, well-considered measures of the Association mentioned in the preceding answer.

Q. What is the name which has been given to it?

A. 'The Association of all Classes of all Nations to form a New Moral World.'[a]

[a] The Association of All Classes of All Nations was founded on 1 May 1835 in order to raise funds to establish a community. Best known as the Rational Society, a shortened version of the Universal Community Society of Rational Religionists, it lasted until 1845, and was principally concerned to enrol members in local branches (most of which were in the industrial Midlands), and to raise funds for the community begun at Queenwood, Hampshire, in 1839.

Q. How is this Association to promote the change of public opinion?

A. By calling public meetings and assisting to extend public lectures and discussions in the Metropolis to promulgate these truths, and by forming lodges of similar Associations in every part of the kingdom, and also throughout other nations until they shall extend over the world. By Associations that shall also protect themselves from pecuniary distress and from all the artificial ills of life arising from the present system of moral evil; or, in other words, produce for themselves all that will be required to insure their permanent happiness.

A

DEVELOPEMENT

OF THE

PRINCIPLES AND PLANS

ON WHICH TO ESTABLISH

SELF-SUPPORTING HOME COLONIES;

AS A

MOST SECURE AND PROFITABLE INVESTMENT FOR CAPITAL, AND AN EFFECTUAL MEANS PERMANENTLY TO REMOVE THE CAUSES OF IGNORANCE, POVERTY, AND CRIME;

AND MOST MATERIALLY TO BENEFIT ALL CLASSES OF SOCIETY;

BY GIVING A RIGHT APPLICATION TO THE NOW GREATLY MISDIRECTED

POWERS OF THE HUMAN FACULTIES AND OF PHYSICAL AND MORAL SCIENCE.

BY

ROBERT OWEN.

"Society can never be substantially improved until all its members shall be well educated, and well employed; and a sound practical education and beneficial employment may be now easily provided, permanently, for all."

LONDON:
PUBLISHED BY THE HOME COLONIZATION SOCIETY, 57 PALL MALL.
AND SOLD BY ALL BOOKSELLERS.
1811.

A DEVELOPEMENT OF THE PRINCIPLES AND PLANS ON WHICH TO ESTABLISH SELF-SUPPORTING HOME COLONIES[a] 1841

CONTENTS

DEDICATION TO GOVERNMENTS

PREFACE

INTRODUCTION

[a] 2nd edn, 1841. This edition was bound with *The Signs of the Times; or, The Approach of the Millennium* (1841), which was also published separately as a pamphlet in two edns, without the illustrative plates. The punctuation of the original, occasionally very eccentric, has been altered here somewhat. The pagination of the contents pages has been altered to accord with this edition.

DEVELOPEMENT

[a] Advertisement omitted from this edn.
[b] Paginated separately in the original edn.
[c] Omitted from this edn.

DEDICATED

TO

THE GOVERNMENTS

OF

GREAT BRITAIN, AUSTRIA, RUSSIA, FRANCE, PRUSSIA,

AND THE

UNITED STATES OF AMERICA

THE SUPREME POWER of the UNIVERSE has, now, placed the Sovereignty of the Earth, for a time, at your united disposal.

To you, is given the High and Mighty Trust, in this your day of power, to effect, by your union, wisely directed, the greatest good that human agency has ever yet attained for man.

You have now, at your control, the means, in the most abundant superfluity, to give such direction to the industry, skill, and mental faculties of the human race, that they shall, speedily, fertilize and beautify the earth; and greatly to improve the character and condition of the present generation; and form all its inhabitants, of the succeeding generations, to be highly useful, healthy, intelligent, essentially good, wise, and happy.

It is the interest, of each individual member of your respective governments, and, more especially, on account of your children, through all future ages, that you, speedily, unite to accomplish this great good, for yourselves, and for the world.

It is a glorious opportunity, – one that angels, as they are described, might rejoice to possess.

Will you not, then, make yourselves immortal, and now, while you have the power, become the glorious instruments of effecting, and permanently securing, more good to the human race than, previously, any mortals could accomplish?

Do you desire to know how, thus, to direct your power? This knowledge may now, for the first time in human history, be easily attained. Put the following questions to the human race, and their obvious reply will be your unerring guide to action; while the practical measures, recommended in this work, will enable you, with ease, to accomplish, gradually, each of these objects.

QUESTIONS TO THE HUMAN RACE

1st, Is it not your interest, that the whole earth should be fertilized, and made healthy and beautiful, in the shortest time practicable?

2nd, Is not the chief obstacle, after you shall have united your powers for its accomplishment, the want of population, in all parts of the world?

3rd, Is it not your interest, that every facility should be given to the increase of population, and of scientific power, to aid man, in all his useful pursuits, and in every department of life?

4th, Is it not your interest, that, as soon as it is practicable, scientific power should be made to supersede slavery, servitude, and all unhealthy and disagreeable manual labour?

5th, Is it not your interest, that every child of man, should be, from his birth, as well trained and educated, as his original organs, faculties, and powers, will admit?

6th, Is it not the birth-right of man, that he should worship the Great Spirit of the Universe in accordance with his conscience, wherever and however that conscience may have been formed for him?

7th, Is it not your interest, that this Religious Liberty should be, now, fully enjoyed, by every individual of your race?

8th, Is it not your interest, that each of these individuals should be placed, through life, within those external arrangements that will insure the most happiness, physically, mentally, and morally, to the individual; and the greatest practical benefit to the whole of society?

9th, Is it not your interest, that the greatest amount, of the most valuable wealth, should be, annually produced, over the world, that each individual may have the largest possible share of it; and that this wealth shall be produced with pleasure to its producers?

10th, Is it not your interest, that this wealth should be well preserved for use; and never wasted, or unnecessarily, destroyed?

11th, Is it not your interest, that this wealth, by arrangements satisfactory to all, should be distributed the most justly, and, of course, the most beneficially for all?

12th, Is it not your interest, that there should be permanent peace over the earth; that none of these well-educated people, or any of this superior wealth, should be, prematurely, destroyed, or injured?

13th, Is it not your interest, that all persons, commodities, and productions, should pass freely over the world, with the greatest safety, ease, and expedition, without local obstruction?

14th, Is it not your interest, that some one language should be decided upon, by you, to be the general language of the world; and that the present local languages, should become among the dead languages, as speedily as practicable?

15th, Is it not your interest, that *Truth* should be universally substituted for *Falsehood*?

16th, Is it not your interest, that *Charity*, for those who have been made to differ from us in opinions, feelings, and conduct, should become the every-day practice of every one throughout the world?

17th, Is it not the interest of the human race, that every one should be so taught, and placed, that he would find his highest enjoyment to arise *from the continued practice of doing all in his power to promote the well-being, and happiness, of every man, woman, and child, without regard to their class, sect, party, country, or colour?*

18th, Is it not your interest, that the governments and people, of the most powerful civilized nations, should, instantly, terminate their wars, and all wars, and now, cordially unite, to carry all the previous objects, gradually and peaceably, into execution?

19th, Is it not your interest, that a congress of these powers, and of such other nations as may be induced, to join them, should be speedily held, to deliberate, and decide upon, these universally important, measures?

20th, Is not the interest of all governments and people, identical with your interest?

If these questions can be answered, only, in the affirmative, then is your course clear and straightforward; – in your respective Dominions, adopt the principles, and pursue the practice, advocated and recommended in the following pages; and use your influence, with all other Governments and People, also to adopt them: – and the peace and happiness of the world will be secured for ever; and the Millennium will become a reality, and no longer remain a mere imaginary state of human existence.

That you may be enabled to appreciate the motives of this Dedication, and be overruled to unite, in a true and permanent Holy Alliance, to carry these recommendations into immediate practice, is the sincere wish of

The Friend to all

Governments and People,

ROBERT OWEN

LONDON, *March* 1841.

PREFACE

It is the truth, the whole truth, and nothing but the truth, that alone can now save the British Empire, and the civilized world, from a revolution of violence, which, if not prevented, by calm and rational measures, threatens to be more dreadful than any revolution that has occurred in past history.

For the period has arrived, when, for the first time in the progress of human affairs, a direct and open conflict has commenced, between moral *falsehood* and *truth*; – between *false* and *real virtue;* – between *force, fraud, and oppression,* and *kindness, honesty, and justice;* – between great *individual riches and luxury* and great *poverty and destitution;* – between *war* and *peace;* – between the *superstitious prostration of the mental faculties*, and *mental liberty;* – in fine, between *misery* and *happiness*.

Who are now the favoured individuals, who have been enabled, by extensive experience, to overcome early impressions; and who possess sufficient knowledge of the world, and moral courage, to enter upon this subject, without fear or local prejudices? These men and women, wherever they can be found, are the prime minds of the world; and, in the first instance, however few they may be, are the only parties prepared, with sufficient experience, to read the following pages with much advantage. It is to this class of minds, therefore, that this work is chiefly addressed.

It will be useless for the inexperienced, or mere localized minds, to occupy their time, at present, upon subjects which must, of necessity, be far beyond their practice, and usual sphere of mental exercise; for, if Man be the creature of circumstances, they could not, yet, have been placed within those which, alone, can prepare them for the task.

Yet this work is intended, essentially, *to benefit the now prostrate mind, and the inexperienced in extensive practice; by preparing the means to raise and elevate the mental and moral faculties; and to enlarge the power and sphere of usefulness in all.*

But the *most experienced minds*, in every department of life, must, first, acquire this new knowledge; that they may be enabled to open and extend the minds of the less informed, to the comprehension of a subject, which is divested of local prejudice and interest, but which, involves the eternal interests and well-being of the human race.

It has been foretold, and, from the gradual advance of the human mind, it is most reasonable to expect, that a period of universal virtue and happiness shall, at some future time, arrive, – a period, when knowledge shall make charity and love extend over the earth – when, in consequence, peace shall be universal, and 'every man shall sit under his own vine and fig-tree,[a] and there shall be none to make him afraid.' All Christians profess to believe that this prophecy will surely come to pass; and that it shall be enjoyed, in a state of existence upon earth, known by the term *Millennium*.

To me, it appears that this period is rapidly approaching: and that great changes, in all nations, are now taking place preparatory to its commencement.

All changes in human affairs are effected by human agency, or instrumentality, but, most frequently, without the agents being conscious of the ultimate results of their own proceedings.

So it is at the present time. The human faculties, for the last century, have been most actively engaged, in bringing forward new inventions and discoveries; and they have, already, succeeded to so great an extent, that society knows not, now, what to do with the surplus wealth which these improvements can supply. And *so great is the magnitude of this new scientific power, that, although it is in its infancy, a small population, with its aid, can supply the wants of a very large population; and, ere long, the inhabitants of a small portion of the earth will be enabled, thus, to supply the wants of the population of the whole world.* The amount of this new power already created, exceeds the imagination of ordinary minds; – it is, however, yet, in its extreme infancy; – but it is the *foundation* on which the Millennium is destined to be erected; – for it will soon be superabundant to provide for all the wants of man; without human slavery or servitude.

This is the *first* step towards the attainment of the Millennium; because, in that state, there can be no human slavery, servitude, or inequality of condition; except the natural inequality of age and experience; which will, for ever, preserve order and harmony in society.*

The *second* preparatory step, is the improvement of the character of the human race; in order to make all intelligent, charitable, and kind to each other. This step can be effected, only, by an *entire* change in the formation of the character of each individual, from birth through life; in order to create that full and complete regeneration of man, which shall give him a *new heart and a new mind*, and, thus, make him a fit inhabitant of the new, or millennium, state of existence.

This *second* step is in preparation, through the new spirit which has been engendered, throughout society, for an improved education for the mass of the people – an idea which, previously, has never existed in the mind of

* See Extract from 'Six Lectures delivered in Manchester,' in the Appendix.[b]

[a] See for example 1 Kings 4:25.
[b] Omitted in this edn.

the priesthood, or rulers, of the world. This desire for educating the people has, already, become almost universal; although no parties appear to know what a right education of the human faculties means; or how it is to be accomplished. Many, however, are sufficiently advanced in a knowledge of the past and present practice of, what is called, education, in all nations, to discover that, hitherto, there has been no real knowledge of education in the world; and, that, at present, *there is not one educational establishment known, that is calculated to train individuals, from birth, to become rational men and women.*

Before this second step towards the formation of the Millennium could be attained, it was necessary that the *science of human nature* should be discovered, to lead to *the practice of forming a superior character for every individual;* – without which knowledge, the millennium state of existence must remain unknown and unattainable.

This Science has been discovered; and the means of forming a superior physical, moral, mental, and practical, character, for every man, women, and child, will, by its developement, be made a plain and certain process.

The *third* step, preparatory to the attainment of the Millennium state of human existence, is the acquirement of the knowledge by which those circumstances, which have, hitherto, created the bad passions, poverty, division, vice, and misery, can be, gradually, but effectually, removed: first, from a part, but ultimately, from the whole of society; in order that, as man ever has been, and must be, the creature of the external circumstances which are made to surround him, no vicious, inferior, or annoying, external circumstance, of human formation may exist; or, which the united knowledge, capital, skill, and labour, of man can remove.

This third step could be attained, only, by the discovery of the *Science of Society;* the science necessary to enable man to *dissect society into its elementary parts; to separate them; to ascertain their past and present incongruities; and to know him to re-combine them in their proper proportions, so as to form a new, consistent, and more perfect, state of society;* – a society, which will, gradually, lead to the long-promised Millennium state of existence.

This science has also been discovered; and, through a knowledge of it, a new scientific arrangement of society may now speedily be formed; – an arrangement which shall unite these original elements, each in its due proportion to the others, in such a manner that all, born and trained within them, shall derive advantages, through life, and experience enjoyments, of which the past and present race of men have, hitherto, had no conception.

The *fourth* step, towards the attainment of the Millennium, *is, the gradual ceasing of the necessity for any of the professions;* the existence of which, until this period, has been deemed to be a permanent part of society.

To those who have been enabled to perceive the wonderful changes which are coming upon the earth, it has been made evident, that 'Peace on earth, and charity and goodwill to mankind'[a] can never be attained – First, So long as any priests teach their opposing doctrines of faith and mysteries: which doctrines have always hitherto produced, and ever must produce, error, only, in the human mind; with hatred, malice, and all uncharitableness, to all who are taught to believe in different doctrines of faith and mysteries, or whose belief is based solely upon *demonstrable facts;* – Second, So long as any necessity shall exist for the continuance of the profession of the law; which, while it shall be maintained, must divide man from man, and prevent the period from arriving, when 'men can love their neighbours as themselves.'[b] Human laws, opposed to nature's everlasting laws, and the Millennium, can never co-exist; – Third, *So long as physical and mental disease shall exist.*

In our progress towards the Millennium, the *discovery of the means, and the adoption of the practice, to prevent disease of body and mind, are necessary;* and the discovery of the means of preventing of physical and mental disease has been, already, made, to a great extent. The practice, where and when least anticipated, has almost miraculously commenced at this period, by the introduction of temperance into Ireland by Father Mathew; and the spread of temperance societies among, the most intemperate of, the British and American population.

The *prevention of disease*, will be obtained, only, when arrangements shall be formed, to well educate, physiologically, every man, woman, and child, so as to enable them to understand their own physical and mental nature; in order that they may learn to exercise, at the proper period of life, all their natural faculties, propensities, and powers, up to the point of temperance; neither falling short, nor exceeding in any of them, or discontent and disease must necessarily follow.

Disease is not the natural state of man. To *prevent disease, among other things*, it is required, that the causes which have, hitherto, created too much anxiety throughout society, should be removed. These are chiefly five, – First, *Religious perplexity and anxiety*, which is produced, and to many, made most dreadful, through the fear of eternal damnation. This fear, which is the most frequent cause of insanity, has been created, and is continued, by the priesthood of the world, either from ignorance or for worldly gain: – Secondly, *Disappointment of the affections;* – This has also arisen from the errors of the priesthood keeping man and woman ignorant of the laws of their own nature; of the best mode of forming the human character; and of the true science of human nature. These disappointments afflict humanity with numerous diseases; and the young with bodily and mental afflictions, which, in females especially, produce the second greatest cause of insanity, and premature death: – Thirdly, *Pecuniary difficulties*, arising from the fear of want, or of sinking in the scale of society and the

[a] See Luke 2:14.
[b] See Mark 12:33.

estimation of our fellows; – These fears arise from the ignorance of the '*science of society;*' and, immediately, from the individual competitive system of carrying on the general business of life. These difficulties must continue as long as this demoralizing and insane system shall be practised, and man shall kept ignorant of his true interests. Pecuniary difficulties, often, extend the anxieties of mind to insanity and suicide: – Fourthly, *Anxiety respecting our offspring:* – This anxiety arises from all the previous causes, with the want of efficient arrangements to well educate and well place all children from their birth: – And, Fifthly, *Intemperance, arising from had habits*, which are often produced by the previous causes, and are equally removable with the causes of all the before-mentioned evils. Intemperance, also, frequently, leads to suicide or insanity.

Now, a moment's rational reflection, will make it evident, that *religious perplexities – disappointment of the affections – pecuniary difficulties – anxieties for our offspring – intemperance*, and the Millennium state, can never co-exist.

The *fifth* step, in the progress to the attainment of the Millennium, is the abandonment of the principles which lead to *war*.

War is the destroyer of true morality in the mind and conduct of all who are connected with it. To talk of *war* and *morality* – of *war* and *religion* – of *war* and *charity* – of *war* and *justice* – or of *war* and *peace and good-will to mankind*, existing, at the same time, in the mind and conduct of the same individual, is only to prove the extent to which the human faculties can be, and have been, made irrational.

War takes from the power of any population to produce wealth, and, in the same proportion, adds to their power to waste and destroy it. War effects more injury, in one year, to the parties engaged in these insane contests, than can be remedied in many years; and before there can be an approach to a rational state of mind and conduct, by the nations of the so-called civilized world, they must adopt measures to adjust all their differences, amicably and justly, without the intervention of brute force; and, thus, *prevent* all the immoralities and misery, necessarily, produced by war.

Until the human race shall cease the practice of war, or the applications of brute force to adjust their affairs, instead of reason and common sense, it will have no real pretensions to the rank of rational beings.

If Christianity be, indeed, a religious or a moral system, intended to introduce into the world, the *spirit* and *practice* of *charity, kindness*, and *love*, then is it impossible that any one *engaged in*, or *promoting, war*, can be a Christian; except by assuming a name to which he has no just title. It is, however, most certain, that war and the Millennium can never co-exist.*

* If it should be possible for an enemy to exist, in opposition to a population known to act upon millennium principles, war may always be prevented, by those who adopt the principles of peace, being, at all times, prepared to resist injustice and oppression; and this preparation may be easily effected by wise arrangements in the education of the young, without any trouble or expense, that would not be amply repaid.

The *sixth* step in advance, preparatory to the Millennium, will be the destruction of the immoral and degrading system of *buying cheap and selling dear, for a money profit*. Individuals trained to this practice, must, of necessity, have their characters formed in an inferior and immoral mould. It is a system to teach the individuals, whom necessity forces into it, the arts of deception; for the more they can deceive those from whom they buy, and those to whom they sell, the greater will be their gain or profit; and those who have acquired the most wealth, by these means, have been the greatest adepts in the arts of deception. The individuals, so employed, are not to be blamed, but to be pitied; being involved within a system which makes it *necessary* for them to acquire this character, and thus, to act.

In a Millennium state of society, there can be none engaged in endeavouring to buy cheap and sell dear, or to take advantage of any one, in any manner whatever.

The *seventh* step, in this preparation for a superior or millennium existence upon earth, will be, the entire abandonment of paying *money wages* by one part of society to another part, for their services, physical or mental. This practice has, now, led to far greater injustice, oppression, degradation, crime, and misery, than existed, at any former period; even when slavery was the *general* practice of the human race. Lodging, food, and clothes, were the birthright of every slave from its owner; and it was the *interest* of this owner, that his slave should never be over-worked, but always healthy and in good working condition. But the *lowest stage of humanity is experienced, when the individual must labour for a small pittance of wages from others – when he is not suffered to have land, from which, by his own labour, he may produce even the meanest necessaries of life – and, when he must find employment, even to obtain this small pittance, or be degraded to a workhouse, or steal, or murder, or starve.*

In the Millennium state, this system, the most wretched of all slaveries, created by money wages, will be unknown; because the physical sciences will have rendered unnecessary all severe, unhealthy, or, even unpleasant human labour.

The *eighth* step, in this progress, will be, to terminate *Idleness and Uselessness*. Every individual who, by arrangements devised by inexperienced and irrational man, has been trained to be idle and useless, has been made to be a serious loss to the human race, an evil spirit to himself, a waster of wealth, a hinderer to its production, an injurious example to all around him, and an object of real pity to every rational creature. It is impossible to calculate the extent of evil that men and women, whose characters have been thus formed, and who are maintained in idleness, by the errors of society, inflict upon the population within their influence.

In the Millennium state, *Idleness and Uselessness* will be unknown in the conduct of a single individual; and yet, no one will ever have his physical or mental powers and faculties over exercised; or exercised beyond the point of temperance, for each faculty. The required exercise of these faculties, physical and mental, will be a continual source of health and enjoyment.

The *ninth* step, in this heavenly progress, will be, to form the external arrangements around every one, from birth, to insure to him the best *physical, moral, intellectual, and practical, education*, that his constitution, or natural faculties, when born, will admit. When these arrangements shall be made, and this practice shall be adopted, and fairly and fully carried into execution, punishment and blame, of every description, will be abandoned, and the character of every one will be as well formed through life, *by society*, as his natural constitution, at birth, will permit.

In the Millennium state of society, every one will be so well trained and educated, from birth, and so well surrounded by superior and rational external circumstances, that an inferior character will be unknown; and individual praise or blame, reward or punishment, will be, not only unpractised, but unthought of; these errors having been previously abandoned in principle, as unjust, useless, and injurious.

The *tenth* step in this divine progress, will be, to terminate at the distinction of *rich and poor*; and the endless evils which this most irrational state of society necessarily, produces. The existence of great wealth and extreme poverty, within the same circle, of what is called by the name of the same religion, as Hindoo, Mahommedan, Jew, Christian, Fo, etc – or, within the same nation, or lesser district, is gross immorality; but, for great riches and poverty to exist side by side, in the same neighbourhood or town, – where one family is wallowing in luxury, to such extent as to create loss of health and of real enjoyment, while a neighbour family often suffers every privation, until its members gradually pine away, and are starved to death, and this, without exciting feelings of horror, of astonishment, or even a thought of its being a crime of the darkest dye, or any crime at all, – indicates, in the language of nature, not to be misunderstood, a degraded state of human existence, which cannot, much longer, be permitted to continue upon the earth, to disgrace the conduct of beings, having the presumption to call themselves rational and religious.

No! In the Millennium state of society, now that science has provided, and offers, the means to create wealth, in the utmost superfluity, for all, none will be permitted to feel the pangs of poverty, or the evils and degradation of inequality of pecuniary condition; or even the least fear of them: for all will be secured, from birth to death, in the use of far more riches, and the enjoyment of much higher, and more rational, pleasures, than all the advantages that the most unlimited wealth can now realize: and no *artificial* means of inequality will exist.

The *eleventh* step, in this progress to the Millennium, will be, to infuse into each heart and mind, the genuine *spirit of charity*, for the varied *opinions, feelings*, and *conduct*, of the human race: until these varied opinions, feelings, and conduct can be amalgamated; and mankind drawn, by the spirit of kindness, directed by judgment, to acquire an accurate knowledge of the sciences of human nature, and of society; when all will be caused to think, to feel, and to act, as much alike on all matters essential to the permanent happiness of mankind, as those well instructed in the science of mathematics, now think, feel, and act, alike, on all things appertaining to this science.

But the *twelfth*, and last step, to be now enumerated, is the chief cornerstone of this magnificent edifice. It is the *abandonment of the principles* from which all *Falsehood* proceeds, and the *adoption of principles* that will establish *Truth*, from birth to death, in the word, look, and action, of every individual; and which, by the destruction of falsehood and deception, which have governed this world while it has been under the dominion of darkness, will, also, destroy war, anger, hatred, ill-will, jealousy, revenge, and all inferior and bad passions; – root out every evil thought and design among men; – and prepare all for that state, when peace and love shall reign over the earth, and man shall be permanently good, and wise, and happy.

In the millennium state, falsehood cannot exist; it will be unknown in the look, word, or action, of any one; and the reign of Truth will then be universal.

The, almost, miraculous decline of reverence for the priesthood over the world; – their insane dissensions in opposition to each other; – and, at this stage of society, their equally insane presumption over their more enlightened fellow-men; – the progress of Father Mathew[a] in Ireland, and the temperance societies[b] in Great Britain and America; – the daily advance of the scientific discoveries; – the new passion for educating the masses; – the extraordinary disinclination to war among the British and other warlike nations; – the easy and rapid communication between the most distant countries; – the general adoption, by civilized nations, of scientific power, to supersede the necessity for severe or injurious manual service; – and the friendly union of governments which, until latterly, have been in great savage hostility to each other; – all, with many other strange and extraordinary occurring events, indicate, with unerring certainty, that a great change is coming over the nations of the earth; and that the wise, the good, the happy, existence of man, approaches with gigantic strides; in fact, that the Millennium is not far distant. And shall irrational man, in any of his present puerile divisions, of class, or sect, or party, or country, or colour, set himself to oppose this great, magnificent, and glorious, change, for the benefit of the human race, now, and through all coming ages? Vain and useless will all such attempts prove! *The decree has gone forth, from the Almighty energies of the universe, that man shall be put in the right*

[a] Father Theobald Mathew (1790–1856): Irish temperance advocate.

[b] Organisations seeking to moderate or ban the consumption of liquor, increasing rapidly after 1800.

path,[a] *now, to become good, and wise, and happy*; and every obstacle in the way of his progress, to this advent of his existence, shall prove unavailing and powerless.

[a] See for example Psalms 16:11.

INTRODUCTION

Mature reflection makes it evident, that the *mind of the world*, which is the aggregate of human acquirements, is more experienced, in the accurate knowledge of facts, to-day, than it has been at any former period. It is also evident, that the world has, hitherto, been in its early or most inexperienced stage; and that its past progress developes no more than the crude, or infant, period, of human existence; – the period, during which the human race has been employed in collecting facts, and striving to overcome the errors of its young uncorrected imagination, when it was filled with the fears of apparitions, ghosts, spectres, witches, and demons; and made *irrational, by the apprehension of future eternal miseries, for convictions over which it had no control; for feelings which it could not create; and for qualities, or a general character, which it did not form.*

These great truths have been, lately, more forcibly impressed on the mind of the author, by the perusal of various statistical publications, emanating from some of the *elite*, or best informed men, of the present day; who have collected a mass of most valuable facts, which open to the public a distinct view of the present state of society, especially of the British Empire.

These authors give evidence of great research, considerable natural abilities, and a strong desire to benefit society; they have, indeed, effected, at this juncture, great benefit to humanity, by searching out, and making public, some of the enormous evils, inflicted upon a large portion of the population, of this, and of other civilized countries, through some causes which *these authors* cannot explain; and which causes their early education and position in society have made it difficult, if not impossible, for them to discover.

They have been educated, like all under the old system of society, to observe, and to occupy themselves with, existing *effects*; having been taught, by everything appertaining to the present irrational system of society, that there is danger in investigating, too deeply the *causes* which produce those effects.

The authors, to whom allusion is, thus, made, are, Dr Alison[a] of Edinburgh;

[a] Dr William Pulteney Alison (1790–1859): prominent Scottish physician.

his brother, the Sheriff of Lanarkshire;[a] Dr Chalmers[b] of Edinburgh; Mr Porters[c] of the Board of Trade; Mr McCulloch,[d] the modern Political Economist; Dr Cowan,[e] and Captain Miller,[f] of Glasgow; Mr Babbage,[g] Mr Rawson,[h] Mr Joseph Bentley,[i] etc etc.

These gentlemen have, with great industry and ability, fully established the facts, that poverty, destitution, crime, and consequent extreme suffering, in the British Dominions, have, under the existing system, fearfully increased; and are rapidly increasing; and that, to prevent society falling into anarchy and confusion, the strongest necessity has arisen for the adoption of some *efficient* measures to stay the progress of these evils, in order to preserve all classes from the crude, yet natural, reaction, of the grievously suffering poor, in opposition to the erroneous government of the rich and powerful.

These talented writers have, also, demonstrated the increased powers acquired by civilized nations, and by this country in particular, to produce wealth, when under right direction, to any extent that the population of this, or any other, country, when made rational, can possibly require.

But, when these learned men begin to write about *practical measures*, to stay the operation of the causes which have produced, and are daily producing, these dire effects upon the suffering masses, and are endangering the safety of all classes, and the rulers of all nations, 'Oh! what a falling off is there' in all useful knowledge, of experience, or of any practical acquaintance with this part of the subject.

Whenever these gentlemen proceed, one step, beyond *talking* of the deplorable *effects* of these evils upon the individuals, and upon society, and attempt to propose a *remedy for* the sufferings which they produce, – although the most ample means to terminate these sufferings are open before them, – yet, like all the pious, the learned, the political economists, the legal, political, or divine, statesmen, who have preceded them, they, at once, prove how little they know of the *practice* which leads to the *only* remedy in nature; – *the only remedy that ever can be found sufficient to accomplish the object.*

'*More Churches, more Priests, and more Religion*,' say some of these parties, 'will cure the evil.'

Will these well-meaning and most conscientious persons, as, no doubt, many of them are, inform the world, *what churches, what priests*, and *what*

[a] Sir Archibald Alison (1792–1867): an opponent of Malthus' population doctrines.

[b] Dr Thomas Chalmers (1780–1847): theologian, preacher and philanthropist.

[c] George Richardson Porter (1792–1852): statistician.

[d] John Ramsey McCulloch (1789–1864): statistician and political economist.

[e] See Robert Cowan, *Vital Statistics of Glasgow* (1838).

[f] See Henry Miller, *Papers Relative to the State of Crime in the City of Glasgow* (1840).

[g] Charles Babbage (1792–1871): mathematician and inventor.

[h] Rawson W. Rawson (1812–99): author of *An Inquiry into the Statistics of Crime in England and Wales* (1839).

[i] See Joseph Bentley, *The State of Education Contrasted with the State of Crime* (1838).

religion, have yet produced, in *practice*, charity and kindness, to all their fellow-men, who have been taught a creed different from their own church or religion? – or, where to find a religion, under which the wealthy, at this moment, do not most grievously oppress and afflict the poor, and ignorant; and also, by their laws, create the poverty, and maintain the ignorance?

'*More Education and Instruction*,' say some others, of these well-meaning writers, 'will effect the desired object, much better than more churches, more priests, and more religion: for these have been tried, again and again, in all countries, and in all ages, and, yet, the evils to be remedied, more abound now, and are more grievous to the sufferers, than at any former time, *although the means of effectual relief are, now, far more ample, than at any former period.*'

Will these advocates for education inform the public, *what are the* PRINCIPLES, *and what is the* PRACTICE, *of that education, which, when the masses must depend for their existence upon wages, – the amount of wages on the demand for manual labour, – the demand for manual labour upon its successful competition with scientific power; – and when, in consequence of the enormous extent and rapid increase of this power, and its greater efficiency and economy than manual labour, little or no employment, and little or no wages, can be obtained for the labourer,* – will prevent the existence, and continual growth, of poverty, destitution, crime, and wretchedness, in any population?

'No,' say others of these authors – 'neither religion, nor education can effect any cure for a redundant population; experience has proved, that religion has hitherto failed to stay the rapid advance of poverty and crime; and, as far as education has been tried, it has, also been unsuccessful.' 'You must diminish the number of the people, by some means, or we, who govern and, now, possess the influence and wealth of the nation, shall be eaten up, or destroyed by the cravings and contest for food.'

'Emigration, to every part of the globe, or starvation through the want of sufficient wages for labour, are the only natural remedies; and, if there are not means to effect sufficient annual emigration, to keep down the numbers of the producing class, then, there is no remedy left, but that the surplus population must perish by some means or other. It is a hard case; – but Nature wills it, and Nature's laws are irresistible.'

These latter are the arguments now most popular, among those who are deemed the least theoretical, and most practical, of British writers on political economy, and general statistics, although another view, of their favourite subject, would have informed them, that *the population* increases, *annually*, at the rate, only, of about *half a million*, in these islands; while *scientific power* has increased, in Great Britain and Ireland, for the last seventy years, at a rate, on the average, equal to the labour of, at least, *nine millions of men annually*.

And this enormous rate of increase, to scientific power, has been obtained, when its progress was commenced at a period when mechanical and chemical knowledge was in a very crude state, compared with the progress since made;

and when the *manual powers* applied to the production of wealth, was not more than *three million*, of men, moderately industrious; – at a period, too, when the old, inferior, mechanical and other scientific, powers, in use, did not exceed the labour of about *twelve millions* in addition, and when these united powers of production produced the wealth, then enjoyed by a population of *fifteen millions*.

But a new and most extraordinary era, in the production of wealth, and scientific knowledge, now opens to the British population: it commences with *six millions* of most industrious *productive labourers*, with upwards of *six hundred and fifty millions* of superior *scientific power*, and with a great advance in the practical knowledge of mechanics, chemistry, and other sciences and arts, compared with the knowledge of these matters at the commencement of the former period. And, yet, with this *enormous actual increase of productive power; and most extraordinary means for its immediate, continued, and* ILLIMITABLE *extension; there are not, yet,* THIRTY MILLIONS *of population to be provided for: or, compared with the gain in the powers of production, not one to be maintained, for every twenty-one seventy years ago; while now, each producer of wealth can produce, at least, five times more in the same period.*

O! most wise governors, statesmen, priests, political economists, and great practical men of business, of the British Empire, who *so ardently* desire to make the population *rich, virtuous, and happy!* How brilliantly shines your wisdom before the astonished world, while it learns that you have succeeded, far in advance of all other nations, in discovering, and bringing into practice, powers of production for the creation of wealth, which, wisely directed, could be, soon, made abundant to supply the population of the world, and greatly to over supply it, and, yet, that with this power at your control, you have, by your *profound wisdom*, created, in a population of less than thirty millions, more poverty, destitution, wretchedness, crime, discontent, and misery, than can be found in any civilized population, of equal extent, upon the globe!!!

The enormous, and, if true, alarming, statements of Mr Malthus,[a] on the subject of population, have, evidently, directed the current of your thoughts in a wrong course; and created the most false and unfortunate notions, in your minds, respecting the industrious classes, and the mode of governing them.

These statements of Mr Malthus were true, only, when man knew not how to use his hand, or his head, except to gather the food which nature spontaneously provided for him; and before he knew how to domesticate animals, to cultivate the soil, or to take fish. But when Mr Malthus wrote his book of errors, prophesying, eternal vice and misery to the human race, man had

[a] Thomas Robert Malthus (1766–1834): opponent first of Condorcet and Godwin, then Owen; author of the immensely influential *Essay on Population* (1798), which argued that population always grew to the means of subsistence, and could be restrained only by want or the prudent marriage of the poor.

acquired the arts of becoming shepherds, and cattle-herds, – of ploughing, sowing, and reaping, – of building boats, and making fishing-nets; and had, even, made some progress in the new manufacturing system, by which such an extraordinary impulse has, since, been given to inventions, discoveries, and improvements, in mechanism, chemistry, and other arts and sciences.

His statements, therefore, at the time when he published his work, were less true then, than they had been, at any former period.

Instead of these statements, if he had possessed practical knowledge, he would have said, – 'Do what you will, *population* can be increased, *annually*, in an *arithmetical* progression only; but you may produce *food*, if there was utility in doing it, *two or three times, annually, beyond its natural consumption;* and this facility, under a wise direction of heads and hands, will continue to enlarge as population increases; that is, for many thousand years; even until the earth shall give forth its full increase, the seas be exhausted, and man's capacity for making a progress in scientific knowledge shall terminate; or, until the earth shall be so full of people that it will not admit of any further increase.'

I would suggest to statesmen, legislators, priests, political economists, men of the world, and men of experience in business, that they stop their present course of legislation; and, before they adopt more stringent measures, to starve out of existence the poor creatures, whose highest ambition now appears to be, to have permission to provide, amply, for the rich man, that they may have the crumbs, or even a part of the crumbs, which fall from his table; that they wait to see the extraordinary advantages that will arise, with the increase of a population, well trained, educated, and employed, for some thousands of years to come; which period will elapse, before the earth can be, thus, well filled with people.

I would, also, suggest to these parties, who now lead and direct the public mind, that much harm could not arise, were they to delay their fears of over-population, until after those thousands of years shall have passed; and recommence the subject of over population, only a few hundred years before the soil, the seas, and men's inventions, shall have been exhausted, and no further increase of population can be supported.

But I blame not the governors, priests, statesmen, political economists, legislators, and men of great business, who have contrived to produce so much wretchedness and crime, with such ample means to produce virtue and happiness; they, like all other men, are the creatures of the circumstances in which they have, by necessity, been placed. They have been, necessarily, influenced, by the false theory of Mr Malthus; who, by his writings, has perplexed and confounded the understandings of those who were without a practical knowledge of society.

As men have been educated and placed, in different classes, they see but a very small part of a most ignorant, artificial, false, and unjust, state of society; they have, therefore, been made incompetent to unravel these palpable incongruities and absurdities.

It is, however, now too evident, that the cup of crime and misery, of the mass of our population, has been made so full, that it is ready to run over; and that the most abundant, nay illimitable means, are, daily, within our power, to ensure to the whole of the population, wealth, wisdom, and goodness, far beyond that which any people have yet attained.

The most lamentable fact is, that those who now govern society, are content with these crude notions of Mr Malthus: for they will not deign to examine any principles or plans designed to give the world the advantage of the late extraordinary discoveries; however true the principles, and good the plans, may be, if they are opposed to the theories of this popular instructor.

It is Mr Malthus, who has filled the public mind with these mental abortions: and it appears to be quite sufficient for the leading lights of the world, to know that an inexperienced, learned, priest, – *and all learned priests are inexperienced* – has said, 'There is a tendency in human beings to increase more rapidly than food; the first increases in a geometrical proportion, while the last increases in an arithmetical ratio only.' If this statement were really true, the population of the world must exist in misery, everlastingly increasing.

And this, well-meaning priest, having said, 'Increase and be miserable,'* legislators have, in direct opposition to the millions upon millions of facts, always at hand, to demonstrate the gross error and practical ignorance of this inexperienced learned priest, acquiesced in the statement; and made their laws and practices in accordance with this error; and carried them into execution, until they have reduced society to the state, so truly described by Dr and Mr Alison, and the other industrious and profound political statesmen, and economists, of the present day.

But is there any truth in this statement of Mr Malthus? If so, farewell, for ever, to virtue, peace, and happiness, upon earth; and to all future expected enjoyment. Happily, however, for the human race, it is as erroneous as any sentence that has ever been uttered; and will remain so, until the soil, the seas, and human knowledge, shall be exhausted.

It will be time enough to inquire, what shall be done, to effect artificial and injurious restraints upon the increase of population, *when the world shall be sufficiently peopled to ensure the greatest advantages, and highest enjoyments, to every individual.*

The plan proposed in this work, to be carried into execution by Joint-Stock Companies, and recommended for immediate general adoption, will provide for the support of four times the population, on the same extent of soil, in twenty-fold more comfort, than they are now maintained. This small beginning is equal to adding, at once, a four-fold increase to the surface of the earth.

* Although other priests have formerly written, 'Increase and multiply, subdue the earth and be happy.'[a]

[a] See Genesis 1:28.

O ye, of little faith in the wisdom and goodness of the Almighty Creating Power of the Universe, and who believe, that That Power cannot, or will not, provide food for man, as extensively as he is created, and that the present restricted quantity of food, is attributable to a deficiency in Nature's stores, and not to man's laws, in opposition to nature's laws! Let a decree go forth, from your governments, offering, upon a sure security, a certain additional profit, of twenty per cent. for twenty, one hundred, or one thousand years, upon the production of food of the best qualities, for the health and enjoyment of man, – its transit to be unrestricted; – and observe, at the end of every year, whether man or his food will increase geometrically.

The knowledge of these, and of many other, facts, compels the writer to pity his poor fellow-men, who suffer ever privation, annoyance, and degradation, while their country, and every country, is overwhelmed with the materials, if rightly used, to terminate, for ever, their poverty, and irrationality; and to make them intelligent, wealthy, and happy beings.

But this state of suffering need not longer continue. To effect the most truly glorious of all changes, that have yet occurred, in the history of the human race, the men of wealth have, only, to form joint-stock companies, to secure, and greatly increase, their wealth – the men of learning, to make these glad tidings speedily known, over the world – and the men of industry, to abandon intemperance, and all unkind, and opposing, conduct, and carry these measures, under the direction of experienced men of business, in the four general departments of life, into immediate execution.

It is true, this change will be, indeed, a RADICAL *change in the principles and practices of society, over the world.* BUT NO CHANGE, LESS THAN THIS, *can, now, produce permanent and substantial benefit to all classes, in all countries.*

The change proposed, will be found, upon full examination, to be competent to effect this result, without the necessity of creating injury, even during its progress, to any individual, class, or country. *It will be a change of unmixed good for the human race.*

It is true, to open the eyes of the public, the author has been compelled, to enable him to effect this great object of his life to use strong language, in describing the professions and classes into which society has been formed; but he has thus written, from no uncharitable, or unkind, feeling, to any individuals of these professions, or classes. For many individuals in all these professions and classes, he has long entertained great regard, and sincere friendship; while he has not the slightest ill-will towards any one of them. He trusts that this statement will remove all unpleasant impressions from the minds of the individuals who, now, necessarily, or accidentally, compose these professions and classes.

In the new state of society, which the author has conceived, and thus far developed to the world, there will be no necessity, except in the first, or transition, colonies, for any of these separate professions, or classes; they will be most advantageously superseded, by a very superior, learned, scientific, practical, population; classified into eight divisions of ages; each division of age having its own most suitable physical, and mental, occupation, in order to keep body and mind in the best state of health, and in the best spirit for the enjoyment of their existence.*

As soon as localized men can be divested of their early, local prepossessions, and can be trained, by new circumstances, to become well-informed, rational, inhabitants of the earth, and to look upon each other, as brothers and sisters of one great family, trained to have a family affection, and a lively interest in each other's well-doing, well-being, and happiness: – and when their minds shall be opened to understand their true, permanent, interests; – all will discover, that separate professions, or classes, tend to divide man from man, mind from mind, interest from interest; and to destroy that open, honest, character, which, without these opposing professions and classes, could be, now, easily created for every one.

The statesmen, priests, lawyers, physicians, and warriors, will therefore, the writer trusts, forgive him, when he speaks of their professions; and the mercantile men, and men of the world of every description, when he speaks of their occupations, as he does in this work; because, when he thus expresses himself, it is on account of the incalculably injurious effects produced, of necessity, by every profession, and every class, throughout society; and he has no intention, by this proceeding, to wound the feelings of any individual whatever.

But, to effect this great and glorious change, it must be made known to the world:

1st, That the necessary character of *the priesthood*, in all nations, is to establish such errors in the human mind, that, while this profession continues, *man, by their preaching and conduct, must, also continue to be, systematically, trained to hate man, and to be uncharitable and unkind to those who differ in their religious prejudices; for all* RELIGIONS, *so called, are, as will be found, on fair investigation,* EARLY-TAUGHT PREJUDICE – *any one of which religions, may be taught to any child, in such manner that he shall, conscientiously, believe it to be most divinely true, and all the others most wickedly, nay dreadfully, false;* –

2d, That the necessary character of *the profession of the law*, is, to maintain the *ignorant* and *most injurious laws of man*, in direct opposition to the wise, and most beneficent, laws of man's nature; evidently formed, by the Supreme Creating Power of the Universe, to ensure to man, when he shall understand and act upon them, health and enjoyment beyond the imaginings of poets; but

* See, in Appendix, the particulars of this new classification of society, explained by extracts from the 'Six Lectures' delivered in Manchester, 1837, by the Author, and published by Heywood, of that place.[a]

---

[a] See *Six Lectures Delivered at Manchester Previously to the Discussion between* Mr. *Robert Owen and the Rev.* J. H. *Roebuck* (Manchester, 1839).

that, as long as the profession of the law, based on the principles on which all human laws have been founded, shall be maintained, *it will prevent the period arriving, when man shall be just to man, when he shall love his neighbour as himself, or when he shall understand his own interest, or, become a rational being*; –

3d, That the necessary character of *the medical profession is*, to form a portion of society into a division, that, like the priesthood, and the law, have an apparent, direct interest, in opposition to the masses; an interest to keep them in ignorance, that they may be, the more easily, imposed upon, and made subservient to the supposed interest of the profession. As long as this profession shall be maintained, men will not be educated, as they, now, easily might be, to understand and attend to their own constitutions, to enable them to learn how to *prevent* disease, render medicine unnecessary, and, ultimately, secure to themselves a good constitution, and sound health, both of body and mind, through their lives; which may, easily, be lengthened many years; –

4th, That the necessary character of *the military profession*, is, to generate a warlike spirit, and a desire for war; making it the apparent interest of those engaged in the profession, not to wish for, or to promote, that period, when 'swords shall be turned into ploughshares, and spears into pruning-hooks;'[a] – and, thus, to perpetuate feelings of hostility among individuals and nations, that must *immortalize immorality*, continue to foster all the bad passions, create confusion and disorder throughout the world, renew such scenes as the late horrifying proceedings, enacted by *Christians*, against unknown individuals, at St Jean D'Acre,[b] and, materially, retard every improvement for extending civilized life; –

5th, That the necessary character of *the individual buying and selling system*, is, to train the human race to acquire the inferior mind of a pedlar and dealer; whose business of life is, to endeavour to procure everything, from others, at the lowest price, and to dispose of everything, to others, at the *highest* price: or in such manner, that he shall secure the greatest amount of money profit, worldly honours, or individual considerations, to himself.

And, in this sense, *all, from the highest to the lowest*, are now trained to become, by the individual competition system, mere pedlars, tradesmen, or dealers: who are constantly endeavouring to obtain the services, and productions, of others, at the easiest rate, and lowest value, and to sell their own services, at the highest, or, to obtain all they can, in exchange for them.

The sovereigns, statesmen, legislators, professional men, military, merchants, bankers, manufacturers, tradesmen, workmen, and beggars, are, now, all, under the competitive individual system, which has hitherto prevailed over the world, engaged in this low, unjust, and degrading traffic, of purchasing

[a] See for example Isaiah 2:4.
[b] See *The Times*, no. 17,631 (30 March 1841), p. 6.

the services of others at the cheapest, and selling their own at the dearest rate; to the incalculable injury of each from the highest to the lowest.

By these means, the most successful, in this inferior and immoral course of conduct, do not obtain a tithe, no, nor a fiftieth part of the permanent, substantial, healthy, enlightened, superior advantages, pleasures, and enjoyments, that, under the united system, *all* may attain and securely possess; without obstruction, competition or contest.

And it is most certain, that while these demoralizing practices, shall be systematically taught, from birth, by, or under the sanction of, the priesthood, to the whole population of every country; and the eyes of the mind of all nations, shall be, thus, kept in total darkness, so as to prevent all useful mental light from entering; that the moral duties, recommended by the professing Christians, and other religionists, will not, because, under such a system of disunion, they cannot, be practised.

The plan, now proposed for adoption, will realize more substantial and permanent happiness than has been promised in the 'NEW JERUSALEM;' and it is, only, within this earthly paradise, that the human character can be formed, from birth, in sufficient charity, wisdom, and purity, to fit it for the millennium state of existence; and, under these new arrangements, in this New Jerusalem, these advantages may be, in part, experienced, even by the present generation, and fully enjoyed by our children's children, not for a thousand years only, but to the end of time.

A DEVELOPEMENT OF THE PRINCIPLES AND PLANS ON WHICH TO ESTABLISH SELF-SUPPORTING HOME COLONIES

The great increase of poverty, destitution, and crime, among the poor and industrious classes of the United Kingdom, with their want of education and employment, is now an authentic record; and placed before the government and the public, in such official form, that the truth of these appalling statements, and the magnitude of the evils they disclose, can be no longer doubted or concealed.

It is, therefore, evident, that society has been hitherto based on false principles – on principles incompetent to produce an intelligent, virtuous, and happy population, If it were not so, whence come to the poverty, the disease, and the crime, by which we are everywhere surrounded? And, especially, when sovereign, statesmen, legislators, political economists, priests, and people, desire to advance their own state in society; and when all have a real interest to improve the general condition of the whole population? How comes it that in London, where there is a population of 1,800,000, one-tenth of the whole are paupers, and 50,000 destitute persons rise every morning without knowing where they are to sleep at night; that in Glasgow, in a population of 280,000, 30,000 are every Saturday night in a state of brutal intoxication, and every tenth house is devoted to the sale of ardent spirits; that in Dublin, in a population of 250,000, 60,000 persons in one year pass through the fever hospital: and lastly, that crimes of a serious nature have, within the last thirty years, increased in proportion to the population, in England *five times*, in Ireland *six times*, and in Scotland *forty times* and that they are every year increasing in a still more rapid ratio?*

* Those who desire to examine these and similar results more in detail, are referred to the Annual Reports of the Registrar-General for 1838 and 1839[a] – the Pamphlet of Mr Slaney,[b] MP for Shrewsbury – Letters of Doctors Southwood Smith and Neill Arnott, to the Poor Law Commissioners[c] – the

[a] See *First Annual Report of the Registrar-General of Births, Deaths and Marriages in England* (1839).

[b] See Robert Slaney, *State of the Poorer Classes in Great Towns* (1840).

[c] See Thomas Southwood Smith, *Report on the Physical Causes of Sickness and Mortality to Which the Poor are Particularly Exposed* (n.d.) and *Report on the Prevalence of Fever in Twenty Metropolitan Unions in 1838* (n.d.); Neill Arnott, *On the Fevers Which Have Prevailed in Edinburgh and Glasgow* (?1840).

Such statements prove the destitute and helpless condition in which the poor, and a large portion of the industrious classes, have been, and now are, throughout the greater part of the United Kingdom; and the unsatisfactory and dangerous state of all classes. But the striking anomaly in the condition of the population of Great Britain, is, that though enormous wealth has been and is constantly created by the industrious classes, it is at once absorbed for the supposed advantage of the few who create none; while the many are daily becoming poorer, more numerous, and more degraded.

For evidence of the general increase of wealth in the British dominions, it is only necessary to refer to the expenditure of the last French war* – the loans of our capitalists to foreign states, and their enormous losses in consequence – the extension of the large manufactories over the United Kingdom – the extension and improvement of agriculture – the roads and canals – the introduction and rapid extension of steam navigation and railways – the increase of superior and expensive private and public buildings in all the large cities and towns in the kingdom – and, above all, to the enormous amount of surplus wealth which could be now exported to all parts of the world, if the appearance of a profitable investment could be shown.

In proof of the increase of the power to produce wealth in the United Kingdom during the last seventy years, it is necessary only to refer to Babbage on Machinery[a] – to the two volumes of the Statistical Account of the British Empire, by Mr Macculloch,[b] in which the rapid growth of this power in all branches of manufactures and British industry is given in detail – and to two volumes on the Progress of the Nation, in its various social and economical relations, by G. R. Porter, Esq.[c]

Journal of the Statistical Society[d] – the 'Principles of Population, and their Connection with Human Happiness,' in two volumes, by Archibald Alison[e] – the Papers read and Statements made by Dr Alison, the Reverend Dr Chalmers, Dr Cowan, Captain Millar, Mr Rawson, Mr Porter, Mr Joseph Bentley, and others, at the Meetings of the Statistic Section of the British Association, held in Glasgow, in September this year[f] – and to the Official Reports made in the last and former Sessions to the House of Commons, on the State of Prisons, Poor, etc.[g]

* The expenditure of the last year of this war was, for Great Britain alone, one hundred and thirty millions.

---

[a] See Charles Babbage, *On the Economy of Machinery and Manufactures* (1832).

[b] J. R. McCulloch, *Statistical Account of the British Empire* (2 vols, 1837).

[c] G. R. Porter, *The Progress of the Nation in Its Various Social and Economic Relations from the Beginning of the Nineteenth Century to the Present Time* (2 vols, 1836).

[d] *The Statistical Journal and Record of Useful Knowledge*, nos 1–5 (1837–8).

[e] Archibald Alison, *Principles of Population, and Their Connection with Human Happiness* (2 vols, 1840).

[f] *Report of the Tenth Meeting of the British Association for the Advancement of Science* (1841), pt 2, pp. 169–86.

[g] See British Parliamentary Papers, *Reports from the Select Committee to Enquire into the Administration of Poor Relief Under the Provisions of the Poor Law Amendment Act* (7 vols, 1837–8), *Reports from Committees. Gaols*, vols 11–12 (1835).

These valuable documents, with other official statements, are abundantly sufficient to demonstrate the rapid, and next to miraculous, increase of scientific productive power within the last seventy or eighty years, as compared with the increase of population in the same period. In 1770, the population of the United Kingdom was fifteen millions, and its producing population three millions; the scientific powers of production equal to about the labour of twelve millions more; or, together, fifteen millions; that is, *as one to one*, compared with the whole population: and the scientific power, compared with the manual power, as *four* to *one*.[a] In 1840, the population does not exceed thirty millions, and the producing population six millions; while the scientific producing powers exceed the labour of 650 millions, or more than *twenty-one to one*, compared with the whole population, and more than *one hundred and eight to one*, compared with the manual power. In Mr Macculloch's work, it is stated that these extraordinarily increased means of producing wealth have been discovered chiefly by 'uneducated men, moving only in the class of common workmen or labourers.'[b]

The industrious classes are, then, the principal authors of all this increased power of producing prosperity. In common justice, therefore, their condition in the scale of society ought to be proportionably advanced.

The documents which have been cited, show, unequivocally, that the industrious classes are now, in a more impoverished, immoral, and degraded condition than they were seventy years ago; and, in consequence, as Dr Chalmers truly stated in the Statistic Section of the British Association, held lately in Glasgow, 'crime has increased, is increasing, and ought to be diminished.'[c]

Now, setting aside all party, class, and sectarian motions and feelings, this is not a condition of society that ought longer to exist in the United Kingdom, if it can be remedied; for it is not only unjust, but extremely cruel, towards the working classes; and most dangerous to the wealthy classes. In truth, all parties are most deeply interested in the change proposed to be effected, from the present most artificial, immoral, and wretched state of society, to one in which these wonderful inventions, discoveries, and improvements may be directed to produce the most beneficial results and to advance and ameliorate the condition of all classes.

To those who reflect, it must be evident that the only remedy for the evils produced by the present system, is a SOUND PRACTICAL EDUCATION, AND PERMANENT BENEFICIAL EMPLOYMENT, for all the industrious classes. Such an education is required to form a substantial, useful, and good character for all;

[a] J. R. McCulloch, *Statistical Account of the British Empire* (2 vols, 1837), vol. 2, pp. 35–139.
[b] Ibid, vol. 2, p. 88.
[c] See *Report of the Tenth Meeting of the British Association for the Advancement of Science* (1841), pt 2, pp. 169–86.

and such employment, to enable each individual, at all times, to create more wealth than he would consume; and thus add continually to the general stock, for the benefit of the Commonwealth. A *good education, and constant employment, would insure a superior conduct from the population, and give them a never-failing supply of wealth; and, without this change in the condition of society, the wealth of the wealthy, or non-producers, and the poverty of the industrious, or producers, must continue to increase; to the great injury and discontent of the producers, and to the increasing danger of the non-producers.*

A strong, nay, an irresistible, necessity, has, therefore, arisen for a general change in society, from ignorance and bad habits to knowledge and good habits, and from poverty to wealth and comfort. The inventions, discoveries, and improvements: which have now been effected, and brought to considerable maturity in the United Kingdom are ample for the attainment of a very advanced and superior state of society – one which shall *prevent*, by *removing the causes that produce*, the poverty, disease, vice, crime, and misery, now so generally experienced, and so loudly complained of, by all classes, – the poor, for their suffering – and the rich, for the danger produced by the sufferings of the poor.

Much has been said in favour of the value and importance of the inventions, discoveries, and improvements of the last eighty years; but their real value is yet but little known. They have hitherto produced much evil with the good. They are capable of producing much more good without any of the evil. Sciences are valuable only in proportion as they conduce to human happiness; and when applied to produce more misery than happiness, they are an evil, instead of a good, to the population of the world.

Now, what are the facts with regard to the application of physical science to the purposes of life in the United Kingdom, under the system of industry and commerce which has hitherto prevailed? Evidently, that it has increased the wealth of the rich, and the poverty of the poor, to the great injury of both.* These sciences have been hitherto applied in the production of wealth, in direct competition with manual labour. Manual labour has had no chance in this contest; and its value has diminished, is diminishing, and, under this system, must continue to diminish, until the sufferings of the producers will become unbearable, and a forced and sanguinary revolution must be the inevitable result, if the experience of the past shall not give a new, and more valuable, and natural, direction to these sciences.

* It is said that Mr Arkwright[a] is possessed of wealth which brings him an income of more than £450,000 a-year, or more than sufficient to establish one of the Home Colonies, advocated in this work, every two years; or sufficient to place 2500 persons at once, and their posterity for ever, in a most prosperous and independent position, without diminishing his fortune or lessening his income. This change could be effected also by all large proprietors in proportion to their wealth.

[a] Sir Richard Arkwright (1732–92): inventor of textile machinery.

A statement of the increase of our scientific power has already been given; and the question is – 'what has been and what may be done with this enormous increase?' for if it were wisely directed, the whole population would individually be benefited in the same proportion; *and poverty, or the fear of it, would not be known throughout the British dominions*. But the increase, enormous as it is, is yet only in its commencement. It may be increased, without difficulty, – not only in Great Britain, but in every other nation, in proportion to its population, – to 50, to 100, or to 1000, to one; and in a comparatively short period. In fact, there is no assignable limit to this increase of difference between manual labour and scientific power; or between the production of wealth and the population.

The physical sciences have already been applied, to so great an extent, in the production of wealth, as to make most kinds of it too abundant for the profitable demand which exists, under the system of individual competition that has hitherto directed the commerce of the world. And these sciences, so applied, will continue to increase this over supply, until the system itself shall be changed, and a superior direction shall be given to these invaluable scientific powers. This state of things tends to the continual decrease of the value of manual labour; and, in the same proportion, to the decrease of the command of the industrious classes over the necessaries and comforts of life. So long as these powers shall be permitted to act in competition with manual labour, the degradation and misery of the producing class must go on increasing: and the producing classes must, of necessity, continue to become more degraded and miserable slaves of the wealthy, than were the Helots to the Greeks.

But a right direction cannot be given to the productive powers of science, except by the abandonment of the principle upon which the commerce of the world has, hitherto, proceeded. That principle is individualism, or individual competition; – a principle which, in the early and crude state of the human mind, was necessary to extort exertion and stimulate invention; but the operation of which, now that these inventions and discoveries have been so extended as to diminish, and soon to supersede, the necessity for manual labour, is in direct, opposition to the interests of all classes. – [*See, in Appendix, the quotation from* Mr *Buckingham.*][a]

Individualism, which has conducted all nations through the period of *ignorant selfishness*, must now give way to the principle of *union*, or of benevolence, or, as really it is, *enlightened selfishness*.

Every living being has been wisely created to desire its own happiness; it is an instinct in all that have life; but in this instinct, there is neither merit nor demerit. Ignorance or inexperience has hitherto given to this desire, in man,

[a] See A *Development of the Principles and Plans on Which to Establish Self-Supporting Home Colonies* (1841), Appendix, p. 15.

an erroneous direction; and disappointment has, of necessity, always followed. It will be for the permanent happiness of all classes, and ranks, that a right direction should be, now, given to this desire.

The knowledge now acquired of physical sciences, and thence of the laws of nature, will lead to, and render inevitable, a true direction of this instinct; and disappointment will no longer be known.

But the inexperienced exclaim – 'how can you create the will to abandon the oldest established prejudice of the human race: – and, if you could succeed in creating a strong desire to bring about this change in the principle and consequent organization of society, how could you carry the desire into practice, without causing great temporary confusion, with loss of property, profit, and comfort, to the older members of the present generation?'

These are questions of grave import; and require to be honestly met, and fairly answered.

To the *first*, the reply is, that the change of principle must be effected in the same manner in which all other general changes have been accomplished; that is, by making it appear, first to the few, and then to the many, that the principle to be abandoned, is producing great evil, and that the one to be adopted, will produce great good. There never has been an old principle to be abandoned, that produced so much evil as the principle of *individualism* is now effecting throughout society; while there never has been a new principle proposed to be adopted, that has produced a good, at all to be compared with the advantages, which cannot fail to be derived from the general adoption of the principle of *union*. The benefits of the principle of union have been, already, largely, experienced, in the combinations to effect great objects; such as the formation of roads, canals, bridges, etc – in the unions to form joint-stock companies, club houses, etc etc – and, in America, in the formation of communities for mutual production and consumption; by which, without anxiety or fear of poverty, more wealth is produced with much less labour. – (*See Extracts from Mr Mellish and Miss Martineau on America, in Appendix.*)[a] Great, however, as the advantages are from these very partial applications of the principle of union, they are a very small part of that which may be effected by a *general and systematic* application of the same principle to the *four* departments of life.

To the *second* question, the reply is, that the change from the one principle to the other shall be proved, to the understanding of all experienced practical persons, to be a measure of easy execution, without creating confusion or disorder of any kind, in any stage of its progress; and that it shall be effected, not only without loss of property, profit, or comfort, to any even of the present

[a] See *A Development of the Principles and Plans on Which to Establish Self-Supporting Home Colonies* (1841), Appendix, pp. 10–15.

generation, but that, on the contrary, all individuals shall speedily become great gainers by the change.

But to accomplish these results in this manner, required the discovery, first, of the 'Science of Human Nature,' or, in other words, a knowledge of the constitution of infant man, of which society forms the matured character, and of the mode by which it may always be well formed, under every variety of original organization; – and, secondly, of the 'Science of Society,' or a knowledge of the means by which men may be united in associations, under such general arrangements as will secure to each, the maximum of good, with the minimum of evil, or the greatest advantages, with the least disadvantages.

These two sciences have been discovered: and an accurate knowledge of them is necessary to enable society to pass, without inconvenience, from the principle of individualism, and the practice of competitive production and partial enjoyment, to the principle of union, and the practice of united production and full enjoyment.

This knowledge is necessary, because, these two sciences form the basis of all the measures, by which it is now proposed to establish and conduct the Self-supporting Home Colonies. All laws, customs, and external circumstances of man's forming, have been, hitherto, founded on the false notion, – most destructive of the rationality and well being of society, – that each individual forms his own character, and is, consequently, responsible for it; while the new laws, customs, and external arrangements, will be formed on the demonstrable fact, that the character of every one is formed *for* him, and that none can rationally, or justly, be made responsible for that of which he is not the willing author. – (*See Extracts from Alison on Human Happiness, in the Appendix.*)[a]

However strong our prejudices naturally become in favour of things as they are, and in opposition to any proposed change, and, more especially, to any great change of principle and practice, it is, nevertheless, incontestibly proved, *by facts*, to be true, that the individual principle of action leads, of necessity, to the formation of the most inferior, and immoral, private and public, character – to the worst motives to action – to stimulate all the valuable propensities of our nature, beyond their healthy and beneficial exercise, into passions which injure the constitution of the individuals, debase many below ordinary animal nature, and cause evil and disorder throughout society. But, above and beyond all, this principle of individualism generates, and perpetually encourages, deception and falsehood, so as unavoidably to make men hypocrites and deceivers of one another; to the utter destruction of all real happiness among the human race.

As long as this unhappy and miserable state of society shall, through want of

[a] See *A Development of the Principles and Plans on Which to Establish Self-Supporting Home Colonies* (1841), Appendix, pp. 44–7.

experience, be permitted to continue, some portion of the human race, must, unfortunately for themselves and the public, be trained to imagine that they have an interest in keeping a large part of their fellow-men ignorant and in poverty, that these latter may be trained to produce wealth for, and to serve, the former, without being made conscious of the injustice they experience, and of their own degradation; and thus will be perpetuated a most inferior and miserable state of existence – one, indeed, most injurious to all, without being really beneficial to a single individual.

On the contrary, a change to the principle of union will soon destroy all motives to deception and falsehood; – all motives to take advantage of the ignorance of any one; – to desire to possess advantages not common to all; – to keep any in subjection, except according to age and experience; – to permit ignorance or poverty to remain among any portion of our fellow men; – or to allow any cause of evil to remain, which the united wisdom and power of society can remove.

The principle of individualism compels those who rule, to govern by force and fraud; and, as yet, there has been no other government in the world. The principle of union will compel those who rule, to govern by reason and kindness, and to adopt decisive measures to *prevent* the existence of evil, by *removing the causes* which produce it.

The individual principle governs by continually punishing the *effects*, permitting, and often encouraging, the *causes* which produce these effects, to remain untouched; while the principle of union, will never *punish the effects*, but will exert itself, without ceasing, to *remove the causes* which produce all injurious effects. The former, can never produce a virtuous or happy state of society; while the latter will ensure permanent goodness, intelligence, and happiness.

As soon as society can be well informed, it will become evident, that *no one* has a real interest in longer maintaining the principle and practices of individualism; while all, without exception of class, sect, or party, in any country, have an interest, truly overwhelming, to introduce and support the principle of union.

That which is now required, from the advocates of this new principle and mode of life, is a practical method of effecting the change, from the one principle to the other, in such a manner, that the prejudices in favour of old institutions, habits, and practices, may be overcome with the least pain and inconvenience to those who have been, from their birth, trained in those prejudices; and who, by the local circumstances of country and district, have been compelled to receive their peculiar geographical prejudices, in whatever quarter of the globe they may have been born; and equally so compelled, whether born or educated in Europe, Asia, Africa, or America; – all men having been, hitherto, made local creatures only, in progress to be formed into rational beings.

The few, whose early prejudices of class, party, and country, have been overcome, are now called upon to use, in the spirit of charity, the best means in their power, to enable the prejudiced to discover the injurious state of mind and feeling, with which local errors have been made to afflict them, from their birth; and to afflict them by blinding their understandings; and perverting, if not destroying, their judgment; both on matters of faith and practice.

To effect this change, in the varied prejudices of all countries, many suppose to be impracticable. It is true, the task is difficult; but strong prejudices, at various times, have been overcome, and thus prove it practicable; and the late increase of scientific discoveries, and especially the acquisition of the knowledge of the sciences of human nature, and of society, will make it more easy of execution, now, than at any former period. Apparent self-interest ever has been, and probably ever will be, the leading motive to action; and, to effect the change now contemplated in the condition of society, means must be adopted to make it evident to all parties, that they will be greatly improved in their character and condition, and be great worldly gainers, by the change of principle and practice, now proposed; and thus will the way be best prepared to overcome the prejudices of education, although these prejudices are not only strong, but almost universal; and necessarily so; because man is the creature of the circumstances which surround him.

It is, therefore, the *interest of all*, that every one, from birth, should be well educated, physically and mentally, that society may be improved in its character, – that every one should be beneficially employed, physically and mentally, that the greatest amount of wealth may be created, and knowledge attained, – that every one should be placed in the midst of those external circumstances, that will produce the greatest number of pleasurable sensations, through the longest life, that man may be made truly intelligent, moral, and happy, and be, thus, prepared to enter upon the coming Millennium.

By the abandonment of the principle of individualism, and the adoption of the principle of union, these beneficial results may be, now, speedily secured, to the population of all countries.

It is, therefore, now proposed, to abandon the principles and practices of individualism; on account of the daily increasing evils which they compel the population to suffer; and from the vexations, and annoyance, which are now becoming more and more severe on the middle class; as well as rendering the condition of the poor and working classes, far inferior, in many respects, to that of slaves, in many parts of the world.

But the change, from the one state to the other, is too great an advance, to be made at once, in the present condition of society; there must be an intermediate, or transition, stage of progress; in which the parties may conveniently learn to pass from the old false notions and inferior habits and practices, to correct principles and superior habits and practices.

This intermediate state, in which, to some extent, private property, and inequality of condition, must be maintained, will alone present any difficulty in practice; and that, solely, by reason of the false and inferior character, which the existing system has forced upon the present generation; and of the incongruous, vicious, inferior, or ill-contrived, arrangements, which have been, hitherto, devised, to form individual character, to produce and distribute wealth, and to govern locally and generally. If these arrangements have been put into practice with the intention of making the population intelligent, and virtuous, healthy, united, charitable and kind to each other, wealthy, and with a desire to promote the happiness of each other, and if these are, now, objects which are sincerely sought to be obtained, then no measures can be more opposed to their attainment, than the principles and practices of *Individualism* and *Sectarianism*, as they, now, prevail in the United Kingdom, and over the world.

The GROUND PLANS, ELEVATIONS, etc, of the PROPOSED COLONIES, at the end of this volume,[a] exhibit the general outline of arrangements for the transition or first stage of advance from individualism to union; and, also, for the second stage; both of which stages will be found, in examination, and comparison with any known system, to be, not only far more economical, but greatly superior in principle and practice.

Superior, however, as is the second over the first stage, yet the first is necessary; and must be passed through, to prepare the parties, born and trained in it, to be competent, – by their superior knowledge, virtuous habits, manners, and general conduct, and by the *universal spirit of charity, and kindness, which will then, of necessity, pervade every mind*, – to enter upon the practice of the second stage; and exhibit, to the world, its innumerable and important advantages.

By referring to these plans, with the accompanying explanations, and studying the estimates of expenditure and profitable results in the first stage, and the greatly increased advantages and profits in the second, the reader, who possesses sufficient experience to comprehend such combinations, will readily perceive the overwhelming advantage of the proposed, over the old, system.

To assist those less experienced to comprehend these new and extended schemes of combination, the following details and additional explanations are given.

GENERAL ARRANGEMENTS OF THE PROPOSED HOME COLONIES

It is proposed that each establishment of these Colonies shall, in the first instance, be the property of a joint-stock company; who, – having purchased the land, and erected thereon the requisite buildings, and furnished the same, – shall let the whole, upon lease, to a company of tenants; the latter having

[a] See *infra*, pp. 416–21.

power gradually to fine down the rents, and ultimately to become the owners, at a stipulated price, to be agreed on between the parties.

Each Colony to be devised to accommodate, ultimately, and permanently, from 2000 to 2500 individuals, of the usual proportions of men, women, and children; but to be so arranged as – without disturbing any of the permanent walls or buildings – to afford accommodation, temporarily, and during the transition state, to a larger number, as will be hereafter explained.

The following is a general description of the buildings and other arrangements of the Colony.

On a suitable site, – as nearly as may be in the centre of AN ESTATE, of about 2000 or 3000 acres, – will be erected the DWELLING-HOUSES and PUBLIC BUILDINGS of the Colonists; forming A SQUARE, inclosing an area of about sixty-five acres.

In front of each side of the square will be (as shown in the block and ground plan) a noble TERRACE OR ESPLANADE, of one hundred feet in breadth, and raised twelve feet from the natural surface of the surrounding land. The length of each side, including the Terrace, to be about 1650 feet.

At each corner of the square will be a large building, designed for a SCHOOL or COLLEGE, – the four constituting AN UNIVERSITY, for the scientific formation of a superior character – physical, intellectual, moral, and practical – from infancy to maturity.

In the centre of each side of the square will be a magnificent building, containing ASSEMBLY and CONCERT ROOMS, LIBRARIES and READING ROOMS, MUSEUMS, LABORATORIES, ARTISTS ROOMS, LECTURE ROOMS, COMMITTEE ROOMS, PLACES of WORSHIP, etc etc.

In the space between these latter buildings and those first described, will be the private DWELLING-HOUSES, 18 in number, on each side of the square. The general plan of these is, –

1st, A Basement Story, to be used as STORE-ROOMS, etc;' as well as for a variety of purposes connected with the apparatus for WARMING and VENTILATING, and supplying with HOT and COLD WATER, and artificial LIGHT, every apartment throughout the whole square.

2d, Above the Basement, will be three other stories, forming suites of APARTMENTS for the adult residents. On each of these stories or flats, will be eight rooms, with closets, and other conveniences; and a spacious geometrical STAIRCASE will run up the centre of each house.

3d, Over these, and forming a fifth story, will be DORMITORIES, and other apartments, for the children and young persons.

Projecting into the corner of the square, from the public buildings forming the centre of each side, will be four magnificent buildings, designed for REFECTORIES; attached to which, will be the KITCHENS. These buildings will contain arrangements much superior in convenience and economy, for the purposes in view, to those of the best Club-Houses in London or Paris.

Attached to these, there will be four massive TOWERS, each 240 feet in height, and of proportionate dimensions in other respects. Among other purposes, these are designed to carry off the smoke and effluvia of the fires below, used for heating the buildings, cooking, etc. They will, also, serve as OBSERVATORIES for astronomical, meteorological, and other purposes; and from near their summits will be reflected, at night, by powerful apparatus, the new Koniaphostic LIGHT, which will brilliantly illuminate the whole square.

Within the square, also, and conveniently situated with regard to the other buildings, will be GYMNASIA, and BATHS.

In the centre of the square will be an immense CONSERVATORY, *of light and elegant construction, with forcing-houses, etc attached.*

The whole of the interior of the square, will be laid out in the most tasteful and scientific manner, as PLEASURE GROUNDS; containing Botanical, Horticultural, and Floricultural GARDENS; together with plots of land for experimental agriculture; the whole intersected with spacious GRAVEL-WALKS, affording abundant space for cheerful out-door exercise.

Running entirely round the interior of the square, at a short distance from the houses, will be a spacious open CLOISTER; *by means of which, access may be had to any apartment in the whole of this extensive range of buildings, without going from under cover; and which will also present opportunities for sheltered exercise in very hot, or wet, weather.*

The surface of the grounds, in the interior of the square, will be nearly on a level with the floor of *the basement story*; whilst the roof of the cloister, which will be flat for the purpose of walking upon in fine weather, will be upon a level with the floor of *the first story* of the dwelling apartments.

Round the exterior of the square, as already explained, will be a noble ESPLANADE OR TERRACE, 100 feet broad, and raised twelve feet from the natural surface of the land; but on a level with the first or ground floor of the dwelling-houses. From this terrace will be seen portions of THE ESTATE belonging to the Colony, laid out in FOUR FARMS, but having the appearance of A PARK, with its hills and dales, its wood and water. These farms will be cultivated, as far as population will admit, with the spade; and kept in the best order and most productive state.

About the centre of each farm will be the requisite AGRICULTURAL BUILDINGS, etc.

At a convenient distance from the square, surrounded by plantations, will be *Manufactories, containing the most complete machinery, with mechanical power, for accomplishing, in the best manner known, such Manufactures and Trades as may be best suited to the locality and other circumstances of the colony; and to make these arrangements complete, there must also be, at some distance without the square; but within* the territory of the colony, GAS APPARATUS; Washing, Bleaching, and DYEING ARRANGEMENTS; with STABLES and COACH-HOUSES; and, in a more remote situation, a SLAUGHTER-HOUSE, as long as it shall be found to be advantageous or necessary for health or happiness, for any portion of the colonists to subsist on animal food.

This, then, is a general description of what may be fairly termed A MAGNIFICENT PALACE, containing within itself the advantages of A METROPOLIS, AN UNIVERSITY, and A COUNTRY RESIDENCE, without any of their disadvantages, and situated within A BEAUTIFUL PARK of 2000 or 3000 acres; the whole most scientifically arranged, and placing within the reach of its inhabitants, at a very moderate annual expenditure, arrangements far superior to any now known, for the production and distribution of wealth, the formation of character, and the government of the population, with innumerable advantages never yet possessed by the most favoured individuals in any age or country.

CLASSIFICATION OF THE FIRST, OR TRANSITION COLONIES

With a view to economy, and at the same time, gradually to overcome existing feelings, arising from inequality of education and condition, with the least inconvenience to all parties, the first or transition colonies, may, most advantageously, comprise four distinct classes: –

First class, Hired Labourers or Servants, – say one-third consisting of single women, who now earn, on the average, £25 a-year; and two-thirds of men, who now earn £39 a-year each. These persons will be lodged, fed, clothed, instructed, and furnished with means of recreation, under circumstances that will gradually improve their language, habits, and general conduct; and, thus, prepare them to become candidates for membership. When they marry, their places, as in old society, must be filled up by other single persons; unless their conduct shall have been previously such as to qualify them to become candidates for membership; in which case, arrangements will be formed for them, and for educating their children, *outside* the square, but, yet, *within* the domain of the colony.

The *second class*, or Candidates for Membership; to consist of mechanics, artisans, and the superior kind of servants, whose services are now paid for at an average of £65 each per annum; and who, when educated and trained, in principle and practice, to attain the full character of members, will be admitted to all the benefits and privileges of members or colonists. In the meantime, they will enjoy many advantages, which they cannot have, in their present state, in old society.

The *third class*, will be the *Members* of the Colony, who will take the establishment, from the proprietors, upon terms to be agreed on between the parties; and who will direct the general affairs of the colony, and possess, with their children, all the advantages of full colonial privileges.

The *fourth class*, will consist of Independent Families, or Individuals, who desire to enjoy all the benefits of a superior home, and society, at a very reduced cost, and without trouble or anxiety; and who do not object to live under the colonial rules and regulations; these rules and regulations having been, previously, framed to secure, most permanently, the happiness of each.

NUMBERS AND COSTS OF THE SEVERAL CLASSES

In the *second* stage, or in a full and complete colony, composed of those who, from their birth, have been trained within the colony, the establishment would accommodate 2448 persons, at an annual cost of £96,360; which amount would insure advantages not to be obtained at present for £277,440. These 2448 persons would consist of men, women and children, in their natural proportions; that is 816 adults, or 408 pairs; and 1632 children. Annual cost of men £55; women £35; and children £20, each.

But in the *first* stage of these colonies, consisting of the four classes above described, each establishment would accommodate 3708 persons, under the following arrangements: –

The *first class*, consisting of Hired Servants and Labourers, to perform the usual services of such parties, but under very improved circumstances for them, will occupy the three first floors of *one half of one side* the square, for their sleeping apartments. These will be, as in the present state of society, unmarried persons. Each floor (as shown in Plate II. fig. 1)[a] will accommodate 32 individuals; or 96 in each house; which, multiplied by 9, the number of houses in half of one side of the square, will give 864; of these one-third, or 288, will be females; and two-thirds, or 576; males. In present society, the average cost in wages and maintenance of these will be, £25 a-year for the females, and £39 a-year for the males, or, in the aggregate, £29,664. In the proposed state, each will cost, for a very superior mode of life, £15 a-year, or £12,960. In the fourth floor, or children's apartments, above these nine houses, 216 children will be accommodated with dormitories, and all other conveniences for children, as in superior boarding-schools, in which, for board and education, £100 a-year each is now paid; but say £70 a-year each, or in the aggregate, £15,120. The children to be so accommodated, will be those of the more wealthy classes, who desire to give their children superior habits, knowledge, and conduct; or in other words, to have them trained physically, mentally, morally, and practically to become in manner, spirit, intelligence, and deportment, superior beings, compared with any whose characters have been, hitherto, formed, or, whose characters can be formed, under the existing notions respecting the formation of character, and surrounded, as all are, by external institutions, laws, and customs, all emanating from superstition, and the error that the

[a] See *infra*, p. 421.

character is formed *by* the individual. These children, in the transition colonies, will be lodged, fed, clothes, thus educated, and rationally occupied and amused, for £30 a-year each, or in the aggregate, £6480; but in the second stage of the colonies, the cost will be less than £20 each.

The *second class*, will consist of Candidates, composed of superior working mechanics, artisans, trades-people, superintending servants, or managers of single departments, in various trades, manufactories, etc, and of small masters. They will occupy, for their sleeping apartments, *the other half of that side* of the square on which the *first* class reside; and their accommodation will be superior to that of the first class. These will, also, be single persons, as long as they remain *within* the square. Each floor (as shown in Plate II. fig. 6),[a] will accommodate 12; or 36 on the three first floors; which, multiplied by 9, the number of houses, gives 324 individuals – of whom one-third, or 108, will be females, and two-thirds, or 216, will be males. In present society, the cost of these females, will be £35 a-year each, or £3780, and of the males, £78, or £16,848, – or in the aggregate, £20,628. In the proposed arrangement, these will cost, on the average, £25 each, or in the aggregate, £8100. In the fourth floor, of the nine houses, there will be superior boarding-room accommodations for 216 children and young persons, who, in present society, will cost, for such board and education, £70 each, or together, £15,120; while, in the proposed arrangements they will cost £30 each, or in the aggregate £6480.

The *third class*, will consist of Tenants to the Proprietors, who will take the establishment on lease, from the proprietors, upon terms mutually advantageous. These tenants will be full Members of the colony, and will direct all its operations. They will occupy, for their private apartments, the *two half-sides* of the square nearest to the side occupied by *the first and second* classes; and will be either married or single; and each married pair or single individual will occupy one bed-room and one sitting-room.* Supposing the three first floors of 12 houses to be occupied by the married pairs, there will be 8 persons on each floor, or 24 in each house, which number multiplied by 12, will give 288. Then there will remain, 6 houses to be occupied each, by single persons; or 4 on each floor; or 12 in each house, which number, multiplied by 6, will give 72, – or, married and single together, 360. At present, the 288 married will cost £80 each, or £23,040; and the 72 single £100 each, or £7200; – in the aggregate £30,240. In the fourth floor, or boarding-house department for children, one side of the square will contain 24 times 18; that is, 24 in each house, or 432 children, which will now cost, as previously stated, for board and education, £70 each, or £30,240. In the proposed arrangement, the married and the single adults will cost £40 each, or 360, £14,400; and the 432 young persons £30 each, or £12,960.

* See Plate II, figs 7 & 8.[b]

[a] See *infra*, p. 421.
[b] See *infra*, p. 421.

The *fourth class* will consist of resident Boarders, or Members of the Family Club, who will pay, according to the rules of this club, for their board, lodging, and general advantages, to the third class, or full members of the colony. These will occupy the remainder of the square: or the three first floors of 36 houses; each floor to be occupied, on the average, by 4 individuals; thus giving a bed-room and sitting-room to each person, male and female; or 4×3 = 12× 36 = 432. Under similar arrangements in present society, each would cost £100, – in the aggregate £43,200. The fourth floor, in each house, will accommodate, as before stated, 24×36 = 864; which at £70 each, present cost, is £60,480. In the proposed arrangements, the 432 adults will cost £50 each, or £21,600; and the 864 young persons, at £30 each, £25,920.

The four classes will thus comprise a population of 1980 adults, and 1728 children, or in the aggregate, as before stated, 3708. And to be as well accommodated and provided for in present society, as the proposed, would thus cost £244,692, while in the proposed they would cost only £108,900, leaving a balance in favour of the latter of £135,792, or upwards of 55 per cent. per annum. (See *Synoptical Table*, p. 381.)

But these colonies, in the next stage, when composed of the individuals born and trained, from birth, within the first or transition state, and when complete in all their arrangements, will contain, as previously stated, 2448 men, women, and children, in their natural proportions – that is, 816 adults, or 408 pairs, and 1632 children; leaving four of the houses to be applied for various public purposes. These 816 adults will have advantages, under these new arrangements, that cannot now be obtained for £200 a-year each, or for £163,200; and the 1632 children and young persons will have advantages not now to be obtained for £70 each, or in the aggregate for £114,240; – these added, make £277,440. In the colony they will cost for the 816 adults, at £50 each, £40,800; and for the 1632 children and young persons, at £20 each, £32,640; or in the aggregate £73,440; making an annual saving, in their expenditure, of £204,000, or upwards of 73½ per cent. per annum, in favour of home colonization, conducted on the principles of union, over the present competitive and unorganized state of society.

OCCUPATIONS OF THE FOUR CLASSES OF COLONISTS IN THE FIRST OR TRANSITION STATE

Of the *first* class, the 288 females will be employed to wash, cook, and clean the rooms of the four sides of the square, exclusive of the children's apartments. The 576 men will be employed, chiefly, in agricultural operations, on the 2000 acres; on the roads and walks, or in assisting in some of the buildings, trades, or manufacturing departments; or in attending to the water, gas, and

SYNOPTICAL TABLE

Shewing the Classification of the Population of a Home Colony, in its First or Transition State; the Numerical Proportion of the several Classes; their several Modes of Accommodation; with the Individual and Aggregate Annual Costs of each, in pounds sterling, in present Society, and in the new Colonies; and the Annual Amounts of Saving effected by the new Combination and Arrangements. Also the Population, etc. of a Home Colony, in the Second State.

The Several Classes of the Inhabitants of a Home Colony, in the First or Transition State	*Numbers of the several Classes*			*Their Domestic Accommodation*			*Cost of Maintenance, etc in present Society*			*Cost of Ditto in the Colonies*		Total Annual Saving of Expense in the Home Colonies
	Total Individuals	Males	Females	Number of Houses occupied by each class	Individuals on each floor	Individuals in each house	Annual Expense per individual: Males	Annual Expense per individual: Females	Aggregate Annual Expense	Annual Expense per individual	Aggregate Annual Expense	
1st, Hired Servants or Labourers	864	576	288	9	32*	96	£39	£25	£29,664	£15	£12,960	£16,704
2nd, Candidates for Membership	324	216	108	9	12†	36	78	35	20,628	25	8,100	12,528
3rd, Members (the Tenants)	360	married, 144 single, 36	144 36	12 6	8‡ 4§	24 12	80 100	80 100	30,240	40	14,400	15,840
4th, Members of the Family Club	432	Variable	Variable	36	4‖	12	100	100	43,200	50	21,600	21,600
„ Children . . .	1728	Variable	Variable	4 Coll. 5th floor of all	„	„	70	70	120,960	30	51,840	69,120
TOTALS	3708	„	„	„	„	„	„	„	244,692	„	108,900	135,792
Inhabitants of a Home Colony, in the Second State												
Adults	816	„	„	68	4	12	200	200	163,200	50	40,800	122,400
Children and Young Persons	1632	„	„	4 Coll. etc 5th floor of all	„	„	70	70	114,240	20	32,640	81,600
TOTALS	2448	„	„	„	„	„	„	„	277,440	„	73,440	204,000

* See Plate II, fig. 1. † See Plate II, fig. 6. ‡ See Plate II, fig. 7. § See Plate II, fig. 8. ‖ See Plate II, fig. 8.

heating apparatus, within and without the square, and to all other required domestic purposes.

Of the *second* class, the 108 females will be employed in making, and washing, the garments of the occupiers of the four sides of the square; in attending upon the infants, children, and young persons, in the fourth story, on the four sides of the square; in the refectory and culinary departments; and in the public buildings. The 216 men will be employed, in part, on the farms, in building, trades, and manufactures; and in the gardens and pleasure grounds; in the water and gas works; in attending to the heating apparatus, and such other parts of the domestic arrangements, as may require the application to them of their respective qualifications, as mechanics, artisans, trades, etc, etc.

Of the *third* class, the 180 women, will be engaged in superintending the nurseries, children's and young persons' domestic departments, in the colleges in part, in the public buildings – in superintending the out-door exercises of the children and young persons – in superintending the apartments and arrangements of the four sides of the square, and, especially, of their own, and the two sides appropriated for the fourth class – and in such manufactures as require their qualifications. The 180 men will be occupied in superintending the same departments, with the addition of the buildings, trades, farms, gardens, and colleges, and all the domestic arrangements of the four classes – in taking care of the landed property and produce – in purchasing and selling, and in all external affairs with the old competitive world – and in superintending the libraries, lecture-rooms, concerts, and assemblies. They will also occupy themselves as artists in every professional department – as conservators of the health of the inhabitants, and of the order of the whole establishment – and in seeing that, at all times, every part of the establishment be kept in high repair, and thoroughly clean; in order that there be no annoyance of any kind, to induce disease, or create discomfort to the most fastidious.

The *fourth*, or Independent Class, occupying two sides of the square, may employ themselves within or without the colony; in any manner the most beneficial and agreeable to themselves; provided they do not interfere with or interrupt the occupations and amusements of the other three classes.

The children, according to age, will be, for some portion of each week-day; employed in acquiring a practical, as well as a theoretical knowledge, of gardening, horticulture, and agriculture; with a practical knowledge of the elements and real substance of the professions, arts, sciences, and some of the useful trades and manufactures, so as to form them to become, at maturity, *superior active moral beings*, each competent to assist, in directing any department within any one of the second stage, or complete colonies.

THE ADVANTAGES WHICH EACH OF THE FOUR CLASSES WILL POSSESS IN THE TRANSITION STATE

First Class, or Hired Servants and Labourers. – *1st*, They will live in apartments within a square, covering about sixty-five statute acres, and the buildings in the aggregate will be superior to any palace, that has ever been erected, or even projected, for securing the advantages and enjoyment of life, from birth to death. The buildings will be surrounded by four park-like farms, of about 500 acres each, to be cultivated in part by this class, under the direction of the third class.

2d, They will be aided, in their various occupations, by the latest inventions, discoveries, and improvements; so as to make their employment as light, healthy, and agreeable as, with such aid, shall be found to be practicable.

3d, They will have no more physical or mental occupation, daily, than will be beneficial to their health, and in proportion to their strength and capacity; for, ultimately, the physical sciences will be made the slaves and servants of man.

4th, They will be lodged, fed, clothed, instructed, and rationally amused; under new and superior arrangements, devised for this purpose, such as have never yet been thought of by any parties for this class; and when they marry, other arrangements will be formed for them, and their children, out of the square, but within the domain of the colony; and in which arrangements, they and their children, will be prepared for becoming candidates for full colonists.

5th, They will have the most favourable means of gradually improving their language, habits, manners, knowledge, and general conduct, so as in time, to advance to the next, or second class; and thus become candidates for full membership of the colony.

6th, They will have the use, in their own side of the square, of the colleges, libraries, lecture, music, and dancing rooms, for instruction and recreation; baths, hot, tepid, and cold, to preserve their health; and chapels for the various modes of worship; but they will be required to adopt the *practice* of pure charity and kind conduct to all, young and old; and this practice, it is anticipated will soon become general in the Colonies, under every profession or form of sectarianism – all religion, without this practice, being sectarian, or merely useless forms and words.

7th, They will have the use of a raised terrace walk, extending in front of their houses and public buildings, about 100 feet wide and 1700 feet long; well laid out and kept in good order, with privilege to extend this walk around the whole square, as their manners and conduct shall improve, until they shall become full members of the colony.

8th, They will have the use of a refectory, where they will have the most convenient arrangements for taking their meals, with comfort equal to that now enjoyed by the well-conducted portion of the middle class.

9th, They will have the use of a covered way, within the interior of the square, from each private dwelling to the other private apartments, and to the public buildings appropriated to their use; also, to the refectories.

10th, They will have the opportunity of witnessing the daily improvement in habits, manners, knowledge, charity, and kindness of all around them, – each striving to promote, by their whole conduct, the happiness of the others; and all actively preparing for a millennium state of existence, for their children, in the third or fourth generation.

11th, They will have the privilege of resorting to educated and well-informed society, as soon as they can acquire the language, habits, and manners, that will make them agreeable associates to such persons.

12th, They will have *free* attendance at lectures, music, and dancing; the free use of places of worship; with a full liberty to adopt any religious forms and ceremonies in accordance with their consciences; not interfering with the same liberty in others.

13th, They will have the liberty of leaving the colony at any time, when a place of greater, or supposed greater happiness; can be obtained.

The Second Class, or Candidates for Membership, will possess all these advantages; with superior lodging room, food, and clothes.

The Third Class, of Full Members of the Colony, will possess these advantages in a still higher degree; will be the tenants of the proprietors, in the commencement: and when the interest agreed upon, and capital, shall be paid to the shareholders, they will become the holders and joint-proprietors with the members of other similar colonies, – all of which, after the interest to, and the capital of, the shareholders, shall be fully paid, will become the common property of all the full members of the colonies for ever; in order, that all property, thus purchased, may be, afterwards, justly retained, undivided, for the general benefit of all the members of this superior commonwealth. This class, will also direct the proceedings of the first and second class of colonists: and conduct the arrangements connected with the fourth class, or independent residents; and see that all the rules of this *New Family Club* are fulfilled by all parties, without partiality. In short, the general government and superintendence of the whole establishment will be in this class; under the inspection of directors, appointed by the shareholders, to see that the conditions of the agreement between them and the tenants are fulfilled, until the interest agreed upon and the capital shall be paid.

The Fourth Class, or Family Club, will be composed of parties who desire a superior mode of living, without the trouble, or anxiety, arising from family establishments, and who may be willing to abide by the rules and regulations of this New Club.

The Club will consist of families, and of single persons, with independent incomes, of good education, manners, and habits. These may have more, or fewer, private apartments, according to their desire and means of expenditure; their meals, may be taken in their own apartments; they will have the free use of all the public institutions, and their children will be educated, from birth, to become far superior, physically, morally, intellectually, and practically, to the past and present race of men. The rules of the club will ensure harmony, continual accession of valuable knowledge, a kind and charitable spirit, and the general happiness of the members; for whatever humanity may require to render it healthy, intelligent, reasonable, and satisfied with the present life, while making the best preparation for any future state of existence, will be obtained in this Club, in great perfection; and at the *minimum* of expenditure, and with little or no trouble to the members.

HOW THE BENEFITS ARE OBTAINED

The advantages of the proposed system of colonization are so numerous, and of such magnitude, that few minds, at first, can give credence to their reality. It is, therefore, necessary, as a means of expanding the mind to the extent of the subject, to explain the *causes* which will produce these results. They are –

I. The *truth* of the principles on which the system has been based, elicited by a knowledge of the Science of Human Nature.
II. The *peculiar combination* of the practical arrangements, suggested by a knowledge of the Science of Society.
III. The *extent* of these arrangements.
IV. The *efficient employment*, of the well trained, physical, and mental powers, and capacities, of each man, woman, and child, beneficially for the individual, for the colony, and for the public, without waste of time or materials, in useless or injurious productions, or for want of useful employment.

Each of these causes requires more extended explanation.

I. THE TRUTH OF THE PRINCIPLES

These principles, are derived from the FACTS which have been gradually accumulating through past ages; and which have been the means of eliciting the sciences of human nature and of society. A knowledge of these moral sciences – when they shall be consistently, and properly, applied to practice – will *prevent the existence of moral evil*, by the *only* means by which it ever can be prevented; that is, *by eradicating the* causes *which produce it, and by replacing those causes with others that shall produce good or beneficial* effects only.

Society, by now adopting these principles, and applying them steadily and consistently to practice, may give to the human race a new character, distinguished by the spirit of truth and charity, and by the light of invaluable knowledge. The sordid, debased, and uncharitable thoughts, and feelings, which now, fill the minds of men, and which are the *sole* offspring of ignorance and superstition, and the fear of poverty, will gradually die their natural death, with the present and succeeding generation. The practical measures, necessary to produce results so desirable, will, under the guidance of these principles, be found to be plain and obvious, and most easy of speedy and general adoption, by all people and nations.

II. THE PECULIAR COMBINATION OF THE PRACTICAL ARRANGEMENTS; *suggested by the knowledge of the Science of Society*

Society ever has consisted, and ever must consist, of four elements, for four natural divisions; that is, –

1st, The *Production* of wealth, –

2nd, The *Distribution* of wealth, –

3rd, Education, or the formation of character, –

4th, Government, local and general.

A large portion of the advantages of the Home Colonization System, will arise from these four elements being, *for the first time in the known history of nations, combined, scientifically, in the due proportions*, –

First, To *produce* the greatest amount of wealth, of superior qualities, in the shortest time, with the least capital, and with pleasure, health, and enjoyment to all the producers; and with the most benefit to all the consumers.

Second, To *distribute* the wealth thus produced, with the least cost of capital and labour, the most advantageously for the producers, distributors, educators, governors; and all other consumers thereof.

Third, To *educate*, or to train each individual from birth, so as to give him the most useful, intelligent, and best general character, that the original germ, organization, or constitution, of the helpless, and unknowing infant, will admit; when it shall be placed within external arrangements, purposely devised to be, through life to death, in accordance with its nature. And *all* may be, thus, trained and educated, to become moral, and valuable members of the colonies.

Fourth, To *govern*, locally and generally, with knowledge derived from this science of society, in the spirit of enlightened charity for the necessary opinions and feelings of all, justly, and, consequently, without partiality, force, or fraud, but according to *true* morality.

III. THE EXTENT OF THESE ARRANGEMENTS; *from which another large portion of the pecuniary advantages will be derived*

These combined family arrangements are, as will be seen by the accompanying plan, upon a scale more extended, magnificent, and complete, than has yet been proposed for practical adoption, at any period, in any country; and, – in virtue of this extent, united with the peculiarity of the combinations, and the truth of the principles upon which the whole rests, with the new mental and moral formation of the character, and the efficient power of each individual, – advantages, *for a superior state of life*, will be obtained, at a far less annual expenditure, that is now required *for a very inferior and comparatively low and miserable state of living, in a most irrational manner*.

The benefits of partial extended combination, are now experienced in the conveyance of letters from one extremity of the United Kingdom to another, at an expense, very much less than a penny per letter;[a] and yet, all parties engaged in effecting this object, are, or might be, well paid; also, in the extended combination of railway travelling; by which, now, in superior carriages, travellers can proceed at the rate of twenty-five miles per hour, at a less expense than they could be conveyed, a few years ago, at the rate of five miles per hour. Again, for an illustration of the same principle, we may point to the fact, that passengers are conveyed by steam, across the Atlantic, in more safety, in twelve or fourteen days, than formerly, in three or four months, of uncertain and dangerous navigation. The large cotton, woollen, flax, silk, iron, and other establishments, over the kingdom, furnish numerous similar instances, of the extraordinary results to be obtained from extended combinations, for the attainment of partial and limited objects.

But these results – insignificant as they are in their immediate bearing upon the great interests of humanity, compared with the object we are now contemplating – have been attained, in the first instance, by the expenditure of large capitals, and could not have been otherwise attained.

In like manner, it is by the outlay of a large sum, in the first instance, that the magnificent advantages will be realised, of the proposed extended arrangements, for the new system of society; – a system which is destined, *ultimately*, to work a great change and improvement in the general condition of all classes, from the highest to the lowest; and, *immediately*, to give relief to the industrious among the working and middle classes. The application of the principle of extended combination, will, in this case, consist in uniting the interests of from one to three thousand men, women, and children, in their natural

[a] The penny post was introduced in 1840.

proportions, under one very superior family arrangement; in which the *individuality* of our nature, as well as its *sociality*, will be *better provided for*, than they have yet been, under any past or present arrangement; by giving to each individual the superior advantage of city, university, and country residence, without the disadvantages of any of these modes of life; with distinct individual arrangements for both sexes, whether married or single. In fact, no individual, or isolated family arrangement, by means of *any* amount of annual expenditure, can give to *any* individual the same extent of benefits, which *all*, after the present generation, will enjoy, in full security, and with the good-will of all around them.

IV. THE SUPERIOR PHYSICAL, INTELLECTUAL, MORAL, AND PRACTICAL TRAINING AND EDUCATION OF THE COLONISTS; *giving enlarged and superior powers and faculties to every man, woman and child, so educated and placed, with permanent beneficial employment for each, according to age and capacity*

These are advantages, of which those involved in the puerile and petty practices, of superstition, and of individual rivalry and competition, can have little or no distinct conception. For in the present mal-arrangement of society, there are to be considered, besides innumerable other evils, –

First, The loss of power and capacity in the mass of the people, arising from a bad or inefficient, training and education, is beyond all estimate. Here is an almost untouched mine of wealth for creating true morality, with superior faculty and power; the amount of which, is not to be calculated by any ordinary means. Were it to be stated, in reference only to the increased power, that could be thus, annually, obtained for producing *wealth of superior qualities*; it would be *greatly* understated, '*at twice the value of the wealth now annually produced, under all the vice and degradation of the individual, opposing, and competitive system within the British Empire.*'

Second, The misapplication of the time and faculties of the poor, for want of capital, knowledge, and a right direction of their inexperienced notions, to produce valuable or useful wealth; and the waste of materials by their crude and ill, or un-taught methods of using them.

Third, The loss of all useful faculty and power, arising from the children of the wealthy, being trained to be, when young, and at maturity, useless in mind and body; or to be actively injurious, by the physical or mental exercise of their faculties; as proved by the wretched condition in which the rich and influential have hitherto kept, and now keep, the mass of the people, their own children, and themselves. This loss may safely be estimated at much more than *one thousand millions sterling per annum, or twice the amount of wealth now produced in the British Empire.*

Fourth, The inferior mind, necessarily formed by the most immoral practice of being trained to endeavour to buy cheap and sell dear; and the time lost by so many, over the kingdom, waiting for customers. The expense, alone, of this class of distributors of wealth, all of which may be most advantageously saved, is not less, including small and large establishments, and their necessary banking and money appendages, than one hundred millions sterling annually; besides the degradation of character produced, by the buying and selling system, in which they are immediately engaged.

Fifth, The loss arising from the producers of wealth producing inferior productions, both as raw material, and finished articles and fabrics; when superior could be produced. This mal-arrangement of society, arising from the individual or competitive system, occasions an annual loss, to the consumers of these inferior productions, that cannot be estimated at less *than the whole amount of the national debt of Great Britain.*

Sixth, The loss arising from the numbers at all times unemployed, or half employed, or ill employed; but who desire to be well and sufficiently employed. This gross error produces a deficiency of wealth, by the maintenance of these parties in idleness, independent of the inferior and immoral habits which they acquire, and the misery which they experience, – *of at least ten millions sterling.*

Seventh, The loss arising from the gross ignorance, and consequent injurious habits, by which a large portion of the people are forced or tempted into crime; making all the paraphernalia of courts of law, lawyers, prisons, and other places of punishment necessary; together with standing armies, police, and other powers of force and coercion to make such a state of society bearable. To this must be added the cost of the priesthood, and all the paraphernalia necessary to delude this mass to submit to force and fraud, from all the professions; to the incalculable loss and injury of every member of these professions, as well as the individuals so degraded and deluded; the deluders having necessarily been previously deceived before they delude the mass. The loss arising from, thus, keeping the people in ignorance, is much greater than that arising from any of the preceding errors; and cannot be estimated, in its direct and indirect influences, at less than *fifteen hundred millions annually;* all of which, might easily, and most beneficially, be saved, by each child being trained, and educated, to become a rational being, and consequently, his own priest, lawyer, physician, and superior soldier, for local or general defence; when cordially united with his fellows.

Let the foregoing suffice; – for, to enumerate the loss now sustained, and evil experienced, by the present superstitious, immoral, disjointed system, and the gain and good to be attained by the moral system of union, or of simultaneous and united systematic effort, is beyond the power or capacity of any one, trained in the error and degradation of the principle of superstition, opposition, competition, and contest, fairly to estimate.

The truth of the principles, – the peculiar combination of the external arrangements, and their extent, – with the new superior formation of the character of each, – and their efficient occupation, physical and mental will secure, to all ages and ranks a union of advantages, in return for the healthy and pleasurable, and much desired, exercise of the physical and mental faculties and powers of the individual, such as no mind has, yet, conceived to be practicable, or possible to be attained, except, at some future and very distant period.

Instead, however, of this period being distant, we have within our sight, and within our grasp, the most ample means, through a knowledge of the preceding sciences, and the inventions, discoveries, and improvements of the last eighty years, to obtain, *for the existing generation*, a full amount, of such advantages, as its present ill-trained, ill-formed, and ill-conditioned state still admit.

But as for the future generations, – who shall be educated from birth, or whose character shall be wholly formed, within these rational Home Colonies, when they shall be governed in accordance with the laws of human nature, – they will possess, in perfect security, advantages and enjoyments, gradually increasing, age after age, as their knowledge shall increase – advantages and enjoyments, of which the confused faculties, and injured state of mind, of the present generation, preclude them, in the absence of some additional aid, to be derived from new and superior external circumstances, from forming any just, or accurate, conception.

Facts, however, with the threatened contentions of nations, indicate, that the period is approaching when this aid has become highly necessary; and when it may be found and safely given; provided it be administered in the spirit of charity, and with the genuine sympathy for the sufferings arising from error, which must always accompany a real knowledge of humanity, and of the science of society.

The limits of a Prospectus will not admit of a *full detail* of the advantages and enjoyments to be derived from the proposed change; they are, in truth, almost endless. We may, however, submit the following short

SKETCH OF THE RESULTS WHICH MAY BE PREDICATED OF THE PLAN OF SELF-SUPPORTING HOME COLONIES

1st, They will tend speedily to unite all classes in good feelings towards each other; and train them to become moral, and rational beings.

2d, They will keep the population in their own country, and support them, at home, in comfort; make them truly good, and ensure their happiness.

3d, They will train and educate each individual, within their sphere, to become a most useful and valuable member of society.

4th, They will arrest the progress of error, superstition, poverty, disunion, vice, crime, and misery, which now disgrace the population of the United Kingdom; and will, for ever, withdraw the *causes* which have, hitherto, produced these lamentable *effects*.

5th, They will reconcile the people to the Government; and enable the latter, beneficially for themselves, to govern, at no distant period, without the use of force or fraud.

6th, They will increase the wealth of the Empire, to an extent beyond the use or wishes of the people.

7th, They will put an end to the wasteful production of inferior character and wealth, when superior can be easily formed and produced.

8th, They will destroy all injurious contest and competition; put an end to wars, and all useless rivalry between nations; and create a new spirit of charity and kindness, which will speedily pervade the daily, and hourly, practice, of every Colony; and, thus, terminate the reign of superstition and immorality.

9th, They will give the *full extent* of civil and religious liberty, and of individual freedom, physical and mental, that will be most conducive to the happiness of each member, and of general society.

10th, They will fertilize and beautify every part of the United Kingdom; and ultimately of the Empire; giving, a sound and wise *practical* example, to all other nations.

11th, Under their influence, the inferior order of minds, which the present system unavoidably generates, by training individuals for a degrading servitude; or to buy cheap and sell dear, for the love of money; or, in a false and injurious aristocratic pride, arising solely from ignorance of human nature, and of society, and from a deficient education; will cease to be formed.

12th, They will eradicate all ill-will, anger, revenge, pride, and covetousness; – infuse a general spirit of universal charity and of real kindness, in *practice;* – and unite all, in a sincere desire to improve and increase the happiness of all.

ADVANTAGES OF THE FIRST OR TRANSITION COLONIES

In the *Transition State*, and until wealth shall, from its superabundance, and the ease and pleasure with which it can be produced, cease to be merchantable, – these home colonies will gradually enhance the value of land, labour, and mines; will give beneficial employment to agricultural labourers, and to agriculturists of every description; afford abundant occupation to manufacturers, builders, engineers, machinists, and to every useful trade; and they will supply advantageous and agreeable employment to the members of the professions, as they become, gradually, useless and unnecessary; and to all who may require employment; and, thus, will they diminish the surplus labour, until there shall be no surplus.

ADVANTAGES OF THE *Second* AND *Third* STAGE OF THESE HOME COLONIES

The great advantage of these Colonies will be, however, *very imperfectly understood*, until they shall be formed of the individuals, *trained from birth*, within the first or transition colonies; and the *full advantages* of this new mode of life, will not be known until they shall be formed of the individuals, *born and trained within the second*; or those who shall be experienced, through life, in the ennobling principles, spirit, and practices, to be derived, only, from a state of equality of education and condition, from birth; and in which obedience and preference has been given, only, to age, knowledge, and experience; and not to youth, inexperience, wealth, or want of useful and valuable knowledge.

In this third stage of Home Colonization, upon these principles, man will learn, *for the first time*, the power and capacity of humanity for the attainment of knowledge, truth, and virtue, and the enjoyment of happiness. For it is, *only*, in a state free from the fear of poverty, and of unjust oppression from wealth, and power, and when placed upon an equality, to the extent of age, with all his fellows, that man can know himself, or the state of excellence and happiness to which he can attain. In this stage, the science of forming a superior character for each individual, and of creating superior external circumstances around all, will be so well known, that the Colonists, in the fourth, if not in the third, generation, will be well prepared to enter upon the promised Millennium, and to become inhabitants of the real 'New Jerusalem;' in which ignorance, disease (except of infancy and old age), vice, and misery, will be unknown; and, in which, happiness, of a much higher order, than any hitherto attained by man, shall be permanently enjoyed by all.

MANAGEMENT OF THE HOME COLONIES, AND EMPLOYMENT OF THEIR INHABITANTS

The next important subject for consideration is, the judicious employment of all the members of these Associations, as they extend throughout civilized society. The nature of this employment will depend, in some degree, on the localities of the situation. In some, the chief employment might be in agriculture; in others, agriculture and manufactures; in others, agriculture and fishing; in others, agriculture, fishing, and manufactures; and in others again, agriculture and employment in mines. It is proposed, however, that agriculture should form the basis in all; and that in each, it shall be carried on to an extent sufficient, on the average of seasons, to supply the whole of the inhabitants with a full quantity of the best food. And it is likewise intended that the clothing and general furniture which they may require, should be manufactured by themselves, that they may be at all times and seasons in possession of the necessaries and comforts of life. But, beyond the creation of food, clothes, and furniture for their own consumption, there will be a large surplus of labour to be employed for the benefit of society, and this will be directed to the extension of agriculture, fisheries, manufactures, or mines – each person being well instructed in agriculture, and at least in some one other art, science, manufacture, or useful occupation. The object of these occupations, as well as every part of the plan, being to give happiness to the whole population, the particular employments of each man, woman, and youth, will be such as may be best suited to their capacities and inclinations. On this principle, all will be taught agriculture and gardening, because these are the most necessary and the most healthy occupations that can be provided for human nature. But there are seasons and periods when employment in the fields and gardens would be useless and disagreeable. It is, therefore, desirable that the parties should be familiar with other kinds of work, which may be carried on at such times within doors: and in some of these they will be properly instructed. It has been generally supposed, that by teaching an individual more than one trade, art, manufacture, or occupation, his powers of production, and his utility to himself and others, would be diminished. A long experience has induced me to come to an opposite conclusion, and convinced me that Adam Smith's principle of the division and subdivision of intellect and labour, has been long since carried far beyond the beneficial limit, and that the world for many years has suffered grievously from its errors in this respect.[a] Under the proposed arrangements, every individual, male and female, will be so instructed, before he shall be twelve years of age, as to have a general knowledge of the earth, and of the animal, vegetable, and mineral kingdoms – of the useful sciences, and of human nature and its past history. There will, therefore, be no obstacle to prevent individuals from learning, if they should be so inclined, as much both of theory and practice in the arts and sciences, as will afford them full employment, and agreeable recreation; on the contrary, facilities will be provided for these pursuits. They will have access to a well selected library, containing scientific and useful works, and possess the means of making experiments, with a view to further improvements in mechanism, chemistry, or any art, science, or manufacture. With such a solid foundation of knowledge, derived from actual facts, it may be expected that the human mind will make a greater advance in a year, than it has hitherto made in many years; and that future inventions, improvements, and discoveries, will be commensurate

[a] See Adam Smith, *Wealth of Nations*, Bk 1, ch. 1.

with the improved and extended cultivation of the human faculties. In the present state of society, how very small – how insignificant, a part of the intellect of the world is permitted to be called into action!

By the inexperienced it may be supposed, that there would be some difficulty in allotting the various occupations to suit the inclinations of the different parties. I would here remark, that human beings have been, hitherto, so circumstanced, that any cordial union among them has been impracticable. They have not been placed in a situation to co-operate in general measures, with a view to obtain increased comforts and advantages for each. Some societies at present existing in the United States of America, do, however, claim to be excepted; for, notwithstanding the many errors and absurdities which attach to their system, and greatly detract from their enjoyments, they present decisive proofs, not only of the practicability of what I recommend, but of the easy and rapid accumulation of wealth, under an association of families united in one common interest.[a] I have indeed no hesitation in saying, that the difficulty which has been alluded to, will speedily vanish when we come to practice. The inhabitants of these villages will fully comprehend that they are occupied as members of a community, the whole arrangements of which are devised to give the greatest amount of good and happiness to each. Human nature, under such circumstances, will be ready to undertake, willingly, far more than it will be necessary at any time to require from any one.

The judicious permanent employment of all the colonists, according to age, as these colonies extend in our own country and over the world, as they rapidly will after the first colony shall have been seen in practice, is a subject of prominent interest in this new arrangement of society, and it has therefore called for due consideration from the projector of these proposed Home Colonies. But as competition, in all the general trades, manufactures, and mercantile occupations, and in the various professions, throughout Great Britain and Ireland, is carried on with so much keenness and excited contest, considerable numbers in every walk of life are now without profitable occupation, and many well disposed among the industrious are continually seeking productive employment, and cannot obtain it.

In consequence, it became necessary to make such arrangements in the first or transition colonies, as should not increase this competition; and yet that their active industry should be sufficiently profitable, by the extraordinary economy of the arrangements, to induce the most respectable wealthy individuals to be desirous of investing their capital in these colonies, on account of the great home security, and the large beneficial return they would afford at the smallest possible risk. To accomplish these results, it is proposed to make the Transition Colonies Educational and Boarding-House colonies, – to effect

[a] Doubtless the Shakers are primarily intended.

which, there must be sufficient extent of these occupations to employ the population, and consume the surplus produce from the land and these first colonies have been arranged accordingly. The profits, under the existing system, will arise from the superior Educational and Boarding-House arrangements which these colonies will ensure to the more wealthy classes, at a reduced cost, and so superior to those now anywhere in existence, that there can no doubt of the eager desire of the wealthy to secure these advantages. The profits arising from these Educational and Boarding-House arrangements have been stated in the previous pages, and also given in a tabular form.

RULES AND REGULATIONS FOR THE GOVERNMENT OF THE COLONIES

In the *first* or Transition State of these Home Colonies, they will be governed, as previously stated, by the *third class* of occupants, or the lessees of the property. These parties will govern the *first and second classes* of the Colonists, as labourers, servants, or assistants, in accordance with the principles of equity, charity, and kindness, previously explained in this Developement; and they will likewise conduct the domestic arrangements and general business of the *fourth class* of colonists, or Family Club, on the same superior principles, so far as they are applicable to an unemployed and independent portion of the Colonists. Their own class will be governed under rules and regulations suited to their position in the *first* or Transition State, and approaching as near as these first or preliminary arrangements will permit, to laws for the government of the *second* or more advanced stage of these colonies, when they shall be based on equality of education and of condition, according to age; each division of age then having its own occupations, and rules and regulations for its conduct, as described in the Appendix. *

The first and second classes will be labourers, servants, or assistants, in the Transition Colonies, under the sole direction of the third class, who will consider them as fellow-workers in the great cause of human regeneration, and who, as such, will treat them as fellow-men, who are to be gradually improved, until they (or if that should be impracticable, their children), shall become full and independent members of the colony.

The third class will be governed under the following

* See Extract from Six Lectures, delivered in Manchester, by Mr Owen, in 1837, – in Appendix.[a]

[a] See A *Development of the Principles and Plans on Which to Establish Self-Supporting Home Colonies* (1841), Appendix, pp. 31–42.

GENERAL RULES AND REGULATIONS

1st. The Members shall consist of persons who have mutually agreed to co-operate with their labour and skill, in measures for producing, distributing, and enjoying, in the most advantageous manner, a full supply of the necessaries and comforts of life, and for securing for their children the best physical and mental education, and the most advantageous permanent employment through life, with a due proportion of rational recreation and amusement.

2d. That, at the commencement, this class shall not exceed the number requisite to conduct and manage the whole business of the colony; and that the great principle of government, to produce efficiency and success, must be the unity of the governing power.

3d. That the whole of the Members above the age of twenty-one years, shall elect, by ballot, a person, deemed the most competent, to direct the general business of the colony; and that such person be authorised to select a Committee of Aid, to assist, under his direction, to manage every department of the colony.

4th. That a sufficient number of officers be appointed by the Governor, to transact the business of the colony, in every department, in the most exact and correct manner; and especially in the financial department, in order that no confusion may ever arise in the accounts, and that all the members may at all times know the state of their property in this respect, until such an amount of surplus wealth shall be annually produced, that poverty, or the fear of it, shall cease.

5th. That the Members shall assist, by all the means in their power, to aid the governing power for the time being to carry its views successfully into execution; and that no opposing forces shall counteract this union of principles and practice, unless it shall prove, by its unsuccessful measures, to be unequal to the task of producing prosperity and happiness.

6th. That the Treasurers be empowered to receive all monies due to the colony, and pay its disbursements, on orders signed by the Secretary; and that they balance and report their accounts every week to the Governor and Committee, who shall appoint two of their number to examine and pass them under their signatures.

7th. That the Secretary shall keep a regular detailed daily statement of all the accounts and transactions of the colony; and that such statement be presented weekly to the Governor and Committee, and submitted to the examination of two of their number, who shall pass it under their signatures, with such observations as may occur to them.

8th. That the books of the accounts and transactions of the Society be open to the inspection of all its members.

9th. That the business of the Colony be divided into the following departments: –

1. Agriculture and Gardening.
2. Manufactures and Trades.
3. Commercial transactions.
4. Domestic Economy; – comprehending the arrangements for heating, ventilating, lighting, cleansing, and keeping in repair, the dwelling-houses and public buildings of the colony – the arrangements connected with the public kitchens and dining halls – those for the furnishing of clothes, linen, and furniture, and for washing and drying – and the management of the dormitories.
5. Health, or the medical superintendence of the sick, – including arrangements to prevent contagion or sickness.
6. Police, – including the lighting and cleansing the square – the repairing of the roads and walks – guarding against fire – and the protection of the property of the colony from external depredation.
7. Education, or the formation of character from infancy. To this department will also belong the devising of the best means of recreation.

10th. That for the general superintendence of these departments, the Governor and Committee shall appoint Sub-committees, from their own number, or from the other Members of the Society. Each of the Sub-committees shall lay a Weekly Report before the Governor and Committee, to be examined and passed, with such observations as may be deemed necessary.

11th. That should there not be, at first, a sufficient number of persons in the colony, fully competent to the management of the different branches of industry which it may be desirable to establish, the Governor and Committee be empowered to engage the assistance of skilful practical men from general society.

12th. That in regulating the employments of the Members, according to their age, abilities, previous acquirements, and situation in life, the Committee pay every regard to the inclinations of each, consistent with the general good; and that the employment be, if possible, so ordered as to permit every individual, who may be so disposed, to occupy part of his time in agriculture. Great facilities will be afforded to agriculture by the power which the Colony will always possess of calling out an extra number of hands, at those times and seasons when it is of the utmost importance to have additional aid.

13th. That as, under the proposed arrangements, every invention for the abridgment of human labour will bring an increase of benefit to all, it be a primary object with the Governor and Committee to introduce, to the utmost, practical extent, all those modern scientific improvements, which if rightly applied, are calculated to render manual labour only a healthy and agreeable exercise.

14th. That the first object of the Colony be to produce a full supply of the necessaries and comforts of life for domestic consumption, and, as far as localities will permit, directly from their own land and labour.

15th. That in regard to domestic consumption, each Member of the colony shall be fully supplied with the necessaries and comforts of life.

16th. That all the Members be equal in rights and privileges, according to their respective ages, under the governing power.

17th. That, to avoid the evils arising from a system of credit, the commercial transactions of the Colony be conducted for ready money only – that these transactions on the part of the colony be always performed in good faith, and without the slightest attempt to deceive buyer or seller – and that, when any individuals with whom they deal, show a disposition to impose upon the colony, all dealings with such individuals shall from that time cease.

18th. That the proportion of the surplus proceeds of the united exertions of the Colony, which remains as the property of the Members, after discharging rent, interest, taxes, and other expenses, be invested to form a fund for the purchase of the establishment from the company of proprietors, upon the terms previously agreed upon.

19th. That in the domestic department, the following arrangements and regulations be adopted: –

1. The heating, ventilating, and lighting, of the dwelling-houses and public buildings, shall be effected according to the most approved methods.
2. An ample supply of water shall be provided, and distributed to each building, for domestic purposes, and as a security against fire.
3. Provisions of the best quality only shall be cooked in the public kitchens; and it shall be a special object to those persons who have the direction of this department, to ascertain and put in practice the best and most economical means of preparing nutritious and agreeable food. Any parties being ill, or desirous of having their meals alone, may have them sent to their private apartments.
4. The furniture of the dwelling-houses, dormitories, and public buildings (as far as the same be provided out of the public funds), shall be devised in reference to intrinsic use and comfort. A similar regulation will apply to the clothing of the colony. Among the children, very essential improvements may be introduced, which will not only save much useless expense; but be the means of increasing, in a very high degree, the strength of the constitution.
5. The dormitories designed for the children above two years of age, and those for the youth of the colony until the period of marriage, shall be divided into compartments, and furnished with the accommodations suited to the different ages.

20th. That the employment of the female part of the colony consist, in preparing and superintending the preparation of food and clothing – in the care of the dwelling-houses, dormitories, and public buildings – in the management of the washing and drying houses – in the education (in part), of the children, and other occupations suited to the female character. By the proposed domestic arrangements, one female will, with great ease and comfort, perform as much as many menial servants can do at present; and instead of woman being a constant drudge and slave, she will have sufficient leisure for mental improvement and rational enjoyment.

21st. That it be a general rule, that every part of the establishment be kept in the highest state of order and neatness, and that the utmost personal cleanliness be observed.

22d. That the following objects and regulations, connected with the department of health, be attended to and adopted:

1. That on the first appearance of indisposition in any of the members, immediate attention be given to it, and every possible care be taken of the patient till complete recovery; – the prevention of serious complaints being always far more easy than to effect a cure after the disease has fixed itself in the constitution.
2. That the complaint of indisposition by any individual shall place him or her on the invalid list, on which the patient will remain until the medical attendant pronounce his or her recovery complete.
3. The arrangements of the apartments for the sick, shall be such as to afford every possible comfort to patients, and provide much more effectual means of recovery than their private dwellings could admit.
4. Removal to the apartments for the sick, shall be at the option of the individual.
5. As the health of the colony may be materially improved or injured by the interior plan of the dwelling-houses, by their situation with respect to other buildings, by dress, food, employment, the temper and general state of the mind, and by various other circumstances – the attention of the Sub-committee of this department shall be continually directed to these important considerations.

23rd. That, as the right Education of the rising generation is the base upon which the future prosperity and happiness of the colony must be founded, the Governor and Committee shall regard this as the most important of all the departments committed to their direction, and employ in its superintendence those individuals whose talents, attainments, and dispositions, render them best qualified for such a charge.

The children will be educated in the schools and exercise grounds provided for them, where they will at all times be under the eye and inspection of their parents, but under the control of their teachers.

By properly conducting their education it will be easy to give to each child, –

1st, Good temper and habits, with as sound a constitution as air, exercise, and temperance can bestow.

2d, A facility in reading, writing, and accounts.

3d, The elements of the most useful sciences, including mechanics and chemistry.

4th, A practical knowledge of agriculture and domestic economy, with a knowledge of some one useful manufacture, trade, or occupation, so that his employment may be varied, for the improvement of his mental and physical powers.

And, *lastly*, a knowledge of himself and of human nature, to form him into a rational being, and render him charitable, kind, and benevolent to all his fellow-creatures.

24th, That when the children of the Members shall have attained their sixteenth year, they be permitted either to become members, or to go out into general society with every advantage which the colony can afford them.

25th, That intelligent and experienced matrons be appointed to instruct the young mothers in the best mode of treating and training children from birth until they are two years old – the age at which it is proposed to send them to the schools and dormitories – that their constitutions, habits, and dispositions may not be injured during that period.

26th, That in winter, and unfavourable weather, a sufficient variety of amusements and recreations proper for the colonists, be prepared within doors, to afford beneficial relaxation from employment and study.

27th, That, as liberty of conscience, religious and mental, will be possessed by every inhabitant of the colony, arrangements be made to accommodate all denominations with convenient places of worship; and that each individual be strongly recommended to exhibit in his whole conduct the utmost forbearance, kindness, and charity towards all who differ from him.

28th, That in advanced age, and in cases of disability from accident, natural infirmity, or any other cause, the individual shall be supported by the colony, and receive every comfort which kindness can administer.

29th. That on the death of parents, the children of the Members shall become the peculiar care of the colony, and proper persons be appointed to take the more immediate charge of them, and, as far as possible, supply the place of their natural parents.

30th. That the Governor and Committee shall not be empowered to admit a new Member without the consent of three-fourths of the Members of the colony, obtained at a general meeting.

31st. That, – although at the period when all the colonists shall have been trained and educated under the proposed arrangements, any regulations against misconduct will probably be unnecessary, and although it is anticipated, that the influence of these new circumstances upon the character of the individuals whose habits and dispositions have been formed under a different system, will be sufficiently powerful to render any serious differences of rare occurrence among them, – yet, in order to provide against such, it shall be a law of the colony, that when differences arise, they be referred to the decision of arbitrators, to be elected by the society, who after hearing the parties, shall decide upon the case.

32d. That if the conduct of any individual be injurious to the well-being of the colony, and it be so decided by three-fourths of the members assembled at a general meeting, the Governor and Committee shall explain to him in what respect his conduct has been injurious, and at the same time intimate to him, that unless the cause of complaint be removed, they are instructed to expel him from the colony.

33d. That any Member wishing to withdraw from the colony, be at full liberty to do so at any time; and the Governor and Committee shall be authorised to allow any such gratuity, as the circumstance of the case may require.

34th. That the Governor and Committee form arrangements by which all the Members shall enjoy equal opportunities of visiting their friends elsewhere, or of travelling for information or other objects.

35th. That the Governor and Committee appoint duly qualified persons to travel from time to time to collect scientific and other information for the benefit of the colony.

36th. That in order to extend the benefits of a system of union and co-operation, which is applicable to mankind in every part of the world, measures be adopted by the Governor and Committee to disseminate knowledge of the new principles and arrangements.

37th. That, as this system is directly opposed to secrecy and exclusion of any kind, every practicable facility shall be given to strangers, to enable them to become acquainted with the constitution, laws, and regulations, of the colony, and to examine the results which these have produced in practice.

38th. That the Governor and Committee be charged with the duty of communicating on all occasions to the Government of the country, an unreserved explanation of the views and proceedings of the colony.

ESTIMATE of the Cost of one of the Superior HOME COLONIES of FAMILY CLUBS

2000 Acres of Land, average quality at £70 per acre (including timber),	£140,000	0	0
72 Dwelling-houses, at £3500 each,	252,000	0	0
4 Colleges for Education, at £4000 each,	16,000	0	0
4 Central buildings, one on each side of the square, for adults, at £8000 each	32,000	0	0
4 Culinary and Refectory arrangements, at £6000 each,	24,000	0	0
Furnishing Houses, Colleges, Public Buildings, Culinary and Refectory Establishments,	60,000	0	0
Water, Gas, and Heating Apparatus for all the public and private buildings and apartments,	60,000	0	0
4 Farm-Houses and appendages for Farms, of about 500 acres each, at £4000 each,	16,000	0	0
Stocking the above, at £4000 each,	16,000	0	0
Baths, Gymnasia, and Cloisters for each side of the square, at £6000 each side,	24,000	0	0
Drainage, laying out the interior of the Square, and Terrace in front of it,	20,000	0	0
4 Towers over the culinary establishments, for chimneys and other purposes, at £5000 each,	20,000	0	0
Contingencies,	20,000	0	0
	£700,000	0	0

£700,000 at 5 per cent.	£35,000	0	0
Annual repairs,	10,000	0	0
Annual cost,	£45,000	0	0

CONTRAST BETWEEN THE PRESENT AND THE PROPOSED SYSTEMS OF SOCIETY,

IN THEIR MENTAL RESULTS, AND IN THE ECONOMY OF PRODUCING AND DISTRIBUTING WEALTH

There are not many men or women whose minds are yet prepared to make a just contrast between the irrational system of society, which has been alone known to all the past generations of our race, and the Rational System which I advocate. Erroneous education respecting human nature, and that, hitherto mysterious, Power which directs the atom and controls the universe, and limited practice in the general business of life, which confines the acquired knowledge of the most experienced, to an imperfect acquaintance with some very partial division of a most heterogeneous, confused, and artificial, state of society, have made men and women incompetent to grasp the conception of two distinct systems for the government of the world; and, more especially, as those systems are founded on opposite principles, and lead to two opposite practices. The one is the present system, which, of necessity, keeps the human race in ignorance and poverty, foments division of opinion about mysteries which no one can comprehend, and thereby creates every uncharitable and unkind feeling from man to man over the earth – errors which produce falsehood, every bad passion, and endless crime and misery; the other system, the one advocated in this work, will, of like necessity, overcome ignorance or inexperience, by judicious arrangements, purposely calculated to secure to each individual, gradually, from birth, a real knowledge of the qualities of all the tangible objects around him, and, as the powers of his mind grow, to enable him clearly to comprehend them, as far as these qualities have yet been discovered by human experience. This system will also give to each individual an accurate knowledge of the qualities of human nature, so far as FACTS have developed them; this knowledge having lately become sufficient to ensure, by its proper application to practice, truth, charity, and kindness, from each to all; also to give to the individual, thus educated, an accurate or scientific knowledge of the elements of society, and of the means by which these elements may be combined, to produce at all times, by the pleasurable exercise of the human faculties, physical and mental, a surplus of wealth for all, without any of the demoralizing effects necessarily arising from the competition and frauds hourly practised in the various attempts to obtain wealth, under the existing system of endless deception and falsehood.

Whenever the unavoidable prejudices of education can be overcome, the extraordinary difference between these two opposing systems cannot fail to make a deep and lasting impression upon all who shall give due attention to the subject; and the difference may be thus shortly stated:

1st. The old system cultivates a small portion only, and that in a most imperfect manner, of the powers and faculties of the human race.

2d. It gives such an injurious direction to the exercise of these faculties, as to produce a most imperfect character, physical and mental, in all: while, by a right education and direction of all our faculties and powers, with much less cost of capital, labour, and good feeling, a very superior character might be insured to each individual.

3d. This old system prevents the creation of an enormous amount of the most valuable wealth; and produces, with a large capital, and great, severe, and unhealthy, labour, a much smaller amount of wealth, while this smaller amount is also inferior or deteriorated in quality.

4th. It distributes this deficient and deteriorated wealth in the most inefficient, costly, and injurious, manner.

5th. This system has created, and now supports, over the world, at a most extravagant expenditure, various opposing systems of *Theology*; all founded upon the wildest imaginations of ignorant and irrational men; – of men before they know how to observe facts, or study the laws of nature, without superstition; while facts now prove that all theologies tend to perplex and confound the mental faculties, and in practice to destroy all real charity and kindness in man. These conflicting and deranging systems of theology, also most powerfully tend to keep the world in ignorance, division, and poverty, and consequently to produce the crime and misery which necessarily result from these three evils. The loss thus sustained, by the human race in character, and wealth, and happiness, exceeds any estimate that can now be made; the human faculties, mistrained as they have hitherto been, are yet unequal to the task. The direct and indirect pecuniary loss to the subjects of Great Britain alone, may safely be stated greatly to exceed a thousand millions sterling annually – or twice the amount of wealth now annually produced in the British Empire. This is a part of the subject which deserves the best attention of the political economists.

6th. This old system has created, and now supports, Codes of *Laws* founded on the imaginary notion that man can believe and feel as he chooses, in opposition to the instincts of his nature, which compel him to believe in obedience to the strongest convictions made on his mind, and to feel in obedience to the influence which external objects make upon his various senses and general organization. Yet man made neither the one nor the other. And individual rewards and punishments with a view to improve man in his character and condition are unnecessary, useless, and injurious; and are the instruments only of man in a state of savage ignorance, governed by irrational institutions. The misery and degradation of character which these Codes of

Laws produce over the world, cannot be estimated; for the evils they produce are, also, beyond the powers of the human mind, as it has been hitherto formed, to trace through all their ramifications. But the pecuniary loss sustained directly and indirectly by this division of the old system, in the British Empire, may also be safely stated to exceed half the amount of loss arising from theology, or much more than five hundred millions annually.

7th. This old system has created, and now supports, the spirit of *war*, and supports the means of carrying the evils arising from wars to an extent that baffles all attempts at an approach to appreciation; but, independently of war demoralizing to a fearful extent all nations subjected to its innumerable evil influences, the wealth which it consumes and destroys, enormous as it is, is a mere bagatelle, compared with the amount which it prevents being created, and which, but for it, would be created. The pecuniary waste and loss arising, directly and indirectly, from this division of the old system, in Great Britain and its dependiaries alone, may be safely stated to exceed the amount both of theology and law. Had the nations of the earth but a correct knowledge of the loss and suffering created by their armies and wars, there is not one individual – prince or peasant – civil or military – who would not abhor the error, and use his utmost endeavour to terminate for ever all motives to war.

8th. This old system, by its innumerable physical and mental errors, fills the world, with *disease and accidents*, and, while keeping the mass of the people in worse than brutal ignorance, renders the medical profession, like the previously named professions, necessary to maintain this old system. The loss to the productive and educational powers of society, by so many naturally talented individuals being engaged in this profession, and so placed as to have an apparent interest in opposition to their fellows, is not only a great evil, by preventing all persons being so trained and educated as to become their own best physician or medical adviser, but also a very large pecuniary loss is thus created and sustained annually by society.

9th. This old system has created, and supports, the most vicious system of *producing and distributing wealth*; a system by which man is greatly demoralized; his best faculties being continually occupied in mercenary speculations to obtain money, first to purchase those things necessary to a comfortable support for a family, and, afterwards, to acquire power and influence in society, to be applied for individual purposes, regardless of the interests of others. The pecuniary loss by this division of the old system, in the British dominions alone, cannot be estimated at less than many hundred millions annually, if not, more correctly, at thousands instead of hundreds; for this system prevents the annual creation of wealth that would be more than sufficient to saturate the whole population with all that a rationally trained and placed people would desire for use, to secure their happiness.

10th. This old system, as long as men shall remain so insane as to support it, in opposition to the highest and best interests of their race, will permanently keep the inhabitants of the world disunited and violently opposed to one another, – will for ever prevent the introduction, *in practice*, of universal charity, or kindness, or a good, intelligent, or rational, character being formed for any portion of the human race. It is based on error, and can produce, of necessity, only deception, fraud, and misery, with a small portion of a low degree of uncertain happiness.

This is a true description, without exaggeration, of the system, which the present generation, through the want of a rational education, so madly desire to maintain, in opposition to the introduction of a system based on truth, that would secure, to themselves in part, but fully to their children's children, to the end of time, the most important permanent advantages.

The proposed New System being based on the everlasting truths of nature, it is an united system, formed of parts all congruous, and perfectly consistent, each part with every other; making an uniform, scientific, arrangement of society, to secure, ultimately, and at no distant period, the happiness, from birth to death, of all its members. And for the following reasons: –

1st. Because in this new system *all* the faculties and natural powers of *all* individuals will be well cultivated, and duly exercised, from birth, in proportion to their strength and capacity; and the most useful and superior character will be thus ensured to the human race, to the extent that their constitution, when born, will admit.

2d. Because it will give a natural, and therefore a right, direction, in the application to practice of all the organs, faculties, and powers, of every individual, in order that they may be, at all times, exercised to the point of temperance, to secure their physical and mental health.

3d. Because, by this training, education, and exercise, of the physical and mental powers, of every individual, such a character will be secured for each, that the necessity for any of the professions will gradually diminish, until they entirely cease. And, thus, besides overcoming the enormous amount of deception, error, and crime, with their consequent misery, which these professions now hourly produce, throughout society, there will be many thousands of millions of wealth saved and produced, which these professions now waste, or prevent being produced.

4th. Because, under this system, by a simple and beautiful arrangement only, a surplus of wealth, all of superior qualities, will be annually *produced*, with great pleasure and advantage to the producers and consumers of it.

5th. Because this wealth, so produced, will be *distributed* with little trouble or expense, most beneficially for the advantage, and to the entire satisfaction, of all.

6th. Because, under this system, *realities*, and not mysteries, will occupy the attention of all; by which change more valuable knowledge will be elicited among mankind in one year, than has yet been usefully introduced in a century.

7th. Because, under this system, *justice* will take the place of *law*; and all differences, if it be possible for such to arise in a rational state of society, will be promptly decided by arbitration, without expense to either party, and with a view also to permanent reconcilement. Individual punishment and reward, after the present generation shall have passed away, and every one shall have been educated from birth in the principles and practices of this new system, will be altogether unnecessary, as well as prejudicial, and most unjust, and, therefore, never adopted. The only code of laws in this system will be nature's laws, made plain to all, easy of adoption, and always beneficial in their practice.

8th. Because, under this system, *war* cannot exist. There will be no motive to it; for man will be cordially united to man, and nation to nation, throughout the earth. All will be made too wise not to perceive the gross immorality, extravagant waste, and loss of property, and utter madness, of war, or of party or individual divisions, to give the slightest encouragement to either of these evils. And, thus, incalculable wealth will be saved to the world and to every individual in it.

9th. Because, under this system, *health* will take the place of *disease* – the *causes* of disease being removed far from the whole of the population; as may be discovered by the inspection of the practical arrangements proposed, and the mode of conducting the business of life, of those so placed, trained, and educated.

10th. Because, under this system, a superior mode of *producing and distributing wealth*, in great abundance, without producing any motive to falsehood or deception of any kind, will be adopted; and by which the interest, prosperity, and happiness, of all, will be essentially promoted; and wealth and power can be no longer objects of contest, between individuals or nations.

In short, the difference between the two systems is the difference, as previously stated, between truth and falsehood, health and disease, morality and immorality, poverty and wealth, union and division; – or misery and happiness; or between a very inferior and a very superior, state of human existence.

Under this view of the subject it must now become evident, to those whose experience enables them to grasp a more extended subject than has ever yet been presented to the human mind, that the difference between the two systems is not to be estimated by pounds, shillings, and pence, or dollars and cents; but even in this respect there can be no comparison; for the general economy, from what has been said, must be upwards of ninety per cent. in its favour; – but with respect to the formation of character, and the enjoyment of superior happiness, there can be no comparison.

THE

SIGNS OF THE TIMES;

OR, THE

APPROACH OF THE MILLENNIUM.

Address to the Tories, Whigs, Radicals, and Chartists;
Churchmen, Catholics, Dissenters, and Infidels;
to all producers of wealth, and non-producers;
in Great Britain and Ireland.

Friends and Fellow Countrymen

Your Country is in danger, from internal dissensions, and external wars.

Your internal dissensions arise from the supersitions which prevent charity for each other's conscientious convictions and feelings; and from the want of permanent employment, with remunerating returns, for the industrious masses of the population.

You have had before you, again and again, in every varied form, from the leaders and advocates of each, the remedies which they respectively offer.

Ask the experienced men of the world, from which of these divisons, is there the slightest chance, of an effectual and permanent remedy, for these daily increasing evils?

Men of research and extensive experience know that the theories of all these parties, have been, often, tried in practice through past ages; and that not one of them, has produced, or ever can produce, a virtuous, united intelligent, and happy state of society; for, not one of them, has ventured to descend, *to the root or real cause*, of the evils of past and present society. There has been, in all, a lack of knowledge, or of moral courage, and of the pure and genuine charity, necessary for this high and important, and now most necessary task.*

* See Extract from Wilberforce's *Primary Charge*, 1840, in Appendix.[a]

[a] See A *Development of the Principles and Plans on Which to Establish Self-Supporting Home Colonies* (1841), Appendix, p. 12.

For the sake of your common interest, and in the name of suffering humanity, I call upon the best minds among you, to pause in your present pursuit, and to ask yourselves, in your calm moments, if the schemes, proposed by any one of these divisions, are likely to imbue you with charity, to unite you in heart and mind, to insure you wealth, or to stay the danger of increased poverty, contention, disorder, and confusion?

As a remedy for the present evils of society, evidently not one of the schemes, advocated by these parties, can give confidence, except to the weak and blindly-led members of the respective sections; for these schemes are, either mysterious, impracticable, or inefficient for permanent good.

Those who reflect, and who have acquired experience, know that these evils arise from *ignorance, superstition, division,* and *poverty;* and that the *only* remedy is, to go honestly and fearlessly to work in right good earnest, to remove the *causes* which perpetuate them; *and this course has never, yet been adopted by any party.*

I, therefore, call upon the truly good men and women, of these opposing divisions, to abandon all party and sectarian proceedings; and to unite cordially, allowing unmolested full liberty of conscience to each, in decisive measures, now, at once, to remove the causes of ignorance, superstition, division, and poverty, for ever, from among us. This is the *only* course, that can ever reconcile man to man, imbue him with universal charity, and enable him to provide abundance of wealth for all, and to love his neighbour as himself.

The task proposed may appear difficult; but it is so, only, to the *misdirected imagination of party, class, and sect.*

Ignorance and superstition, may now be overcome, in the whole population, *by a sound, good, practical, education for all;* and poverty, with the fear of it, be destroyed, *by permanent beneficial employment for all.*

This education may, now, be given, and this employment may, now, be found, for all who require them.

The British Empire, above all the nations of the earth, abounds in the most ample means to give, and permanently secure, both, to the whole of her population.

To the British Empire, above all the nations of the earth, it is now become an object of imperious necessity, that the people should be so educated and employed; or open rebellion, or secret severe vengeance, may be justly apprehended, – and

1st, Because, this empire contains within its dominions more scientific knowledge, with more ignorance, superstition, and immorality, than any nation upon the earth.

2d, Because, it exhibits more riches and ignorant pride, with more *party, disease destitution,* and *degradation of mind,* than can be found in any other nation.

3d, Because within its territories, there is not wanting one single material, or ingredient, of the means requisite to convert, in a short period, this mass of immorality, pride, corruption, ignorance, disease, destitution, crime, and misery, into a sound, healthy, united, intelligent, highly moral, wealthy, and happy society; – a society, not indeed to be *envied* by surrounding nations,' but to be an example to be followed by the nations of the world; – a society, which shall hold out the hand of fellowship to every other people, and, willingly, assist them, in the attainment of the same advantages – the same permanently increasing prosperity; – thus, exercising an influence, which will tend to create, and maintain, a cordial, and most beneficial union, among all nations.

4th, Because, the Government of this country, with all its immense power to create wealth and virtue, is, owing to its erroneous system of governing by force and fraud, now producing more poverty, crime, and misery, than is produced in any other nation upon earth, while, with ease, under a system of united interest, it may produce more permanent good and extended happiness.

5th, Because, there is in the British Empire, a greater expenditure, for the support of a religion to produce charity and affection for the human race, than is expended in any other country; while less of both is evinced, in practice, than in any other part of the globe.

6th, Because, throughout the British Empire, there is more superstition, hypocrisy, bigotry, and moral weakness, and less simplicity, honesty, moral courage, and *true religion*,* than in any nation upon earth.

7th, Because, in the British Empire, a greater expenditure is incurred than in any other, professedly, to govern it, in a very superior manner; while, with the talent, industry, capital, and materials. at the command of its government, wherewith to produce a superior character in the people, and create permanent prosperity, and general happiness, it is, of all nations, the most inefficiently governed; for the great mass of the population could not be in a more demoralized, destitute, and degraded condition, than are, at this day, the

* *True religion*, it is now evident to common sense, consists *in the practice* of producing the greatest amount of happiness to the human race, and to all that have life upon the earth. Man never has benefited, nor, by all he can do, is it possible for him, in any manner whatever, to benefit, that Incomprehensible Power, which, 'by searching, no man can find out,' or which, by searching, it is certain, no man has yet found out. If there be presumption, ignorance, and blasphemy, in man, according to any rational notions of blasphemy, it is when mere mortals, who are now, evidently, by their general conduct, less rational than most animals, pretend, or attempt in any way, to '*do good*' to God, to '*glorify*' him, and to '*magnify* his holy name.' Can worms magnify or glorify man? – and is not the difference between the Deity and man, infinitely greater than that between man and worms? Such notions and conduct must surely proceed from the very last stage of insanity in the human mind; and the public exposure of their gross absurdity, it is to be hoped, indicates a speedy change to rational principles in the whole population. The old ceremonial forms for the worship of this Power are evidently the invention of the early priesthood of the world, when the people were in the depths of mental darkness; and it is now continued soley for the intended benefit of the priesthood; to the prostration of the human mind, and to the incalculable injury of the priesthood themselves, and of the whole human race.

majority of the people of the United Kingdom, without being instigated to revolt, or maddened into open rebellion.*

8*th*, Because, the demoralization, destitution, and degradation of both sexes, in the British dominions, are the necessary and unavoidable results, of the want of a *sound practical education, on principles in accordance with human nature; and of permanent beneficial employment, and occupation,* for all classes; and the want of general arrangements, to place *high and low, rich* and *poor*, within better and more virtuous external circumstances; – seeing that the human race ever have been, are now, and ever must be, the creatures of the external circumstances, whether good or bad, which man makes to surround his fellows.†

9*th*, Because, the sciences of forming a virtuous and superior character, for all men and women, and creating a superfluity of superior qualities, of wealth for all, *are now known, and may be most easily applied to practice.*

10*th*, Because, there is now, from one end of the kingdom to the other, one general demand for relief, from an ignorant, and crude, system of force and fraud; – a system of *universal deception*, by which all classes are kept in physical or mental slavery to each other, and by which they are interdicted from the incalculable advantages of a system of *truth*, that may now, with ease, and in a short period, be extended to the whole population.‡

11*th*, Because, throughout these dominions, all are *actively engaged* in doing that which they ought *not* to do; while they leave undone that which, for their interest and happiness, should be done.

12*th*, Because, the change, proposed in the author's 'Developement,' will effect the great revolution, preliminary to the commencement of the regeneration, which, about this period, so many nations expect; to relieve the population of the world, without force or fraud, from the poverty, destitution, contention, prostitution, crime, and misery now so prevalent throughout all countries, and which evils, as published in so many authentic and official documents,§ are daily increasing, under the present system, throughout Great Britain and Ireland.

* The British Government takes more from, and does less for, each individual of her population than any nation in Europe; while the Austrian Government takes less from, and does more for, each individual in Austria, than any other nation in Europe. – The one is called free, the other despotic.

† See Mr Alison on Human Happiness,[a] and Dr Alison on the Management of the Poor in Scotland.[b]

‡ See the Preface, Introduction, and the Author's Developement and Plans for Joint-Stock Companies.

§ See writers referred to in the Author's 'Developement,' and especially Dr and Mr Alison's late publications.

---

[a] See Archibald Alison, *The Principles of Population, and Their Connection with Human Happiness* (2 vols, 1840).

[b] See William Pulteney Alison, *Observations on the Management of the Poor in Scotland* (1840).

Now, no one is justified in thus finding fault with *what is*, without having an effectual remedy to propose for immediate adoption.

A remedy is now offered, to the Government, Priesthood, and People; in the establishment of the author's proposed Joint-Stock Companies, for forming Home Colonies; – one that will be safe for the two former, and beneficial to the whole population.

This remedy, and mode of carrying it into execution, will be, speedily, made more generally known to the public, by various means, in order, that every class, sect, and party, may learn what it really is, and thus, be enabled to judge for itself.*

But, it will be asked – who is he, who, thus, arraigns the whole proceedings of the British Empire, in all its separate divisions, and as a whole, – an Empire said to be 'the first in wealth, in science, and in arms,' and to be 'the envy of surrounding nations, and the admiration of the world?'

A plain practical man, who, from his birth, has been made to love his species before all other considerations; who, regardless of wealth, honours, present popularity, future fame, or life, has devoted himself to the discovery and removal of the obstacles which ignorance, or inexperience, has placed in the way of making all of human kind highly intelligent, truly good, abundantly wealthy, and happy as humanity, with these qualities, can be made; when it shall be governed by its own laws, well understood, and surrounded by superior external circumstances, in accordance with those laws.

A man, whose organization at *birth*, and character *from birth*, has been formed *for* him; and whether it has been made *inferior* or *superior*, to that of other men, or *between these extremes*, he takes no blame, he takes no praise, to himself. What he had been through life, and what he now is, the Power which moves and governs the universe, whatever that power may ultimately be discovered to be, if it ever shall be discovered by man, has made the author of this Address. If there be merit or demerit in his organs, faculties, and qualities, either at birth or subsequently, – to that mysterious, and, as yet, to man, utterly Incomprehensible Power, the merit or demerit solely belongs.

Were the human race now *rational*, this statement, on this part of the subject, would be sufficient and complete.

But, as humanity ever has been, and yet is, in a most pitiably irrational state, another step to prepare the way to overcome this irrationality, and to make man, *in future, a rational creature*, must now be made.

To retard, and, if possible, to prevent the ultimate advance of high and important truths – truths on which depend the happiness or misery of the

* That full information may be given to the public on this subject, so deeply interesting to all ranks and classes, an Office, designated the 'Home Colonization Office,' has been opened at 57 Pall Mall, London; where a Committee attends daily, from ten to four o'clock, to answer any inquiries, and give whatever further explanations may be required. Letters addressed to the Secretary, at the Office, will be attended to.

human race – all the usual arts and cunning of the old system, based on error, falsehood, and deception, have been, for years past, set to work, and, latterly, with greatly increased activity, to vilify and defame, by every kind of means, the man who has been made to have more pleasure in preparing a superior state of future existence for his fellow men, than, in any other pursuit, throughout the whole of his life; and who, by a singular combination of external circumstances, has been, evidently, in an especial manner, prepared, by that Incomprehensible Power which directs and overrules all within the universe, for this most difficult, dangerous, and extraordinary task.

But the principles which this man has been compelled to believe to be eternal truths, forbid him to blame, and make him to pity, those who have been made, thus, to act.

In truth, those men have, unconsciously, done much good in their day. They have, now, effectually, called the attention of the civilized world, to the all-important facts, and self-evident deductions from those facts, which are necessary to be known, before man can be 'regenerated and born again,' or prepared to enter upon a superior mode of life.

It is, however, necessary to be well understood, that it matters not what may be the qualities, or qualifications, of the agents of this All-pervading Incomprehensible Power, which may be the immediate cause of imparting high truths, leading to permanent happiness for the human race, it is sufficient that the happiness be secured.

Most insignificant, therefore, is the question, who or what Robert Owen is, or how he may have felt, thought, or acted, through life.

Yet, as the world, in its irrational state, has been taught to attach much consideration to individual reputation, according to its geographical notions of right and wrong, the author of this Address is most willing to gratify the present error of the human mind to its full extent; and to have whatever, from his birth to this period, he has thought, said, or done, wrong, made as thoroughly public as it can be made, – upon the simple condition, that the charges shall be made openly and publicly to himself, and that he shall have a fair opportunity, publicly, of replying, fully, to each accusation.

To any parties, therefore, who think they have an interest in finding, or who desire to find, error or evil in his conduct through life, lie now offers the means of tracing that life, from birth to the present time. (*See Appendix*)[a].

Robert Owen claims not to be faultless, according to the prevailing conventional notions of right and wrong, in the geographical position of this country; but he is most willing that the whole of his sayings and doings, year by year, and day by day, shall pass through the ordeal of a comparison with the sayings and doings of all or any of his accusers, during the entire lives of the parties.

[a] The reference is presumably to the excerpts from Owen's own writings in the Appendix (pp. 17–44).

Nay, more; to bring this senseless question to a point, and to set it at rest for ever, the author of this Address, who, as already stated, claims no merit, and takes no demerit, for what he has been, is, or may become, is most ready and willing to have his life – of now nearly three-score years and ten – most strictly scrutinized, and compared with the life of any other man, religious or infidel; and, so that the comparison shall be justly made, he is indifferent what manner may be adopted, to ascertain the true conduct of each, as son, brother, husband, and father, apprentice, servant and master, citizen, and public instructor, and friend to the human race, even according to the present notions of the world; although his convictions of what is right or wrong, or good and bad, have been made to differ, very widely, from the prevailing irrational notions, as taught to the ordinary mind of the, so-called, civilized portion of society.

Let none, therefore, on account of who or what Robert Owen is, be longer frightened by mysterious names, or mysteries of any kind, from striving to attain the high and important station to which all of the human race are, ultimately, destined to rise; for, upon close examination, these mysterious names, or mysteries of any kind, will be found to be mere sounds, unsubstantial as the visions, ghosts, and witchcraft, of our ignorant, superstitious, and, therefore easily deluded, ancestors.

These mere words, signifying nothing, have been the invention from time to time, of mystics, priests, or politicians, and have, powerfully, tended to keep society in a state of abject mental slavery: and in consequence, the world is now overwhelmed with ignorance, and superstition, and division, and all the vices and miseries which are their unavoidable results.

What then is to be done to relieve the human race from these great evils? Are the mystics, and priests, and deceived politicians, to be for ever the incubus of the world; and is man, everlastingly, to remain the slaye of senseless superstitions, and be kept more ignorant of his nature, and, thus, be made less rational, more degraded, and more miserable, than any of the tribes of animals who live in accordance with their nature?

No! This cannot be. The Grȩat Spirit of the Universe, – or The God of the nations of the world, – That Power, from whose mysterious operations, all life and intelligence proceed, – has evidently decreed, that the reign of the mystics, the priests, and the ignorantly selfish, should now cease; by exposing their ignorance, in their opposing creeds, contradictory mysteries, love of gain, and internal dissentions for worldly honours and individual advantage.

But, as the dominion of this world has been, so long, under the direct or indirect influence of their mystics and priests; who, by their assumed power over the consciences of men, enslave the minds of all, *and especially of the women*, who are thus made to assist the priests still more effectually to enslave the men – how is this gross mental darkness to be overcome?

Is it possible that this victory, – the greatest of all victories that man can attempt, – can be gained, over bigotry, superstition, fanaticism, and mystery, without a serious contest with those who, for worldly or conscientious motives, are now trained, and educated, to maintain the permanent supremacy of the causes which produce these evils?

Shall any one dare attempt, at once, to snap asunder these mental bonds, which have enslaved the population of the world for unnumbered ages, and not be made a victim for his temerity, and, by the priesthood, made to suffer death?

It shall be tried; – if a contest of this description cannot be avoided, and if a victim be necessary, to appease the anger of those who preach peace, charity, and kindness to all, and even the love of enemies – let the conflict come; – and if the sacrifice of a life, in this all-glorious cause, shall be necessary, to secure mental liberty to the human race, the victim is prepared.

In this case, on which depends the misery or happiness of man, through all future ages, I am now, as I ever have been, ready and willing to sacrifice my life; and if by so doing I can ensure the permanent well-being and progressive excellence and happiness of my poor, deluded, oppressed, and, therefore, miserable, fellow men, I shall consider the sacrifice a great privilege – a privilege the highest that man can enjoy; *because the termination of the reign of the priesthood upon earth, would ensure the well-being and happiness of the human race; and their, immediate, entrance into a new, or millennium state of happy existence.*

ROBERT OWEN

LONDON, *March* 1841.

EXPLANATION OF PLATE I.

Fig. 1. View of Exterior of one side of the Square.

Fig. 2. View of Interior of one side of the Square.

Fig. 3. Block and Ground-Plan of the Square.

A A A A
A A A A } ..Dwelling-Houses.

B B B B
B B B B } ..Colonnade.

C C C C ...Public Buildings.

D D D D...Schools.

E E E E ...Play Grounds and Gymnasia.

F F F F ...Refectories, &c. &c.

G G G G...Towers.

H H H H
H H H H } Baths.

I I I I ....Conservatory.

K K K K...Arbours.

L L L L
L L L L } ..Terrace.

PLATE I.

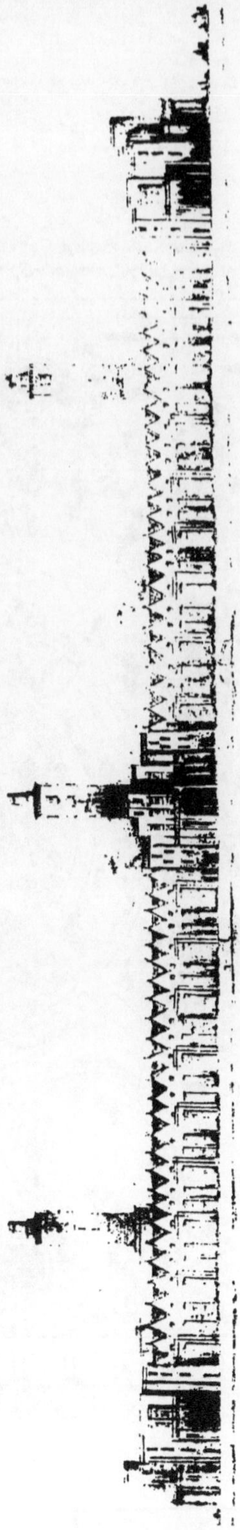

FIG 1

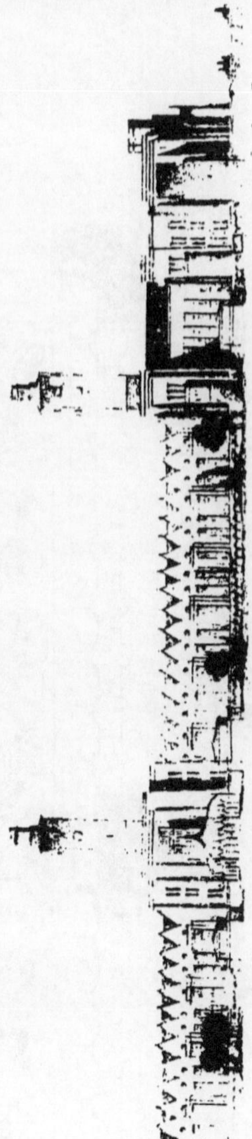

FIG 2

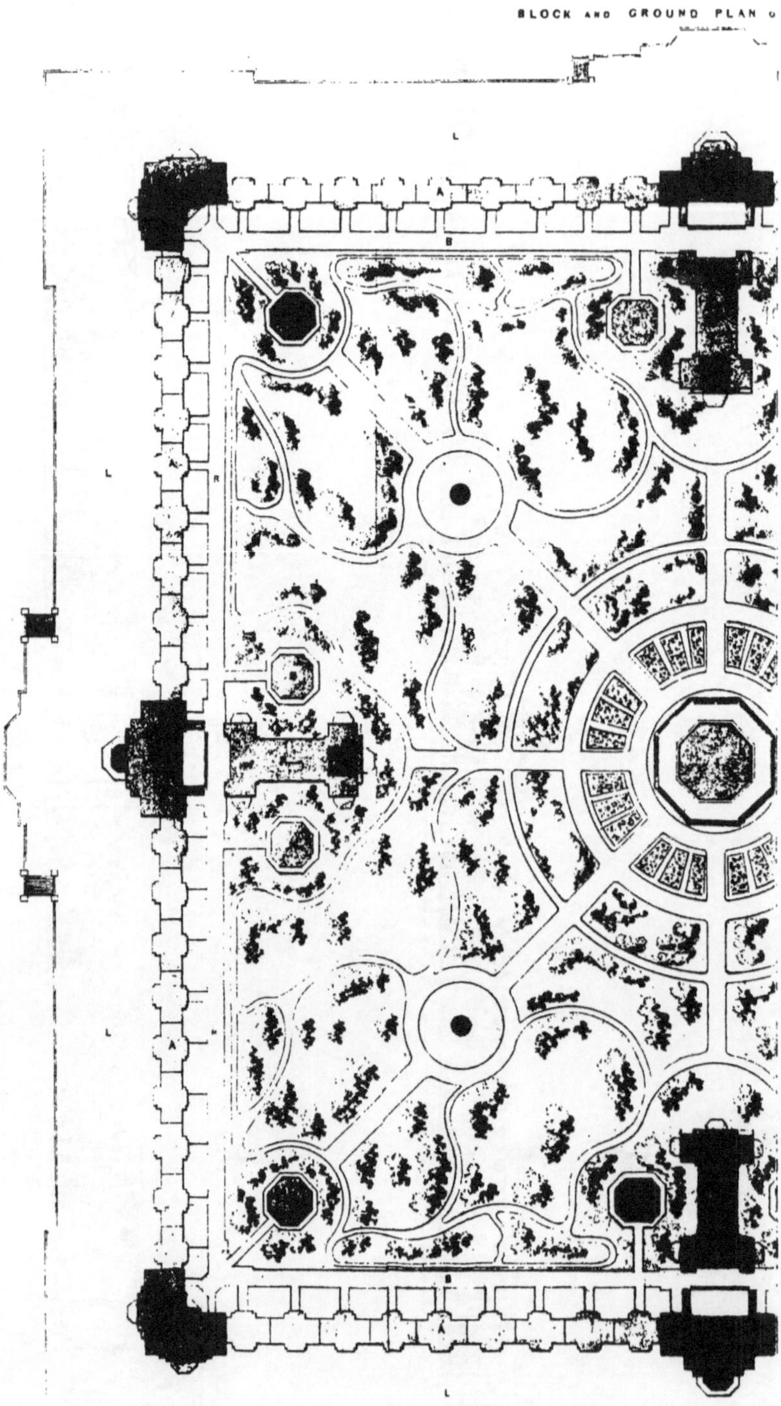

FIG. 5.

OUND PLAN OF THE SQUARE.

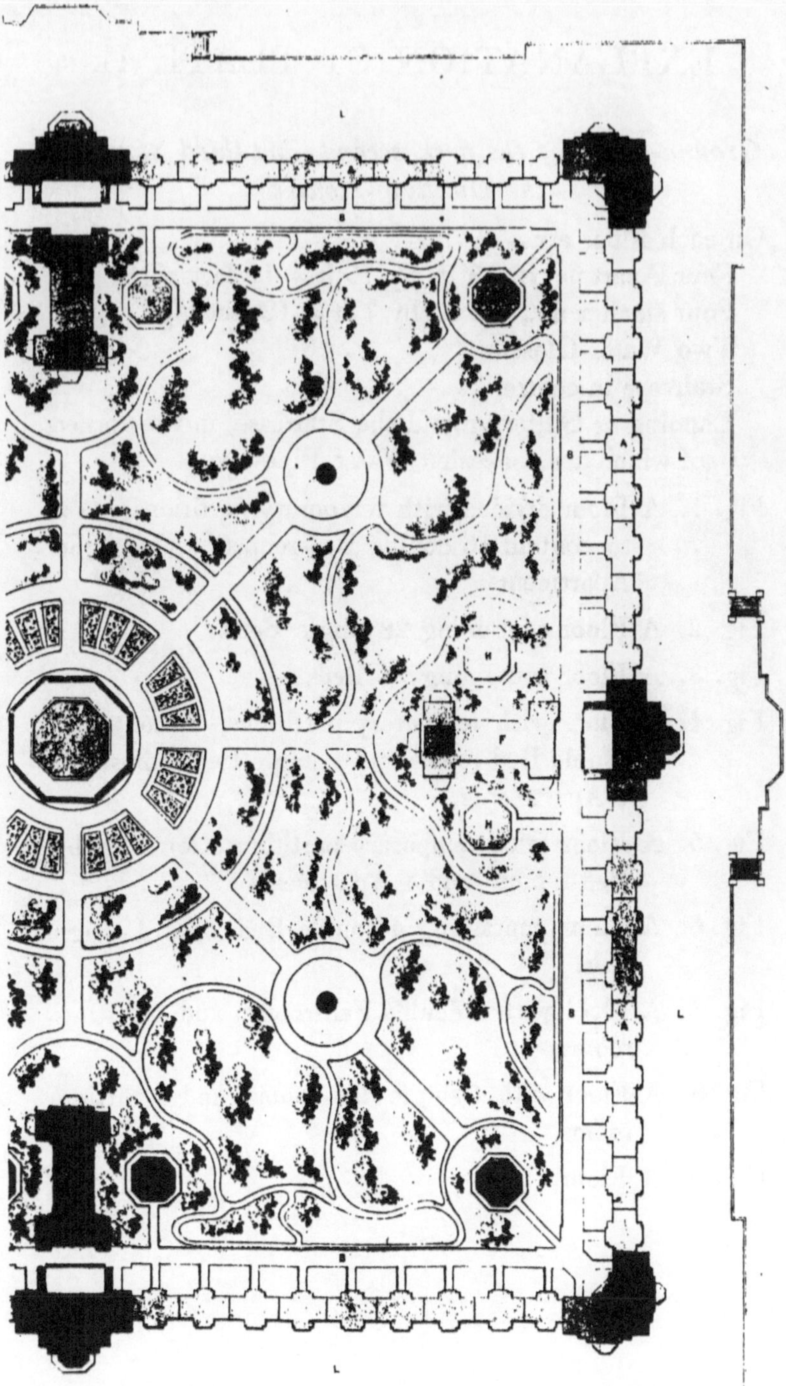

FIG 5

EXPLANATION OF PLATE II.

Ground-Plans of the first, second, and third Stories of the Dwelling-Houses.

On each Floor are—

Four Apartments, 18 ft. by 16 ft.—12 feet high.
Four smaller do., 11 ft. by 7 ft.—12 feet high.
Two Water-Closets.
Staircase in centre.
Landing or Gallery round the Staircase, in the corners of which are concealed Water Pipes, &c.

Fig. 1. A Floor divided with temporary partitions, so as to contain 16 double Bed-rooms, with 4 other Apartments.

Fig. 2. A Floor containing 28 single Beds.

Fig. 3. A Floor containing 24 Beds.

Fig. 4. A Floor with temporary partitions, to contain 8 double Bed-rooms and 4 single Bed rooms, and 4 Apartments.

Fig. 5. A Floor with temporary partitions, for 8 double Bed-rooms, and 4 Apartments.

Fig. 6. A Floor containing 4 double Beds and 4 single Beds.

Fig. 7. A Floor with 4 double Bed-rooms, and 4 Sitting-rooms.

Fig. 8. A Floor with 4 single Bed-rooms, and 4 Sitting-rooms.

Fig. 9. A Floor.

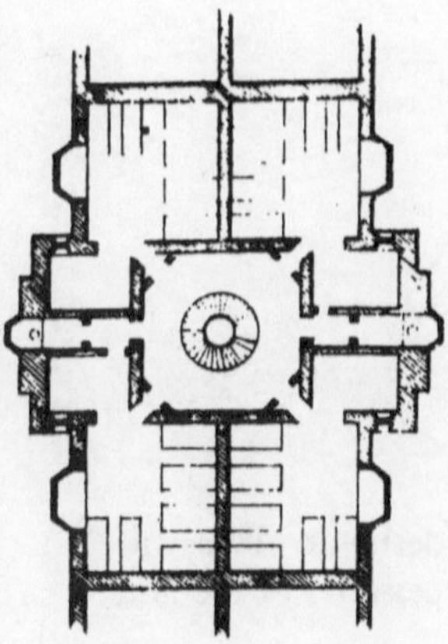
Fig. 3.

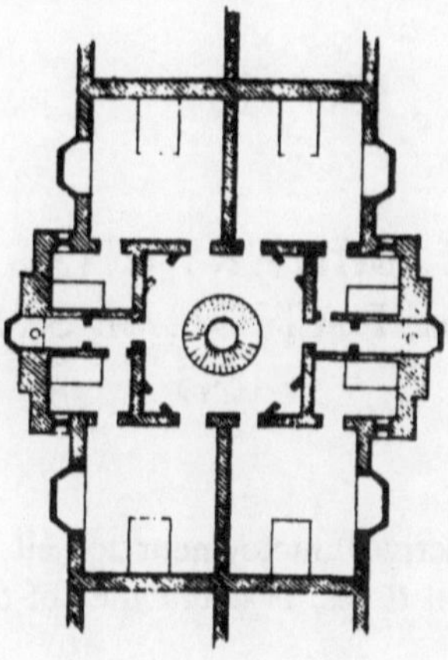
Fig. 6.

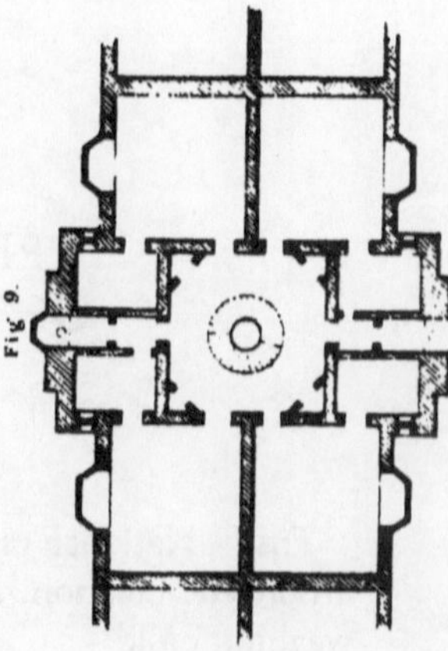
Fig. 9.

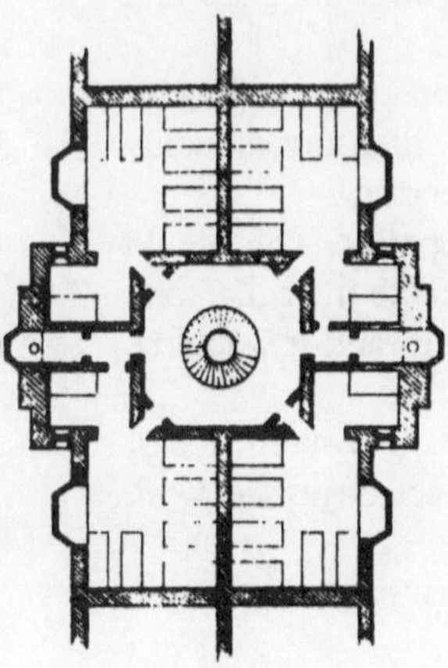
Fig. 2.

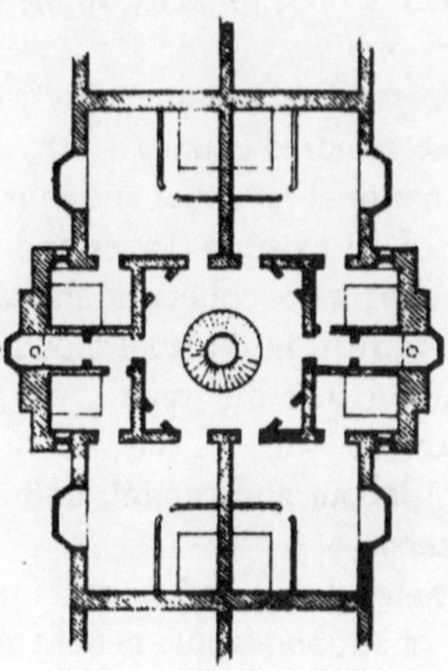
Fig. 5.

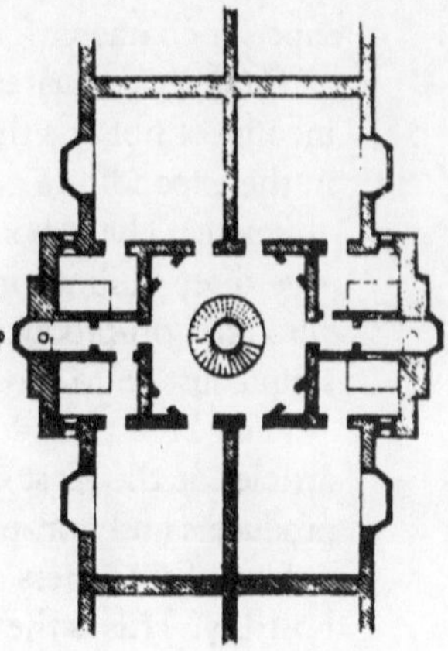
Fig. 8.

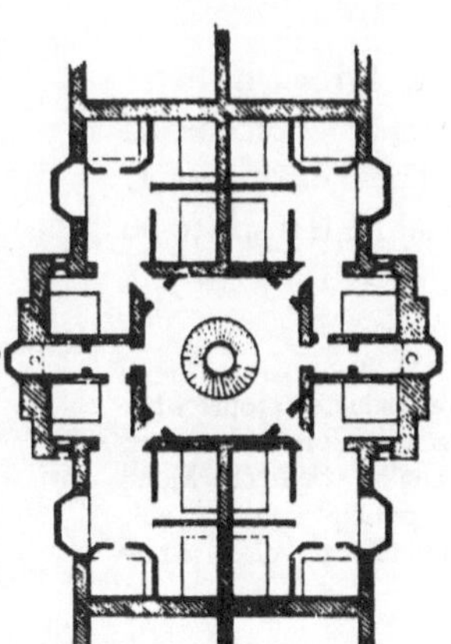
Fig. 1.

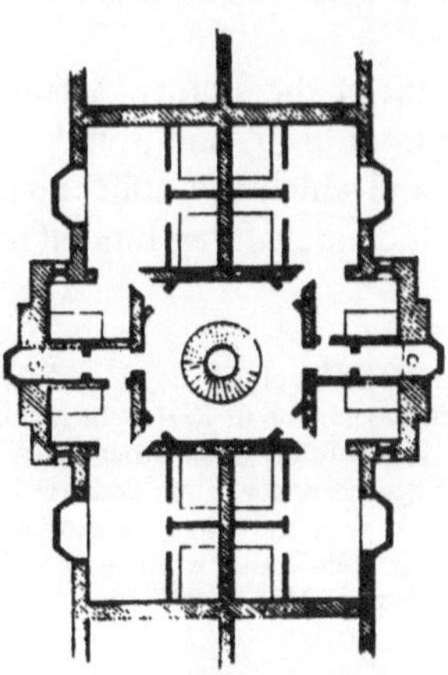
Fig. 4.

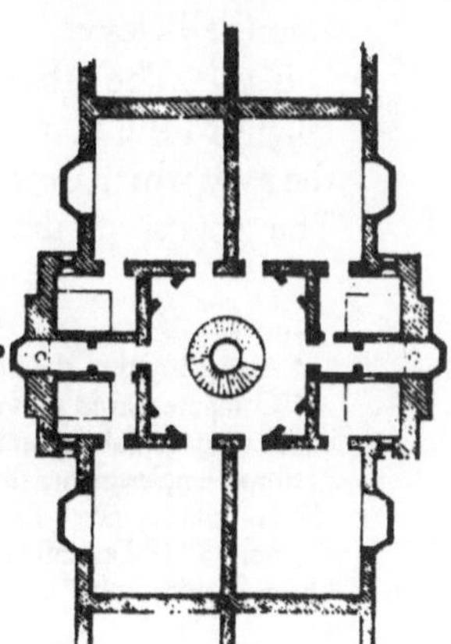
Fig. 7.

PRELIMINARY CHARTER OF THE RATIONAL SYSTEM[a] 1843

First.[b] National productive Employment for all who desire it. This will ensure the creation, at all times, of abundance of the necessaries of life and wealth for all.

Second. National unexclusive superior practical Education for all who require it. This, well understood and properly applied, will ensure a good and superior character for every one.

Third. A graduated Property Tax, commencing with properties yielding an income of not less than two hundred pounds a year. This will ensure economy in the expenditure of the national revenue, and in its collection.

Fourth. The Abolition of all existing Taxes and Monopolies. This would save three millions in the expense of collecting the taxes; make the collectors, who are non-producers of wealth, into actual producers of it; and it would be simple justice to those who produce the wealth.

Fifth. Free trade in all things, with all the world. This will ensure the best articles at the least cost of labour and capital, and be an act of justice to all producers and non-producers.

Sixth. Free Egress and Ingress to all natives and foreigners, except to foes in hostility. This is the right of all, and would benefit all.

Seventh. Unrestricted Liberty of Speech, Writing and Publication. This will prepare the way for the language of truth, and for a superior state of morality among all classes.

Eighth. The Abandonment of the Trinity of Fundamental Errors, hitherto taught to the human race from birth, and from which errors have proceeded the evils which ever have, and which now afflict mankind. These errors are, 1. The supposition that each individual forms himself to be what he is made to be

---

[a] Also printed in the *New Moral World*, vol. 11, no. 32 (4 February 1843), p. 253.

[b] Compare Owen's seven-point programme in 1841, which called for a graduated property tax equal to national expenditure; the abolition of all other taxes; free trade; national education; national employment; liberty of speech and writing; and freedom of religion. See *New Moral World*, vol. 10, no. 1 (3 July 1841), p. 3, and Owen's discussion of these principles in ibid, vol. 10, no. 25 (18 December 1841), pp. 196–7; and the nine-point 'Transition Charter' discussed by Owen in ibid, vol. 10, no. 43 (23 April 1842), p. 387.

by the power which creates all his faculties, and by society which forms the chief circumstance that subsequently cultivates and directs those faculties: 2. The supposition that man is originally formed with power at his control to believe or disbelieve as he pleases, and that there is merit or demerit in any belief or disbelief attributable to the individual possessing the one or the other: and 3. The supposition that each individual has been created with power to like or dislike, to love or hate persons and things at his pleasure. This trinity of fundamental errors has introduced, and hitherto maintained, sin and misery throughout society: and is now the real cause of all falsehood and deception, and of the universal want of charity for the feelings, opinions, and conduct of others.

Ninth. The Adoption of the opposed three great fundamental Truths: 1. That man does not form himself: 2. That he cannot believe or disbelieve at his pleasure: and 3. That he has not the power to like or love, or dislike and hate, in obedience to his wishes. This knowledge will destroy the sin and misery of the world, and for ever maintain the practice of truth, charity, and kindness in all for the benefit of all; and lay a solid foundation for real wisdom, and for an illimitable increase to an accurate knowledge of facts and just deductions from them.

Tenth. The Abandonment of the practice of creating *anything inferior*, when it may be made *superior*. By this means, a new combination of superior external circumstances of man's formation may be made to surround all of every age and condition. And as man is to a very great extent, the creature of circumstances, he will thus be made to become the creature of superior, instead of inferior circumstances, and consequently be formed into a superior and happy being.

Eleventh. The Abandonment of all foreign and artificial-made money, and the adoption of national-made money, to represent the exact value and no more, of exchangeable wealth deposited in the national stores,[a] and always ready to be exchanged for such money; and that money, instead of being the cause of injustice and oppression throughout society, will become the instrument of justice and benefit to all.

Twelfth. The Exchangeable Value of all Wealth to be decided by properly qualified officers, appointed by the nation, who will have no private interest to bias their judgment; and then the inferiot character of deception, created by men being regularly trained to endeavour to buy cheap and sell dear, will cease, and men will be easily formed to become honest.

This Preliminary Charter of the Rational System, when it shall be fairly and honestly carried into execution, will materially prepare the way, 1. To terminate poverty, or the most distant fear of it, for ever: 2. All division of mind

[a] Owen's discussion of 'national stores' here may well be indebted to the proposals of John Gray. See especially Gray's *The Social System: A Treatise on the System of Exchange* (1831), and my *Machinery, Money and the Millennium* (Princeton: Princeton University Press, 1987), pp. 117–29.

between individuals and nations: 3. All wars, civil, religious, and national: 4. The creation of all the inferior passions, with all uncharitableness: and 5. Put an end to the now unnecessary sufferings of the millions proceeding from causes, all of which may now be removed, and their recurrence prevented.

Kilmarnock, Ayrshire, Jan 25th, 1843 ROBERT OWEN

TO THE MEN AND WOMEN OF FRANCE
1848

Friends, – A great responsibility has suddenly fallen upon you.

In consequence, great foresight, wisdom, forbearance, and charity are required from you by the public mind of Europe, which will now look to you for a superior example worthy of general imitation.

This opportunity, wisely used, is glorious beyond all precedent. It has been well said –

'For forms of government let fools contest,
That which is best administered is best.'[a]

Any government based on false principles must be supported by force and fraud, and produce evil continually.

All governments hitherto have been based on falsehood, and have of necessity been supported by force and fraud.

You may now establish a new government based on truth alone, which shall be an example for the world and beneficial for every individual of the human race.

The result of a government so based will be to establish –

1. Perpetual, beneficial, physical, and mental employment for every one, according to age and strength of body and mind.

2. Universal training and education from birth, so as to draw out and cultivate in the best manner known the physical, mental, moral, and practical powers of every one, according to their respective qualities or organisations when born.

3. As all religious and imaginary notions are the necessary results of the great circumstances belonging to the various latitudes and longitudes over the earth, all religious opinions should be equally free, without any one having more advantages from legal power than another. Thus, and thus alone, will error die quietly its natural death, and ere long truth will universally supersede and reign triumphant.

4. Universal liberty of speech and writing, and also of action, when it does

[a] See Alexander Pope, *Essay on Man*, Ep. 3, l.303.

not interfere with the happiness of those trained to become rational in mind and conduct.

5. Equality of training, education and condition, according to age, so far as birth-born capacity will admit.

6. No tax except a graduated property tax, until wealth shall be annually created to become superabundant for all.

7. As man, by the laws of his nature, must be the creature of the circumstances in which the folly or wisdom of society shall place him, and as wisdom says, 'replace all the inferior by superior,' such should be the immediate practice for adoption.

8. As isolated and disunited men cannot effect this change from inferior to superior circumstances, principles of unity and rational association should be introduced for practice, making due allowance for the habits of isolation in which all of the present generation have been trained.

9. *Self local governments* in each new-formed division of men and women, based on the previously stated principles and practices, and each of these divisions not to exceed the number most advantageous in one establishment, or scientific arrangement of society, to enable all to be well employed, to create the most valuable wealth, and to distribute it the most advantageously; to be well trained and educated from birth, and to be well locally governed. All should be taught to know that these results can be attained only when the parties shall be *properly placed* to secure their all-important objects.

10. To be as pleased they must be formed into new practical arrangements, by which, through their own well-directed industry, they will be supported in comfort and respectability, without fear of falling back in the world, which, to great numbers, is a source of daily bread and misery.

11. The American government, in principle, with some essential modifications in their practice, will be a good present model with which to commence.

12. Non interference by any foreign power, except as mediator to stay hostilities; but it will be wisdom in all nations to preserve peace and a good understanding with you.

13. To be an armed nation for self-defence, but not to interfere with other nations.

The knowledge, therefore, which has to be required and put into practice is, how to devise and execute such arrangements as will gradually admit of all being so placed as in the best manner to create and distribute wealth; to have a superior character, according to natural qualities, formed for them; and to be well locally and generally governed.

This is the comprehensive new social change required by the world; and with the enormous new productive scientific power at the disposal of society, for the benefit of all nations and people, this new placing of the population of all countries may be peaceably and most advantageously effected.

You have now the best opportunity that has ever occurred in the history of nations to accomplish this great and glorious social change, and thus to establish charity, peace, kindness, amidst a rapid annual increase of wealth and knowledge through France, and it would soon become an example for all nations and people to follow.

Be moderate, be merciful to your enemies and opponents, be just to all, and your triumph will be glorious, great, and permanent.

Your Friend,

ROBERT OWEN.

London, 27th February, 1848.

P.S. I will prepare, and submit for your consideration, a full and complete constitution, with detailed reasons for each of its laws.[a]

[a] Owen developed these proposals over the next months in the *Northern Star*, arguing for a European parliament elected by universal suffrage. The final result was published in *The Revolution in the Mind and Practice of the Human Race* (1849), especially pp. 56–71, 'The Universal Permanent Government, Constitution, and Code of Laws, For All Nations, and For Each Township, and Federation of Townships'. In France, he also published several other pamphlets, most notably the *Dialogue entre La France, Le Monde et Robert Owen* (Paris, 1848). The best account of this period in his life remains Chushichi Tsuzuki, 'Robert Owen and Revolutionary Politics', in Sidney Pollard and John Salt, eds, *Robert Owen. Prophet of the Poor* (Macmillan, 1971), pp. 13–38.